When
Talk
Works

◆ ◆ ◆ ◆ ◆ ◆

When
Talk
Works

. . . .

Profiles
of
Mediators

Deborah M. Kolb and Associates

Jossey-Bass Publishers
San Francisco

Substantial discounts on bulk quantities of Jossey-Bass books are available to corporations, professional associations, and other organizations. For details and discount information, contact the special sales department at Jossey-Bass Inc., Publishers. (415) 433-1740; Fax (415) 433-0499.

For sales outside the United States, contact Maxwell Macmillan International Publishing Group, 866 Third Avenue, New York, New York 10022.

Manufactured in the United States of America. Nearly all Jossey-Bass books, jackets, and periodicals are printed on recycled paper that contains at least 50 percent recycled waste, including 10 percent postconsumer waste. Many of our materials are also printed with vegetable-based ink; during the printing process these inks emit fewer volatile organic compounds (VOCs) than petroleum-based inks. VOCs contribute to the formation of smog.

Library of Congress Cataloging-in-Publication Data

Kolb, Deborah M.
    When talk works : profiles of mediators / Deborah M. Kolb.—1st
ed.
        p.   cm.—(The Jossey-Bass management series)   (Conflict
resolution series)
    Includes bibliographical references and index.
    ISBN 1-55542-640-9
    1. Mediation—United States. 2. Conflict management—United
States. 3. Dispute resolution (Law)—United States. I. Title.
II. Series. III. Series: Conflict resolution series.
HD42.K65 1993
303.6'9—dc20   93-48667
                                                                            CIP

FIRST EDITION
HB Printing   10 9 8 7 6 5 4 3 2 1   Code 9433

Contents

. . . .

PART TWO
Builders of the Field

PART THREE
Extending the Reach of Mediation

Conclusion

Index

Preface

· ·

Mediation is one of the oldest and most ubiquitous forms of conflict resolution in American society and throughout the world.
As long as people have had disputes with each other, mediators
have counseled the use of reason over arms, the benefits of compromise over adjudication. While the role is an old one, only in
the last ten to fifteen years has mediation become a formal complement to dispute resolution in a wide array of social arenas.
Traditionally an adjunct to labor and international negotiations,
mediation is now prominently used in divorce proceedings; in
civil, consumer, and commercial relations; for the purposes of
environmental planning and siting; and to assist the development of governmental procedures and regulations. The possibilities for using mediation are continually expanding.

As mediation has grown, there has been an outpouring of
works designed to help would-be mediators learn the tactics and
techniques necessary to find agreement in the midst of intransi-
gence. While the events of mediation are often emotional and
dramatic, most of the books and stories we read are detached and
abstract. They reduce practice to a series of technical formulas
that seem far removed from the experience of a mediator caught
in the heat of a conflict between a couple, co-workers, towns, or
nations. Our purpose in this book is to animate the mediation
process by bringing the work of some of its exemplary practition-

ers into detailed focus so that others can appreciate what they do and learn from it.

Mediation has always been something of a mysterious art. Behind closed doors, skilled individuals somehow find ways to work out compromises among people who disagree about intense and important matters. In contrast to other works that focus on the structure and process of mediation, we turn the spotlight on the mediators as the pivotal players. Mediators are not passive participants in any sense. Rather they actively construct the ways a dispute will be handled and what kinds of behavior are expected from the parties. They participate in the definition of the problem, choreograph the agenda and meetings, exercise control over communication and information, and have direct input into the types of agreements that are possible. The profiles in this book bring the reader behind the scenes to witness what occurs there.

When Talk Works is a product of an interdisciplinary research team that worked together for several years under the auspices of the Program on Negotiation at Harvard Law School. Each member of the team has studied, analyzed, and written about mediation according to the canons of his or her respective discipline. We brought these different perspectives to the project, viewpoints that have enriched our dialogue and our understandings of those we have profiled. The profiles bear the imprint and richness of these various viewpoints.

What connected us in this common endeavor was a curiosity about the details of the mediation process and how those who are leaders, with either local or national reputations, think about what they do, carry out their practices, and work through some of the inherent contradictions of the role. Our challenge has been to work with the mediators on an ongoing basis and use that relationship to learn more about the practice of mediation. We introduce the mediators through their work and bring the readers into the room with us to watch and listen to what the mediators do and how they reflect on their work.

The book is organized according to the kinds of practice each mediator pursues. Some are full-time professionals—Howard Bellman in the public policy arena, Frances Butler in the Essex County (New Jersey) Court, Patrick Davis in the Massachusetts Department of Education, William Hobgood in labor-management grievances, and Patrick Phear in divorce and family mediation. Others divide their time between mediation and other related activities—Albie Davis in the community field, Eric Green in the corporate sector, and Lawrence Susskind in public policy. Finally, there are people who use mediation from time to time when it suits other purposes they are pursuing—Juju Atkinson in a North Carolina small claims court, former U.S. president Jimmy Carter as a private citizen, Linda Colburn in a public housing project, and Joseph Elder as a peacemaker in Sri Lanka. Each chapter profiles the practice of one of these mediators based on interviews and, in many instances, from direct observation of cases.

Mediation is proliferating at a rapid rate. Almost weekly a new book appears that is intended to guide, comment on, and/or evaluate some aspect of mediation and the ways it is used in various arenas. The problem is that mediation is a complex social process. It is difficult for both users and would-be practitioners to appreciate the detail and nuance of what mediation entails. The profiles in this book bring people into the process in a way that has never been done before on this scale.

Conflict resolution "consumers" (divorcing couples, union or management leaders, community groups, and so on) who are deciding to use a mediator (or actually engaged in the process already) will be interested in the convincing and detailed picture this book draws of what they can expect in mediation. Mediators, would-be mediators, and others who manage conflict (such as managers, therapists, and educators) will be interested in the particulars of the process covered in the profiles, the tips about techniques, and the failures, choices, and dilemmas that the mediators face. Those involved in educating and training people to do mediation will find this book invaluable. In law, business, and other professional schools, mediation and dispute resolution is increasingly finding its way into the core curriculum. Currently existing handbooks are used to assist students to understand and learn something about the techniques of practice. The profiles in this book will be a worthy substitute for what is now in use, for students are always curious about how the "pros" do it.

The Program on Negotiation at Harvard Law School supported the research team with great enthusiasm and resources in the work that led to this book. Jeffrey Z. Rubin, executive director during the period of the team's collaboration, has been an important advocate and critic, and we gratefully acknowledge all his contributions. We also acknowledge the Steering Committee of the Program on Negotiation for its support of the project. Elaine Landry worked as the project coordinator until her own work moved her in other directions. Her organizational skills, knowledge about everybody and everything, and wit could not be replaced. J. William Breslin took on many roles in this project—most recently the herculean task of editing the profiles. He should merit a profile in his own right, as he practiced the fine art of mediating between profiler and profilee. Heather Pabrezis and Linda Underwood coordinated the activities of this diverse group; our meetings and retreats went off smoothly thanks to their efforts. Finally, I want to thank the research team, especially Sally Merry and Susan Silbey, who helped assemble the group. It took us a while, but the challenge of working together and the fun we had in the process have made this a memorable project.

January 1994   Deborah M. Kolb
Cambridge, Massachusetts

The Authors

Eileen Babbitt is deputy director of the Program on International Conflict Analysis and Resolution at the Center for International Affairs, Harvard University. She is also associate director of the Public Disputes Program at the Program on Negotiation at Harvard Law School, where she teaches a seminar in mediation theory and practice. She received her M.P.P. degree from the Kennedy School of Government, Harvard University, and her Ph.D. degree in planning and public policy from the Massachusetts Institute of Technology.

John Forester is professor of city and regional planning at Cornell University. He received his Ph.D. in city and regional planning from the University of California at Berkeley. His recent books include *Planning in the Face of Power* (1989), *Making Equity Planning Work* (1990, with N. Krumholz), *The Argumentative Turn in Policy Analysis and Planning* (1993, with F. Fischer), and *Critical Theory Public Policy and Planning Practice* (1993).

Lavinia E. Hall received her M.A. degree in linguistics from New York University and her J.D. degree from New York Law School. She is a mediator and consultant on negotiation and dispute resolution. An attorney by training, she works exclusively as a neutral on public and private sector issues. As a mediator and as a consultant on conflict, Hall helps resolve disputes and assists parties to be more effective negotiators. Before starting her own practice, she was a senior mediator with Endispute, and served as director of the cross-disciplinary Specialization in Negotiation and Dispute Resolution.

Christine Harrington is associate professor of politics at New York University. She is author of *Shadow Justice: The Ideology and Institutionalization of Alternatives to Court* (1985), coauthor of *Administrative Law and Politics* (1990, with L. Carter), and co-editor of *The Presidency in American Politics* (1989, with P. Brace and G. King). She has published articles on legal ideology, constitutive and interpretive sociolegal theory and empirical methods, dispute processing, alternative dispute resolution and informalism, regulatory litigation, and the relationship between law and state formation.

Deborah M. Kolb is professor of management at the Simmons College Graduate School of Management and executive director of the Program on Negotiation at Harvard Law School. She received her B.A. degree from Vassar College, her M.B.A. degree from the University of Colorado, and her Ph.D. degree from the Sloan School of Management, Massachusetts Institute of Technology, where her dissertation won the Zannetos Prize for outstanding doctoral scholarship. She is an authority on gender issues in negotiation and other forms of conflict management. Kolb is the author of *The Mediators* (1983) and co-editor of *Hidden Conflict In Organizations: Uncovering Behind-the-Scenes Disputes* (1992, with J. Bartunek). Other recent publications include "Her Place at the Table: A Consideration of Gender Issues in Negotiation" (1991, with G. Coolidge, in J. W. Breslin and J. Z. Rubin, *Negotiation Theory and Practice*, Cambridge, Mass.: Program on Negotiation Books); and "The Multiple Faces of Conflict in Organizations" (1992, with L. Putnam, in the *Journal of Organizational Behavior*, Vol. 13, pp. 311–324). She is a member of the editorial boards of *Negotiation Journal, Journal of Conflict Resolution, Academy of Management Executive,* and *Journal of Contemporary Ethnography.*

Kenneth Kressel is professor of psychology at Rutgers University, Newark, and acting director of the Teaching Excellence Center. He is a fellow of the Society for the Psychological Study of Social Issues and of the Division of Family Psychology of the American Psychological Association. He received his B.A. degree from Queens College, CUNY, and his Ph.D. degree from Columbia University in psychology. He is author of *The Process of Divorce: How Professionals and Couples Negotiate Settlement* (1985) and co-editor of an issue of the *Journal of Social Issues* on the mediation of social conflict (1985, with D. Pruitt) and *Mediation Research: The Process and Effectiveness of Third-Party Intervention* (1989, with D. Pruitt). He is currently associate editor of the *International Journal of Conflict Management* and is on the editorial boards of *Negotiation Journal* and *Mediation Quarterly.*

Sally Engle Merry is professor of anthropology at Wellesley College. She received her Ph.D. in anthropology from Brandeis University. She is the author of *Urban Danger: Life in a Neighborhood of Strangers* (1981), *Getting Justice and Getting Even: Legal Consciousness among Working-Class Americans* (1990), and co-editor of *The Possibility of Popular Justice: A Case Study of American Community Justice* (1993, with N. Milner). She has published numerous articles and review essays on legal ideology, mediation, urban ethnic relations, and legal pluralism in scholarly journals such as the *Law and Society Review, American Ethnologist, Urban Affairs Quarterly,* and *Harvard Law Review.* She is president of the Law and Society Association.

Neal Milner is professor of political science at the University of Hawaii, and formerly director of the university's Program on

Conflict Resolution. He received his Ph.D. degree in political science from the University of Wisconsin. His most recent research and publications focus on folk definitions of rights and ownership, including "Ownership Rights and the Rites of Ownership" (1993, in *Law and Social Inquiry*, Vol. 18), and *The Possibilities of Popular Justice* (1993, with S. Merry). He also works as a mediator.

William M. O'Barr is professor of cultural anthropology and sociology at Duke University, and adjunct professor of law and anthropology at the University of North Carolina, Chapel Hill. His research and teaching interests include law and language, legal anthropology, and cultural studies of public institutions. He is author of *Linguistic Evidence: Language, Power, and Strategy in the Courtroom* (1982), and coauthor of *Rules Versus Relationships: The Ethnography of Legal Discourse* (1990, with J. Conley) and *Fortune and Folly: The Wealth and Power of Institutional Investing* (1992, with J. Conley). He is founder and co-director of the Duke Law and Language Project, and co-editor of the Language and Legal Discourse Series for the University of Chicago Press.

Thomas Princen is assistant professor of international environmental policy at the School of Natural Resources and Environment, the University of Michigan. He has also taught negotiation and conflict resolution at Harvard, Princeton, and Syracuse Universities. He received his Ph.D. degree in political economy from Harvard University. He is author of *Intermediaries in International Conflict* (1992) and co-author of *Environmental NGOs in World Politics: Linking the Local and the Global* (in press).

Austin Sarat is William Nelson Cromwell Professor of jurisprudence and social thought at Amherst College. He received his Ph.D. degree from the University of Wisconsin and his J.D. degree from Yale Law School. He has published articles in *Law and Society Review, Yale Journal of Law and The Humanities*, and *Yale Law Journal*. His most recent publications include *Law's Violence* (1992) and *Law in Everyday Life* (1993, both co-edited with T. Kearns).

Susan S. Silbey is professor of sociology at Wellesley College, and a liberal arts fellow in law and sociology at Harvard Law School. She received her M.A. and Ph.D. degrees in political science from the University of Chicago. She is currently studying the ways in which conflict is understood and mediated in the informal daily life of Americans. She has published numerous articles on dispute processing and conflict management in such journals as the *Law and Society Review, Law and Policy, Justice System Journal, Denver Law Review*, and *Actes de la Recherches en Sciences Sociales*. She is currently co-editor of *Studies in Law: Politics and Society* (with A. Sarat), a research annual that brings together work in the social sciences, humanities, and law.

Introduction

. . . .

Another Way to Settle Disputes
The Practice of Mediation

Mediation is increasingly being used to resolve differences in our families and communities, where we work, at (and between) many layers of government, and in our relations with other countries. One reason for this growing popularity is that many people believe mediation promises a better, more satisfying and harmonious, more efficient, and perhaps less costly way for society to deal with its conflicts. For couples who are divorcing, mediation provides opportunities to find workable agreements that meet the needs of both parents and children. In the business world, mediation helps parties avoid costly litigation and/or arbitration. Mediation has become important in the field of public policy because it can bring all interested parties together to work out solutions to seemingly intractable siting and development issues. With large caseloads and delays in the court, the alternative of mediation often delivers agreements that are reached sooner and are more implementable than resolutions obtained through other methods. Finally, mediators have had notable success in the international arena when other means of resolving differences have failed.

This book reports on these developments by profiling some of the people who have been at the forefront of the mediation experiment. In essence, it is a book about people who mediate— the people who make talk work.

The project that led to this book had its beginnings in my own work on labor mediators, completed a decade ago. At that time, mediation had begun to expand beyond the traditional realms of collective bargaining and international relations into courts and communities. Mediation was the technique most prominent in the alternative dispute resolution (ADR or "alternatives") movement that began in earnest in the 1980s. ADR proponents then and now have worked to bring a different kind of process to the problems of overcrowded and unsympathetic courts; to changing, conflict-ridden communities; and to the stalemates that accompany long and contentious struggles over public policy and international affairs. Many of the members of the research team that produced this book began their own work on mediation during this time.

Experiments and demonstration projects sprang up everywhere. The neighborhood justice center, the multi-door courthouse, negotiated investment strategies, the mini-trial, and regulatory negotiation were among the most visible of these experiments. Practitioners who were involved in designing these programs and/or actually mediating some of the disputes sang the praises of these innovations. Building on their experience and enthusiasm were several major evaluative research efforts that showed mediation to be a satisfying, efficient process that produces implementable agreements.

Also during the past ten years or so, there has been a coherence and convergence of thinking about exactly what mediation is, or at least what it is not, for that is how most definitions have been framed. Mediation is not, in contrast with such legal procedures as arbitration or adjudication, a process where the mediator is empowered to make decisions for the parties. Thus, many argued, the parties retain control over their dispute; nobody compels them to give in to what they do not deem to be in their best interests. Mediation is not compulsory. That is, parties decide on their own whether to try mediation but do not give up the option to pursue other avenues. Mediation is also supposed to be fair, and those mediators who are most successful are the ones who adopt a neutral stance. Parties need not fear that mediators will pursue their own agenda or favor one party over another in the process.

Claims about the advantages of mediation were debated in print and public forums. The debates took place, however, within the context of the shared understanding about the nature of mediation. That understanding focused on the attributes of the process, its structure and techniques. Many practitioners—Jay Folberg and Allison Taylor, John Haynes, Christopher Moore, Lawrence Susskind, William Simkin, and Susan Carpenter, among others—wrote about their experiences in guidebook form. Although each may have specialized in a particular area— divorce, labor relations, public policy—the advice they offered would-be practitioners was that mediation, in its basic forms, was applicable across the spectrum of all social conflict. If you learned how to mediate, they argued, you could do it almost anywhere.

As time went on, the field began to become more specialized in its practice. Many areas, such as divorce/family and environmental/public sector mediation, expanded rapidly. Practitioners more often than not specialized in a particular area. Organizations like the Academy of Family Mediators and the Society of Professionals in Dispute Resolution emerged to support this growing professional activity. Debates about the differences between areas of mediation became more prominent. The process of mediating in a labor contract, for example, was viewed as very different from that required when multiple parties were convened to agree on the site for a toxic waste dump. A career in one field was not necessarily translatable to another.

This focus on diversity in practice was given a significant boost by the kinds of scholarship that began to appear. Social scientists moved beyond evaluation toward investigating how mediation worked in the context of the social systems of which it was a part. What we got, in part, were comparisons between mediation and the alternatives it was meant to replace. But these comparisons were not solely based on the differences in satisfaction and cost between mediated and nonmediated disputes; they also focused on mediators at work.

What we learned was that mediation is an adaptive and responsive process; in fact, it is altogether a rather loose process that captures considerable diversity under its label. In certain settings, such as small claims mediation, mediation has more in common with the court procedure it replaces than with its counterpart in labor-management relations or public sector decision making. We learned that even within similar fields, little consensus is apparent on how to practice mediation. It became increasingly clear that the forms mediation would take were highly dependent on the economic and political structure in which it occurred, the status and experience of the parties to the process, the professional experience and organizational affiliation of the mediator, and a host of other factors. Critics also began to question mediation's ability to meet the needs of the disadvantaged and disempowered who were referred in overwhelming numbers to the process. Rich people did not seem very interested in this alternative.

By the end of the decade, mediation was still expanding at a rapid rate into new areas of social life—the schools, business firms, and very notably, government agencies. This expansion was often fueled by new legislation at the federal and state levels that sometimes mandated, and in other situations recommended, the use of mediation to resolve conflicts. Would-be practitioners with quite varied backgrounds were lining up to enter this emerging profession, even though the possibilities of making a living at it were still considered slim. At the same time, the consensus that existed about what mediation is and what it could accomplish was starting to unravel. Our research project team began its work at this turbulent time.

The Project: Scope and Method

The intellectual and practical crosscurrents of the late 1980s influenced how we came to define the critical comparisons and methodological choices in our study of mediation. We hoped to portray some of the diversity in mediation practice by investigating it in the different social fields in which it is used and by focusing intensively on a few individuals. It is important to understand why we made these choices and the implications they have for the profiles we have produced.

Our agenda was to capture in its variety what looked like an emerging profession. One of the central debates concerned the degree to which mediation could be considered a generic skill similarly plied in all fields, or if the tenets of practice varied according to the field in which it was used. On the basis of work already carried out by some in our research group, we began with the latter assumption. That is, public policy mediators like Lawrence Susskind and Howard Bellman would have more in common with each other than with practitioners in the divorce and family domain, like Frances Butler and Patrick Phear. Our reasoning was clear. First, we knew from much of the current work that conflicts differ among the settings in which mediators work. Some are interpersonal disputes; others involve many groups and organizations. Some occur once between strangers, while others punctuate ongoing relationships. We also knew that the relationship between the mediator and the mediated is not the same in different arenas. That is, sometimes the mediator knows the parties (or at least their representatives) well because they have had many dealings in the past. In other settings, they are meeting for the first and only time. We believed that these particular aspects of individual disputes would make a difference to the mediators and might help to distinguish the forms their practice took.

On another level, we knew that mediation complements or replaces some other way of resolving differences—court proceedings, legislative hearings, arbitration, violence, and so forth. If mediation does not result in a settlement, then the parties will pursue these other alternatives. We knew that mediators relied on this other, no-agreement possibility as one means to persuade parties to settle. We reasoned, therefore, that the differences between mediation and the procedure it could replace, or be an alternative to, would be blurred. And, if this were the case, then the mediation process in each arena might have more in common with its distinctive alternative procedure than it would with mediation in a different arena.

While there are some obvious differences when the disputants are a husband and wife and when the disputants are company and union representatives in a labor grievance, our hypothesis—that practice would vary substantially according to the setting in which it takes place—was not generally supported by our work. As we learned from watching mediators and talking with them about their work, we came to see themes that joined the practice of some of the mediators and differentiated it from others.

First, there are divisions in how practice is organized. Some mediators are full-time professionals, others are entrepreneurs interested in building a field, and still others do not define themselves as mediators at all but, rather, use mediation as a resource in other work that they do. The field is divided about the purposes mediation is intended to serve and the specific aims mediators hope to achieve. Practitioners disagree about technique and the stance of the intervenor, about the role of mediation in society and the value of their individual work, about the future of the profession, and about whether they as individuals will continue doing what they do.

Our second decision was to orient the project to the work of individual practitioners. There were several reasons for this decision. First, we were reacting to the state of existing scholarship.

What we had were predominantly policy-oriented evaluations that contrasted mediation with other procedures, laboratory studies that tried to isolate microtactics used by college students when they try to mediate, and a plethora of handbooks written by practitioners that purported to tell people how to do this thing called mediation. We wanted to build on some of the in-depth field studies of practicing mediators that were beginning to appear. It was our conviction that the aims of this emerging field, in both its scholarly and practical tracks, would be advanced by a close investigation of some important individuals in the field. In this way, what mediation is and how it is used could be opened up to public scrutiny for better or worse.

The profiles of practice that we produced capture some of the struggles of a group of dedicated individuals who are making a place for themselves in a growing and changing profession, perhaps clarify their thinking a bit about what works, and explore the consequences of what they do. What we learned is best seen in the context of the individual stories of these remarkable practitioners of a new (or is it old?) profession.

Our selection of the twelve mediators was systematic but does not conform to the statistical rigor of scientific selection. However, a number of principles guided our choices. All of us on the project team had experience in the field, either as researchers of mediation and dispute resolution or as practitioners, or both. We are familiar with the literature and know many of the people who are active in the field. When it came time to choose, we had an idea of the domain we wanted to specialize in and the type of practice we wanted to profile.

We had several collective selection criteria. First, we wanted to make sure that most of the major arenas in which mediation is practiced were covered—the mediators we chose to study needed to be seen as part of the community of practitioners in each domain. Second, we were looking for a certain kind of mediator. We wanted people who would be able to converse with us about their practice, to be able to infuse their work with meaning and purpose, moving beyond recitations of technique and tactics. Finally, we wanted mediators who would be self-reflective and interested in putting their work into a larger social and political context.

We wanted a mix of various types of mediators: those who are prominent in the field because they write and lecture about it, and those who do it full-time for a living; those who are involved in the profit-making end of the business, and those who work for public or nonprofit organizations; those who see themselves as professional mediators, and those who use mediation in the context of their work. We also wanted to ensure that our profiles were not only about elite practitioners but that they would also reflect something of the gender and socioeconomic mix in the field at large, so we discussed situations in which well-known mediators were not involved, yet in which competent, expert, and self-conscious people were working. This discussion considerably narrowed the field.

Our final decision-making process was often idiosyncratic, reflecting the specific interests of the group and its members. Christine Harrington was interested in regulation. She had already studied mediation alternatives and court management practices and when she found that mediation experiments were taking place in the regulatory arena, she was interested. Some very well-known mediators work in this area, and Harrington asked Howard Bellman (whom she had never met) to participate after hearing him talk engagingly at a conference about the limits of mediation. They were an unlikely pair. In contrast, in the same domain of public policy, John Forester and Lawrence Susskind were more or less colleagues. The choice was really a natural for Forester because it was Susskind who had influenced his own introduction to this field.

Ken Kressel was committed to studying divorce mediation. With the growth in this specialty, there were many suitable candidates. It became clear that Kressel was not excited by the prospect of studying one of the leaders in divorce mediation who had already written extensively about their work. He had been working with Frances Butler as part of a larger study on divorce mediation in the courts and came to respect her as one of the finest mediators he had ever seen. Given his interest in helping family mediators become more competent at what they do, the chance to work with somebody whom he thought was so good motivated his choice of subject.

For many of us, in fact, something unique about the person inspired our selections. In her work in the schools, for example, Susan Silbey had heard about a special education mediator, Patrick Davis, who had a reputation for caring and commitment in the face of a cold bureaucracy. Neal Milner met Linda Colburn at a neighborhood justice center. Later, when he learned about her attempts to take mediation out of an institutional setting and put it to use in her management job, Milner saw it as an opportunity to extend his own work on mediation as a social movement. In the end, I believe we provide a snapshot of mediation as it exists in the United States in the late 1980s and early 1990s.

Organization of the Book

Some people describe mediation as an entrepreneurial venture with the lure of high returns; others see it as a social movement that promises significant social change; still others see it as both. Mediation is viewed as a profession by some and as a set of tactics and techniques that have widespread applicability by others. All of these perspectives are represented in the profiles that follow.

We have tried to group the profiles in ways that approximate some of the social organization of this developing field. Some mediators are full-time professionals, others mediate but are also concerned in a public way with the building of the profession, and still others do not consider themselves mediators at all but find elements of mediation practice useful in their work. By organizing the book according to the ways in which mediation "fits" into the professional lives of those we have studied, we can begin to make sense of some of the diversity that we find in their work.

The first group of mediators—the professionals—are people who work full-time in the field and are known either nationally or locally for their competence. Three of them—Howard Bellman, William Hobgood, and Patrick Phear—are in private practice. They talk about their market niches and how their work is different from or similar to that of their colleagues. Frances Butler and Patrick Davis are government employees, and securing cases to mediate does not concern them; they have too many already. But they worry about their clients and the caprice and dehumanizing effects of government.

The second group of mediators—builders of the field—are practitioners, but are equally known for their public activities in support of mediation. This group is actively involved in influencing the field through their writing, their training activity, their work on professional standards, and their visibility in the field as advocates. Eric Green and Lawrence Susskind write extensively and have been instrumental in introducing mediation into professional education. Albie Davis also writes, but is known more for her efforts to develop mediation programs, her development of training programs, and her role as a national spokesperson for mediation. These practitioners share some of the same concerns with the professionals but are also interested in the overall growth of the field, reflecting on it, and improving the state of practice.

The third group of profiles features people who do not describe themselves as professional mediators but use mediation to achieve other ends. In effect, they are extending the reach of mediation. Juju Atkinson and Linda Colburn are trying to make the institutions in which they work meet the needs of the people there. The existence of a professional activity such as mediation helps them label what they do. In a similar category but on a broader scale, Jimmy Carter and Joseph Elder are trying to do good in the world to make it a safer and more peaceable place. All of these mediators are concerned with finding methods that will work to solve the problems they face.

Collectively, the profiles tell us about the diverse meaning of exemplary practice in mediation and about the struggles these practitioners face in an evolving professional culture. The work they do is fraught with contradiction between public expectation and the pragmatic challenges of the dispute. Still, it is a practice that has captured their attention and the attention of thousands of others in the United States.

In our final chapter, we summarize some of the major themes in this new profession. But the real stories are in the profiles. The mediators are very open about their work, and we have tried to capture what they think and say in a way that brings the reader into their practice with all its challenges, rewards, and failures. It is hard to be neutral about these stories. There is much to applaud in their work, but also much to criticize. It is easy to see the potential for good, but also for harm. What we can learn from their experience is compelling to those of us who study and practice. And as new people enter this field, they will look to mediators such as these to figure out the various ways in which talk works.

Deborah M. Kolb

PART ONE

. . . .

The Professionals

Professional mediators work in many places. Indeed, long before mediation became a popular complement to other forms of dispute resolution in courts, communities, and families, mediators worked in labor-management relations as private practitioners and employees of state and federal agencies. Now, too, the world of professionals is divided between those who work on their own in private practice or as part of a private dispute resolution firm and those who are full-time employees in public agencies. What they have in common is that they do mediation for a living, or for most of their living.

Making a living as a private practitioner is not easy. Although mediation is a part-time avocation for many, full-time private practice is now starting to become a reality for mediators who specialize in family and divorce, corporate, and public policy disputes. Private practitioners must rely on their reputations and referral networks to get cases. Many are listed on panels or referral lists that are put together by the American Arbitration Association, the Center for Public Resources, and the Administrative Conference of the United States, among other organizations. Other practitioners affiliate with private firms or consortiums to get clients or (for large cases) to bid on projects. Keeping busy means developing a network of lawyers, government officials, and businesspeople.

Private practitioners generally have established reputations in their community and/or fields of specialization. Their reputations and networks therefore are likely to be more local. Private practitioners may not be known outside their particular professional community. However, because of their success at building a professional role, they are often the role models would-be practitioners look to emulate.

Obviously, many private practitioners could be profiled. However, finding them means being familiar with either a particular geographic locale or a specialized field of interest. We have profiled three prominent private practitioners: Howard Bellman, William Hobgood, and Patrick Phear. Two of them, Bellman and Hobgood, come from labor arbitration and mediation backgrounds but have moved into broader arenas of practice. Phear was one of the first family mediators to build a full-time practice in Boston. The profilers—Christine Harrington, Deborah Kolb, and Austin Sarat—identified these mediators because of their reputations and through referrals in the professional community.

Mediation is also the mandate of many federal, state, and local agencies. Particularly at the state and local levels, agencies employ full-time mediators to handle labor, family, education, business, real estate, and many other kinds of disputes. Typically, some type of legislation sets the context for the activities of these agencies. Parties may be required to try mediation before they can pursue their disputes through other means. There are several distinguishing factors of the mediators who work full-time for these agencies. These mediators have the most local of reputations—that is, the quality of their work may not be much known outside the boundaries of their practice. Salaried mediators often work against the most difficult odds. Resources are frequently tight, and caseloads tend to be very large. It is in this setting also that both practitioners and parties have the least discretion over their decision whether to be in mediation. In many jurisdictions, parties are required to have their divorce, labor, educational, and other disputes mediated before they can go to court or walk out on strike. Similarly, the mediators must take on the cases that come before them. This is not mediation under the most auspicious of conditions. And yet there are practitioners who, under these circumstances, manage to do their work with distinction.

There are probably many mediators across the country who fit this description. Identifying them requires intimate local knowledge about the work of specific agencies and institutions. Two of these mediators, Frances Butler and Patrick Davis, exemplify the agency side of mediation. Kenneth Kressel and Susan Silbey decided to profile them because they knew firsthand that even under the most difficult of situations, Butler and Davis mediate in a caring and professional manner that others will find interesting.

It is in the practice of the full-time mediators that many of the issues facing this profession come into play. They face the challenge of working full-time to bring often difficult and recalcitrant parties to the table and a possible agreement. This tends to make the professionals rather pragmatic in their outlook. They do not have the luxury, like the field builders, to pick their cases. Further, the professionals are more likely to work in settings that constrain—by the law, by contract, or by accepted practice—their range of options. Pros are unlikely to depart from the agenda given them by the parties. Because they do it regularly and because their practice is made up of similar cases, they are likely to develop a more consistent approach to mediation.

People attracted to the profession by the field builders can see in the profiles of the professionals how the promise is translated into daily practice.

"Most people in parenting conflict are totally incapable of explaining their situation to you in a rational way—together, in the same room, on a first meeting."

—Frances Butler

1

. . . .

Frances Butler
Questions that Lead to Answers in Child Custody Mediation

R obert and Barbara Jansen[1] wait in a corridor of the New Essex County Courts Building, seated across from a sign that says "Family Mediation Program." Robert is a tall, lithe man with crew-cut red hair. Barbara is blonde and nearly as tall. Her face is pretty, but shows the wear and tear of months of legal wrangling. The corridor is home to the overflow of an understaffed, overcrowded probation system—bulging cartons of files of uncertain origin and vintage; a metal coat rack with two bent and tangled wire hangers; a large grimy fan waiting for the first humid days of summer. From the open cubicles around them comes the sound of conferences between probation officers and young felons, some of whom also wait in the corridor, slumped and wearing baseball caps and worn sneakers, with half-insolent, half-attentive looks. On another day, the Jansens would have elbowed past the drug-addict crowd waiting to enter the patrolled bathroom at the end of the corridor to deposit urine samples.

The Jansens wait in these uninspiring surroundings because, for the last year and a half, the Essex County Family Court, with assistance from the New Jersey Administrative Office of the Courts, has been experimenting with custody mediation as an alternative to the traditional legal approach for resolving disputes between divorcing parents. The idea is simple: instead of the adversary posturing of attorneys trying to "win" a victory for one parent over the other, why not try to reach a settlement with the help of a neutral third party trained in the skills of conflict management?

When the Jansens separated two years ago, Barbara had no job and no money, and she was living with her parents. Driven by the fractured circumstances of her life, she signed an agreement that gave Robert legal and physical custody of their two children, a boy and a girl, now eight and nine years old. Although she has seen the children with increasing regularity and now has visitation rights every weekend, there have been frequent conflicts with Robert about the children's upbringing and Barbara's role in their lives.

Six months ago, Barbara and Robert petitioned the Family Court to grant them a final divorce. Barbara, now employed full-time as a hairdresser and in a stable relationship with a man with whom she lives, has requested either sole or joint legal custody. In effect, she wishes to reclaim the parental rights and opportunities she signed away at the time of separation. Robert has been unwilling to agree to any such changes.

In routine fashion, the judge who heard the initial pleadings of lawyers for both Robert and Barbara ordered the probation department to conduct an evaluation of parental fitness, a so-called "best interest investigation" (BII), to help him decide whether changes in the prevailing custody arrangement should be made. He also ordered an independent psychological evaluation of the children. The BII recommended that the children should be returned to Barbara's full-time care, with liberal visitation for Robert and joint legal custody. The psychologist, taking a different tack, recommended no immediate change but noted that if Barbara became "more stable," the children might eventually live with her. The major theme in the psychologist's report was the signs of serious emotional problems in the children—especially the little girl, Ann, who was described as being seriously depressed and in "urgent" need of psychotherapy.

At this point in their dispute, the Jansens' case would ordinarily have been returned to the hands of the judge and the lawyers. Because they reside in a county with one of the largest backlogs of divorce cases in the state, Barbara and Robert Jansen could have waited as long as eighteen months or more for their day in court. In fact, the "day in court" would most probably have been a string of days caused by delays that would have had little to do with any formal legal proceedings. The Jansens would have been primarily anxious onlookers as their attorneys ran the legal gauntlet on their behalf: attorney conference with the judge; attorney presentation before an "early settlement" panel of volunteer attorneys (to obtain an advisory opinion on any economic issues related to the dispute); hallway conferencing between the attorneys; return of the attorneys to the judge's chambers for further conferencing; more hallway conferences; return next week for assembly in the courtroom; and so at last to a "final" settlement that probably would have made at least one if not both of the Jansens dismally unhappy. Such is the fate—in Essex County and in much of the rest of the United States—of divorcing or divorced parents who cannot agree.

Essex County, New Jersey, does not represent the vanguard of the thesis that custody mediation may offer divorced parents more cheering vistas. States like Minnesota, California, and Florida have offered divorce mediation services for nearly a decade; in Maine, it is mandatory that couples in a contested divorce go to mediation. But the process is still something of a mystery, even to its ardent proponents. Custody mediation has gained acceptance in many family courts, but staff turnover is often high—nearly everyone agrees the role is inordinately stressful. And professional meetings of family mediators often revolve relentlessly and inconclusively around questions about the "best" way to mediate and the proper role and attitude of the mediator—to get settlements regardless of the merits, to be a spokesperson for the children at the risk of alienating a parent, to never take sides? Researchers beleaguer parents with questionnaires and interviews about "mediator behavior" and dissect tape recordings of mediation sessions in painstaking search of those mediator utterances ("requests information," "expresses empathy") that perhaps predict mediator "success." Yet, with the exception of certain common themes (the importance of rapport, the ability to create win/win solutions) the fundamental mystery remains: How does a skilled mediator *do* it?[2] The Jansens are about to partake of the mystery. Their guide will be Frances Butler.

．．．．．．．．

Fran Butler and I have been colleagues for more than three years at the Essex County Custody Mediation Project. With our two co-workers—Linda Fish, an experienced matrimonial attorney, and Sam Forlenza, another probation officer assigned to the Family Court—we have been mediating cases and meeting regularly to improve our skills and develop a workable, teachable approach to mediation. As the researcher on the team, I feel a special responsibility to codify our experience and relate it to research on the mediation process.

This is familiar territory for me. I have been studying mediation since my days as a Ph.D. candidate in social psychology. As I sit, carefully making a verbatim text of Butler's work with the Jansens, I also feel a bit uneasy. Can I make any reasonable claim to objectivity, studying a colleague with whom I have worked so closely and on a project with whose success I am more than a little personally involved? What kind of social "science" can this be that so blurs the lines between investigator and participant?

I try to comfort myself with the idea that I am following in the venerable tradition of "action research," a path emblazoned by no less an icon than Kurt Lewin, the father of social psychology, whose dictum was "If you want to understand how something works, try to fix it." The spirit of my activity, however, is probably much closer to Mark Twain's observation that "If you grab a cat

by the tail, you will learn things you can learn in no other way."
This project will not be the cool, objective "science" in which I
was trained but, rather, cat grabbing.

Fran Butler is a very successful divorce mediator. Her settlement rate is high (75 percent, the highest on a team in which the
low end of the settlement range is about 50 percent), her agreements noteworthy for their detail and creativity, and her couples
the most satisfied.[3] A woman in her late thirties, Butler has a
bachelor's degree with a major in sociology from St. Peter's
College in Jersey City, not far from the blue-collar neighborhood
where she was raised. For a year and a half, she worked toward a
master's degree in criminal justice at Rutgers University in
Newark; but, as a single parent, she gave it up to spend more time
with her two children, Meghann, who was less than a year old at
the time, and Jon, then ten.

She has been a probation officer for twelve years, the first
eight doing criminal supervision. She was then transferred to the
family division. For the first year, she spent most of her time
doing BIIs. She liked this work and felt she was good at it, but
later she accepted the opportunity to help develop a new service
in something called "nondissolution" mediation. In that capacity,
she and Sam Forlenza have been handling hundreds of cases a
year between nonmarried parents or other family members from
Essex County's poor African-American and Latino communities.
These are cases that lawyers and judges want little part of. The
parties cannot afford legal representation and are often baffled
and intimidated by the legal system. The disputes are nonetheless
often heart-rending—the wish of a grandmother to have legal
custody of her AIDS-stricken daughter's child, or the frantic
struggle of a mother to win her child's safety from the brutalizing
but legally empowered father. Except for a week of general orientation to mediation conducted by New Jersey's Office of the
Public Advocate, Butler had no formal training in mediation
when she began her nondissolution assignment.

When the Family Court was awarded a grant from the Administrative Office of the Courts to mediate disputes between divorcing or divorced parents, Butler added the assignment to her nondissolution workload. She has just finished a morning of nondissolution work.

Her office, in which the Jansens are now seated, is crowded with institutional furniture, including a long table piled with folders. In counterpoint to the institutional clutter is clutter of another sort: a large assortment of children's toys and stuffed animals piled one on top of the other at the back of the room. On one wall is a large poster of Albert Einstein that reads, "Great spirits have always encountered violent opposition from mediocre minds." Bordering her desk are several family photographs. On the wall alongside the desk are taped an assortment of Meghann's drawings, notes, and greeting cards to her mother. One of these is endorsed to "The worlds Gratist Meedeator." The object of these sentiments sits behind the desk, facing the Jansens with an expectant air and a direct, frank gaze.

· · · · · · · · ·

A week before today's session the Jansens had attended a pre-mediation workshop aimed at providing them with basic information about mediation procedures and objectives. Butler was one of the speakers at the workshop and arranged today's appointment with the Jansens at that time, with some difficulty. At the workshop, Butler thought the "climate" between Barbara and Robert was extremely tense. Robert appeared especially angry and wary. However, before the first meeting, Butler received telephone calls from both Jansens that seemed to promise a favorable attitude toward working with her. The gist of the calls was that the Jansens now agreed on the general goal of trying to expand Barbara's time with the children; they remained far apart, however, on how this could be done. Indeed, Robert was skeptical that it could be accomplished at all but was willing to try.

The first mediation session opened with Butler asking the Jansens if either had any questions left over from the workshop. After Robert jokingly inquired who was responsible for burning the popcorn, Barbara asked why, after already going through lawyers and the courts, they were now in mediation. Butler replied:

> That's a real good question. Your situation is kind of unique. Your mediation procedure is out of synch with the procedure as we described it in the workshop, very definitely. Why did that happen? Well, it has something to do with the particular judge that you are with. He has done that before; he waits for the professionals to get a hand in it and to bring back their reports, and then he sends people to us. Quite frankly, that puts a different focus on mediation, because what it means to me is that the opinions the judge got are causing him some concern; in other words, the solution to the situation is not readily apparent, if I may be very frank with both of you.

Butler suddenly interrupts her train of thought, switching to a faster pace of speech and a slightly lower pitch of voice—a signal that something important is being said. "I think what it really is, if I may be very honest with you, is that the judge is still hoping that if he gives you one last chance to sit down, you can grab that chance and make a decision, and not force him to come down with an order that I guess he feels is going to contain things that neither one of you are going to like—that 'win/lose' thing that we talked about before. . . . So you're absolutely right, Barbara, normally mediation should have occurred prior to the best interest and prior to the psychologicals. However, although you're unusual, you're not alone."

This brief speech is vivid, engaged, and without hint of condescension. Butler makes direct personal contact with each party and sets a relaxed, warm tone (as in the shared laugh over the burnt popcorn). The looming image of the judge, "hoping" they will "grab" this "one last chance," graphically reinforces the theme of self-determination that underlies the whole opening discourse. The mediator has also underscored her expertise about the court system (how judges think, what normal procedures are) and coupled it with tempered, empathic optimism that the Jansens and she can succeed if they work together on a settlement.

Butler moves immediately from this opening episode into a series of questions about the parties' knowledge of the court-ordered evaluations. She quickly ascertains that both are aware that the best interest report and the psychologist's evaluation reached somewhat different conclusions about custody. More questions follow concerning how the Jansens came to the initial custody arrangement and the basic chronology of the physical separation period. She learns that the decision that the children would remain with Robert in the marital residence was a joint one; however, for about three-quarters of the time, the children were cared for by Robert's mother, while he spent time repairing a "handyman's special" he purchased shortly after the separation. Butler then moves to the sensitive issue of Barbara's renunciation of custody.

"Back then," Barbara says, "I didn't realize we didn't have to settle custody of the kids. But in the lawyer's office I said to him that I want the kids back after I get my own place. And he and the lawyer said, 'Don't worry about it; we'll take care of it when the time comes.' And I didn't worry about it. I just signed the paper."

Butler asks about the specifics of the custody agreement,

which had been drawn up by a lawyer-friend of the couple.

"It gives Robert total custody," says Barbara.

"Does it say 'temporary'?" Butler asks.

"No," Barbara replies.

Robert believes there is an implication that Barbara was "railroaded" into giving him custody, and he tries to correct that impression. He notes that she always retained the right to negotiate for custody and implies that it was her own failure to act sooner that brought about the current dilemma.

More questions from Butler ascertain that, when Barbara filed for the divorce, the judge allowed the initial custody arrangement to stand but began the series of evaluations that have ultimately led to the current impasse. Her survey of the postseparation period also discloses that a visitation plan had been set up for Barbara; that, in general, the plan has worked reasonably well and with some flexibility on Robert's part; that visitation began to expand when Barbara moved into her own apartment; and that she currently has the children from Friday evening until Sunday afternoon.

There are several things about Butler's performance so far, approximately fifteen minutes into the session, that are not part of what most people regard as traditional mediation. First, Butler has not offered the parties an opportunity to "tell their story." It is a common theme in the mediation canon that, in the initial moments of mediation, the parties should be given such a cathartic invitation: it will make them feel "heard," release tension, and help establish the mediator's credentials as one who "listens."

I myself have been following this enshrined dogma routinely, in spite of the fact that the consequences have been more or less predictable: I would turn to one of the parties—the wife, for example—and, in my warmest therapeutic manner, utter something along the lines of, "So, Mrs. Smith, why don't you give me your perspective on why you are here and what you hope to accomplish, and then we'll get your views on the subject, Mr. Smith." Mrs. Smith would accept my invitation with relish, explaining that they were here because Mr. Smith was a worth-less lout who cared nothing for his children or common decency and had been vilifying and humiliating her for years. For all she knew, he might also be an alcoholic and child abuser. His cross dressing was a matter of record. She was in mediation by order of the court and was certainly willing to do her best to encourage Mr. Smith to "finally be a father" but was, shall we say, skeptical. Whatever the tonic benefits of this outburst for Mrs. Smith, for Mr. Smith and myself the results were clearly unhappy: he would be provoked into an apoplectic rebuttal and I into a dismal con-templation of other lines of work. Yes, I exaggerate. But only a little.

What shocks me even more than my habitual use of such an unproductive opening gambit is that it took me months of work-ing on the transcript of the Jansen session to realize that Butler had not used it—and that her departure from custom might be of more than passing interest. In preparing a final draft of this pro-file, I asked Butler to explain her thinking. "I think that most people in parenting conflict are totally incapable of explaining their situation to you in a rational way—together, in the same room, on a first meeting," she said. She laughed wryly and con-tinued: "If they're that conflicted and that worked up and that involved in the legal situation, how can they possibly, in a vacu-um, frame their conflict for you in any kind of constructive way? It's inconceivable to me, unless they're extraordinarily sensible people—and if they were that, they probably wouldn't be in this predicament." She laughed more openly, as if enjoying her own contemplation of the hazards of the job. Her solution to the "tell your story" dilemma? Structure and control.

"There has already been an enormous amount of unstructured ventilation by parents to various listeners," she said. "That's part of the problem, and it is also part of managing conflict: to realize how tangential and irrelevant and confused their discussion has become. The structure begins with my explaining the process and taking control *right* from the beginning, and telling them what my expectations of the process are. Then I make it immediately clear that although I am not going to throw an open invitation to ventilation, I am *extremely* interested in what's been happening and the way I'm going to find that out is to ask you a series of questions. The message I am sending, consciously or unconsciously, is that my experience makes me know exactly what I need to know, and what we need to be talking about. That, combined with what I hope is very evident interest in their problem, is a much safer way to start. The risk of losing control is greatly minimized. Not losing control is what the process is all about."

True to these words, and representing her second major departure from the canon, is her disavowal of the hortatory approach to mediation with which so many of us try to inspire, socialize, and restrain disputants—the "lectures" we give on the value of cooperation and compromise; the invocation of the curative powers of mediation (especially compared to the horrible alternatives of lawyers and courts); the sage critiques and advice on why such-and-such an action or plan was or would be ill advised. By contrast, and with very few exceptions, Butler's interventions have been exclusively in the form of questions—more than forty of them. The interrogatory mode is a hallmark of her style. In the opening phase, this style works to involve the parties actively in the give and take of mediation and to begin the process of gleaning information about each side's perceptions that may have been obscured so far.

"My style is heavily interrogatory," Butler notes. "But I try to put the questions in such a way that the people want to talk. I almost never tell anybody that they are wrong in what they are feeling. I might tell them that I don't understand—would they explain it to me a little better?—but I try not to tell them they're wrong. People don't generally feel angry when they leave mediation with me. My perception of my style is that it's very directive, but it's quiet; it's friendly."

Her interrogatory style derives partly from her experience as a best interest investigator, an experience that made a profound impression on her. "My style is highly nonjudgmental, caring," she said. "I guess that's because I've seen people abused in the investigatory process by social workers and court personnel in general who just don't have the right attitude in asking you about such important issues as where your child is going to live and who's going to have responsibility for caring for that child."

The interrogatory style is also central to the mediator's third major accomplishment in these opening minutes: the firm anchoring of the dispute in legal realities. The professional ethos of divorce mediation, in general, retains an unwitting neglect of the legal realities, partly because divorce mediation has been promoted as an "alternative" to the legal system and partly because some of its most influential theorists began working outside the courts, of whose procedures they were often wary (not to say ignorant). However, according to Butler, the workings of the legal machinery are not a mere hazard; a knowledge of the legal mechanism can also be a significant benefit by helping to point the way out of the legal quagmire into which the parties have tumbled.

Before she even meets with the parties, she reads their court file thoroughly, "even if it weighs half a pound." Nobody else on the Essex County team, myself included, paid nearly as much attention to the court files as Butler. Indeed, when I came to the project, I purposely avoided contact with the file. My training in family therapy and my doubts about the objectivity of lawyers, judges, and even other mental health practitioners who might have become embroiled in the conflict, made me keenly suspicious of what the "official" record might have to say. I would come virginal to the fray, my objectivity intact. Indeed, even now, after three years of working with Butler and somewhat won over to her views on the subject, I was skeptical. I asked her pointedly whether she might not be in error on this issue: Would it not be better to skip all that "he said/she said" nonsense?

Her answer was an emphatic no. She was confident that a careful reading of the file does not expose her to much risk of becoming biased because the typical file contains an abundance of detailed accusations from both sides. Moreover, whatever small risk of contamination is involved is more than offset, she believes, by the gains in rapport: her knowledge of their case is greatly reassuring to the parties, most of whom have become aware that an attentive familiarity with their legal record by other actors in the legal system is not to be assumed.

Most importantly, knowledge of the file is a logical extension of her view of herself as a legal problem solver and guide. She is under no illusion that the file will give her an objective picture of the conflict. She reads it for "historical perspective": How long has this been going on? Who are the key players? Who is the moving party and where are we now? Is there a previously established co-parenting order that somebody wants to change? Was there never an established co-parenting order?

She is also intent on forming hypotheses about what is generating the conflict, trying to understand where in the legal maw the parties have become entangled, speculating how attorney or judicial intervention may have created strategic imbalances of power that will have to be dealt with, turning over in her mind possible areas in which trade-offs and compromises may be possible. All of this thinking is highly subject to revision once the actual human beings are before her, but it gives her a sense of direction and shapes her initial interrogatories.

Her knowledge of the parties' legal history is also meant to convey that they are now in a new kind of arena. "This is not you talking to some sympathetic friend or a brother-in-law or sister; this is not you screaming and arguing with each other," said Butler. "This is a brand-new ball game, I tell my clients. This is an interaction and a dynamic that is, I hope, going to astound and delight you. I think that being educated about the conflict is essential to being able to do that. I don't see how you can escape it."

Concerns about creating a new context for the parties in which they can communicate are also behind Butler's strong dislike of another icon in the mediation canon: the use of separate caucuses between the mediator and each of the disputants. She recognizes that caucusing may occasionally be inevitable, but rarely calls one. In her view, caucuses continue for the disputants the themes of secrecy and private strategies that typify the worst elements of the adversary legal arena. For Butler, nothing could be worse than re-creating such prospects in mediation.

Once a mediation begins, Butler continues to use her legal expertise to shape and direct the negotiations. She does this now with a question to Barbara, who is the moving party in the legal proceedings. The deliberate vocal stress on each of the first dozen or so words, as well as the questions themselves, seems almost like a signal that the preliminary phase of mediation is ending and a new phase is simultaneously commencing.

. . . .

"Barbara," Butler requested, "explain to me now, if you would, what the present legal situation is. What are you seeking now in these legal proceedings? What is the ideal situation that you would like to see come out of this?"

Barbara then lists her objectives. Her first choice would be to reverse the current arrangement. She would have the children Mondays through Fridays, and Robert would see them on weekends. She has discussed this plan with Robert, who has turned it down. She is willing, therefore, to pick up the children after school on Wednesday on her way home from work and keep them until Saturday evening when Robert would pick them up.

This, she says, is her effort to meet him "halfway." She then begins to express worry about her daughter, Ann, who is "having a tough time in school," is "going through puberty," and "needs to be with me." Barbara reports that Ann has no friends in school and is constantly being teased by the other children because "she doesn't have a mother." According to Barbara, "She really, really needs to be with me. She says she hates her grandmother. She seems very unhappy and very depressed. Frankie [their son] might feel the same way, but he doesn't show it; he's not that emotional."

Butler notes that Ann apparently talks to her mother about her desire to be with her and about being unhappy in school. "Does she talk to you about it, Robert?" Butler asks.

Robert, in a kind of rhythmic sing-song voice, says, "Certain times she does and certain times she goes the opposite way. It all depends on who she's with, how she feels, what has occurred, and what she's heard. She's very perceptive of what goes on around her. She puts two and two together, draws her own conclusions, passes them along to her brother. Her brother is right now making up his own mind on a lot of things. More or less, he's becoming independent. It's good because, for his sake, he doesn't rely on his sister."

This response is highly characteristic of Robert's verbal style, which tends toward vagueness and the abstract positing of contrary possibilities. This particular utterance has an additional confounding power because of the hypnotic rhythm with which it is uttered. Robert continues, more to the point, by saying, "As far as the issue of the time that she would have them, it works out on paper, but not in real life, mainly because—I've already had comments from Frankie and Ann that they want their own separate rooms—they can't get along together in one room. Where she's at now, they're in one room, on a day bed."

Barbara and Robert quibble, with Barbara arguing that since she puts Frankie to bed a few minutes before Ann, privacy in the bedroom is not an issue, and Robert contending that such a schedule is unfair. Robert then defends his mother's role with the children. As he sees it, the kids exaggerate, like to play one side off against the other, and are sometimes simply misperceiving Grandma's motives.

His remarks elicit an impassioned response from Barbara:

> His mother is always putting me down. She puts the kids in the middle all the time. I never say anything about Robert, the grandmother, anything. I get remarks from Ann—and I know that it's the grandmother saying it, because Ann couldn't think of it— that "Grandma says you're an asshole"; "Grandma says you're stupid." I have a little piece of paper that Ann left on my bed that says, "Grandma says she hopes you die." She says I'm going to die because I left the father, because I never wanted to be with him, I only married him to get out of my own house, I never wanted Frankie and Ann to begin with. She's always playing mind games with the kids. As far as I'm concerned, she's mentally abusing them.

Robert responds by saying, "Don't talk about mentally abusing them, if you want to get technical [with an ominous chuckle]; don't talk about abusing them."

Butler then asks both parties to "let me back up a second" and turns to Robert and says she's not sure that she understands his response to Barbara's proposal for her to have the kids from Wednesday until Saturday. "With the exception of the sleeping arrangements, do you have any problems with that?" she asks.

This intervention sidesteps the rising tensions and potentially explosive material that has begun to surface. As I listened to this segment, I wondered whether it would not have been wiser to inquire further into the "Grandma issue" and Robert's allusion to other forms of "abuse." The route chosen by Butler, however, is more pragmatic: the parties have asked her to help them correct an initial custody agreement that has brought them nothing but trouble. If the custody plan can be amended quickly, without the risk of exacerbating the conflict by delving into ancient history, so much the better.

However, it is immediately apparent that Barbara and Robert are not yet prepared to follow this tack. The oscillation between Butler's search for a negotiating focal point and the Jansens' need to air their differences results in a series of "episodes" in which first one party, then the other, gets a turn at being heard on an important issue.

The first episode revolves around Robert's concerns for the children's safety while they are in Barbara's care. He describes "constant abuse" of his son by Arthur, Barbara's live-in boyfriend. Frankie has had large bruises on his behind as a result, according to Robert, of Arthur's pinching. Robert claims that before that, both children were disciplined with straps and spoons.

"And now the spoon doesn't have a crown on the end of it; it's down to nothing but a stem," he charges angrily. "Getting punched in the arm: what kind of man is this? And I'm afraid for those kids. If you're not supervising them, God knows what could happen." He adds that "Ann tells what happens to Frankie. She never admits that she's ever been hit. I don't know what she's concealing. For a while there, they would tell us things. Now there's like hush-hush; they look at each other and it's, 'Don't tell him'—that kind of look. I don't know what's going on."

Barbara does not deny the accusations but tries to justify her and Arthur's behavior. When she and Arthur first began having visits with the children, she reports, they were being disciplined with a belt because, according to her, Robert was telling them that they didn't have to listen to Arthur. The children were calling Arthur a "jerkoff" and were defiant of any authority that she and Arthur tried to exercise. "They were just laughing at us. We had to show some kind of discipline," Barbara says.

Now she feels that things are better. Arthur has begun to ignore the children when they misbehave. Barbara also notes that the children "love" to play with Arthur; he takes them to the park and plays sports with them—something Robert never did with them. Furthermore, Frankie often initiates the pinching on the behind with Arthur. "He pinches Arthur; Arthur pinches him back. It's not what Robert is trying to make it sound like," she says.

Butler now faces the dilemma of maintaining rapport with Barbara while at the same time protecting the children from physical abuse. Speaking "both as a mediator and an officer of the court," she expresses her "personal opinion" that the use of belts and spoons "should never occur."

The mediator, quietly but emphatically, tells Barbara that she "needs to assume control of this situation by explaining to Arthur that he would be hurting your chances of gaining custody or gaining a larger period of time with the kids if he ever does that again. . . . We are living in a time when the courts and DYFS [Division of Youth and Family Services] are becoming very watchful of all forms of corporal punishment, especially any kind that would leave a mark on a child. If those marks were reported by a school nurse or a teacher, there would be intervention by the state. I realize that what you are saying is that this happened by way of roughhousing, but it should never occur at all. Do you agree with that assessment?"

The closing question offers Barbara an opportunity to clarify and give additional perspective on the violence. Such information is obviously important, especially since Butler is obligated to report suspected abuse to DYFS. (In one of her recent cases, she terminated a mediation and notified DYFS after the first half hour disclosed the strong likelihood that there was ongoing child abuse.) The question also softens the implied criticism of Barbara by offering her an opportunity to save face.

Barbara acknowledges that the physical punishment was wrong, but when the children were first back in her care it was "hard to get them under control." Robert sharply reminds her that it is her responsibility to control the children, not Arthur's.

The information about the physical abuse has also alerted Butler that she needs to reassess the idea that a viable settlement can be built around Barbara's proposal for more time with the children. She begins a series of pointed questions, asking Barbara why she thought it was so difficult to control the children when she first had them for visits? "Because of the things they were hearing. They were so confused. 'Your mother doesn't want you.' 'Your mother doesn't love you.' 'You don't have to listen to Arthur.' 'He can't hit you.'"

In retrospect, were there any better ways that she could have gained control of the situation other than by allowing Arthur to use physical punishment on them? "I guess what he's doing now; just ignoring them . . . and they've been pretty good lately." How long has that technique been working? "Oh, a couple of months." Do the children have any more of a respectful attitude toward Barbara? "It's not really so much me. They apologize and he won't talk to them until they say they are sorry. It seems to be working okay now."

The questions Butler asked here intrigued me. She herself believed that these were some of the key questions she had posed in the session, and I could hear clearly from the tape the productiveness of her interventions. However, I knew from painful personal experiences just how difficult it can be to pose useful questions to parents in the midst of emotionally roiling material. I asked her to explain her motives. She sketched them with no trouble: first, she wanted to make sure that Barbara had a solid grasp on the requirements of decent parenting; second, she wanted Robert to be able to hear for himself that Barbara understood that violent discipline was unacceptable; third, by getting Barbara to verbalize why her children had been initially so difficult to manage, she was hoping to help her "integrate intellectually a lesson she knows in her guts—that children being hard to manage is common in situations like hers and the causes are known"; and finally, she was trying to educate Robert to see that he, too, was playing a role in the children's unruly behavior.

In contrast with this easy retrospective sketch of her own motives, Butler's inner experience at the time was anything but intellectually neat and organized. "It's all intuitive," she said. "It comes from a very strong conviction that I understand how to help them manage their conflict; that I understand how to learn about it, and, once I know about it, how to help them understand it better and possibly resolve it." Beyond this visceral belief in her own powers, not much else was clear to her. "Now I know, looking at it, why I asked those questions, but it was instinctive." I then asked her what she was thinking as she listened to the Jansens in that sequence.

"I got a little sick to my stomach. . . . What does he mean, 'physical abuse'? . . . Are these children being hurt? So now I'm scared, to some extent I'm anxious," said Butler. "But I never lose sight of the fact that I want to keep this thing going; that I'm not ready to jump ship just because he threw out a 'physical abuse' charge. I want to find out, but I want to find out in a way that doesn't send everybody running out of the room."

By the time she had received answers to her questions, Butler realized that Barbara did understand the requirements of more effective discipline and that the plan to give her more time with the children was still viable. (Nonetheless, Butler brought the information about the physical discipline to a team conference a few days later. We agreed that I, as team psychologist, would review the tape of the session. These reviews endorsed Butler's handling of the session. She had made clear the unacceptability of the discipline methods; also, Robert and Barbara had agreed to seek therapy immediately, so there was assurance of ongoing monitoring of the children.)

Switching to an entirely new tone, bright and crisp, Butler addresses Robert: "Let me ask you a question now," she says. "One of the beauties of mediation, Robert, is that when someone raises concerns like, for example, the ones you have raised, we can address those concerns on paper, in the agreement. So, for example, if you were inclined to give Barbara more time with the kids along the lines that she is saying—and I'm not recommending that you do that—I'm just explaining how this would work."

This intervention encapsulates many aspects of the Butler style (that is, the veiled but strong push for a particular substantive direction, the use of language to emphasize a possible future settlement—"we can address that concern on paper"). However, the intervention is stillborn. Robert is still not ready to proceed along those lines, and Butler defers as a new, related episode of parental conflict unfolds.

Robert describes an occasion from last summer when Barbara had the children. He claims Barbara screamed over the phone that she wanted the kids "out of here," that she couldn't "stand 'em." Despite this, Robert left the children with Barbara. The next morning, he says, Barbara telephoned him at work and said she did not mean anything she said; she was "upset" and asked him "not to go telling my lawyer or taking it heavily."

"For two days I was upset," said Robert. "I didn't know what way to go. Should I listen to my lawyer or go get the kids? What should I do?"

"What did you do?" Butler asks.

"I let her have them," said Robert, chuckling. "I took the chance. Luckily they came through."

Once again, Butler channels the dialogue around the central issue of Barbara's parental competence. She begins by asking Barbara to describe what was going on during the period in question.

Barbara explains that all three children (her two and Arthur's son, Keith) would vie for Arthur's attention. On the weekend in question, they had gone to the Statue of Liberty. She stresses that "everybody was included" but that since Arthur is so good with children, they all fought for his attention. At times, things got tough because the three children were not used to being with each other. In addition, Frankie did not always understand that Arthur's son was only roughhousing. Robert interjects that Frankie was complaining of getting punched in the stomach and being kneed in the groin—and this from a boy two years older than he.

"What was going on the night that you called Robert?" the mediator asks.

"My kids were all fighting with Keith and it was just tough in the beginning," Barbara said. "They weren't listening to me or Arthur. I just got a little on edge because I hadn't had the kids for a while. But we worked things out and it was fine the next day."

Butler then asks Barbara, "If you were to have them for another month, now that you are six, seven months into that relationship and into what you describe as a better situation with the kids, do you think that the month would be as rough as it was then?" Barbara says no, "because we were trying to think of things to keep the kids busy, and now they go to school; it's like a schedule now. I think it would be alright."

Butler has allowed Barbara to advance her case for expanded visitation: There were reasons things went so badly then; now things are better.

· · · · · · · · ·

Robert then wants to know "what about if I were to agree to this Wednesday to Saturday, or whatever? What about during the summer or the time they have off from school? What happens then? What are you going to do with juggling your schedule then?"

Barbara acknowledges that "yeah, that's a problem."

Butler's patient tracking of Robert's concerns and the use of the interrogatory mode to camouflage her orchestration of the proceedings has begun to pay off: Robert is now discussing the initial proposal that Butler had unsuccessfully tried to float a few minutes earlier in the session. However, a major new set of issues is about to erupt.

Robert makes it clear that, in regard to summer or holidays, he allows Barbara to have the children if he "feels comfortable" with how things are going. When he is not comfortable, he feels he has a "right" to hold the children back. The articulation of his authority and control propels Barbara into her longest and most detailed statement thus far. She recounts alarming worries:

> Sometimes I feel uncomfortable with your mother. Ann keeps telling me that in the summertime she locks her out of the house in the yard. She told me twice about that. . . . Ann broke out crying uncontrollably in church one day. She misunderstood something he had told her, that "you'll never see your mother again." It was the first missed court date. She over-heard something. And Ann will hear the last part of a sentence and she'll fill it in. They had to bring her out of church; she was crying uncontrollably. I went to speak with his mother. She denied saying anything about me. "I never locked the kids out," she said. Things that I heard Ann say, that I questioned her about. Ann says, "Grandma lies. She locks us out in the yard." Ann is so afraid of her grandmother her hands get sweaty and clammy. She had lice in her hair because her hair is not properly taken care of.

The most explosive issues of the session are now on the table. From this point until the episode ends, Butler will remain entirely within the interrogatory mode, carefully probing for information about Grandma's role in the family.

Both parents recognize the need for counseling for the children. Robert has gone so far as to get the name of a counseling agency, but has deferred seeking help until the custody issue is resolved; he has not been sure that Barbara would follow through on the counseling if she got the children. Barbara declares softly, but with determination, "I want to get the kids away from his mother. They hate her."

Butler now begins to explore the Grandma issue, which has been simmering throughout the session. She has tentatively concluded that Barbara's concerns are legitimate. Barbara's complaints about Grandma are detailed, and Robert has said little to change the mediator's impression. Rather than waste more time eliciting additional details from Barbara (and risk worsening the climate significantly), Butler begins to test her hypothesis by testing Robert's perceptions.

"Robert," she asks, "what do you feel truthfully about their relationship with your mother? Do you think its a good relationship?"

"I think it is," he replies determinedly.

"Do you see any evidence of Ann being fearful or anxious about your mother?" asks Butler.

The mediator appears to be hoping that Robert will either throw new light on his mother's role or will exhibit some capacity to distance himself from his dependence on her for child care. He does neither, responding instead with a rambling monologue to the effect that when Grandma is properly stern with the children—as when they are not doing their homework—they "shy away" from her; but when she is indulgent, they like her. In his view, being with his mother does no more harm to the children than being with Barbara and Arthur. Barbara begins to take exception to this conclusion.

Butler is now aware that she has been pursuing an unproductive trail. And perhaps an unnecessary one. She switches back to a discussion of the children's frame of mind when they see either parent—for example, when it is time to leave Robert and go to Barbara's.

"It's not that they're happy," says Robert, "but they're excited. Because when she comes—originally she would wait outside in the car—and they had to move; it was like the adrenalin started pumping in them. Not that it was 'Oh Mommy.' They gotta go; they gotta go."

An irritated Barbara says, "That's not true; it's not true. Why don't you tell her about when I drop them off; how they stand by the door and wave until they can't see me anymore? How they blow me a million kisses."

"What do you think they do when I come home at night?" asks Robert loudly.

"So they're anxious to see you. But they're anxious to see me too," chimes in Barbara.

"That's what I'm saying; it's equal," Robert states.

There is a sudden, dramatic silence, as if everybody has been caught off guard by Robert's sudden turnabout—first denying that the children are happy to see Barbara at all, and then agreeing that they are. Butler has what she was hoping for, but the somewhat zany way she has obtained it seems to have temporarily dazed her.

• • • • • • • •

With Robert's words of agreement about the children's happiness at seeing both parents, Butler snatches back the conversational ball. "Okay," she says, taking a deep, audible breath, and then pauses. Before she can begin, Robert embarks on another statement about the need to get the children in therapy, his lack of money to do so, but his determination to somehow make it happen. Butler gives him room to talk, but it is apparent from her more frequent than usual "uhmms" as he speaks that she is anxious for him to finish his thought so that she can return to her own interrupted purpose.

"Okay," she begins again, with a tone that seems surer and more authoritative this time, as if his interruption has given her the chance to solidify her thoughts and the determination to speak them. "Let me see if I can frame this thing for you a little bit in time," she says. "First of all, you and Barbara can make a plan if you want to, for a very short term, that would stop your involvement with the court, stop your legal expenses, and have some sort of a structured plan that you all could live with for whatever period of time you set it up for. What I am trying to say is that you don't have to decide today or next week what you're going to do about your kids for the rest of their lives, okay?"

She says that about half the couples she deals with "just need to know more about the situation in order to feel good about making any changes in their children's lives. And frankly, Robert—correct me if I'm wrong—I think that's what I hear you saying: there are some good things going on; yes, they'd like to see their mom, but I have some concerns about what's going on over there. And you're *both* telling me that the kids are acting out in ways that are not absolutely healthful."

Butler has planted the first of a sequence of ideas that will come rushing out of her in the next few moments. The parties will be permitted to respond and comment briefly, but only long enough to confirm that they do not seriously disagree. In the next few moments, Butler will synthesize for them everything she has learned and thought about the conflict that is germane to finding an expeditious path out of it.

Butler does not subscribe to the view that the mediator is primarily a benevolent but nondirective presence, whose job is to improve the "climate" in which the parties search for their own solutions to the conflict. This earnest but essentially passive conception of the mediator's role has had an unusually persistent life among the first generation of family and community mediators. Nonetheless, successful mediators enact a far more directive vision of the role. The persistence of the nondirective theology owes much to the insecurity and lack of experience of the first generation of family mediators and the uncertainty within the field as to how to draw the line between the mediator's mandate to resolve disputes and, at the same time, avoid the act or appearance of favoritism or strong-arming. This problem does not trouble Butler. Halfway through the first meeting, she has formulated a plan for the terms of final settlement. From this point forward, she will get the parties talking along the substantive lines that she has determined are sensible.

The first part of her proposal contains several other characteristic elements. First, she introduces a time perspective and gives the parties a notion of the flexibility and control over their own destinies that the mediation process can afford. ("You don't have to decide today . . . what you're going to do about your kids for the rest of their lives.") Second, she holds out temptingly the motivational "carrot" of ending the legal quagmire (they could "stop" their involvement with the court and "stop" their legal expenses). Finally, her remarks reflect her attention to the legal realities. Custody and physical control of the children rest with Robert. She addresses him because, if the conflict is to take the path that she has come to feel is reasonable, it is Robert who will have to take the first step. Barbara is the first to speak after the mediator's remarks, asking Robert directly if Arthur is the problem in giving her custody. Robert angrily says "no," then mentions the size of her apartment. Butler listens attentively to this exchange but has more to say.

We could have a plan where Barbara's time might be expanded—and again, I'm not suggesting this, I just want to walk you through this—and while it's expanded to whatever degree you feel comfortable with, you get the kids involved in therapy, so that you can get some feedback from a professional as to what's best for them. If they are unable to verbalize for you now what they really need and want, maybe what you need is the input of a professional; and I don't mean a one-shot evaluation like you got from the court-appointed psychologist. I mean somebody who will really listen to both of them and help you make a longer-range plan.

Okay, what you could do, if you wanted to, is come to some agreement on perhaps a slightly expanded time frame—if you can live with that, Robert. And then put that in place. What we would do is, we would ask the judge to memorialize that as an order of the court. It would say, "At this moment in time, this is what Barbara and Robert want to do with respect to their children." With the clear understanding, in writing, that the children are going to enter therapy and that we will meet again with the mediator in whatever time frame you want that to be—three months, six months—or you could leave it open-ended.

The appeal of the mediator's plan is built on a number of factors. It is, first, a modest proposal (a "slightly" expanded time for Barbara to have the children is all that is being suggested). Second, the message leans heavily on themes of autonomy and control. (They will only expand the time with Barbara "to whatever degree you feel comfortable with"; the proposed therapy is designed so that they can get some "feedback" from a professional who will "really listen," so that they can decide what is best for the children; they will decide when to come back to mediation.) Third, the plan is made more comprehensible and tempting by the use of visual imagery and concrete language ("What we would do is, we would ask the judge to memorialize this as an order of the court"). Finally, the presentation positions the mediator as a powerful ally (what "we" could do) and as one who is more than willing to defer should her judgment be found wanting ("I'm not suggesting this; I just want to walk you through it.")

From the beginning of the session onward, Butler has not so much been generating a process of joint problem solving by the parties as she has been conducting one inside her own head. Barbara and Robert gave her the initial charge; in theory they were both willing to consider expanding Barbara's time with the children. In practice, however, it has been the mediator's focused questioning and her continuing flow of substantive ideas that have moved them toward the goal. What will prevent such a highly directed process from leading to "solutions" toward which the parties will have no genuine sense of psychologicalownership?

The answer would seem to lie in two directions. The first has to do with the degree to which Butler's proposal is rooted in an accurate and fair understanding of the parties and their circumstances. On this count her suggestions seem responsive to the facts: the parties themselves have been expanding Barbara's time with the children, and Robert has signaled that he is not, in principle, opposed to continuing to do so; both parents acknowledge that psychological help is needed; and only temporary, short-range plans would seem appropriate, given the uncertainty as to what underlies the children's troubling symptoms.

The second criterion for judging the appropriateness of the mediator's directive control is the extent to which Robert and Barbara will be allowed to explore and modify the proposal that the mediator has put into play. It is around this issue that the next major phase of the session will revolve.

. . . .

Butler works quickly to elicit Robert's evaluation of her ideas. As he articulates his doubts, she helps Barbara respond to his concerns. With the exception of an occasional "uh-huh" from the mediator, nearly all of this work is done through questions.

Robert says that he has two "negatives" about expanding Barbara's time with the children. Before he can describe these, the couple begin to squabble over Robert's assertion that a prior plan to give Barbara time with the children on Sundays "never materialized" because she began working on Sundays. Butler gives them a moment or two to argue, then pushes them back to Robert's "two negatives."

The first issue he raises is the size of Barbara's apartment and the fact that Ann and Frankie share a sleeping area at Barbara's, while at his house they each have their own space. The conversation continues at length; at one point, Robert suggests bunk beds for Barbara's small apartment, and Barbara agrees she could afford the bunk beds.

Robert's second worry is what he describes as the "manhandling" of the children by Arthur. He wants Barbara present at all times when the children are in her care. Although Frankie is no longer complaining about being pinched on the behind and punched, Robert says he is still not comfortable with the situation. By way of analogy, he reminds Barbara that she used to express displeasure when her brother used to bounce Frankie on his stomach; he characterizes her as feeling that "something sexual" might have been going on.

"People are strange nowadays," says Robert. "I'm not saying anybody is, but sometimes people get certain kicks out of doing certain things. I'm not a psychologist; I'm just telling you how I hear it."

Butler, in a deliberate tone, notes Robert is making concrete statements about how he feels about Barbara's plans for custody. "My job as mediator," she says, "is to take Robert's statement and ask you how you feel about it. I don't want you to assume that inherent in my asking is my telling you that you must go along with it, or that I believe that this is true. Remember that you and Robert are their parents; I don't even know these children. Don't assume that you have to agree to each one of these proposals just because I'm throwing it back at you. Do you understand that?"

Barbara agrees, then Butler adds, "What he's saying is that he would like you or your mother to be physically present with or near those children for the entire time that they are with you. And I would suggest that we say, 'Except in case of an emergency.' Is there any problem as far as you are concerned with any one of those things?"

After a brief silence, suggesting genuine reflection, Barbara says no. Butler then asks whether she is sure.

"What if my mother is not available?" Barbara asks. "Could we say I can confer with Robert and come up with an agreement at that time?"

"Sure," says Butler. "So if your mother is not available, you will confer with Robert about alternate plans?" Both Barbara and Robert agree such a condition is fine.

Butler continues to channel the dialogue between Robert and Barbara on other particulars that are helping them form an agreement.

Barbara begins to outline her proposal: she says she would like to pick up Ann on Wednesday mornings and take her to school. Robert immediately objects; this would be "too hectic" for him. Barbara appeals to Butler, explaining that she would like to do Ann's hair in the morning. The children pick on Ann at school and Barbara feels that if her hair was done nicely Ann "would feel better about herself." Robert disparages this approach, saying that changing a child's appearance is not going to change anything. Barbara sticks to her guns, continuing to appeal to Butler. "That's why I feel the kids are picking on her, because she wears her hair parted down and just pulled back." Robert labels the idea of a morning pick-up as impractical: "There isn't enough time to work on her hair at eight in the morning." He also takes exception to the idea that Ann is socially isolated.

"She has all kinds of girlfriends," says Robert. "They come over to her house; she goes over to their house. I don't know what you're talking about. I've been taking them over myself. . . . I don't understand that, including Frankie too. I don't understand where you come off saying they have no friends. They get along with everybody."

To Butler, Barbara says, "She just looks so 'blah' and depressed." Robert interjects with "That's your opinion."

This exchange suggests part of the problem underlying the dispute: as the primary caretaker, Robert is sensitive to any implication that his parenting is defective. In this exchange, however, it is Barbara who seems more in touch with Ann's misery. Butler tries a compromise to ease them past this tension point. "Well now, let's see. She's nine, right? If you had her for longer periods of time—my daughter is going to be nine next month—could you teach her how to style her hair herself in the mornings?"

The suggestion does not take. Barbara says she has tried to teach this to Ann on weekends, but her hair is too long for her to manage it on her own. Robert disagrees that Ann is interested in changing her looks. She prefers being plain, like Laura in "Little House on the Prairie," her favorite TV show. There is some light-hearted banter, with Butler joining the parties in a chuckle about the appeal the show has for children. Robert begins a monologue about how he used to wash and style Ann's hair. His account gets increasingly tangential, with reminiscences about the school's misdiagnosis that the children had head lice and the strenuous consequences.

Butler allows him to talk, while she, half-listening, asks herself what the chances are for Robert to agree to Barbara's plan for a Wednesday morning pickup. "Not good. He is clearly against it," she thinks. "His talk about his mother's devoted housecleaning is not a good sign either; too defensive and provocative—he knows Grandma is a sore spot with Barbara. How crucial to the children and Barbara is a Wednesday A.M. pickup? Probably not crucial at all. The key thing is to get her more involved in their lives. This is not the time to let a fight start. Skirt the issue and move toward agreement."

Butler then asks about the possibility of an after-school Wednesday pickup. Both parties meander about in conversation, occasionally taking jabs at one another, but finally agree to that time for Barbara to get the children. Then they move on to when Robert should pick them up and, after a similar conversation, settle on Saturday evening after dinner.

Barbara's initial proposal, modified to meet Robert's major concerns, is now, sixty minutes or so into the session, on its way to becoming a reality. Butler, not Barbara Jansen, has been its principal architect. Having helped to uncover the major piece of the settlement puzzle, Butler presses on. She lays out a number of additional issues that they need to consider: do they want to specify a return to mediation at a specified future time or should the agreement indicate a return to mediation only if new problems arise that they cannot solve on their own? They also need a clause on getting the children into therapy.

Robert assures her that he will take care of the therapy. He realizes that therapy for the children is essential because "they're starting to hush up on me." Butler remarks that part of the "hush-hush" may have to do with the children's awareness that their parents are negotiating a new custody arrangement. A brief argument erupts. Robert feels there is no need to tell the children about the co-parenting negotiations. Barbara believes the children's anxiety would be relieved if they knew what was going on.

As the argument proceeds it emerges that, in her exasperation with their unruly behavior, Barbara may have frightened the children by threatening that she would stop taking them. She plaintively notes that they are always embroiled with one another. By way of response, Butler reflects humorously on her own parental trials. As she talks, Robert and Barbara are agreeing and laughing. For an instant, the room contains three parents contemplating the joy and puzzlement of raising children.

As Butler finishes, Barbara inquires if she has the right to say what happens to the children while they are at Robert's house. She recounts an episode from last summer when Frankie almost drowned in Robert's pool because Robert's sister, who was ostensibly in charge, was in the house rather than outside supervising the children. Robert retorts that this is a nonissue. He found out about it, and it will not happen again. Another argument starts. However, it has none of the charge and meanness of spirit of the earlier disagreements.

Butler immediately agrees with Barbara that specifying child care arrangements is a legitimate matter for mediation. However, with a laugh, she announces that before they can address the matter, she needs to call her own young daughter. In a mock serious tone, Robert accuses her of taking away from their valuable time. Seeing that she has not realized the tease, he tells her warmly that he was only kidding.

The "working through" phase of the session nears its culmination with a final episode. Should they break for the day or continue? The parties, particularly Barbara, are unsure about where to go next. Butler tells them, "Amazing as it may seem, you already have before you what I perceive to be an agreement. By that I mean, if this is what you want, and this is what Robert will agree to—with certain conditions—then . . . the next step, after we hear your concerns, would be for you to decide on a time frame. By that I mean whether you want this to be for a given period of time or whether you want it to be open-ended. And

then I would report to Judge L. that you have reached an agreement. Okay?"

Barbara and Robert agree to continue working. After inquir-
ing if both are represented by attorneys, Butler says she will draft
this agreement and give each of them a copy. "I would send it to
your homes in typed format, and then you take it to your attorneys," she says, "telling them this is what you agreed to in mediation and asking their opinion. They might fine-tune it or suggest
minor revisions," she continues. "And then one of them will sub-
mit it to the court and say, 'For this moment in time, this is what
the Jansens want to do about their children.' And at that point,
you would be disengaged from the legal process, as I said. There is
no more issue before the court." Without further discussion,
Robert and Barbara begin productively working on the few additional issues remaining for their draft agreement.

As I observed her in this case, Butler is intensely settlement-
minded. Her years of experience in the courts have made her
painfully aware that the state is often a dim-witted, clumsy parent. She knows that it can be as much of a menace as the
parental dispute itself. She also knows what can happen in
divorce disputes if the constructive moment is allowed to pass.
Notwithstanding the settlement drive, the tenor of her remarks,
as always when she is taking a strongly directive tack, is also rich
with references and reinforcements to the parties' autonomy. If
they are tired, she will defer; if they want to think things over,
she will go along; theirs is the right to review "away from this
setting."

Finally, there is the element of personal involvement. She
makes explicit her willingness to help them, and she is adroitly
self-disclosing about her own family life. In this case she uses it
not only to establish her "credentials" on parenting but to form
an implicit, supportive helping alliance, particularly with
Barbara, whose maternal insecurities and guilt threaten the entire
plan.

The children will not be left unattended while they are in the care of either parent, and mutually acceptable substitute caretakers are specified; the children will be allowed one ten-minute telephone call per day to Barbara when they are in Robert's care and vice versa; neither parent, nor any family member or friend, will be permitted to say critical things to the children about the other parent; therapy for the children will be made a priority. Although minor skirmishes erupt, the tone stays largely cooperative and the agreements flow with relative ease. Butler's contributions continue along familiar lines: she skillfully uses questions to involve both parties, elicit relevant information, and encourage commitment. When necessary, she suggests a compromise.

The last episode blends imperceptibly into one final phase of the session. This last phase is an oasis of tranquillity after the hard work that has gone before. Its defining characteristic—and a striking contrast with what has preceded—is that, for the first time, Butler does the lion's share of the talking. Although an agreement to return to mediation in six months is worked out during this phase, the majority of the time is taken up by a series of mediator "mini-lectures": the importance to the children of parental cooperation and respect; the value of relying on their own and each other's judgment rather than deferring to the judgment of others (such as Grandma or the attorneys); the importance of realizing that all children have problems and fears (this discourse seems aimed primarily at Barbara); and the need for both of them not only to seek therapy for the children but to be actively involved in selecting and working with the therapist.

Speeches of this type are common among the custody mediators whose work I have been privy to, including my own. Typically, they begin early and continue like a background hum, with periodic rises in exhortatory intensity. Experience suggests that such talk often signals mediator anxiety or the absence of a clear idea of what else to do; I think of it as mediator "chatter." For Butler, talk of this kind has an altogether different purpose: it is a confirmation of what she and the parties have achieved together and a respite from their labors. She also appears to want to lend her own determination and belief in the settlement to Robert and Barbara. Listening to the tape, I imagine them bent slightly toward her in their chairs, eagerly attending to her words, nodding and speaking their confirmation that she is correct, that it all makes sense.

"I cannot overestimate to you the value of that last provision: not to speak against each other to the kids," Butler advises. "We're not stupid in mediation; we've seen all kinds of conflicts. I personally have been divorced—I know what it's like. And I know that it's hard to speak positively about a situation that pained you, or about a person that caused you pain. But every bit of evidence that we have says that, if you can bring yourself to either say nothing or say something positive . . . it's like antibiotic to an infection, you know? It just does so much good for the kids to feel that 'it's okay for me to go and enjoy Dad,' 'that Mom's not mad at me for doing that,' and 'it's okay for me to enjoy Mom because Dad's not mad at me.'

"It's really scary to lose the affection of one of your parents," she continues. "It's probably the most scary prospect in the world for a child. I can't even get to that place in my head—what it must be like for them to feel that if they are kind to one parent they will risk losing the love of another parent." Both Robert and Barbara agree.

＊ ＊ ＊ ＊ ＊ ＊ ＊

"Structure" is perhaps the most characteristic of all the elements that constitute the mediation style of Fran Butler. The empathy, the adroit and persistent use of interrogatories, the graphic language, the personal involvement—all of these occur within a distinct series of logically connected movements and clearly demarcated episodes within movements.

None of the rest of us on the team produced mediations with as much organization and structure. The pressures and constraints of the court setting do produce what might be called the "bureaucratic style"—an approach as distinctive as Butler's, but without its organization. The defining characteristic of the bureaucratic style is a preoccupation with "settlements," settlement being the currency that the court setting most easily recognizes. If the field of mediation was developed enough and the product less ephemeral and mundane, the musical analogy of structure and movements could be extended: Butler is an exponent of the "classical" style in custody mediation—feeling, but unsentimental; dramatic, but disciplined; flexible, but conforming to a distinctive plan. The plan is only partly conscious; Butler recognized it as typical of her work when it was described to her, but it was not, as far as she can tell, premeditated. It is a creative piece of cognitive work, all the same, and in a way more strikingly so because the material to be shaped is a human social interaction in which the "notes" can scarcely be taken for granted.

* * * * * * * *

Five months after the session recorded here, Robert and Barbara called Butler with a request for further mediation, per the agreement in the first go-round. This second stage of mediation involved two additional sessions of approximately two hours each. In the first of those meetings, the children were invited in and had a brief separate caucus with Butler.

These were difficult meetings, especially for Robert. Since the earlier mediation, he had lost his job and was on unemployment. Perhaps more crucially, he had lost his mother's psychological and practical support. She had made it increasingly clear to him that her condition for continuing to help him care for the children was that Barbara cede the mothering role to her. If Barbara was back in the picture—the manifest result of the first round of mediation—Grandma was out. The sessions also confirmed for Butler the strong suspicion she had formed in the first round of mediation: that Grandma was treating Ann in an emotionally abusive way. Grandma was neglecting Ann's physical care to the extent that teachers were noting that Ann smelled of body odor, she was dressing Ann in unstylish clothing, and she was openly disparaging of her physical resemblance to Barbara. Robert's sister, who was also living with his mother, echoed the implacable hostility to Barbara's reemergence into the lives of the children. Robert was thus trapped between his own very deep attachment to the children, on the one hand, and his greatly diminished ability to make a home for them, on the other.

Barbara, in the meantime, had become better stabilized. Between the first and second round of mediation, she had married Arthur and had been managing her expanded visitation with the children reasonably well.

The first mediation had also set several useful currents in motion. Cooperation between Robert and Barbara had increased, and therapy for the children had been in progress for the last two and a half months. Robert was a potent force behind this counseling, as he had promised he would be. He religiously took the children to their appointments and had attended several of their sessions. He also gained a degree of objectivity about his mother's influence on the children and was able to empathize with Ann's distress at how Grandma sometimes scapegoated her. Butler felt that the therapy had helped the children be more direct with their parents about their needs, and their exposure to therapy may have facilitated their willingness to talk with Butler about their wishes—a move that somewhat eased Robert's uncertainty about ceding even more authority to Barbara.

Reflecting on these changed circumstances and building on the firm working alliance that had been established in the first round of mediation, Robert and Barbara reached a new accord to replace Robert's sole legal custody with joint custody. Barbara was given sole physical custody of the children. Butler transmitted this final mediation agreement to the judge, and it was made into an order of the court.

Several months after this new agreement was reached, Robert and Barbara were contacted by the research arm of the project for their views on the mediation services. Their reports were extremely favorable. Both of them listed themselves as "very satisfied" with the mediation and could not think of anything they were dissatisfied about. Barbara's views were especially glowing. (The interviewer described her as perhaps the person most pleased with mediation of the thirty or so with whom he had spoken.) Her only regret was that mediation had not come much earlier.

"I saw a lot of pain in the kids," she said. "Had [mediation] come earlier it would have saved lots of headaches. As a couple we never could communicate. Through the mediator my point of view was heard. As soon as mediation started I paid off my lawyer. I didn't need him once mediation began. . . . Fran was great! She was very personable. It was easy to open up and talk to her. In mediation it seemed like the people cared about me. It was not like with lawyers, where all you see is your money flying out the window."

Robert was not as effusive in his praise, but he too was laudatory. He appreciated the mediator's "total involvement" and felt the mediation was helpful "right from the start." He felt that "if more couples tried mediation the courts would be in better shape."

Mediation did not, however, solve all of this family's problems. Within a month of these positive evaluations, the children were again posing discipline problems for Barbara, and Robert was wondering whether he had made a mistake in allowing her to become the primary caretaker. However, their faith in Butler was unshaken, and both of them reached out to her for guidance. With Robert's wholehearted consent, Butler arranged for Barbara and Arthur to come in for a meeting to explore the source of the discipline problems with the children. I was invited to attend as consulting psychologist. Careful questioning clearly indicated that the use of physical discipline had not reoccurred. The meeting resulted in a plan for Barbara and Arthur to seek counseling to help them work more effectively as a parental team.

Although the Essex County Family Mediation Project is now complete, Butler's dedication to family mediation remains strong. Promoted out of the nondissolution program, Butler continues consulting with members of the mediation team, examining the mediation process extensively and training others in its skills. As she does so, her commitment to mediation as an alternative for parents in conflict grows continually stronger.

Kenneth Kressel

Notes

The project on which this chapter is based was funded by a grant from the New Jersey Administrative Office of the Courts. The views expressed are not necessarily endorsed by the funding agency.

1.   Names and identifying information about the family have been altered to protect the anonymity of family members.

2.   Among the better-known examples of work on the "nuts and bolts" of mediation are Folberg and Taylor (1984), Haynes (1981), and Moore (1986). As is often the case, the research community lags behind the practitioners. For a recent account of the status of mediation research, see Kressel, Pruitt, and Associates (1989).

3.   The empirical data supporting these conclusions and the description of the research of the Essex County Mediation Project will be found in Kressel, Butler, Forlenza, and Wilcox (1989) and Kressel and others (in press).

References

Folberg, J., and Taylor, A. (1984). *Mediation: A comprehensive guide to resolving conflicts without litigation*. San Francisco: Jossey-Bass.

Haynes, J. M. (1981). *Divorce mediation: A practical guide for therapists and counselors*. New York: Springer.

Kressel, K., Pruitt, D. G., and Associates. (1989). *Mediation research*. San Francisco: Jossey-Bass.

Kressel, K., Butler, F., Forlenza, S., and Wilcox, C. (1989). Research in contested custody mediations: An illustration of the case study method. *Mediation Quarterly, 24,* 55–70.

Kressel, K., Frontera, E., Forlenza, S., Butler, F., and Fish, L. (in press). The settlement orientation vs. the problem-solving style in custody mediation. *Journal of Social Issues*.

Moore, C. W. (1986). *The mediation process: Practical strategies for resolving conflict*. San Francisco: Jossey-Bass.

• • • • • • •

"*There is a drawback with 'mediation technicians' wearing the techniques of mediation as a foreign appendage. One must make the skills one's own; light your own torch from others' candles, but make the skills fit your person. . . . Try to be whole.*"

—Patrick Davis

2

. . . .

Patrick Davis
"To Bring Out the Best . . .
To Undo a Little Pain"
in Special Education Mediation

I didn't know much about Patrick Davis when I first met him for lunch on the lakeside terrace of the Wellesley College Club, in late April 1989. I was not, however, unfamiliar with mediation processes, special education programs, and, in particular, special education mediation. I had raised two children, been a veteran activist in local PTA organizations, and been elected to serve three terms on a local school board. The relations between parents and schools about children had been a large part of my life for more than a decade.

During this first interview with Davis, however, I began to realize that my usual methods of sociological inquiry might not work in this project. As I attempted to push the talk toward topics appropriate for this profile, questions about the economics and law of special education, Davis's training as a mediator, and his goals in the cases he handled, he insisted on questioning me. He insisted on that reciprocal exchange and informational intimacy that constitutes good conversation but threatens professional distance and objectivity. This was dangerous territory. I feared being taken in, losing my critical edge. Yet I began to like this man.

In the end, I did not feel undone, but not because sociological inquiry is impervious to individual agency or resistance. Rather than obstructing my project, Davis's persistent effort to engage me created the opportunity to experience his skill personally.

Rather than being told about his techniques and simply observing his methods, I became his subject. He helped me see that
interviewing ought not be a one-way process and that it was
important that we talk about ourselves together; most important,
he allowed me to feel safe in this collaboration.

This first interview set a leisurely pace for the lunches we
would continue to share over the next year and accustomed me
to the form and tone of the mediation sessions I would later
observe. More telling, however, that first lunch suggested some of
the themes that would be revealed and regularly reenacted in the
mediation sessions, themes of exposure, pain, and incongruity,
the experiences that too frequently constitute the legacy of raising a "damaged" child. In this contested ground, Patrick Davis
calmed the spirits. But perhaps I am getting ahead of the story.

◆ ◆ ◆ ◆ ◆ ◆ ◆

Mediation is an optional stage in Massachusetts' step-by-step
process of determining the educational program for children identified with special needs. The process went into effect in 1974, two
years after the passage of a landmark Massachusetts law popularly
known as "Chapter 766," which later served as a model for the
1975 federal Education for All Handicapped Children Act. Very
briefly, both of these laws (with the Massachusetts version being
more inclusive and stringent) *require* states and local communities
to pay for the costs of educating children with special needs.

Both the state and federal statutes were, in part, a response to
the widespread and systematic exclusion of children with disabilities from mainstream schools and classrooms. Challenging conventional practices, the new laws demanded that disabled children were to be integrated with nondisabled children "to the
maximum extent appropriate." To meet these goals, the federal
government would provide funds to states that complied with the

provisions of the statute.

Both statutes require parents' informed consent for all decisions, in most cases ensuring parental (nonprofessional) participation directly in the education of children with disabilities.
Parents must approve all aspects of the special education process:
the initial identification of the child as potentially having special
educational needs, referral for special assistance, administration
of any tests or other evaluations, the specification of the impair-
ment following testing and evaluation, the enumeration of
behavioral and educational goals, and the design and operation of
a program of instruction. Parents must accept the program of
instruction, or individual educational plan (IEP), in writing
before it can be implemented.

The parental role in the decision-making process is further
enhanced and safeguarded by the parents' right to invoke an
elaborate appeals process when they believe their child's needs
are not being adequately perceived or addressed. Over forty states
now include or are developing mediation as an optional step in
the process for appealing and resolving disagreements that arise
in the special education decision-making process. Massachusetts
was among the first states to incorporate mediation into its
special education system.

Although mediation is not mandated by the federal statute,
the legislation reflects the general ethos behind the mediation
movement. It insists that substantive rights (and better education) should be created through open, nonexpert, often informal,
deliberation—exactly what mediation advocates claim it provides. In effect, the law tells parents, "We cannot say exactly
what sort of education your child is entitled to, but we can ensure
your right to have a say and to challenge important decisions"
(Engel, 1991, p. 17). And even when the mandated collaboration
and decision making fails to secure agreement among all the parties—school systems, professional educators, and parents—medi-

ation of special education disputes provides another forum to try, informally and collaboratively, to forge a local consensus about the child's needs.

Patrick Davis is one of the six full-time mediators employed by the Commonwealth of Massachusetts to mediate special education disputes. When I first began meeting with him, most of the mediators were assigned to a regional office; Davis was one of the two exceptions who shared jurisdiction for the most heavily populated region. Davis and his colleague were then each handling approximately two hundred mediation cases per year. Since the state's fiscal crisis worsened, regional offices were collected into a central state office of special education mediation.

By the time a special education case comes to mediation, the parties have usually been in conflict for months, sometimes even years. Davis confronts people who feel frustrated and powerless, sometimes angry, and often tired of dealing with each other. All other conciliatory efforts have failed, and the parties have dug in their heels. In addition to whatever constraints plague special education generally, mediation of special education disputes is made even more difficult by this personal history of disagreements and failed compromises.

Lately, the incentives to dispute and litigate have been shifted by changes in the judicial interpretation of special education legislation. New court decisions rereading the original statutes have made parents less willing to make agreements without exhausting all administrative procedures and school systems more cautious in shaping compromises. This is a domain in which the bargaining is not merely in the shadow of law, but the law and institutional practices made available by law are *actively* shaping both the mediation and the outcomes.

The cases that come to mediation are now noticeably more complex, and parties more intransigent; there are generally fewer prospects for agreement. Consequently, Davis has found mediation to be increasingly difficult. What I found remarkable was his persistent effort where success seems to be so elusive. I realized, after a while, that the mediation process was herculean, if you regarded it *only* as a means of dispute resolution. Davis did not. He believed his job did indeed offer opportunities to reach agreement as well as "bring out the best" in children, parents, and schools, and "undo a little of the pain" along the way.

· · · · · · ·

It is August now and Patrick Davis and I have arrived ten minutes early for a mediation session in Greenly, Massachusetts.[1] The administrative offices of the Greenly public schools occupy a fading red brick building whose history is etched in the pediment inscribed "Thomas Lowell School." Once the home of two dozen elementary school classes, the Thomas Lowell School building is now office space for the budget manager, curriculum planners, physical plant manager, superintendent, assistant superintendent, and the system's special education director. Set among three two-hundred-year-old beech trees, a fifty-foot Douglas fir, and several acres of playing fields, the Greenly administration building welcomes visitors with a restrained exhibit of the town's particular combination of wealth and Yankee frugality.

In this pastoral setting, the town of Greenly is markedly different from its closest neighbor, Waterville, where school administrators also occupy a now-unused elementary school. However, instead of sitting on a green hill above rolling fields of conservation land, the Waterville school offices offer views of Kentucky Fried Chicken, Midas Muffler, and ABCO Carpet Sales along an aging strip of retail stores. Despite the obvious differences in the wealth and populations of these neighboring towns, the two school-become-administration buildings retain the unmistakable marks of their previous inhabitants.

Alongside offices with bright new formica desks and filing cabinets, plush carpeting, and banks of telephones are large empty rooms with dull pastel walls, marble-chip floors, black-boards with chalk trays, and hard birch tables and chairs just slightly too low for adult comfort. Remnants of posters describing the four food groups, the metric weight system, and America as a melting pot of peoples and cultures hang precariously on abandoned bulletin boards. The corridors with yellow-tiled walls are poorly lit and cluttered with stacks of empty bookshelves. There are echoes of children everywhere, but no children. The unused classrooms feel like tombs.

The mediation session is scheduled in the administrative conference room, a spare but brightly painted and carpeted space carved out of one of the old classrooms. In the past, I have accompanied Davis to sessions in an old classroom, with parties sitting on children's chairs around a hastily constructed table. Davis does not seem optimistic about the upcoming mediation: "This is one of the more difficult types of cases," he has explained to me several days earlier. "The parents have enrolled their daughter, Heather, in the Roberts School, out in Duffield. Heather's parents, Richard and Susan Donnelly, want Greenly to pay the tuition and transportation to the Roberts School. [The Roberts School is reputed to be one of the finest private schools for learning-disabled children; it is located on the grounds of a regional public high school, making it a particularly attractive choice for many families.] Greenly's position is that the Suburban Educational Collaborative in Waterville—or SECOOP, a cost-sharing collaborative among suburban communities—is the appropriate program."

The Donnelly case, like most appeals, began with a disagreement about the IEP developed to meet Heather's "behavioral deficits and educational goals." Revised annually, such plans are the subject of discussion at the required yearly team meeting. The special education team includes regular classroom teachers, psychologists, social workers, special education specialists, and principals; they are expected to work and consult, in a group, with parents to develop the IEP. In most school systems, the annual meeting of the team has become the central locus of school system-parent consultation.

Heather Donnelly's team met in April with the expectation that Susan and Richard Donnelly would agree to the team's recommendation that Heather would move next fall from a SECOOP classroom in Riverside, neighboring Greenly on the south, to another SECOOP classroom in Waterville, east of Greenly. The Donnellys did not agree and promptly enrolled Heather in the private Roberts School in Duffield. Whether she attends school in Waterville or Duffield, Heather will need transportation.

. . . .

When parents reject an IEP, the local school system is required to forward the rejected plan to the Bureau of Special Education Appeals and to the appropriate district mediator. In some cases, parents waive mediation and proceed directly to a formal hearing (Budoff, Orenstein, and Kervick, 1982). Because mediation is regarded as an optional and voluntary process, no one is required to use it, and both parties must agree to participate. However, according to the director of the state Special Education Bureau of Appeals, 90 to 95 percent of the disputed IEPs go to mediation. More than 50 percent are resolved there (Singer and Nace, 1985).

Some school districts have created additional internal responses that precede the appeal to the state process, which thus further extends the appeals process. When a parent seems about to reject an IEP, a school system special education director will often intervene to see whether some agreement between the parents and the team can be worked out. These are the school administrators with responsibility for overseeing special education programs and supervising school-based teams. The director's intervention is regarded as part of a school system's local remedy for disputes that arise between parents and the team.

Mediation occurs late in the process for social as well as procedural reasons. Although the right and processes of appeal are clearly specified, parents are reluctant to bring appeals, even though they may disagree with a proposed IEP. The decision to appeal a local decision or education plan may mean that a child goes without services entirely. Parents are also reticent to appeal lest they end up antagonizing the people with whom they share decision-making responsibility during a child's educational career, people who must authorize continuing service and who will regularly provide direct service to the child. Retribution almost never happens, but parents still do not want to chance alienating school personnel. Other parents seem reluctant to make special claims for their child at what they perceive to be the expense of other children.[2] Thus, cases forwarded to the state for appeal and mediation have usually been through an unsuccessful, local dispute resolution effort. By that time, the parents have generally overcome any initial reluctance to dispute the professional assessments and recommendations made for their child. They are ready to do battle.

These dynamics obviously shape the mediation session; the mediation begins, so to speak, midstream. The participants are almost always well known to each other, yet Davis introduces them as the session begins. Moreover, their claims have been repeatedly explored in previous conversations between the parties one on one or in small groups. Davis's mission is to loosen these positions or more often, he claims, to get the parties to better understand each other's positions.

On one side of the table sits George Livingston, the special education director in Greenly; Sam Noble, representing the SECOOP in Waterville; and Joan Miller, Heather's teacher in the SECOOP class in Riverside. Richard and Susan Donnelly and Jim Carroll, the director of the Roberts School, are sitting

across from them. Davis is at the head of the table, and I am sitting off to the side. The Donnellys have brought new diagnostic
reports, which Davis distributes to the school personnel. While
they leave the room for a few minutes to read these materials,
Davis engages the Donnellys in conversation about their children:

Susan Donnelly: If we don't get this, I'll have to go to work to
get the $23,000 for the tuition.

Davis: Yes, that's a possibility. Parents sometimes say, "We
can't afford to do it and we can't afford not to do it."

Susan Donnelly: If only you could see how lonely Heather has
been, and isolated!

Davis: But then again, the Collaborative would be a fresh start
too; maybe she'll make connections. You never know. Both
schools would be a fresh start.

Susan Donnelly: She'd be so happy at Roberts, I just know it.

The small talk continues. Richard Donnelly explains that he
must be out of the meeting by noon to make it to the airport on
time. Although his manner does not suggest any immediate
urgency, Mr. Donnelly nonetheless announces his independence
from the process by setting a time limit for the meeting. In this
opening move, he reinforces the initiative that he and his wife
established by enrolling Heather in the Roberts School. The
Donnellys are relying on both timing and placement—the key
elements in special education—to get the town of Greenly to pay
for Heather's tuition at the Roberts School.

About timing: mediation of special education disputes begins
when the mediator contacts the parents to explain the process
and schedule a mediation session. State regulation requires the
school district to report the rejection of an IEP to the State
Department of Education's Bureau of Special Education Appeals
within five days after the parents have rejected the plan. Within

five more days, the bureau must send the parents and the school a packet of materials describing the appeals process. The mediator then contacts the parents and the school to explain the process and schedule a parent-school conference (mediation session). At this point, the mediator may begin informal efforts toward resolution that include collecting and offering information, and clarifying regulations and confusions. If the mediation session does not result in a settlement of the disagreements between the parents and the school system and an agreed-on IEP, either party may request a full formal hearing before a special education hearing officer.

In the Donnelly case, discussions with the Greenly special education director did not change the situation. The appeal was filed. Although federal law requires a formal hearing to be scheduled within twenty days of the request being filed, these deadlines may be waived at the parents' request. Parents sometimes request a delay to obtain independent evaluations and other preparations for the hearing. Such a delay further postpones the formal hearing and any intermediate mediation if it is attempted. Often the parties already have a date set for a formal hearing—in this case, two weeks following mediation—so that no additional time will be lost.

The delay between filing appeals, arranging mediation sessions, possibly continuing on to formal hearings, and then obtaining decisions has become a regular feature of special education, with direct, often detrimental consequences for children. Although statutory protections attempt to limit foot dragging, some is initiated, as indicated earlier, by parents seeking additional evaluation and consultation about alternatives.

Other delays result simply from the rigidity with which school officials move through the academic calendar. Although time can be measured in a variety of ways, school officials assess children primarily within the confines of the academic year (Engel, 1991). Under this academic calendar, special education programs are put into place in the fall and assessed at the end of the academic year in the spring. Two consequences follow from the need to fit the children's lives and development into calendars fashioned for other purposes. First, there often is insufficient time between the beginning of the school year and the early spring to adequately measure and assess changes in the child's performance. Thus children subject to this annual review process are often kept in situations for longer periods than are effective, to create documentation of the child's experience. Second, because the assessments and team meetings cluster in the last months of the school year, the number of appeals from rejected IEPs also cluster in the late spring and summer. In a typical year, for example, Davis's caseload went from a low of eleven cases in January and twelve in December to a high of sixty-five in July. This irregular pattern means cases sometimes cannot be resolved before the start of the next school year. Many special education students thus begin the school year without a fixed or new program, and again their movement to a more suitable situation is delayed.

About placement: the Donnellys, like an increasing number of parents who have learned how this process works, have altered the balance of power that arises from the rigidity of the school calendar and the slowness of bureaucratic procedures and appeals. It is probably worth noting that the entitlements under the special education statutes seem to have produced a disproportionate benefit for more affluent families like the Donnellys who know how to negotiate the rules and processes to obtain resources for their children. The Donnellys are unwilling to allow Heather to continue in a classroom of children whom both parents and school personnel agree she has outgrown; that would happen, nonetheless, if a new IEP were not signed. The Donnellys are equally unwilling to sign an IEP that would place her in the Waterville classroom, which the Greenly schools claim will provide an excellent program for the child. They contest the professional judgment of the Greenly schools and have enrolled

Heather in the Roberts School without waiting for the outcome of the appeals process.

More and more parents have chosen this route, and many, in the early years of both the state and federal legislation, found it a successful strategy for obtaining what they considered appropriate education for their children. With this action, the parents try to create greater leverage in their negotiations with the school system. Although it cannot be determinative, the child's existing placement is a factor in a hearing officer's consideration. If a child is functioning and progressing well, hearing officers will be just that little bit more reluctant to move the child, even if the current location was the result of a unilateral placement by the parents in a private school. A successful experience in the new placement creates evidence that the child is doing better in an alternative situation, even though the school was chosen by the parents, which makes the burden of proof for the school system a bit more difficult.

While the school personnel are out of the room reading the Donnellys' new diagnostic report, Susan Donnelly talks about her family. Her oldest child, Steven, is now twenty-two and training for the Olympic pentathlon. "He works out ten hours a day, six days a week. Steven will be going to Poland to train in fencing for three months. He is an all-around athlete," she says. Richard Donnelly worries about Steven's life after sports. The Donnellys have another daughter, Elizabeth, who is twenty, and then Heather, who is fourteen. Davis encourages Mrs. Donnelly to talk more about her family:

Davis: Is Heather into sports too?
Susan Donnelly: No, she's a great booster. Heather was a choice, you know. We waited five years after Elizabeth and we wanted her. We watched her develop and respond. We observed and watched her. We've tried to create lots of avenues for her, for all our children. She's artistic . . . musical, every medium. I used

to push athletics, but I've stopped. Right now, she's having fun learning to apply makeup.

Davis: You can't push on all fronts.

Susan Donnelly: Steven used to have special ed tutoring; he had organizational and auditory processing problems.

Davis: Ask me about it! I have another Steven and I know what your side of the table feels like! It's so much easier to talk about someone else's child. It was an eye-opener for me. . . . Some kids put so much energy into not succeeding. But the school response was amazing. I mean, they really went the extra mile. He's doing better, but it's a long haul.

Richard Donnelly: The sports is a great boost for Steven. . . .

Mrs. Donnelly seems nervous and keen to explain herself and her children. There is a defensive, guilty tone that emerges amidst her congratulatory rhetoric about the children. The professional staff return, having read the new reports. According to George Livingston, "There is nothing surprising here; it's worded differently. It was done by the head of neuropsychology at Children's, Robby Cohen's boss."

It is now 9:30, forty minutes after we arrived. The small talk is over, and the proceedings immediately take on a more formal and, to a certain degree, less anxious character. Davis speaks softly and though not slow, his cadence is measured and lyrical. His Irish brogue feels comforting. He begins by explaining to the school personnel that Richard Donnelly must leave by noon.

By announcing Mr. Donnelly's time constraint, Davis may have been simply noting a fact of life; he also reaffirmed the Donnellys' position. They would give this mediation just so much time but no more. They were prepared to go to the full formal hearing; they had little interest in compromising. By commenting that the neurological report contained nothing new, the special education director indicated that the Greenly Schools' position had also remained unchanged. His side, so to speak, affirmed its

previous position. Moreover, Livingston's reference to the head of
neuropsychology at Children's Hospital, Robby Cohen's boss, created an image of wider and prestigious professional support for
Greenly's position. Livingston, in effect, claimed that he is a
member of the community of specialists, a relatively close-knit
club who call each other by diminutive first names. The director
shares some of the prestige and authority of the larger community
and brings, this tone suggests, additional resources to his position.
Davis explains:

> Placement must be discussed within the context of
> two mandates. Heather is entitled to a program in the
> least restrictive environment—that is, the most nor-
> mal educational setting. She is also entitled to a pro-
> gram that will provide her with the maximum feasible
> benefit. Whether you make the decision or a hearing
> officer decides, this is the context. The law and regula-
> tions place great emphasis on inclusion [Davis puts an
> equal weighty emphasis on each syllable of *inclusion*];
> however, if the school system is satisfied that no public
> school program fits the bill, they must look elsewhere,
> and that decision is reviewed by the Department of
> Education, so strong is the mandate for inclusion.

Davis continues the meeting, noting that he "cannot emphasize enough the need to avoid letting your beginning positions get
in the way of listening. There is ample room for differences of
opinion. The special ed law is not written like an insurance policy that addresses every conceivable situation. The law is very
broad.

"Also," he says, "we are not dealing with a question of a broken, difficult, or inadequate home. We are dealing with a complexity of issues—cognitive, emotional, perhaps physical—and
maybe a combination of all three. You who know Heather are in

the best position to make a sound educational judgment, and I hope that in this informal, confidential forum, we have a candid exchange, and hopefully, an agreement."

Although Davis's few interventions until now—his informal conversation with Susan Donnelly, his reiteration of the time constraint—seemed to provide a platform for the Donnellys, these formal opening remarks emphasize the fragility of the Donnelly position. He frames the question by insisting on the necessity of review for any outside placement for Heather. He is, in effect, saying that no matter what preemptive action the Donnellys have taken by enrolling Heather in the Roberts School, that decision cannot be *the* decision.

This opening illustrates, in the context of the preliminary exchanges that seemed to bolster the Donnellys, Davis's effort to keep all parties equal players. Being equal players may require, however, giving very special attention to the absent child:

Davis: Let us begin by seeing whether we can agree on who Heather is, what are her needs and perhaps then move on to where these needs can best be met.

Susan Donnelly: It's hard to know where to begin.

Davis: Tell us the salient points . . . the highlights of the evaluation from your perspective.

Mrs. Donnelly hesitates and seems unable to begin. She breathes heavily and her hands fidget.

Davis: Mrs. Donnelly, tell us who Heather is.

Susan Donnelly: Heather is a great kid. She's our third child.

Mrs. Donnelly immediately begins describing the spacing of her children, how Heather had been planned and wanted, and is very much loved. She describes her child as she knows her and in her own words rather than the mystifying and self-consciously impersonal language that will occupy a good part of the next few hours. On another occasion Davis has explained to me that he believes part of his job is to give parents a chance to say and hear good things about their child. Interactions between school personnel and parents about their "special" child are often suffused with anxiety and an overwhelming sense of guilt. It takes a while to realize it, Davis has said, but what parents sometimes feel as the teachers, principals, and psychologists "talk *at* you about your child" is that somehow the parents are responsible for this problem, this "defective" and "inadequate" human being. To respond to this experience, and perhaps to alleviate the tension, Davis will sometimes talk about his own child and how children will defeat one's best efforts.

Davis seems to have energized Susan Donnelly by the request to "tell me who Heather is." What had been nervously exposed during the preliminary chat is now legitimately exhibited. It almost seemed as if Davis had also orchestrated the revelations:

Susan Donnelly: Heather didn't speak until she was three, and we began to think that something was wrong. She was tested at four years old by the head of Children's. Maybe it was one of his protégés, whatever. But we had all three tested when we moved here. Heather, she learns slowly. She's not a slow learner; she has language deficits. She's a good storyteller, compassionate, and oh boy is she organized. She could run a house.

She wants to learn, but she learns differently, from experience, TV, and music. She's an observer; she likes to travel. We've been to Israel and to Iowa. Reading is difficult, though. She's an experiential person.

Heather spent one and half years learning at home after the third grade. She had been in a special class, but we didn't think it was going well. Halfway into the third grade, we decided she would learn better at home. After that, she began in Riverside [the SECOOP class].

Davis: Tell us more about Heather's language needs, explain more of that.

Richard Donnelly: Heather has an unusually strong interest in learning. For example, she is right now crazy about sharks and spends a lot of time on that. Compared to the other two kids, her motivation is high; she has more interest than the average kid. She also has academic interest. She does not give up. She is tenacious! Heather is not like our son, who has mild learning disabilities. Heather's teachers have also noticed and commented to us how strong Heather's interest in learning is. Heather knows she has language deficiencies and knows that she needs to have phrases repeated. Susan studied speech therapy in college and understands these language deficiencies, knows that Heather needs to have consistent use of phrases and experiential connections to language.

Davis: Jim, could you amplify on this?

Jim Carroll [of Roberts School]: I'd like to do something different. I've diagnosed and feel I know her. She does have language processing and short-term memory deficits. But I'd like to know Riverside's experience with her. That I don't have.

Davis: I'd like to get as complete a picture as possible of Heather from this side of the table before getting a reaction from Greenly. Let's have a picture of the family, of Heather's language needs, the slow learning, the interactions with adults rather than peers. Let's fill out that picture. Tell us what you do know, minus the experience factor.

Davis seems to have an agenda that he will not let the participants derail. He is trying to make more space for the Donnellys' position by calling on their "expert" to support their picture of Heather. From what has been said thus far, he has picked up that Heather may be a slow learner but that there may be some parental denial. He wants to get the Donnellys' expert to offer his professional evaluation of Heather, either to help the parents to better accept the diagnosis or to have an alternative construction put before the school system.

Jim Carroll, however, attempts to deflect Davis's effort. Why Carroll does not immediately grasp the opportunity to talk about Heather is not clear. Although I had a sense that he was not very well prepared for the meeting, I suspect that there is something more fundamental underlying Carroll's reluctance to offer his own account of Heather. He has little experience with Heather, while the experience of the Greenly and Riverside staffs is far more extensive and of longer duration. I suspect that he is unwilling to be the first "professional" to characterize Heather, lest his lesser experience be revealed and his professionalism made suspect. While the Donnellys may be clients of the Roberts School, and Jim Carroll their professional representative, the informal alliances among professionals and their status within that community may be much more important than the relationship between client and professional.

The tension between professional and parental interests, and the tendency for professionals, even those representing opposing interests, to ally against the nonprofessional parties is, in fact, a central issue in special education. It is also one of the concerns that animated the collaborative design of the decision-making process and the legislative requirement of parental consent. As a result, both the state and federal laws specifically empower parents to share what had, until the passage of these laws, been professional prerogatives. By requiring parental involvement, the statutes specifically challenge professional claims to exclusive and expert knowledge about the educational needs and goals of children. By demanding extensive consultation and collaboration in the development of a child's IEP, the statutes empower parents to challenge the routinized application of general norms by technical experts who may have interests other than the specific needs of a particular child.

By pressing the reluctant Carroll to "fill out the picture" of Heather, Davis is attempting to interject some of this professional expertise on the Donnelly side of the table and thus possibly reduce the divide between parent and professional:

Jim Carroll: Heather is a complex child, of average intelligence but with a difference. She has special language needs. There are two areas of need. There are language deficits, and, at this point in time, there are social deficits. She has low self-esteem that was revealed in the projective tests but is apparent in meeting her. The modern world just doesn't offer the time for children like Heather; the problem is not entirely hers. With regard to language, we have to see this as three pieces: written, reading, and output of the two. Heather is able to organize the world, but not through language; she has decoding deficits and is unable to pull information from print. Therefore, her reading is seven to eight years behind, not just a year. She is reading at the third- to fourth-grade level and is thus very disabled for a fourteen-year-old. This infiltrates and frustrates all areas of learning. Content and concepts need a lot of work. Conceptually she can succeed, but we need to take into account her inability to take in information. Heather also needs work with her identity as a disabled child. We tend to judge people on reading, not ability to think. She needs to think about and assess her future and her projections for life after high school.

Davis: Jim, can you elaborate further on the issue of "average intelligence" yet seven- to eight-year reading gap? This is unusual. Are we looking at more than a problem of language?

Jim Carroll: I can only repeat: Heather is a complex child, disabled for a fourteen-year-old. She reads at the third- to fourth-grade level.

Davis: Let's have a reaction from Greenly, Riverside, and Waterville. How do you see Heather?

George Livingston [of Greenly]: We see Heather similarly. She is a language-disabled child with neurological etiology. This relationship between the nervous system and the use of language comes out in two ways. First, using language for communication and social interaction is difficult. Two, because language is such a deficit, it brings in other factors such as in reading. Heather can take in information but has trouble with inferential thinking. Language is so difficult that her thinking breaks down. However, Heather is a self-advocate; she can work with the system and get what she wants and needs. Our view is that she is a language-involved child. Thus, we have placed her in language classes, where the learning is experiential.

Davis: Is this the same as I am hearing from Mr. and Mrs. Donnelly and Jim Carroll? There is some agreement that progress has been made and will continue, within existing limitations?

Both the diagnosis, the child's "deficits," and the appropriate remedial program need to be agreed to in the development of an IEP. Here Davis is trying to sharpen the differences in the diagnosis, making the points of contention more explicit. If he can secure an agreement on the profile, he is more likely to secure consensus on the remedy. He has two goals in this profiling or specification stage. If an agreement is to emerge, there will be movement or adjustment by the parties in these framing issues. If agreement is unlikely, which is what Davis suspects, the Donnellys and the schools will be better prepared for the next stage of their appeal by having a clearer sense of the parameters of the case: the disputed diagnosis. In response to probing by Davis, the session continues:

George Livingston: No. There are differences between us on the degree of language involvement and the degree of experiential learning, reading with content, inferential thinking, syntax, semantic word retrieval. . . . We cannot see her as a third-grade reader without these. It is very doubtful. Jim talks as if this is a matter of language delay. It is not.

Jim Carroll: No, no. We could never get this kid up to grade level. I don't see that we are speaking of that.

Susan Donnelly [directed toward George Livingston]: What do you mean by self-advocate?

George Livingston: She can pull from her environment what she needs.

Susan Donnelly: She was taught! I trained her to do it!

George Livingston: She is learning pragmatics in Riverside. She is learning to say, "I don't understand that, tell me in different words."

Richard Donnelly: But you sound like she is not learning! She has learned to use these tools in environments she feels comfortable in; she can learn.

Susan Donnelly: She needs to feel comfortable, be one of the group and secure in the group, to function. At the Roberts School, she was comfortable. She functions better where she knows why she is there.

This is a critical juncture. The Donnellys are hearing that their child is incapable, unable to learn or progress. They respond vehemently and defensively. Mr. Donnelly is adamant and appears angry. Mrs. Donnelly wants the others, who now appear as a wall of hostile forces, to see Heather as she can be seen. She wants them to understand that Heather's abilities may be related to place and pedagogy and that, therefore, the particular placement is absolutely crucial to her future. Yes, Heather *can* pull from her environment because Mrs. Donnelly has taught her to do it; the new school must also do this.

This exchange is difficult to observe passively; the Donnellys' pain and hurt is apparent. This unmasking—this revelation of personal anguish—occurs much earlier than one might expect in what will turn out to be a three-hour session, but it is not unusual in special education mediation, in which, as I have already indicated, the parties have been involved in continuing negotiation for many months and years. In this case, the struggle between the Donnellys and the school personnel to agree on a common perception of Heather has been ongoing for nearly a decade. This familiarity contributes to the sense of artificiality of the mediation but also enables a personal confession:

Joan Miller [Heather's teacher from Riverside]: My view is not different than the consensus emerging here. It is a question of deficits versus delays. Heather has spent three years in Riverside and has made significant progress. We will miss her here; she is an appealing child and makes strong connections. The staff will miss her.

Davis: The staff?

Joan Miller: Perhaps the staff more than the students.

Davis: Is there is a general consensus on Heather's needs and that she made growth? Would you agree, Mrs. Donnelly, that she made progress?

Again, Davis is attempting to find places where shared perspective and consensus can be declared. The more the Donnellys and the staff provide consistent descriptions of Heather, the more Davis can claim a common ground.

Susan Donnelly: Yes, but her subject matter growth is slow. There have been different teachers and a lot of different structures. She does not attach to all of them. And she was out twenty-three days with medical problems. We have taken care of some of that with strong allergy shots, but there are migraine headaches. We are developing strategies for dealing with these. And there was a disruptive boy in class.

Davis: So the reviews are mixed. Would it be fair to say that, given the degree of need, mixed reviews would continue?

Joan Miller: Mixed reviews might be produced by different perceptions of the situation and the projections. I don't see her moving to a high level of inferential reasoning, as you may see her. How much more could she do with her ability? In areas of pragmatics, we taught her to adapt and use compensatory strategies. But in all subject areas, primary focus was on language; content has been relatively incidental.

Susan Donnelly: Agreed. There has been attention to language.

Davis: How about social and emotional . . . ?

Joan Miller: When she first came, almost nonverbal, we worked to get her to engage.

Richard and Susan Donnelly [simultaneously]: Any new situation is like that if it's not church or at home. That's why the Roberts School is a surprise.

Joan Miller: Maybe.

Davis: There is some consensus, but also serious disagreement on the school side about social issues, and the evaluation is vague there. Did she make as great strides socially and emotionally as she did academically?

Joan Miller: Yes. This is not to say that she is not sometimes depressed. But she is more socially adept; she was used to being alone, and more social interaction was needed.

Davis: I don't follow.

Joan Miller: She is less able to be alone now.

Richard and Susan Donnelly: She's almost fifteen; she's adolescent. Heather thinks as our whole society did thirty years ago.

Joan Miller: She's beginning to see herself next to her peers and she sees the difference. It is hard for her. I think she's making progress. I think it's depression.

Davis: Joan, are you implying that the mainstream was uncomfortable for Heather, that she feels inadequate in contrast with other kids? How was her mainstream experience at Riverside?

Joan Miller: I know the issue you raise. She certainly liked her mainstream classes; she won an award there.

Richard Donnelly: The reason she won the award, to no small degree, was because of the life skills she learned at home. She is a leader in the kitchen, to start off with.

The Donnellys sustain their conviction that Heather should be placed in the Roberts School by asserting and reasserting, as Mr. Donnelly does here, that Heather's learning is almost entirely a product of home instruction and influence. By implication, the schools have failed Heather; thus, an alternative placement is justified.

Susan Donnelly: Mainstream classes were a success, but she had no friends. These are her areas of success not because they are mainstreamed but because they are her areas. Yet she has no friends. I used to ask her to bring home a friend. I guess I pressured her, but there were none.

Davis: There seems to be some consensus that she had a good experience in Riverside. Did she know . . . ? [cut off]

Joan Miller: Yes. We'll miss her.

Richard and Susan Donnelly: Yes, yes.

George Livingston: We are addressing the issue of friendships.

Joan Miller: It is important for Heather to be in a program for kids like her. We don't have any girls next year, therefore we recommended Waterville. . . . She needs a controlled, predictable and structured environment for friends.

Davis: Friends need to be part of the program?

Davis is continuing his efforts to shore up the few points of consensus. Whenever he finds that common ground, he reiterates and emphasizes the point. George Livingston, the Greenly representative, is unwilling to acquiesce in this developing accord; as

he resists Davis's proclamation of consensus, the special education teacher, Joan Miller, attempts to offer independent support.
Davis repeats that emotional development and friendships are
becoming a central feature of Heather's current situation. The
absence of available peers at the Riverside school justifies a
move; even Greenly can agree to that. The question now is about
which placement will offer the best peer opportunities.

These exchanges illustrate a piece of the painful irony inherent in the special education system. Engel (1991) points out that
"it is a central irony of the [federal special education law] that
each child who seeks to benefit from its 'mainstreaming' provisions must first be classified as fundamentally different from his or
her peers" (p. 24). Thus, the first hurdle to being *included* within
the community of all students is the requirement to be *excluded* in
the category of special student.

In their effort to maintain their conception of Heather and
resist the professionals' implication of her difference, her incapac-
ities, the Donnellys are caught in this distressing contradiction.
How can they find Heather a place, even in an alternative world,
when there is an insistence that she be understood and measured
by what she is not? Referring to Heather's need for a friend, Mr.
Donnelly's response makes this contradiction and his heartbreak
palpable:

Richard Donnelly: One will do it. She has no real friend, just
the one in her head. She doesn't talk a lot. She's like my father,
who is a farmer. We visit cousins about every six weeks, regularly.
She thinks they are friends.

Susan Donnelly: When we visited the Roberts School, and
also the Hallmark School, she made friends.

Davis: Clearly there are signs of consensus on that aspect of
Heather's self-esteem, lack of friends. Heather has academic
needs but also social needs.

Susan Donnelly [interrupting]: When we face things, we learn that we have to put some things aside and get on....

Davis: Yes, we do. Yes [Long pause]. To the degree that there is some consensus about Heather's social and academic needs, we need to turn now to the question: which program can best be tailored?

At this point, Davis begins a significant transition. He has been seeking consensus on the specification of need, and each time he states it, there is assent and then slippage as a particular elaboration is offered. Yes, she had a good experience at Riverside, but she had no friends. Yes, the school system acknowledges the need for emotional relationships and has consequently decided to transfer her to Waterville. The moments of consensus when the parties explicitly say that they see Heather similarly seem to evaporate as they keep talking. Davis now shifts the conversation by suggesting that we "seem to have some consensus on who Heather is." Nothing further seems likely to happen; he moves to a discussion of the new situation, the future. Davis opens exploration of this new placement that all agree is necessary. He inquires about the size of the class at Roberts, the composition and mix of children and needs, the staffing that will be provided.

Jim Carroll describes the program at the Roberts School. He details the teacher-student ratio, the subjects that will be covered, and the efforts that will be made to increase inferential reasoning. There is mainstreaming in physical education, in collaboration with some local public school systems who share facilities. Similarly, the school emphasizes participating in community projects with the homeless, shoveling sidewalks, and visiting the elderly in nursing homes. This sounds like a general pitch for the school, yet it does not specify the details of Heather's program. Joan Miller inquires about the training of the staff at the Roberts

School and the availability of speech therapists, language special-ists, psychologists, and the particular approach that will be used in the language-centered classes. There is a fast recounting of the variety of specialists, tutors, and skill-building techniques available. Most of it is special education jargon.

Richard Donnelly seems to be losing his way in the long list of specialists, hours, techniques, and the shifting talk about disability and language deficits. Davis intervenes to resist what is beginning to sound like a technical professional debate. "I need some help here," says Davis, announcing his own incapacity and, at the same time, asserting that this distant rhetorical style needs to cease. Davis is also deferring to the public school personnel, who general-ly perceive themselves to be more professional and experienced in special education than private school personnel, who often have less training and certification. His interjection allows the conversa-tion to turn to the public school programs, expertise, and services.

The conversation turns specifically to the program available at the Waterville School. Sam Noble of Waterville describes the benefits of Heather's placement in a public high school, where she can have many mainstreaming experiences. Again, the talk turns to the number of minutes per week Heather would receive language instruction, the amount of time she would spend with a speech therapist, how many staff would be shared among how many children:

Sam Noble: I concur on Heather's needs. I think we all do, and indeed there is enormous similarity in the programs at Waterville and at Roberts. We have, however, 850 students at Waterville High School—that is a small school for a comprehen-sive high school. But we have all kinds of students and lots of variety. We have a learning-disabled resource class where there is much attention to language processing and learning disabilities. We differentiate this from the mentally retarded and emotionally disabled. The students in Heather's class exhibit similar need; they each have language processing difficulties, their skills are similar, but some are at a higher level.

Davis: I hear distinctions between learning disability programs versus language programs. Is there a distinction and what is it? Can we clarify the terms here? We need some help. Is it dyslexia?

Jim Carroll: We'd all give it a different definition.

Davis: One element of a program is the question of compatibility. This may be especially important, given the general consensus about Heather's feelings about herself.

Jim Carroll: You seem to suggest that Heather will be one of the more impaired in the class of eleven.

Sam Noble: She will be in the bottom third of the class; there are three or four like her. She represents a challenge, but we're prepared for it.

. . . .

At each stage of the mediation process, the child is being verbally constructed, known through the descriptions and words each of the speakers utter. She is understood simultaneously as an object to be educated, a vessel to be shaped and molded by expert hands, and also as an independent, acting subject of capacity, will, and emotion. Parents struggle to insist on and sustain a positive image of the child, who is perceived and regularly spoken about negatively by the professionals as a problem. The Donnellys insist that Heather has talents, interests, capacities. The professional language seems to impede their effort to talk about Heather as a person, with a fully developed personality, sensibilities, wants, desires, and identity. But sometimes professional language provides a welcome fortress against the inescapable recognition that the child is seriously impaired. Although Davis sees himself creating opportunities to celebrate children, as he did at the outset for Susan Donnelly, he some-times, as now, colludes in the technical talk when it seems to offer a needed shelter in an increasingly emotional atmosphere.

The talk next moves to questions about the certification of the staff, previous training, types of techniques they will use, and the amount of time devoted to each learning and social activity:

Davis: You described a learning-disabled language-based resource class, a self-contained class. Is that rather than a resource room?

Sam Noble: But for some things the kids are there only 50 percent of the time.

Davis: Is the ratio actually less than eleven to one then? Do you have other non-Waterville kids in the class? Will Heather be the only non-Waterville student?

Sam Noble: Not in this class, but in other special classes we have non-Waterville kids.

Susan Donnelly: What is the ratio of girls and boys? What was it last year?

The conversation continues on the gender ratio, which will be five girls and six boys. Susan is worried that Heather will not have sufficient opportunity to create friendships among so few students like herself and in a class where all the other children live in a different, and distant, town. Davis then calls for a break, noting he plans to caucus with the Donnellys and Jim Carroll, then meet with the Greenly Schools officials.

As the other school personnel leave the classroom to have their own caucus in the hall, the Donnellys and Jim Carroll exchange soothing words. Carroll asks Davis what the cost differ-ential to Greenly would be if Heather goes to Roberts or Waterville. Davis says he doubts that the money is a factor but says he will ask. The mediator then lays out the case for the Donnellys as he sees it.

Clearly, there are a number of discrepancies as to how each party sees Heather. We have heard learning disabled, language impaired, differing expectations. And we have also heard pros and cons about both the collaborative program at Waterville and the Roberts program.

I see striking similarities in the physical settings and the distance. Roberts could be offering a greater intensity of teaching, Waterville some larger time in a mainstreamed environment. The case for Roberts, however, is strong because of its location on the land of a public school; you might have less of a case if you wanted a placement, for example, at the Hallmark School, where no mainstreaming is available. But with Roberts, because it is unlike the usual sharp division between public and private [the Roberts School sits on the grounds of a suburban public school], it's one of the toughest cases I've seen. Here is a private school adjacent and sharing facilities with a public school. The discrepancy I see, however, is in socioemotional development. I didn't get a picture from the schools of a sad, depressed, and isolated kid.

Davis identifies the disadvantages of the situation facing the Donnellys. Without some agreement here, they face a long, protracted, and unpleasant hearing; in that hearing they are challenging a placement at the regional collaborative in Waterville that is not all that different from the private Roberts School in Duffield. Finally, Heather does not seem so misplaced, unhappy, or depressed as a result of public placement in Riverside to justify removing her from the public system. It seems to be a difficult case because the Roberts School shares space with a public school and provides opportunities for mainstreaming, yet those features are also offered in Waterville.

Susan Donnelly is unpersuaded, unwilling to accept Davis's characterization of the similarities in the two schools; she insists that there are significant detriments in the Waterville placement. She reiterates her concerns about the transportation, too much mainstreaming, and lack of emotional support. Jim Carroll of the Roberts School reinforces her claims. The Donnellys are immovable, as Davis predicted they would be. They announce their unwillingness to compromise by characterizing the Greenly Schools representatives as intransigent.

Rather than validate the Donnellys' description of the Greenly Schools system, Davis plays it back against them by labeling them inflexible. Having acknowledged their position, and his inability to alter their position, Davis asks for their help in altering the Greenly position. He seeks their support. In so doing, however, he is nonetheless again inviting them to rethink their position, because they must once again name the advantages of a placement for Heather at the Roberts School and correlatively the disadvantages of a placement at Waterville.

Davis: The bottom line is that Heather has a spot at Roberts. She is going there. You're going to work. . . . Can you give me anything to persuade them to go along?

Susan Donnelly: Quality! I've observed their program, I've checked their experience, in both schools. Waterville just doesn't have teachers that are professional enough.

Richard Donnelly: Talk about their presentation. They are unprepared and are just winging it.

Jim Carroll: The program is disjointed. They haven't a sufficient group for Heather. In our program, she will be in the lower fifth, but at least there will be a group of similar kids. And there will be more comprehensive content. They are not addressing these issues.

Richard Donnelly: They are not experienced. The program is only one and one-half to two years old.

Susan Donnelly: It is too risky. They haven't the experience. In Riverside, she had a parade of teachers in just her first three years. That is relevant to us.

Davis: You have outlined a number of points about Roberts: the mixture of kids in the class, the ratio of teachers to students, the gender division, the math issue, the concreteness of the social studies curriculum, study skills, work-study community service programs, adaptive physical education, potential for mainstreaming since Roberts is situated in a public school building. . . .

Richard Donnelly: I looked carefully at the kids in the class in Waterville. They are like Waterville. I worked there. There wasn't a kid she could relate to there. These are inner-city type kids, although they live in a suburb; they are not motivated the way she is. I can get her trained; that's not what she needs. There are educational possibilities, not to mention higher education.

Susan Donnelly: The potential involvement with other kids is important, so important for her self-esteem. There is none, zero in Waterville.

Davis: If you mentioned the issue of involvement with other kids, they would agree; they have agreed. Isolation is equally a concern of the public schools. She is going to a new placement, why rule out the possibility of friends?

Jim Carroll: He's got the salient points.

Having failed to move the Donnellys, Davis nonetheless encourages them to believe that they have had a caring audience and that he has heard their concerns (see Handler, 1986). Davis now meets privately with the school personnel and attempts to see what movement he can make in their position. He begins by acknowledging their authority and deliberation, asking what conclusion they have reached. George Livingston, the Greenly special education director, notes that the regional cooperative in Waterville is similar to the program Heather had been attending in Riverside.

Davis then reviews the case as he had described it to Susan and Richard Donnelly and Jim Carroll. He lists the virtues and weaknesses of both the Roberts School and the Waterville School. There is talk about the substantially separate classroom, its classification and Heather's.[3] Does the classification of the classroom in Waterville match Heather's designation? Technical discussion begins again about the differences between neurologically language disabled versus learning disabled and the appropriateness of the Roberts placement at a school for learning-disabled children. Several school representatives jockey for authority, but Davis responds in kind.

Davis knows that the school administrators are reluctant to see the case move to the formal hearing stage. He also knows and reminds them that, although the technical discussion may suggest ambiguity, there are possibilities, in fact probabilities, of heavy costs to Greenly, in terms of both personnel time and high-priced legal services. In addition, appeals can have cost-intensive systemic consequences for the school district. An appeal lost by a school system may require a response for a whole category of cases, not merely the single child who is the subject of the appeal. If a due-process appeal is lost, the school system may be required not only to change an individual IEP but to develop a generally available program for a pattern of disability. The school system may also be required, as some observers advocate, to change the pedagogy for all "normal" children so that it is equally accessible to children with disabilities, who could then be "mainstreamed" and educated in the "least restrictive setting" (see Minow, 1990). Systemic changes and new programs mean large commitments of financial resources for school systems.

Thus, Davis knows that Livingston, the special education director, is generally reluctant to move to the due-process hearing and court review of that, where the resolution can provoke possibly far more expensive remedies. His job performance, at least in part, is measured by his success at limiting the number of hearings and the costs.

Nonetheless, Livingston is reluctant to make concessions. Rightfully, he does not believe that Heather's case is likely to provoke a finding by the hearing officer that requires changes in Greenly schools. The stake is limited here to the cost of Heather's tuition. Had this case arisen eight or nine years earlier, Livingston knows that Greenly would have been in a more vulnerable position; now, however, Greenly—like its neighbors— has taken steps to limit its liability by developing collaborative programs.

In the early history (during the 1970s) of Chapter 766 in Massachusetts, school systems lacked internal resources to provide for the varied needs of their population (see Hausmann, 1985). Parents were regularly "winning" appeals that required services not available in schools; winning a case for a parent meant that the school system would pay the tuition for private education, often at schools with programs designed for specifically classified disabilities. The school systems found themselves with escalating budgets for private school placements. Special education directors were given explicit instructions to create programs within the public school systems. But public school systems designed to provide a standard education for normal children are often less well equipped to provide programs tailored for every child with a unique collection of impairments and needs. No one school system is likely to contain within its jurisdiction sufficient numbers of children with like disabilities. Thus, George Livingston, like most special education directors, found himself with the increasing cost of private tuition, a mandate to create programs in-house to reduce costs, and insufficient numbers of children with each particular disability with which to build a program.

As a consequence, in the late 1970s Greenly, Waterville, and a half-dozen other towns in the suburban area created a collaborative system to provide special education programs for learning disabled children whom they could not adequately service within the separate towns but could handle collectively among the several communities. The SECOOP classroom in Waterville, to which Greenly wants to send Heather, is an example of this effort to create public alternatives to the private placements. Because of the SECOOP programs, parents have won fewer appeals, and in time the number of appeals in general has decreased. School administrators have begun to feel they have greater control over their special education budgets. Livingston believes Heather's previous placement in the Riverside collaborative classroom and proposed placement in the Waterville collaborative demonstrate appropriate responsiveness on the part of the school system and thus limit the possible effects of an adverse decision by a hearing officer or court. Between 1980 and 1987, parents in the position of the Donnellys would have been unlikely to win an appeal ordering Greenly to pay tuition at the Roberts School. Livingston knows that, and to some degree is hoping that the Donnellys also know that.

But, as Davis indicates, the law has very recently changed. "As you know," he tells the school officials, "we are now looking at a standard change. The maximal feasible benefit issue, in addition to the least restrictive environment, which is sometimes less of an issue in cases like this, makes this a difficult case." Davis describes changes in the law that have created new and serious disadvantages for Greenly. A 1987 decision of the First Circuit Court of Appeals reinterpreted the state standards and provisions, shifting the burdens of proof for the appropriateness and adequacy of IEPs. What this means is that it is no longer sufficient for Greenly and other communities to provide disabled students with an education *equal* to that provided nondisabled students. The court determined that the legislature had intended the special education law to provide not merely equal education for children with disabilities but an educational program that offered the *maximum feasible benefit* for the disabled child.

This new standard has made it less likely that Greenly will win in a formal hearing since it will have to prove not only that the proposed placement in Waterville is appropriate for Heather, offering her an education equal to that received by nondisabled students (the standard under which the cooperative programs were designed), but also that it must be the very best possible placement for her, providing the "maximum feasible benefit." This new standard fosters closer scrutiny of programs, encourages school systems to settle disputed IEPs more often, and makes the remaining cases that go to mediation the "really tough nuts," where it is difficult to resolve the remaining differences between the school system and parents.

As the talk continues, George Livingston interjects that he will offer a concession. "I will offer to monitor the situation in Waterville. That's my concession," he says. Knowing that this is Livingston's legal obligation in any case, Davis tries to pin him down about how much time he would spend each week monitoring the situation and Heather's development.

Davis: I realize that financial considerations ...

George Livingston: Money has nothing to do with this.

Davis: . . . cannot determine programs for special needs students, but sometimes public schools, sometimes in the interest of relationship, work out solutions. For example, acknowledging that both programs may meet Heather's needs, but since the parents have bought heavily into Roberts, Greenly may contribute to Roberts what the collaborative plus transportation would have cost Greenly. While you consider this, let me speak with the parents.

Davis, having provided a summary of the positions, offers a compromise that may settle the case. He drops a hint for them to pick up, a way for the costs to Greenly to remain constant and for the Donnellys to share the expenses at Roberts. He reminds them of this piece of the agenda and returns to speaking with the Donnellys:

Davis: I'm sorry to keep you waiting. The school people had a lot to say and that is sometimes encouraging. The sense I have is that Mr. Livingston has pressures on him. . . . This often happens when a collaborative is involved. Although he didn't say it in so many words, he may have the feeling that the SECOOP program is one designed specifically for kids like Heather—low incidence....

Susan Donnelly: Low incidence?

Davis: I mean, not many students like Heather would be in any one town, so there is a collaborative. . . . We seem to be at an impasse.

As Davis communicates the possibility of the shared expenses Greenly and the Donnellys could have at the Roberts School, Susan Donnelly jumps into the conversation in mock song:

Susan Donnelly: Heigh ho, heigh ho, it's off to work I go.

Davis: Hey, maybe Susan could go into show business.... Let's take one final look at how this may evolve. For you, as you well know, there is the possibility of tuition, transportation, and legal fees. If you prevail, Greenly would be responsible, including perhaps for your legal fees. For Greenly, likewise, there is substantial cost or, if they prevail, none. Rather than continue to argue the relative merits of Roberts versus the SECOOP in Waterville, perhaps you might consider putting that aside. A possible solution which I have seen adopted in situations like this is, for example, that Greenly contributes towards Roberts what the collaborative plus transportation would cost. That may be as much as 50 percent of the Roberts School costs.

Richard Donnelly: Have you proposed that to Greenly?

Davis: I asked them to consider it, give it some thought, and I would urge you to please be sure to run it by your attorney.

Davis finds Mr. Donnelly's response encouraging and, because he is looking for a long-lasting agreement, asks the Donnellys to speak with their lawyer. He is unsatisfied with agreements that fall apart as soon as the lawyers look at them. Because they are making a major decision and committing large sums of money as well as the future of their child, Davis does not want the Donnellys to think that he misled them into thinking it was an all-or-nothing situation.

The Donnellys and Jim Carroll reenter the room, and the entire group reforms around the table. Davis then thanks everyone for their patience, and the meeting slowly dissolves in talk about the hearing date, the names of the lawyers, and which hearing officer is scheduled to hear the case. Richard Donnelly and George Livingston are separate from the group, together and speaking. Two weeks later the parties sign an agreement placing Heather at the Roberts School, with costs of transportation—which are considerable—paid by the Greenly Public Schools, while the Donnellys pay for Heather's tuition.

· · · · · · ·

By attending to the concerns of persons made outsiders by virtue of their differences, Patrick Davis also places himself outside. Although Davis conceives of himself as a professional mediator, he neither reads little about dispute resolution nor is involved in efforts to institutionalize mediation or the dispute resolution community. "There is no problem with studying mediation, reading the literature, being the best one can be," he says. "What are the prerequisites? Law, special education, process? There is a drawback with 'mediation technicians' wearing the techniques of mediation as a foreign appendage. One must make the skills one's own; light your own torch from others' candles, but make the skills fit your person. That is best. Avoid compartments. Try to be whole."

Many themes animating debates about the consequences of various forms of collaborative dispute processing (such as authority and control issues) are alien and, it turns out, uninteresting to Davis. Seventeen years of experience and success at special education mediation is unique; he is reluctant, however, as he has encouraged me to be, to generalize to other mediation efforts.

Other matters that often structure the delivery of mediation services—the generation of a clientele, the maintenance of a caseload, the satisfaction and agreement of the parties—are also alien simply because of the nature of the job. Unlike other successful and accomplished mediators, Davis does not work in plush offices or with people of influence and power. Special education mediation takes place in schoolrooms and administrative offices carved out of abandoned schoolrooms. The usual settings of special education mediation are unlike the lush green lawns that formed the background of our introductory lunch, and those surrounding the administration building in Greenly. The barren classrooms, stale corridors, and child-sized furniture devoted to adult negotiations symbolize the relative lack of importance of children, particularly those with disabilities, in the general scheme of social values.

Although Davis locates himself with children, their parents, and school personnel trying to respond to children and their parents, he is a public employee, a functionary in a state bureaucracy. While he does not associate himself with power or affluence, he is part of that increasingly institutionalized environment that he sees as part of the apparatus that defines children with disabilities as a special problem. This inherent contradiction informs Davis's practice as he tries to make room for individuals in a world dominated by institutions.

If Davis cannot resolve or remedy these incongruities, or succeed in meeting the bureaucratic criteria of success-mediated
agreements, then what does he do?

He attempts to bring out the best in the parties to the dispute,
provide an opportunity for parents to speak well of their child,
and thus undo a little of the pain. Davis wrestles with the experience of having a disabled child, of what it feels like to face others
who constantly treat you as if you did something wrong, as if you
yourself are profoundly defective, rather than the normally less-
than-perfect. He is concerned about the parents' guilt and shame.
They are the object of a poorly concealed loathing because they
are in the position that every parent fears: they have an impaired
or "abnormal" child. He invites parents to announce their pain,
without facing an accusing authority, and to celebrate the child
before a receptive, generous audience.

Thus, in this three-hour mediation session with the Donnellys
and professional staff from three school systems, much of the language is about Heather's achievements, her needs, her progress.
There is an implicit agreement to speak well of her; Jim Carroll,
the Donnellys' advocate, referred to Heather as having average
intelligence but being a complex child. It took more than two
hours for me to realize that Heather was a child who was develop-
mentally delayed, not merely one who was having reading and
language-processing difficulties.

In another case, Davis described the difficulties facing special
education directors, arguably one of the most difficult positions in
education. Faced with decreasing or frozen financial resources
and the unrelenting and often legitimate demands of parents,
advocacy groups, and lawyers, these administrators are between
the proverbial rock and hard place. Unlike other human service
agencies, public schools cannot excuse themselves with claims
that "the school committee did not appropriate the funds." So
these school officials share some of the stress and pain the parents

experience and feel forced into uneasy compromises. Davis's concern is not limited merely to the formal outcome of a specific mediation. He is sensitive to the pain and stress along the way, concerned with the means as well as the ends. Davis explained this to me with a quote from Gandhi: "The means are the end in embryo."

Davis's manner is not surprising. He began his professional life preparing for the priesthood. He has done many things since then, including teaching, social work, fathering and raising children. I asked him if he would agree that there was continuity in the path he had taken. His life's work was "not the church," he said, but "some useful service." When I asked him to describe his mission, he said, "There is a continuity to it—the priesthood to mediation—in that it is aimed at alleviating a little pain somewhere." Pain, in fact, is a pervasive theme. I had considered various topics I might discuss in this profile, among them issues of concern to professional observers, promoters, and critics of mediation. For example, I had intended to write about the mediator's efforts to balance unequal power, eschew or use authority, hedge or confront issues of legal rights. I ran the transcripts of several mediation sessions through a computer program that counts words, to identify the places where parties made claims of right; arguments about law, rule, or statute; threats to turn to litigation or courts; claims of authority and expertise. I found that there were few references to law, few claims of right or obligation or related words. The most frequently used word, other than prepositions and articles, was *pain*.

Indeed, the insistent renunciation of authority stands out in my mind as I think about the interviews with Patrick Davis and the mediation sessions in which I observed him at work. He does not claim special expertise, nor does he make a display of extensive knowledge of the state bureaucracy, special education programs, or children's needs. He portrays himself as a cog in a machine rather than an overseer of people and an important process. He identifies with all the other cogs. He talks about trying to create a balance of power and authority between the two parties, which may at times lean away from neutrality and toward advocacy, and that, he worries, may threaten mediation. But he does not seem interested in talking at length about the techniques or ideology of mediation. He is a lover of people, not processes.

Compassionate for others, Davis is, at the same time, rather hard on himself. He is not self-congratulating; he seems to be a man for whom good is never good enough. It may come from his deep Catholicism. But his Catholicism is not about the church or Catholic institutions. He is less interested in the church than in a personal spirit and a Christian formula for living. Davis seems to break everything down into smaller units, and he views those units as more important than the overall picture. It is not the institution of the church but the Christian spirit that is important, not the process of mediation but the individuals—family, school, and child—in each case.

In the end, he finds much to celebrate. For Davis, each case is child-specific, and the most successful agreements—as many as 70 percent, he believes—benefit the child in obvious, even measurable ways. In the remaining 30 percent of the cases, however, mediation may indeed produce what some of its critics suggest: another obstacle between a child's needs and an appropriate educational response. For a few minutes, however, some parents may experience a respite.

Susan S. Silbey

Notes

I would like to thank Joel Handler, Deborah Kolb, Sally Merry, Brinkley Messick, David Engel, Austin Sarat, Scott Saul, and Elizabeth Schuster for their generous reading and advice. I am especially indebted to Patrick Davis, not only for allowing himself to be scrutinized and possibly misrepresented but also for trying to save me from folly and error. That I am unredeemed is none of their responsibility.

1.   This name is fictitious: there is no Greenly Public School district in Massachusetts. As a condition of the permission to observe mediation sessions that I received from the Department of Education of the Commonwealth of Massachusetts, Patrick Davis, and the school officials and parents whom I observed, I agreed that no parents, school districts, or local school administrators would be individually identified.

2.   David Engel (1991) identifies the reluctance of some parents to exaggerate their disabled child's difference by demanding a disproportionate share of the public resources.

3.   The federal and state laws create a system of diagnostic labels for classifying special needs children by the proportion of weekly time spent in special education services. Four of the six ranks range from less than 10 percent to more than 60 percent time in special services; the fifth category defines children in out-of-district, day-school programs; the sixth category classifies children in residential, twenty-four-hour care programs.

References

Budoff, M., Orenstein, A., and Kervick, C. (1982). *Due process in special education: On going to a hearing.* Cambridge, Mass.: Ware Press.

Engel, D. M. (1991). Law, culture, and children with disabilities: Educational rights and the construction of difference. *Duke Law Journal,* 166–205.

Handler, J. (1986). *The conditions of discretion: Autonomy, community, bureaucracy.* New York: Russell Sage Foundation.

Hausmann, B. (1985). *Mandates without money: Negotiated enforcement of special education regulations.* Unpublished doctoral dissertation, Brandeis University, Waltham, Mass.

Minow, M. (1990). *Making all the difference.* Ithaca, N.Y.: Cornell University Press.

Singer, L. R., and E. Nace. (1985). *Mediation in special education.* NIDR Reports no. 1. Washington, D.C.: National Institute for Dispute Resolution.

"*I do what is necessary to get to my goals, not theirs.
. . . The pursuit of closure is a neutral goal.*"

—Howard Bellman

3

· ·

Howard Bellman
Using "Bundles of Input" to
Negotiate an Environmental Dispute

The Nuclear Regulatory Commission (NRC) ventured into several unknown areas when it chose to use "regulatory negotiation" instead of conventional administrative rulemaking procedures to develop a licensing procedure for the first high-level nuclear waste dump in the United States. The proposed NRC rule was, in fact, an historic event. It was an effort to invent a legal means for handling the garbage from the first generation of nuclear weapons and nuclear power plants, as well as for the second generation of these plants, now being constructed, in part, through this very rule. The rule creates a procedure to adjudicate the U.S. Department of Energy's (DOE) application for a license to receive and process high-level radioactive waste at a geological repository to be built at Yucca Mountain in Nevada.

Although it is not certain, Nevada will probably be a party in the licensing application procedure, given its substantial interest in the dump site. Yucca Mountain is a hundred miles northwest of Las Vegas, just outside the Nuclear Testing Site where atmospheric testing went on from 1951 to 1962 and underground nuclear tests are still being carried out today. It is near the California border and the Death Valley National Monument. Approximately fourteen hundred people, including a ranch run by prostitutes, live near the site.

Beyond the obvious reason—the attempt to develop a method to deal with a highly dangerous, highly controversial substance— why was this a precedent-setting event?

First, the NRC has a procedure for licensing commercial power plants, but not for licensing the storage of high-level nuclear waste.[1] The absence of such procedures is an outgrowth of government's and industry's overall approach to nuclear waste, dating back to the establishment of the Atomic Energy Commission in 1947: avoidance, or what might be called the "politics of neglect." A second and perhaps equally daunting unknown in this case is that Congress has, for the first time, required the nuclear waste producer, the Department of Energy, to get a license for its garbage.[2] Under the Nuclear Waste Policy Act of 1982, DOE is the administrative agency required to locate and develop the nation's first high-level nuclear waste dump. Since the invention of the atomic bomb, nuclear weapons sites throughout the United States have disposed of high-level radioactive waste secretly. The proposed Yucca Mountain dump will, however, receive both commercial and military waste. Publicly and privately generated nuclear garbage will be brought into one repository under the same licensing scheme. This single regulatory process pierces the once-sacred shield of secrecy surrounding nuclear waste disposal.

Then there is the use in this rulemaking procedure of a still relatively unknown alternative dispute resolution process called *regulatory negotiation*, or "reg neg" for short. Reg neg is a process for developing federal agency rules through negotiation with the parties affected by a regulation. Recommendations issued by the Administrative Conference of the United States (ACUS) in 1986 encourage agencies to "review the areas that they regulate to determine the potential for the establishment and use of dispute resolution mechanisms by private organizations as an alternative to direct agency action" (ACUS, 1986, p. 86). Facilitators or mediators are selected from outside the agency to help the parties reach an agreement on a rule.[3] Once a consensus is reached, the rule is published in the *Federal Register*, and then a period for public notice and comment is set.

Regulatory negotiation may be initiated by either an agency or one of its constituencies. The agency designates a "neutral convener," a mediator or facilitator, whose job it is to identify the interested parties and relevant issues. First, the convener undertakes a "feasibility analysis" to establish whether the parties, including agency actors, will agree to negotiate a rule. In a number of cases, the agency will empanel the interested parties as an advisory committee, under authority from the Federal Advisory Committee Act of 1976. If negotiations produce agreement among the parties, a rule will be announced in the *Federal Register* (see Susskind, Babbitt, and Segal, 1993).

As with other proposals for alternative dispute resolution, the advocates are highly enthusiastic about the advantages of rulemaking through negotiation. Specifically, they see the following advantages: (1) negotiated rulemaking offers the parties direct participation in the process; (2) the mediator is more active in "outreach" to the parties affected by regulation than in the "customary rulemaking route" (Harter, 1984, p. 4); (3) the parties are engaged in direct substantive decisions rather than appearing as expert witnesses testifying before the agency; (4) the costs of participation are reduced because the parties need not prepare "defensive research" (Harter, 1982); (5) the quality of participation is richer because the parties are in a setting that provides incentives to rank their concerns; (6) and finally, according to reform activists Susskind and McMahon (1985, p. 159), regulatory negotiations cannot fail: "At the very least, conflicts can be clarified, data shared, and differences aired in a constructive way. Even if full consensus is not achieved, the negotiation process will still have narrowed the issues in disputes." Regulatory negotiation is most successful, according to its proponents, when the agency participates. They argue that the parties are more likely to

participate in negotiating a rule with the agency rather than
without, to avoid the uncertainty of agency review.

. . . .

Howard Bellman of Wisconsin was the mediator who tried to
tie together what he called "bundles of input" in the reg neg process involving the licensing procedure for the nuclear waste
dump. Bellman, a lawyer (as were all the parties in this negotiation), convened and facilitated the year-long reg neg sessions.[4]

Bellman graduated from the University of Cincinnati Law
School in 1962, received a master of law degree from New York
University in 1963, and worked as a staff attorney for the
National Labor Relations Board in Detroit until 1965. He then
worked for the Wisconsin Employment Relations Commission as
a staff mediator, arbitrator, and hearing examiner for eight years
before becoming the commissioner of that agency for three
years. Bellman then became the vice president and project director for the Wisconsin Center for Public Policy, where he worked
on environmental mediations, including cases involving the siting of solid waste and hazardous waste management facilities. At
the same time, he continued his practice in employment relations.

In 1983, Bellman was appointed by Governor Anthony S.
Earl of Wisconsin to serve as the state's secretary of the
Department of Industry, Labor, and Human Relations. He did so
until Earl, a Democrat, lost a reelection bid in 1986. Since then,
Bellman has been a mediator and consultant in numerous public
policy cases, most of which involve state or federal agencies and
environmental conflicts or labor relations. Based on his extensive
background in environmental and labor mediation with state and
federal agencies, Bellman has established a national reputation in
the field of public policy negotiation.

What does the negotiation of the high-level nuclear waste

dump licensing procedure tell us about Howard Bellman's practice?[5] What is his theory of practice? These questions are difficult to answer because Bellman does not believe his work as a negotiator and mediator is guided by a single, comprehensive set of practice rules that can be applied to different cases. Indeed, Bellman rejects the conventional distinction in the mediation literature between theory and practice, which postulates that broad theory is applied to particular practice. He has little use for general abstract, formulaic theories of mediation, preferring to think of his practice strictly in case-by-case pragmatic terms.

Over the course of the year I observed Bellman, however, I saw him construct what I will call a mediation practice *within* the context of negotiating nuclear waste licensing. That is, I understand his "practice" as primarily constituted by the particular and peculiar context of the case. The story that follows is, therefore, about how negotiation practice is built from the conditions of conflict—in this case, from Bellman's interpretation of how far the parties are willing to "march toward consensus," a phrase he uses to describe the negotiation.

• • • • • • •

The selection of what issues to negotiate is the basis for deliberation in any mediation. In this case, determining those issues was perhaps as unsettled as the policy for burying nuclear waste is contested. Should the deliberations include concerns about locating or siting a dump, or is that a foregone conclusion, an established national policy? The process of determining what to negotiate, separating out what the parties could negotiate (licensing procedures) from what could not be negotiated (whether to bury nuclear waste in Nevada), structured the negotiations themselves.

Through the reg neg, both Bellman and the NRC made a concerted effort to distinguish issues dealing with the politics of locating a site for the nuclear dump from questions about the process of licensing it. They sought to focus group discussions on the question of how a generic high-level nuclear waste repository should be licensed, not specifically the Nevada site. The broader policy conflict over the construction of a high-level nuclear repository in Nevada was not subject to negotiation—at least not at this reg neg. Yet over time, the boundary between these two questions blurred as some of the parties rejected this distinction as a legitimate starting point for the negotiation process. Statements by representatives of the state of Nevada (such as "The dump is an act of genocide against the people of Nevada") shattered the artificial wall between licensing procedures for a nuclear waste dump and the reality of having yet more nuclear materials come into the state. The reg neg thus served as a means for people to figure out how either to contest or bury nuclear waste (depending on whether one opposes nuclear production or produces the waste materials).

In December 1986, the NRC published a notice in the *Federal Register* announcing that it intended to conduct a negotiated rulemaking process to establish a licensing procedure for a high-level radioactive waste repository. The NRC also initiated government contracting procedures to procure the services of a private mediator for the proposed reg neg, ultimately hiring the Conservation Foundation in Washington, D.C., to serve as its referral agency. Howard Bellman is on the foundation's list of "qualified mediators" and, at the time of the NRC contract, was a senior fellow there. The foundation selected him and three other individuals to serve as a team for negotiating this case.

By the time the reg neg got under way, one person who initially had been on the negotiating team, a technical adviser, dropped off because of a conflict of interest in the case. Now there were two people working with Bellman on the reg neg: Timothy Mealey, a young environmental specialist at the Conservation Foundation, who wrote and distributed the minutes from each negotiation session and summarized and clarified proposals at the meetings; and Matthew Low, a lawyer with substantial experience in NRC practice and administrative agency procedures, who answered questions about particular provisions in the draft rule and aspects of agency practice. Although the term *team* was used to describe the threesome of Bellman, Mealey, and Low, it is fair to say that Bellman was acting alone as the mediator for this reg neg.

The siting of the dump is of paramount political and economic concern for almost every state in the continental United States, because radioactive waste will be transported across many states en route to the dump. Initially, the DOE identified ten states as possible locations for the dump, but before the *Federal Register* notice was published, the DOE announced that it was now only considering three locales: Deaf Smith, Texas;[6] Hanford, Washington; and Yucca Mountain, Nevada.

The process of convening parties for the reg neg was as charged as the process of locating the nuclear dump site. In August 1987, the NRC announced that it was forming a high-level waste-licensing support system advisory committee, also known as the negotiating committee. Under the Federal Advisory Committee Act, agencies have the power to set up advisory committees composed of people whom the agency thinks are informed and interested parties. Bellman used responses to the initial *Federal Register* notice to identify a range of interested parties: Native American tribes, state governments, local governments, environmental groups, utility companies, and federal agencies (the only federal agency was DOE).

Before the negotiation committee was finally established, a group of about thirty-five people, including representatives from state radioactive waste review boards, state attorney general offices, environmental groups, the utility industry, and Native American tribes, attended a negotiation training meeting held at a Washington, D.C., hotel in October 1987. The main purpose of

the meeting was to familiarize prospective parties with negotiation "principles and techniques." Bellman was present, but the
training session was run by consultants from Endispute (Jonathan
Marks) and the Conservation Foundation (Suzanne Orenstein).

What was supposed to be a training session was, in fact, a picture of disorder and chaos; people were talking to each other during the presentations, walking in and out of the room, reading
newspapers, and paying little attention to the negotiation simulations the consultants asked them to play. Only a few people were
listening to the trainers and following their instructions. Bellman
told me he did not share the trainers' philosophy, which claimed
that negotiation functions according to certain principles.
However, he did say he liked the training process because he
believed it produced a congenial "atmosphere" among people
who do not usually work together.

The situation changed in December 1987, when Congress
amended the Nuclear Waste Policy Act to focus on licensing *one*
site. Nonetheless, the parties believed that what was negotiated
for Yucca Mountain would be a model for future sites.

After Congress designated Yucca Mountain to be the prospective site, the number of parties in the reg neg dropped from
thirty-five to five: the NRC, the DOE, industry, the state of
Nevada, and an environmental coalition. Groups representing
local Nevada governments and the National Congress of
American Indians petitioned to participate in the reg neg. Both
requests were granted by the five parties.

As the sponsoring agency, the NRC's main goal was to create
a licensing procedure and then use it to process a license application from DOE within three years. Since it takes on the average
twelve years to license a nuclear power plant, the three-year goal
was viewed by other parties as exceedingly optimistic. The NRC
wanted to cut down the licensing time by reducing what it called
the "time-consuming" discovery process, which in this case
includes the physical production and on-site review of documents

by parties in the high-level waste licensing proceeding. The NRC's chief negotiator and legal counsel was Bill Olmstead, an avid supporter of the reg-neg process. Indeed, midway through the reg neg, he accepted a position with the Administrative Conference of the United States, a federally funded agency, to develop and expand reg neg in federal administrative practice once this reg neg was concluded. Francis "Chip" Cameron, another NRC attorney, also represented the NRC in the negotiations.

The DOE, the federal agency seeking a license for the dump, was represented by its spokesperson, Jerry Saltzman, and alternate, Stan Echols. Periodically, Barbara Cerny, a DOE computer specialist, attended the negotiations and provided technical information. The negotiation strategy of the DOE representatives and their substantive interest throughout the reg neg was to streamline the procedure for getting a license. Given the history of military secrecy and broad discretion surrounding the disposal of nuclear waste, this strategy was no surprise to the other parties and did little to instill legitimacy or trust in DOE.

Industry's position was represented by three utility organizations: the Edison Electric Institute (EEI), the Utility Nuclear Waste Management Group, and the U.S. Council of Energy Awareness. This trio of utility company organizations was represented by Steven Kraft and Jay Silberg, both attorneys with EEI. As one industry representative noted at the beginning of the reg neg, "Our main interest is in promoting nuclear power." At this point in the development of the nuclear power industry, that meant finding a place to dump the waste. Industry tended to support DOE positions more often than any of the other parties since it too wanted to streamline the licensing process. Its way of achieving this was to limit public access to the process.

The state of Nevada, where atmospheric and underground testing of nuclear weapons has gone on since the early 1950s, was the fourth party in the reg neg. According to the people representing Nevada in this reg neg, it is a state that has been "sold down the tubes by its former senator and close friend of Ronald Reagan, Paul Laxalt." Ironically, Nevada, the state where most nuclear weapons activity takes place, has no local resources for dealing with the NRC, because nuclear energy in Nevada has been under the auspices of the DOE. In short, according to the two attorneys from the same Seattle law firm who were hired to represent Nevada in this reg neg, the state has little expertise in the field of law that most directly affects its future. The Seattle lawyers, Mal Murphy and Jim Davenport, both have experience in power plant licensing procedures and have argued before the NRC.

The environmental coalition in the reg neg included the Environmental Defense Fund (EDF), Friends of the Earth, and the Sierra Club. In my view, the most skilled negotiator in the reg neg was Melinda Kassen of the EDF, who was also the only woman regularly participating in the negotiations. Kassen, a young graduate of Dartmouth and Stanford Law School, articulated her constituencies' positions extremely well in the face of considerable opposition; anticipated the impact of suggested compromises for future challenges environmentalists were likely to make during the licensing process; and, at the same time, was able to broker deals between other parties.

The National Congress of American Indians was represented by a young white lawyer, Dean Tousley, from the Washington, D.C., firm of Harmon and Weiss, who participated little in the discussion but worked closely with the environmental coalition. The Nuclear Waste Policy Act of 1982 recognizes the sovereignty of American Indian tribes and considers them as equal to states. The DOE's final environmental assessment of potential nuclear waste disposal sites concluded that only one site, that in Hanford, Washington, could potentially affect Native American tribes (the Yakima Indian Nation, the Nez Perce, and the Confederated Tribes of the Umatilla Indian Reservation). However, critics of the assessment argue that the Paiute and Shoshone tribes could also be affected in Yucca Mountain (Stoffle and Evans, 1988, p. 751).

It is difficult to say much at all about the local Nevada government representatives, other than how and why they came to be a party in the reg neg. The state's representatives did not speak at any of the meetings. The local government group, formed after a heated battle with the state of Nevada,[7] included representatives from Nye, Lincoln, and Clarke counties, all of which are located in the southern part of the state. All were nonlawyers. The local government representatives hired Mike Baughman, who has a bachelor's degree in economics, to advise them. Baughman told me that they did not have the resources to represent themselves adequately, not even to hire a lawyer.

Although the local government group frequently went outside the meeting room and did not say anything during the negotiations, their silence was a subject of discussion among the other parties. I asked them, "Why aren't you in there? What's the deal?" They indicated they did not feel competent in the discussions and that they believed the state of Nevada was representing their concerns. One of the local representatives added, "We want to remain a separate entity so that during the licensing procedure we have the option to oppose Nevada if need be." Some participants in the reg neg were continually discrediting these people by joking that they were only interested in coming to the Washington, D.C., meetings to "play around." Others worried that, in the end, the local government people could pull out a manifesto and move to sabotage the entire reg neg.

. . . .

As I sat through the reg-neg meetings, I watched the local contingent go in and out of the eastern hotel conference rooms in their western wear—tan cowboy suits with contrasting stitching across the shirt pockets, large cowboy hats, and cowboy boots. In stark contrast, representatives from industry and the government, as well as Bellman and his assistants, all wore navy blue suits, typically with light blue shirts and red ties. The environmental and Native American representatives were markedly younger than the other participants and tended to dress more casually.

According to administrative rules, the agency must ask whether there are any comments from the public at the end of each meeting. Since I was the only person from "the public" (that is, not affiliated with any of the parties), the executive secretary for the reg neg, Donnie Grimsley (an NRC employee) would say, "Christine, have you gotten anything yet?" This was, in fact, the main way I was introduced to the group as a whole. I told individuals whom I interviewed that I was a professor of political science at New York University and I was studying Howard Bellman. This seemed to make them feel a bit easier—that I was studying Howard Bellman and not them. Some people found out I was originally from Los Alamos, New Mexico, a hometown that generated much interest.

The parties always sat in the same places, whether the tables were arranged in a square or a rectangle. Bellman and the two facilitators, Low and Mealey, sat at tables referred to as the "head of the table." Bellman often paced behind his chair or walked around the front of the room while the parties spoke. The other parties sat at tables around and across from Bellman. The NRC representatives sat to the left of Bellman with several individuals from the agency (who periodically provided the representatives with information) sitting behind them. NRC appellate judges attended a few of the meetings as well. The DOE representatives sat to the right of Bellman and also brought consultants to the meetings. Industry representatives sat next to DOE on the same side of the room, while the environmental coalition and Native

American representatives sat together next to NRC representatives. The representative for Nevada and the local government group sat next to each other at tables across from Bellman.

Each party had one vote, but rarely were parties asked to vote; instead, they operated as coalitions in the negotiations. The state of Nevada and the environmental group, along with the Native American representative, functioned as a coalition on most issues. Industry and the DOE were more often than not joint partners. Depending on the issue at hand, NRC moved back and forth between these two distinct coalitions.

· · · · · · ·

In addition to the already mentioned unusual aspects of this rulemaking procedure, two unique elements to this reg neg arose. First, the NRC invented an information-gathering and -sharing program that it calls the licensing support system (LSS). The LSS is an electronic information management system that will transmit and store data during the licensing process. Parties to the licensing procedure, as well as interested intervenors who meet the test of standing, will input data, ranging from geological site reports to environmental impact studies and notations of cultural and historic artifacts from the site.

During the reg neg, the parties negotiated over what information would go into the LSS and who would have access to it during the licensing procedure. All of the information is declassified. Initially, the NRC and DOE's plan was to have all data available on ASCII files (universal) accessible at the public document room where the licensing was taking place. However, the environmental coalition and the representative for the state of Nevada fought to expand points of access to individuals and groups who might not be able to travel to the public document room. In the end, they did not win on this point.

The main controversy over this part of the rule concerned the scope of participation and access to the LSS. In the beginning, it looked like DOE wanted to control the LSS, and the other parties mobilized against this idea. The environmental coalition and the representative for Native Americans wanted to ensure maximum access to and participation in the LSS. Industry wanted to limit participation to parties in the licensing process who agreed in advance to share all their documents. The environmentalists and Native Americans argued that it would be more efficient to accept expanded access to the LSS now than face legal challenges down the road. Since industry representatives regularly used the language of "efficiency" to characterize their positions, they found the environmentalists' argument about political efficiency difficult to brush aside.

The NRC, DOE, and state of Nevada said little during this exchange between industry and the environmental coalition but gave some indications that they supported efforts to maximize the legitimacy of the LSS. They were not representing the groups who would be most affected by limited access—the environmental coalition spoke on behalf of those groups. However, the coalition of what might be called "government groups" (the NRC, DOE, and the state of Nevada) ultimately joined the environmental and Native American coalition to support an open-access, open-participation position.

The second unique aspect of this rulemaking concerns the licensing procedure itself: discoveries, interrogatories, and contentions. The NRC, DOE, and industry wanted to limit the number of interrogatories and eliminate oral contentions, while Nevada and the environmental coalition argued to maintain these features, all of which are part of other licensing procedures, such as those used to license nuclear power plants.

Everyone participating in the reg neg seemed aware that these two issues both raised a common controversial question: how public should the process for licensing the nuclear waste dump be? Yet, as Bellman often commented to me, issues of access and participation were often buried in the minutiae of the meetings and rarely aired in a forthright manner. Instead, negotiating over words and sentence construction was a vehicle for venting yet controlling substantive political conflict in this reg neg.

The parties established a set of protocols at the beginning of the process that outlined how they would reach a consensus. Essentially, the protocols said that in order for this reg neg to produce a rule that the NRC would adopt, *all* the parties had to reach a consensus. This meant that no one could dissent. Unanimity is typical of how reg negs work. It is one way of keeping people in the negotiation: tell them it is an all-or-nothing rule, and hope that they will want to preserve what they have created. In the end, this all-or-nothing bargaining turned out to be the major bone of contention.

. . . .

Except for the one local government representative from Carson City, Nevada, all the people involved in this reg neg were lawyers. In addition to establishing the LSS, the rule they negotiated created an adjudicatory proceeding (that is, a licensing process). So Bellman mediated among lawyers who were negotiating an adjudicatory process.

I asked him at one point how he felt about mediating such a process. "We are, after all, in the final analysis dealing with lawyer-like behavior," he said. "For better or worse . . . there is a lot of lawyer-like behavior here that is a better way of capturing what we are seeing here than anything else I can think of." These lawyers were also considered experts in the field of NRC practice.

One might have expected the NRC to play a leading role in the negotiation process, because, as Bellman said, "the parties *are* mediating state law." Most other reg neg mediators, however, have insisted that the state agency should not play a leading role but merely be one of a number of parties (see Harter, 1982, 1984; Susskind and McMahon, 1985). Bellman rejects this view, and his practice challenges the concept of state regulation implicit in it.[8] He argues that the sponsoring agency (the NRC in this case) was the laboring oar in the negotiations. By this he means that the state agency must be fully committed to the negotiation process and willing to put the text of the proposed rule on the table for others to discuss, challenge, and change. Bellman counts on the state to carry the burden of working toward a consensus, in part because he thinks the parties are working from the perspective that the state has the ultimate authority over rulemaking. The responsibilities that come with being the laboring oar are substantial in Bellman's view, and he cannot manage those responsibilities for the state. "If the sponsoring agency is either in bad faith, incompetent, wavering, or has any deficit at all, attitudinal deficit or competence deficit," he observed, "the whole thing is in terrible jeopardy. Now, if you find that out 90 percent into the case, you've got your hands full. There is nothing I can do to make bad-faith people into good-faith people or incompetent people into competent people, or whatever the deficit is."

From the beginning and throughout the negotiations, people in the reg neg asked how committed the NRC was to making a negotiated rule. During the final hours of the reg neg, Bellman told me, "Everyone here from time to time was worried about what was coming out of the sponsoring agency. I found myself worried today about whether the sponsoring agency was going to subvert its own exercise . . . by a whole set of things . . . what I would call tactical behaviors that were not consistent with my goals—which they ought to be because they hired me . . . not the kind of stuff that keeps you marching toward consensus."

So, if the state is the laboring oar, how is this form of rulemaking any different from the conventional process? In the beginning, everyone was talking to the NRC; the conversation appeared to be a set of dialogues between the NRC and the parties. At first this looked a lot like a typical notice-and-comment proceeding except that oral comment took place *before* the rule was announced in the *Federal Register*.

Over the course of the reg neg, however, Bellman elicited responses from the NRC and turned them into points for negotiation. Thus, through Bellman's practice, the agency was continually moved into a leadership position, a position that was itself subject to negotiation. In other words, the NRC did not just present its rule and collect comments from interested parties; the NRC negotiated with parties over particular provisions of the licensing rule as did the other parties negotiate among themselves. Bellman claims that the state has to answer more questions and engage in a more probing and open discussion if they take seriously the laboring oar rule.

The state's "authority," however, is not viewed by Bellman as naked power to coerce others to act.

> One thing I always tell people in prenegotiation conferences is that you have to have an iron fist and a velvet glove. . . . To me that is an extremely important thing. Now if the iron fist shows through the knuckles of the velvet glove, you have got yourself a problem. The iron fist is terribly important and the velvet glove is equally important. The mastery of the situation is to have both. . . . If you get too easy or if you get too tough, either way, you lose it. Today [the last day of negotiations], I think you saw people getting too tough. . . . It is a judgment, it is an art and not a science a little bit, it is like taste. . . . I cannot say to someone, say this and not this.

Bellman believes that the reg neg requires more of the state by way of participation and commitment to making a "good" rule than conventional agency rulemaking. He is not critical about the role of the state in the way that Susskind, Harter, and other advocates of alternative dispute resolution are. Bellman views the state neither as neutral nor as a biased, mission-oriented actor. He takes a pragmatic view, arguing that the best he can do is to try to make the parties have some autonomy, although they know about each other's dealings in advance of the reg neg. He sees reg neg as an opening for interested parties to make their demands clear and get the state to do its work in a setting he believes more fully exposes the state.

This aspect of Bellman's practice could be characterized as an unorthodox orthodoxy. That is, he rejects much of the new "theory" about reg neg and hence thinks of himself as unorthodox. At the same time, however, he embraces a traditional welfare state perspective on regulation. On both accounts, he places considerable responsibility with the sponsoring agency. Bellman describes this as a "problem" for him in the contemporary alternative dispute resolution (ADR) community. He thinks that most practitioners do not go along with his view of mediation because he relies heavily on the capabilities of the parties, particularly the sponsoring agency.

Given how Bellman staged the deliberations—his strong effort to place the laboring oar in the hands of the state—the parties may appear to be doing all the work. Some even told me about midway through the reg neg that they were getting annoyed with Bellman because they felt they were doing all the work. But that is exactly what Bellman wants them to do: he wants to set them up to make them work with each other. When they cannot work with each other, when they get to the point of shouting at each other, he sees the need for a mediator.

. . . .

For most of the reg-neg process, representatives of industry, the environment, Nevada, the NRC, the DOE, and everyone else were not shouting at each other but quietly editing sentences out loud, crafting a rule they hoped would be to their own advantage in future litigation on the dump application. The conversations between the parties went back and forth between editing sentences and speculating on how future generations might live with "their" rule. Critical questions about the impact of nuclear waste on future generations surfaced periodically; however, most of the negotiations, in Bellman's view, were simply over "minutiae." The participants, he said later, "do seem attracted to the minutiae. . . . It is an escape. . . . They prefer the trees to the forest. . . . They can grasp it." Much of their work focused on substituting *and* for *or*, which might seem to be only a marginal input. But, from the perspective of how law is crafted, the *ands* and *ors* were viewed as important markers for determining the meaning of the rule. Commenting on this "lawyers' talk," Bellman observed that they were all "jockeying for advantage in the context of litigation and making deals where it seems like the best thing to do in the context of the litigation. . . . I think we are seeing a lot of lawyers representing a lot of clients here."

Bellman participated very little in the debates over sentence construction. He yawned, leaned back in his chair, stared at the ceiling, and even walked out of the room. His associates, Low and Mealey, kept track of suggested changes in the text of the draft rule, along with Cameron, who had primary responsibility for ensuring that all editing that resulted from the negotiations was incorporated into the text. Bellman did not oversee or participate in the editing itself. Instead, he focused on issues concerning the pace and tone of the discussions.

When parties got stuck on a word for ten minutes, Bellman said, "C'mon, c'mon," urging the parties to decide on *and* or *or*. He remained, however, distanced from the motives different parties might have for insisting on one word over another. Although managing lawyers' talk of this sort is a big part of Bellman's mediation practice, he does not think that it is his business to sort out their language. "In the vast majority of my experience [mediating], most or all of the parties are represented by lawyers. [However], I rarely have had an experience where lawyers are negotiating over the law; this [reg neg] is a real dose of that. Not only are lawyers there, entering an enforceable agreement that brings lawyering out in anybody, but we're also talking about a legal process. The substance of what we are talking about is one layer of lawyering. . . . That is pretty rare."

Nor does Bellman think it is his business to resolve technical conflicts that came up in the process of negotiating the licensing rule. "The more technical something becomes, the less of a role mediators have when experts are negotiating. . . . I would attempt to justify my staying out on that basis. I cannot just leap in there with common sense and tell them how to set up a computer system just because I am dispassionate." Bellman says he just lets the parties play out their lawyering habits among themselves as long as they do not threaten to break the consensus process or stall negotiations.

Bellman did intervene in lawyers' talk when major disagreements occurred, as when someone said something like "No way in hell will this be changed." At such contentious points, Bellman said, "Let's move on." Bellman does not postpone differences of opinion so much as isolate those parties who seem responsible for either threatening a consensus or dragging on a "boring conversation." For example, when major disagreements about wording arose, Bellman encouraged those parties most at odds with each other to spend a half an hour to an hour, apart from the other parties, writing new language. He then said, "Look it, you are holding up the scene; if it's important to you, deal with it and get back in the room." This is an effective means of getting the parties to work with each other, and then, as "partners," to present their new language to the larger group.

According to Bellman, the parties in this case have a history of talking and arguing with one another. They are familiar foes and "skilled negotiators" who rarely turn to an outsider like him for strategies. They are also part of a "community" of lawyers who litigate before the NRC. Importantly for Bellman, this community of lawyers is comprised of ordinary human beings. "There is not a party here," he says, "who has had any influence at all who I have not seen make some kind of a deal with any one of the other parties. Despite the fact that it seems that sides have formed on an issue-by-issue basis, every combination has occurred, and that is what makes it work. . . . But it also makes it very clear that we are dealing with pretty ordinary human beings doing ordinary human business, and once in a while the flag gets waved."

How does Bellman activate these "ordinary human beings"? Does he get them to negotiate by teaching them "people skills" to negotiate or empowering those without power to bargain? No, Bellman brushes aside what he calls the "inflated claims of ADR entrepreneurs," claims that mediators can impart special skills to parties and "balance" the power inequities they bring to the table.

Although, as mentioned earlier, Bellman likes the "atmospherics" training can create and believes it "bodes well for a collaborative style," he does not think training necessarily makes effective negotiations.

> The idea that you are going to devise a method that obscures power imbalances is grossly unrealistic. And [you] should not begin on an unrealistic basis. None of it [the Conservation Foundation training] is stupid or detached from reality in some crazy way. I think it tends to magnify reality in ways that people would prefer . . . sugar coated. I don't want to attack ideals, but when you get closer [to the training material] there is a tendency to reduce the importance of power.

All of my experiences and limitations have to do with power and recognizing it, and then doing something about it. I say to people, this is the best you can do in negotiations, take it or leave it. I hope you take it because you don't have enough power to do better. If you want more power, organize, collect money, lick envelopes, whatever. I tell them to go outside negotiation if you want power. And then bring it in and it will articulate. [It is] hard to expand someone's power if you're neutral. And that is what I *have* to be, and that is how I get entry. Otherwise it would be fraudulent.

It takes more than an afternoon to change people's operational styles—[it's] unrealistic [to say otherwise]. This is high-stakes stuff, and people rely on conventional methods when the stakes are high. They are not risk takers.

Bellman sees himself as a bit of a rebel when it comes to the orthodoxy of mediation practice, in particular the assertion that mediators can impart special skills to the participants. He says, "I do speech making, not training. . . . I don't have a game . . . in my briefcase. I must be regarded as some kind of a heretic because I am not putting paper up on the walls," he says, apparently referring to the ubiquitous flipchart in mediation sessions. "Everybody in the world insists on doing that but me. I said we are not going to do that. . . . It is a distraction, it is not necessary. . . . I don't know why we have to do that."

In continuing to explain his aversion to flipchart-noted lists of options, he adds, "I know the pat answers, but they don't come out of this case. Also, I want this to be as much of the parties' process as humanly possible. I want to be as light-handed and nonintervening as humanly possible. I want to be sure that the only time I am intervening is when they need it."

At points in the negotiation, Bellman told some parties to "toughen up, make demands ... tell them what you are going to do if they don't go along with you." He exhorted the parties not because he "sympathizes" with them but because he says it is in the interest of speed, sometimes, for parties to express their threats. If they make clear their limits, it may help move the negotiations forward. This kind of intervention is not, in Bellman's view, meant to put him in the role of a broker standing between the parties: "I don't feel like somehow I am entitled to be the broker of everything, particularly in a situation like this where this is a tiny fraction of all their relationships," he says. He does not caucus much either. The parties caucus with each other. Early on, the parties learned that this is the way Bellman operates, and if they wanted to challenge something, they had best not wait for Bellman to do it.

The key to Bellman's practice is to normalize mediation and the process of negotiation. Without a "game" in his briefcase or the pretensions of a trainer, Bellman says that "one of the things you will see happen is that people eventually come to the conclusion that I am not doing anything. . . . So if I don't come to the meetings, it does not matter." He says that the parties "see me over at the end of the room staring into space, and they think, 'Jesus, that is not bad work.' . . . They feel a lot of pressure, and they see me picking up a check." To Bellman, this perception is "some indication . . . that I did it right because if I have a real success here, not only will there be an agreement . . . but the next time somebody has the impulse to do this negotiating, they will just go ahead and do it and they won't have to have some third party."

He describes his attitude toward mediation as "ad hoc, glib stuff, not deliberated on. But when I do think about it, it is a matter of degree in the pursuit of closure, not in the pursuit of justice. I do what is necessary to get to my goals, not theirs. . . . The pursuit of closure is a neutral goal." Bellman is confident he has a good sense of what is supposed to happen in negotiation. He conveys this confidence by acting as if the negotiation process is an ordinary and normal form of deliberating. This reassures the parties, who are working with unknowns and who question the meaning and impact of the reg neg on future policy. Bellman's reassuring stance is key to how he activates the parties.

• • • • • • •

If Bellman is able to normalize the process of mediating an adjudicatory rule, how does he then get parties who distrust one another to move toward a consensus? As Bellman observed, "It would be hard to identify a more conflict-ridden community on the day I entered. . . . [There was] a history of fighting at the highest level." During the negotiations that followed, Bellman did not attempt to convince the parties that they could or should trust one another, nor did he place himself between them and act as a broker. His efforts at shaping a consensus were far more subtle.

Handling or mediating around deep distrust between the parties was critical to Bellman's practice in this case. He made no secret of the fact that negotiations would be taking place in an environment of distrust. "I was told not to say this in my convener's report, but I did anyway. Among the now significant impediments, in addition to the need to separate this negotiation from the siting issue, is that no one trusts DOE to be truthful or competent. NRC said not to say it in the report. I said it because I felt a professional responsibility not to make something look easier than it is, or more appealing than it is. Everyone said it [how they distrusted DOE] to me but DOE, and to leave it out of the list of factors, I don't know what they would have made of me if I had done that." Bellman made the issue of DOE distrust an important aspect of the reg neg by insisting that it was a formidable barrier to reaching a consensus. As he said, it is "not for me to revise the history in order to get the case done," nor does Bellman believe he can get the parties to revise their history of distrusting DOE.

A striking example of how distrust permeated the negotiations and how Bellman handled it occurred during the third meeting of the reg neg participants as discussion turned to public access to the licensing process and review of documents in the electronic licensing support system (LSS). The NRC representative was concerned about imposing limits on who could participate and wanted to require that parties who challenge the DOE during the licensing process must first make all their documents available on the LSS. The environmentalists and representatives for Nevada argued that NRC's "incentives" for full disclosure of documents shut out members of the public who might want to enter into a licensing challenge later in the process. Excerpts from that session follow:

Bill Olmstead (NRC): It was my concept that if it wasn't an agency record, if it belonged to some private party—EEI, EDF, or somebody else—they would have to get that document the same way they always get that document, namely they would have to ask that organization.

Jim Davenport (Nevada): Bill, we have created a system that ought to be beneficial to as many people as possible. Why not . . . ?

Melinda Kassen (Environmental): The other problem is that there is the following section which says that you guys [DOE] are not going to let in most of the people from the public who might want to be participants because you are going to restrict it to people who qualify for intervention. So, on the one hand you are saying, "Well, if they want to play they have to be asked to be admitted." On the other hand, you're saying they cannot be admitted. So what you are really doing is denying the public access.

Olmstead: Look, I'm sorry, you don't trust us and I don't trust you. . . .

Kassen: We'll give you all our documents.

Olmstead: I don't believe that for a minute, quite frankly.

Kassen: What is it about the public that you don't trust? I don't understand that.

Olmstead: Well, "the public" I probably trust. The organizations that intervene in our proceedings are not exactly the most forthcoming organizations in the world in the discovery process. And so I want some incentives to insure that they have submitted to the jurisdiction of the licensing board so that, when I want to object to their tactics, I am informed to do that.

Chip Cameron (NRC): It isn't necessarily even a case of mistrust. We are not trying to limit the public's access—we are giving them enhanced access through the headers [headings on LSS to identify topics included]. If people who volunteer in this process want their documents also to be available, hard copy at the public document room, we can do it that way. We were not really sure that anybody who was granted participation rights would want their documents to be sitting in the public document room. If that is not a problem for Nevada, EDF, or whoever else, then we can do it that way.

Olmstead: Look it, the issue here is what is the incentive for a nongovernmental unit to participate. . . . What is it?

Mal Murphy (Nevada): Well, that isn't the only issue here. The other one is the statutory language about public participation. The whole object is to enhance the public's knowledge about what is going on here, so they are going to like getting rid of Jay's [DOE] garbage.

Olmstead: It *is* being enhanced. They are going to have more information....

Jim Davenport (Nevada): Then why not put it in the public document room?

Olmstead: I fail to understand what nongovernmental agency will subject itself to the jurisdiction of the licensing board at all.

Jay Silberg (Industry): A court may ultimately decide this issue, but if you want to make that clear here. . . .

The conversation continued, then facilitator Matthew Low asked whether "there are any other thoughts on the issue of public access that separates us." The reply and resulting conversation offer some dramatic evidence of the "old boys network" attitudes that surfaced at times during the negotiations:

Olmstead: Well, does it really separate us or are we being pinged on here?

Kassen: Just being what?

Olmstead: Pinged on.

Stan Echols (DOE): I think Melinda [EDF] is just having one of those days. . . .

The men in the audience sounded a collective "Ohhh" while the women all booed.[9] The exchange then continued:

Olmstead: Look it, this is a major controversy within the federal government today. Can the government, through the use of automated systems, enhance the value of documentary material and then turn around and give it to the public? There is a sizable congressional delegation that says we cannot even do that. . . .

Bellman: The question is whether . . . [attempted cutoff by NRC's Olmstead]. The answer you are giving is that you . . . [attempted cutoff by representatives of NRC, DOE, and Nevada]. We have to take a short break.

It appeared that order or just plain decorum simply broke down at this point, so Bellman called for a short break. During the break, he worked to repair some of the damage done during this exchange, particularly the harm caused by the sexist attack on the woman representing the environmental coalition (Kassen). Kassen first confronted Bellman, letting him know that she would "not stand for" those kinds of negotiation tactics. "Is it the job of the mediator to control sexism, or do I have to do that?" she said forcefully. He responded that the DOE person was "out of it" and that the public access issue was the important issue to focus on. Unwilling to let the sexist remark go without comment, she said, "If you don't take care of this . . . if it's not part of the reg neg, then I'll take care of it myself."

As it turned out, there was no public discussion of the sexist remark, nor did the group confront the problem of using sexism to put down an opponent in negotiation. However, Bellman did work to take care of at least the damaging impact of the sexist remark. During the break, he got Melinda Kassen and Bill Olmstead (NRC negotiator) to work together on some language about access to the LSS. Within a half hour, the environmental coalition and NRC caucused and returned to the table with a written agreement to provide "full headers" on the LSS, a format issue they had differed on earlier. The environmental group said it understood NRC's concern about commercial interests, and they would be satisfied with full headers.

In the end, the rest of the parties agreed to the language the environmental group and NRC had worked out. During the discussion of their proposed language, however, Bellman played a more active role in supporting concerns raised by the environmentalists, such as the need to provide funding for public interest groups to access the LSS. By active role, I mean that Bellman kept the floor open for Kassen (environmentalist) to express her position fully. As Bellman said to me following this episode:

> I jumped in the middle of the room to save this . . . to help people through the issues. . . . DOE came after me [afterwards] and said I was no longer a neutral. I

was cross-examining DOE on their resistance [to support public interest funding]. . . . Ultimately, she [the representative for the environmental coalition] settled for a hell of a lot less than I thought she would. . . . I had overinterpreted her position. . . .

There is a culture of distrust of which this [incident] is just the tip of the iceberg. . . . It is remarkable that in this context they are still getting this much done, and lots of people have said publicly that this is the first episode [negotiating the LSS] in the whole history in which they have been able to do anything together.

In addition to keeping the floor open for parties who he thinks are "ready to walk," Bellman also continually reminded all parties of what they had already invested in the reg neg and used this to keep them moving toward a consensus.

. . . .

The process of getting parties to realize their investment in agreement was a combination of two strategies. The first was continually reminding the parties that if they did not agree to one part of the reg neg, they would destroy the whole rule—this was an all-or-nothing procedure. The second strategy was encouraging the parties to stay by telling them "you can leave anytime." Bellman led the parties to believe that if they wanted to reach an agreement, it must be an agreement on the whole rule, but they could "opt out at anytime." His approach to consensus building thus extracted a general "commitment" from the parties to accept the whole rule but gave them the freedom to "exit" the reg-neg process whenever they wanted to. It seemed to many that they had little to lose by participating. However, as the reg neg drew to a close, many of the parties felt that, by that time, they had invested too much in the negotiation to withdraw. This did not mean,

however, that all of the parties felt equally invested in the deliberations. In the end, industry did indeed pull out of the agreement, but only after it had secured substantial changes in the
adjudicatory process for licensing the nuclear waste dump.

Bellman says he does not believe he can equalize power
imbalances that exist among parties. But his practice of investing
the parties in deliberation, and ultimately a consensus, does
attempt, if only indirectly, to overcome power inequities.

For example, at the second to last meeting, Bellman said, "We
have one more meeting in Reno, so you're all going to have to go
back to your constituencies and whatever, and get yourselves
lined up, and get ready to commit." At the same time, Bellman
asked the NRC representatives if they would go back to the commission and request additional funds for another meeting in case
an agreement was not reached in Reno. Bellman attempted to
build in some flexibility while pressuring the parties to clarify
their bottom line on a consensus rule. Bellman's use of time was
essential in getting the parties to realize their investment in the
reg neg. As the following account shows, he also uses timing to
invest the parties in a consensus.

It was the last meeting, held in Reno. During the first day,
industry representatives said they probably could not agree to the
licensing rule because of their concern with the costs.[10] This position enraged the Nevada representatives and the environmental
coalition, who believed they had made significant compromises
with industry that allowed for some streamlining of the discovery
process. Mal Murphy of Nevada, addressing the industry interests,
said, "You're trying to get the reforms of the licensing procedure
that you've been unable to get for twenty years in court or before
the Nuclear Regulatory Commission, and we're not going to give
it to you here now. Period." The rejoinder from Olmstead of the
NRC was, "Well, that's why we're here. . . . We're here to reform
the licensing proceeding. After all, isn't that what reg neg is
about?"

"No, it's to enhance it," said Murphy. "It's to make it the smartest thing, you know, more information stuff." When industry began to pull out of the reg neg on the second day, Bellman's job really began:

Bellman: We have been through a zillion elements of this work in which you all [referring to industry], and lots of other people, have made *countless* changes. . . . And it seems to me that we are now at a point where, unless those changes are betrayed in the drafting, which I think they won't be, at least deliberately, then what you are going to have to say is, considering all the changes you have made and agreed to—indeed, were the source of—it is still too expensive for you.

Now you have that right. . . . I do not want to be misunderstood about that, but that is where we will be left. We will be left with a lot of language to which everyone else has agreed and to which you have agreed, but for the cost of it. Now I happen to think that if that is the product of this group, it is a worthwhile product.

Olmstead (NRC): We'll accept that a lot of the compromises that have been made in order to attempt to secure this item of consent. We'll probably go back and change if we don't get the consent we need. If they are not going to give us their consent, a lot of things will be drafted differently.

Bellman: Thanks [laughter from the group].

Olmstead: Not necessarily. It's just that they [environmentalists, state of Nevada] mentioned it first.

Silberg (Industry): Well, this is a very interesting point, a very interesting point. Our understanding was from the very beginning that if the consensus simply did not work in the end, the NRC is left to its own devices.

Bellman: Right. But I am saying to them [industry], okay, just me saying to them, it is a hell of a device to have the support of everybody but one.

Timothy Mealey: And there are other possible scenarios. Like if EEI says, "We think that this is the best rule it could be, but we nevertheless have some reservations because of costs." In other words, if you were able to commit in that fashion rather than back away completely, that is also something.

Cameron (NRC): That is a good point. You don't have to give up all your consensus on the text. We could register EEI's concern or objection in the supplementary information that, although you support the rule or whatever, that you . . . think it is too costly or something.

Silberg: But I want to go back to this other point about what happens if there is no consensus. . . . I don't quite know how all this fits, if there is somehow a continuation of this process, albeit informally in Dallas.

Bellman: That is always a possibility no matter what happens.

Olmstead: Sure is. That's right.

As the negotiations progressed, Bellman attempted to speak to a number of parties at once and, in all cases, sought to guide them toward realizing their own investment in a consensus. This was a challenging task as there were a number of different interests and agendas at work. Bellman wanted to reassure industry that, in the end, the rule may not "tie" them into an agreement; but at the same time he pointed to their work on the rule. Bellman told the industry representatives that they had created expectations in others, had justified certain positions, and would lose credibility if they walked then. He subtly conveyed that industry runs the risk of violating the very expectations it created if its representatives backed out of a consensus. It is this material that Bellman used to invest them in a consensus:

> I think the formal process is going to expire, either in
> a few hours or after this next meeting. The informal

process was going on a hell of a long time before we started and is going to continue, I presume, for decades.

Now it seems to me that we can end this with some sort of a bundle of input that all of you may or may not fully like ... but hopefully is a consensus as initially defined. But even if it isn't, there is this terrific amount of input which is available at least to the NRC people here as they report, as they propose and recommend. I mean, I think it would be squandering, frankly, not to take advantage of it.

The industry representative failed to respond directly, and the negotiation appeared to head off in a different direction. Representatives from Nevada then expressed their concern that if a consensus was not reached, if industry did pull out, the NRC would take charge and write the rule it wanted, leaving out the input of Nevada and the environmentalists. The dialogue continued:

Davenport (Nevada): That [what Bellman has just stated above] is an argument that Bill [NRC] also made. He said, "I am going to scrap all of this and do whatever we want."

Bellman: I am trying to make my argument in front of Bill, just like the rest of you. . . .

Olmstead (NRC): Let me respond to those arguments. This *is* the last meeting. The only reason for having another meeting is because there is a belief that something productive other than nonconsensus will come out of it. And while it was allright for you to say all along that this a process that people could withhold [withhold consensus] until the last minute. . . .

Bellman: We would not have gotten them engaged otherwise.

Olmstead: I understand that—that is fine. The amount of time that we have allocated to this process has expired and it is time for people to say where they are. I will accept the cost issue from EEI, they have been upfront about it all the time. . . . In other words, we go into the next meeting with the reservation that EEI still has not decided whether they think it is cost effective but Stan [DOE]. . . . They think that the objectives of the rulemaking are useful and that they are willing to achieve consensus forgetting cost.

Bellman was now attempting to mediate two separate disputes at once. One conflict was between Nevada (with support from the environmental coalition) and the NRC over whether the process should conclude that day or go on. The Nevada delegation believed that consensus could be worked out with one more meeting, since it did not look like one would be reached today. The NRC wanted industry to show its hand now rather than wait until another meeting when, in the NRC's view, industry was likely to withdraw from the process. The second dispute was between industry and all of the other parties except the NRC. Industry was ready to walk away, and Bellman was telling its representatives, "You're too invested. . . . You've got too much in this to walk away. . . . You've basically written this rule, and everybody's agreed to it. If you don't go along with it, it's going to be . . . a bad deal." The other parties, most vocally the Nevada representatives and the environmental coalition but not excluding DOE, wanted to have their investments in this reg neg realized in a consensus rule—with or without industry.

After some back-and-forth discussion, the negotiations shifted back to the first dispute between those who wanted another meeting to give one more try to reach a consensus (Nevada and the environmental coalition were the most vocal) and the NRC, which seemed to be pressing people to decide at this meeting:

Davenport (Nevada): You [NRC] are holding hostage the next month's meeting, adhering to a very rigid time schedule for a rule that will not be implemented for a significant amount of time, except for these interim things like the technical review panels and this type of thing. But the guts of it isn't happening until 1991. The charter for this group I do not think ends for another year under FACA [the Federal Advisory Committee Act], and you're saying, "Well, we are not going to meet next month because I don't have everything lined up the way I want it, like it. I don't see the productivity." I think that is an unrealistic. . . .

Murphy (Nevada): Let me suggest something else too, that I think is in here. . . . Assuming the scenario plays out like we suggested it and the language of the rule is agreeable to everybody, including EEI . . . except for the cost problem, you [industry] can simply not give your consensus. If this group can take another day, day-and-a-half meeting to produce a document to which the environmental organizations can agree, to which the state of Nevada can agree, to which the Department of Energy can agree, you are going to be the first person in the country to be able to go to their commission and say, "I have secured the agreement, the cooperation of the Department of Energy and the state of Nevada, *and* as pepper on the salad, I throw in the national environmental organizations . . . and the Indian tribes, yes, the Indian tribes. . . . "

Cameron (NRC): And the local governments.

Murphy: You're going to do that, we all know you're going to do that, and be a candidate for the Nobel Prize [laughter from the group].

Murphy: And the fact that the utilities, that you, the NRC has wrongly been accused of being in bed with, who don't agree with it, it is just probably a benefit [very loud laughter from the group].

Davenport: And we all know that if you can buy us off, if you can get Jerry [DOE] to sign off and if you can get Melinda [EDF] to sign off, *that's* the language that is going to the commission. And I am suggesting that if we cannot do that by three this afternoon, it might be worthwhile to try one more day. Plus you're in a win-win position. If it doesn't, you'd say, "My God, what more could I have done?"

Olmstead: Can I get all your signatures to this speech? [laughter from the group and lots of people talking at once]

Bellman: Okay, have we beat on your [NRC] heart strings enough? [laughter from the group]

Dean Tousley (Indian Tribe): Please . . . do we get to come to another meeting?

Bellman: Pretty please, huh?

Olmstead: You're recommending?

Bellman: Absolutely!

Olmstead: On the grounds that. . . .

Bellman: That I think there is going to be a very worthwhile product, which is either going to be a consensus or very close to it.

Davenport: I'll tell you, let us go to the commission next week and tell them because you skipped out of the meeting we need another meeting [very loud laughter from the group; lots of people saying, "That is the real issue"].

Olmstead: I've been threatened here . . . [laughter from the group].

Bellman: We have to know what the answer is. . . .

Olmstead: I haven't heard EEI [industry] respond to my suggestion.

Silberg: Well, why don't you repeat it?

Olmstead: I understand that you are reserving the cost issue, but I need to know where you stand on the rest of the rule. As Howard has pointed out, you have had a heavy hand in the negotiation and one of the things I have to decide, quite frankly, is if I don't get a consensus what do I do about the text rule? One option which has been suggested is to renegotiate with all the parties. The other option is to go back . . . and to have another meeting or not.

Silberg: Well, all those considerations affect our processes here.

Olmstead: Is it reasonably likely that we can get a statement from you that you approve of the rule without approving of the costs?

Silberg: I think the answer is pretty much the same as the answer I gave you before. We really don't know at this point. That is the nature of the negotiation process. It was still understood by us at the beginning that once the negotiation process followed its nature, it was done. We then would each have a chance to sit down, read over the entire rule and prepare a strategy by ourselves on what we think is going to be the outcome and test it against the costs, and then have the industry in its selective group judgment tell us which way to vote. We haven't done any of that. We are still working through the text of the rule. We need to go back and start that process of going through the text of deciding where things stand in the text. And that judgment, for our purposes, has to be a fairly reasoned activity.

Olmstead: I will agree to another meeting, but I want to make some points very quickly. There have been meetings outside of these meetings that I know about [between industry and commission members], and I know what was said at those meetings. Okay? And there have been meetings with the other parties and I know what they said. . . . If what you are doing is trying to yoke this rule one last time to get every last ounce of blood out of it, I am saying that isn't going to work because I am going to go back and rethink some of the concessions we made in some of those areas.

Davenport: My proposal is intended to be responsive to that, that in our last meeting we only address these last paragraphs.

Olmstead: I have no disagreement with you on that.

Bellman: I don't think any of us should go into the next meeting having compromised any of the rights we agreed to in the protocols. I think that is all you are asking for, and that what EEI is asking for . . . is that the protocols continue to prevail. In addition to that, I think it serves us well to occasionally verbalize the realities, in addition to the protocols, and that is what we have been trying to do. Some of the realities are beginning to become pretty forceful here. . . .

Olmstead: Right.

Bellman: The protocols are still governing. . . .

Olmstead: There will be no meeting beyond the next one?

Davenport: I don't think anyone in the room wants that.

Bellman: Okay now, at the last meeting we scheduled on a very tentative basis to meet in Reno [many on the negotiation committee objected to traveling back to Reno]. . . . I don't want to go through that conversation to be perfectly honest with you. If anyone in the group wants to become the travel agent, fine. Let's have lunch.

Bellman has reminded the parties of their investments in a consensus rule, investments that *he* has orchestrated all along. For instance, Bellman allowed the parties unlimited time to fuss over words as part of investing them in the deliberations and, ultimately, creating the basis for asking them for a commitment. He let the parties spin out a rule, and then he turned back to them and used this fact as a basis for tying their "bundles of input" together. Because they have somehow participated in this conversation, they now have some obligation, too.

Furthermore, Bellman himself is invested in consensus. "I get sucked into the thought of having a success," he told me. "We took so much advice from EEI, and I think it will be totally untenable for them not to go along with it in some psychological, in some political way. I want their words all over that thing, every nook and cranny. I don't care how trivial it is, how much of a pain in the butt it is."

Yet, characteristic of his self-image, Bellman does not think he *controls* the parties. They reach closure when they exhaust what possibilities they have for reaching a consensus. When I asked him whether the ending of this reg neg was arbitrary, he replied, "Yes, and of course that [industry's insistence on cost-benefit information before it could commit to the rule] did not make it any easier. What you are seeing here is a particular style of mediation. Someone else would probably abhor what I am saying here now, 'cause they say that mediation is something that permeates negotiations from the beginning to the end and makes the negotiators act differently from the beginning to the end. And I just don't presume to do that . . . very much, maybe a little . . . but not as much as some of the doctrine."

Bellman says he does not want to get himself caught in a situation where he is stating what somebody's interests are. He certainly never would want to be caught in the situation where he feels he has to tell somebody that their interests are A and not B. The closest he seemed to come to such direction was when he told industry representatives that they had an interest in supporting a rule they had had a large role in creating.

In general, Bellman's style is close to that of Colombo, the television detective: he helps set the stage for letting the parties implicate themselves through their own deliberations, and, when they have played out their respective positions, he attempts to hold them responsible for the consensus to work.

While I know that Bellman would probably not want to characterize himself according to a particular type of mediator, and I too think he has a unique style, he did construct a "practice" over the course of this reg neg—a practice that is, perhaps, best described in his own words:

It is familiar to me, although I think it bothers other people, that sometimes a mediator doesn't seem to really be doing anything until the last minute and then they wonder what the hell you have been doing there all that other time. There is something to that.

With a few exceptions I think that today [the last meeting in Reno] was a time when there was an indispensable third party role. . . . I feel very restrained about what I can talk with you about because what I am doing now really deals with the personalities and my sense of the attitudes of the parties . . . and that is what I was trying to manipulate. . . .

Accusation of bad faith were made today, and you heard me say, for tactical reasons, that I did not think anyone was in bad faith. . . . I had specific reasons for saying that. . . . Today we were getting down to the short strokes, and people were going to have to confront the risks of negotiation. It was evoking behaviors on the part of particular human beings that I, as the advocate of consensus by now, had to try to overcome, hopefully legitimately and not by trickery. Where I had to keep their eye on the ball and give them every conceivable reason to reach an agreement.

In the end, at the last meeting held in Reno, industry withdrew and would not join the others in making a consensus agreement. This act was described by Bellman as "dicey," but "none of us had the right to be shocked by their behavior."

A caucus was called by all parties except industry, at which they agreed to abide by the rule. Although this reg neg did not produce a consensus rule, Bellman said it produced "postconsensus behavior"—the NRC will publish the rule and the parties will not challenge it.

Feelings by the environmental and Nevada representatives that industry had unfairly gotten concessions from the negotiations were, in Bellman's view, not strong enough to make them want to go back and change what they had spent over a year negotiating. Industry clearly did secure concessions from the environmental coalition and Nevada that others would accept to save the rule—the postconsensus behavior—without a commitment from industry that they too would abide by the reg neg.

Much could be said about the power dynamics of the reg-neg process in this case. However, much of that story would focus on the power inequities among the parties, inequities they bring to the negotiations and that Bellman cannot erase. Instead, Bellman's practice relies on his ability to normalize deliberations between conflicting parties and to lead them toward investing their word, ideas, and interests in a text. The bundles of input he helps put together are represented to the parties as investments they can realize by reaching a consensus.

Christine B. Harrington

Notes

I would like to express my appreciation to the Program on Negotiation at Harvard Law School for funding this research and to members of the Building Theory From Practice Project for listening to rough observations and reading earlier drafts. In particular, I want to thank Deborah Kolb for her valuable comments and Bill Breslin for his editorial suggestions. I would also like to thank Tim Mealey of the Conservation Foundation for generously providing materials necessary to complete this chapter and Kelley Bevans for her research assistance. A special thanks to John Brigham for his reading of this work. Finally, I greatly appreciate Howard Bellman's candid reactions and the time he devoted to discussing his work with me.

1.   High-level nuclear waste is produced by nuclear weapons plants and spent fuel rods from nuclear power plant reactors. Critics have noted that the term *spent fuel* is "perhaps the most misleading term in the nuclear lexicon. Uranium

assemblies are removed from commercial reactors after three years' 'burnup' but not because their radiation is in any way 'spent': rather, they are removed because they have become too radioactive for further efficient use" (Shapiro, 1988, p. 61). Low-level waste is described in the literature as including "work gloves, tools, medical isotopes, and radioactive tailing from uranium mining and processing" (Karkut, 1988, p. 302).

2. When Congress created the AEC in 1947, it gave this commission complete authority over nuclear energy use and management. The AEC was dissolved by Congress in 1974, and its responsibilities were delegated to two new organizations, the NRC and the Energy Research and Development Administration (ERDA). The NRC assumed responsibility for regulating nuclear power; ERDA took over all research, promotion, and military aspects of nuclear energy. In 1977, ERDA merged into the newly created Department of Energy (Karkut, 1988).

3. A few agencies, such as the Environmental Protection Agency, have in-house mediators.

4. I attended four out of seven negotiation meetings (three in Washington, D.C., and one in Reno, Nevada). Of the three meetings I did not attend, one was in Denver and two were in Reno. I read the minutes from those meetings. I interviewed and spent time with almost all of the parties in this regulatory negotiation. As in all extended negotiations, many interactions among the parties and among some parties and Bellman took place outside of the reg neg meeting. I did not observe these discussions.

5. The scope of this article does not address the congressional politics of the Nuclear Waste Act, nor does it address the larger political and legal issues associated with nuclear waste disposal.

6. Deaf Smith, Texas, is a farming community just west of Amarillo, where natural foods peanut butter is produced. When the DOE announced that it was a possible site for the nuclear dump, I was told that the natural foods peanut butter company went out of business.

7. Nevada created a county, which encompassed Yucca Mountain, called Bullfrog County. It established extremely high property taxes for this county so that if the dump was built, the state (not the counties) would collect lots of money from it. The counties took the state to court, and a state judge overturned the legislation that created Bullfrog County.

8. The concept of state regulation in the dominant view of reg neg supports

the trend toward deregulation and embraces a minimalist regulatory state. See Harrington (1988).

9.   The audience was mainly women who work for the NRC. They sat behind the representatives and passed them information during the negotiations.

10.   The DOE had not completed its cost-benefit report by the time of this meeting. While the rule that this reg neg developed would have cost-benefit impacts, a cost-benefit analysis was not part of this reg neg.

References

ACUS [Administrative Conference of the United States] (1986). Agencies' use of alternative means of dispute resolution. Recommendation 86–3, Washington, D.C.

Harrington, C. (1988). Regulatory reform: Creating gaps and making markets. Law & Policy, 10(4), 293– 316.

Harter, P. (1982). Negotiating regulations: A cure for malaise. Georgetown Law Journal, 71(1), 1–118.

Harter, P. (1984). Status report on project on "The uses of alternative means of dispute resolution in the administrative process." Memorandum to Committee on Administration, Administrative Conference of the United States, November 19, 1984.

Karkut, J. E. (1988). Nevada v. Herrington: An ineffective check on the DOE. Journal of Energy Law & Policy, 8(2), 301–318.

Shapiro, F. C. (1988). Courts, legislatures, and paternalism. Virginia Law Review, 74(3), 519–575.

Stoffle, R. W., and Evans, M. J. (1988). American Indians and nuclear waste storage: The debate at Yucca Mountain, Nevada. Policy Studies Journal, 16(4), 751–767.

Susskind, L., Babbitt, E., and Segal, P. (1993). When ADR becomes the law: A review of federal practice. Negotiation Journal, 9(1), 59–75.

Susskind, L., and McMahon, G. (1985). The theory and practice of negotiated rulemaking. Yale Journal of Regulation, 3(1), 133–165.

"By the time the problem gets to the mediation process, it has had what I call double reinforcement. . . . Both parties have convinced themselves that they are right and can't back away from it because of the positions that have been taken all along the way."

—William Hobgood

4

. . . .

William Hobgood
"Conditioning" Parties
in Labor Grievances

B ill Hobgood is one of America's busiest and best-known
mediators of grievances between labor and management. A
lawyer by training, he has worked as either a mediator or an arbitrator in the labor-management community for most of his adult
life, beginning as a field mediator with the Federal Mediation and
Conciliation Service (FMCS) in rural, coal-mining areas of
Kentucky and North Carolina. His roots in this area of the country are apparent both from his accent and in the feelings he
expresses for the coal industry and the people who work there: "I
have a high regard for the values of both labor and management
in the coal industry. They are trying, under really tough conditions, to reach out, to come up from 'underground' and try new
processes and systems. It's tough, but they are trying."

Hobgood arbitrates coal industry cases but spends more and
more of his time mediating grievances there. In early 1990, along
with William Usery, his former boss at both FMCS and the
Department of Labor, he mediated the settlement of the Pittston
Coal strike, one of the most acrimonious and costly in recent
memory.

Friends and colleagues describe Hobgood as both talented and
incredibly patient. "What might drive other people crazy doesn't
seem to faze Bill," says a lawyer who has seen him handle scores
of cases. "Bill just sits and listens. He lets them talk as long as

they want." Another colleague, a labor-management consultant, compares Hobgood's style with that of other mediators who also can work as arbitrators: "Bill doesn't confuse mediation with arbitration. He doesn't push people, make pronouncements, or use pressure tactics to get them to compromise. He uses questions to get at their interests."

With these kinds of recommendations, I looked forward to observing and learning from this mediator, which I would do over a period of months as he handled eleven separate cases, including that of Rosie Bracken. After each day's work, we would meet for dinner and a debriefing interview at one of Hobgood's many favorite restaurants. A ruddy-complexioned runner, Hobgood is a gray-haired, youthful man who apparently doesn't need to watch his waistline; in fact, he loves to discover new places in the neighborhood where he is working that specialize in ethnic or regional cuisine. The excitement of such discoveries is not unlike the feeling he gets when he settles on a "fix"—finds the key, or at least *a* key, to a tough case. Fortunately for me, in addition to enjoying a good meal, Hobgood also enjoys talking about his work. This chapter will move back and forth between my observations of him in action (in a real case that has been disguised) and Hobgood's reflections on his work.

. . . .

At 9 o'clock in the morning, mediator Bill Hobgood, with me in tow, entered the living-room section of a room in an Embassy Suites hotel on the outskirts of Birmingham, a city long associated with the coal industry and the mines that supply it. The furniture was motel provincial and the wallpaper velvet-flocked. (Earlier Bill had told me that meetings in hotel conference rooms are generally more convenient for all the parties than a trip to the coalfields.) Fourteen people were crowded into the room, drinking coffee, smoking cigarettes, and reading the morning papers. Seated on one side of a small table in the center of the room were three large, burly men dressed in jeans and plaid flannel shirts: shop stewards Mike Henderson and Dick James, plus Eddie Paulson, president of the Mineworkers' Local in Mine 18. With them was a tall slender man more formally dressed in jacket and tie; he was Pete Graves, district representative of the Mineworkers. On the same side of the table but at the end, slightly apart from her union brethren, was a thin, blonde woman, the grievant Rosie Bracken.

Directly across the table sat three men, all dressed in blazers and gray slacks. Closest to the head was Harry Maines, the industrial relations representative at Mine 18. Next to him was Buddy Edwards, a manager of industrial relations at the corporate office, and his boss, Wayne Roberts, vice president of industrial relations for The Coal Company, or TCC as it is commonly known. In the corner of the room were a couch and several chairs, where three people were seated: Mike Downes, the company's newly hired vice president for safety; Jim Grant, the manager in charge of safety at Mine 18; and Alice Barry, a member of the industrial relations support staff.

They were all there for Hobgood's grievance mediation of Rosie's case. Grievance mediation is the most recent in a long line of innovations intended to make the grievance procedure more responsive to worker and management concerns. It is often said that the multistep grievance procedure, with its provision for arbitration by an outside neutral, is at the very heart of a collective bargaining agreement because it provides workers and managers with a mechanism to interpret their labor contract in light of day-to-day operations and to settle work-floor conflicts short of strikes. A multistep grievance procedure with provision for arbitration is now a fixture in 98 percent of collective bargaining agreements in the United States.

Rosie Bracken's case is typical. She hurt her back lifting some wood on the job. After she returned from medical leave, she received a "final written warning" from the company, which stated she would be dismissed if she had any more accidents at work. Upset and fearing she would lose her job, Rosie, through the union, "grieved" the company's warning, contending that the accident was not her fault, that the wood was too heavy, and that she should not be punished for the accident.

Rosie's case went through three different steps in the grievance procedure: between her supervisor and the shop steward; between Harry Maines (the industrial relations representative at her mine) and Eddie Paulson (the president of the Mineworkers' Local); and finally between Buddy Edwards (the manager of industrial relations for TCC) and Pete Graves (the union's district representative). At each of these stages, the grievance was discussed but not settled. The company maintained it had the right, based on company rules, to take disciplinary action against an employee with "unsatisfactory injury records." The union countered that the company is required to prove that the employee is at fault in order to take such severe disciplinary action. Against this background of no agreement, the company and union agreed to mediate Rosie's case.

Bill Hobgood sat at the head of the table, introduced me, then told a joke about divorce mediation. After the chuckling subsided, Hobgood described the process and his goals:

> Mediation is an informal process designed to get the parties, who have the best understanding of the contract and the relationships, involved in finding a solution to the problem. We will have an open and frank discussion about the background of the dispute here in a joint meeting, and try to resolve it. . . . We hope this dispute can be resolved. But if no agreement is reached, as it states in your contract, I will advise you on how I think an arbitrator would rule on the case. If

> we do not resolve the grievance and you do go on to
> arbitration, nothing we discuss here will be used at
> that step.

If the mediation provision was not in the contract, the parties, as is the situation in most collective bargaining relationships, would have gone from the third step cited earlier directly
to arbitration. Labor arbitration is often cited as a major success
story in U.S. employee relations. Independent arbitrators, who
are jointly selected by representatives of union and management,
hear cases concerning discipline, contract interpretation, and
other workplace issues. On the basis of these hearings, the arbitrator writes a decision that is final and binding on the parties.
Over the years, TCC and the Mineworkers have taken many
safety-related grievances to arbitration. Indeed, at the time of
Rosie's case, each side had an arbitrator's decision in hand that
supported its position in the mediation.

Despite its contribution to industrial peace, arbitration is
sometimes criticized for its failure to deliver fast and inexpensive
resolutions to workplace problems and to do so in a way perceived as fair and responsive by all sides. Critics claim that
responsive resolution of disputes is an almost impossible goal
because of the delays and high costs. It is not unusual in some
firms to have grievance backloads into the hundreds and sometimes even thousands of cases. Adding to the delays are such
"legalese" factors as hearings that include rules of evidence,
examination and cross-examination of witnesses, and submission
of written briefs, posthearing briefs, and written transcripts.
Arbitration has become almost as formal a process as litigation.

From Hobgood's perspective, however, the problems with
arbitration go deeper than a consideration of its transaction costs
or the satisfaction of the parties.

The job of the arbitrator is to determine who is right or wrong. Even though you as an arbitrator may want to know about extenuating circumstances, most arbitrators will tell you that very often they walk away from a case without knowing the full facts because the parties chose not to bring them forward.

The goal of the players is to win. So, you play it in a way that is going to achieve that, and that's not to give the arbitrator the benefit of the extenuating circumstances. After all, you don't want to help the opposition build its case. So nothing about extent, frequency, fault, type, or other extenuating circumstances will come out. . . . You just want the arbitrator to rule on this particular issue; you don't want him to open it up.

The mediation process, on the other hand, is aimed at *solving* a problem rather than rendering a decision. "Mediation," Hobgood says, "gives you the capacity to either keep the agreement as narrowly defined as possible or, because an issue will come up again and again, you can broaden it to the policy question and see if it makes sense so that we can deal with it in a different way. At least you have the luxury to do that. At least you're not shooting craps and letting the arbitrator decide on it. *You're* still in control of the process." He adds that mediation also "allows you to say, 'Look, if you did go to arbitration, this is what's likely to happen, this is the likely outcome, even if you do win.'"

Hobgood became intrigued with grievance mediation while working at the Department of Labor in the early 1970s. He met Northwestern University Law School Professor Steve Goldberg during the national coal negotiations in 1974, and they both served on President Jimmy Carter's Coal Commission in 1977. During his tenure as assistant secretary of labor-management relations at the Department of Labor, Hobgood funded an experiment that Goldberg proposed, to try grievance mediation in the coal industry—a project that resulted in scores of articles and several books. Goldberg, his wife and colleague Jeanne Brett, and William Ury (coauthor of the best-selling book *Getting to YES*) all have become very well known for their grievance mediation work in the mines. Hobgood, however, has his own views about what grievance mediation does.

> Goldberg started off with the idea that the process would be like a preliminary arbitration hearing, that the real focus would be the advisory opinion the mediator would give the parties about what would happen in arbitration. Once they heard this opinion from an experienced arbitrator, settlements would follow. . . . I argued that the advisory opinion could be an element, but that the real success of the process would be the mediation part. So that they would have to train the arbitrators who would use this to be better mediators. I don't know whether I was the only one who argued this, but in some ways this debate is still going on.

Despite the advantages Hobgood and others claim for grievance mediation, they still have to "sell" labor leaders and Local management on the idea of including mediation as an additional process in the grievance procedure, taking place after the third step and prior to arbitration. In collective bargaining relationships such as the one between TCC and the Mineworkers, this provision must be included directly in the contract or as an appendix to it. Hobgood notes he spends at least a few days every month trying to convince parties to try grievance mediation. His experience with TCC and the Mineworkers is typical.

At the time of Rosie's case, Hobgood had been mediating grievances with the company and the Mineworkers for about a year. In general, the coal industry has been receptive to using grievance mediation, in part because mediators like Hobgood, Steve Goldberg, and Rolf Valtin (another arbitrator-turned-grievance-mediator) have extensive connections with labor and management in the industry as a result of their previous work as arbitrators. Managers of industrial relations and union officials usually hear about grievance mediation through their associations with others in the industry. One of TCC's competitors in the state, for example, was the first to experiment with the procedure, and others, hearing about its success, gradually followed suit.

Getting a company and union to agree is a "sell job," and success often depends on the kinds of experiences union and management have with grievances and arbitration. Eighteen months before the Rosie Bracken case, Hobgood did a "sell job" before TCC and union officials. "We did the usual presentation about the costs of arbitration and a simulation on how grievance mediation works, using a discharge case," he says. "Some of the people from management in a few of the mines were skeptical, and so was the union leadership; but they were under pressure from their rank-and-file to try it. That's because arbitration does not work well here."

According to Hobgood, many problems have come up between TCC and the Mineworkers over the grievance process itself, including arbitration and even mediation. It is currently not clear whether the union and management will continue to use mediation. According to Hobgood:

> This company and union have many grievances. The company has a very aggressive labor relations policy, and so there's a high degree of conflict and a lot of grievances. This is compounded by the politics on the

union side. Everybody is elected, so it's one of the most political unions I know. As a result of the frequent changes, the union really is not very good at screening grievances. Not screening grievances makes problems. The union would win only 20 percent of the cases, and then accuse the arbitrators of being dishonest. The union has also had experiences with arbitration, where arbitrators were once on the company's payroll. Their experience is adversarial—it's a win-lose mentality, and the company would win most of the arbitrations. Not a lot of trust, as you can imagine. . . . There is another problem—getting qualified arbitrators to hear the cases. Their contract says that all arbitrations have to take place *at* the mine site. The mines are in rural areas and are hard to get to.

Despite the disenchantment with arbitration, Hobgood says getting mediation to "take" at TCC has been difficult. At first, the union was reluctant to use it because there was no provision in the contract. Once a letter of agreement was appended to the national agreement, union leaders agreed to give it a try. In contrast with other mines where the parties agree to mediate all cases, at TCC mediation is only by mutual agreement and on a case-by-case basis. Hobgood said this means the grievances he mediates at TCC are ones where one side or the other thinks its case is weak or wants to avoid arbitration for one reason or another. This is especially true on the management side: "If you are sure that you will win, there's probably not much reason to mediate," according to one TCC manager.

In Rosie's case, Hobgood was convinced almost from the outset that both parties could reach an agreement in mediation because both the company and the union had incentives to settle, not all of which concerned Rosie. The union complained, and TCC officials privately acknowledged, that there were serious problems with safety in Mine 18, a situation that could result in a serious accident, leaving the company vulnerable to the potentially high costs of a damages lawsuit. Hobgood believed mediation could provide a convenient venue for the company to deal with the broader safety issues in Mine 18. Union representatives felt there were two reasons to opt for mediation: Rosie, with her accident record, was a weak case to take to arbitration; and if Rosie's case were lost, an earlier arbitration award that was very much in the union's favor could be overturned.

. . . .

Hobgood regularly mediates grievances for several companies and unions primarily in the coal, utility, and energy industries. Generally, he schedules two days per month for each company and union and plans to mediate three grievances each day. The schedule changes frequently, either because there are no cases to mediate or because the parties indicate that a certain case may take longer than the typical one-third day allocated to it. That is what happened with Rosie's case; it was the only one scheduled for that day. Hobgood understood this to mean that the case had some significance, not only for the grievant but also for the organizations involved. The fact that so many senior people were present at the session from the management side reinforced his hunch.

Hobgood asked the union to begin its presentation. Pete Graves, the district representative, gave him a copy of the grievance, saying, "Even though this is a disciplinary case, I have no trouble going forward. The grievant, Rosie Bracken, received a final written warning about excessive accidents, that any further accidents would result in dismissal. We know the company has problems with employees being hurt, and that they have to control it. But as the union, we have a problem with how this was handled, with the disciplinary action taken on Rosie. We want the company to withdraw the warning."

For Hobgood, the major factor that distinguishes mediation from arbitration is the latitude a mediator has to move beyond the issue of who is right or who is wrong. The mediator can, in Hobgood's words, move from this "kind of black-and-white approach to one where the focus in on the parties' interests," in order to find an agreement that meets these interests. The difficulty is that the parties present their case in mediation very much as they would in arbitration—as a matter of who is right or wrong. They do so because, according to Hobgood, this perception has been continually reinforced throughout the grievance procedure: "By the time the problem gets to the mediation process," he says, "it has had what I call double reinforcement. The supervisor makes the initial decision and it's probably already been checked all the way up to the top. Then step 2 reinforces step 1, and step 3 reinforces step 2. By the time the mediator arrives on the scene, both parties have convinced themselves that they are right and can't back away from it because of the positions that have been taken all along the way."

Pete Graves's presentation of Rosie's case exemplified this tendency to present the issue in terms of right and wrong. He passed Hobgood a copy of the warning that Rosie had received. It stated that "your accident rate is excessive and if it is not brought into line you will be fired." He then passed Hobgood a copy of Rosie's accident record. It was a chart that listed her injuries and the dates that they occurred. The list included a series of muscle and back strains, a broken toe, fractured fingers, specks in her eye, and other minor accidents. The issue, Graves went on, was not the number of accidents that Rosie had but whether they were her fault. "The issue from the union's point," he said, "is whether the employee is at fault or not. Did she drop a rock on her foot or did she get back strain because the company asked her to pick up a four-by-four? We have an arbitration award, and it clearly states that the company must *prove* that the employee is at fault if it takes disciplinary action."

Hobgood interrupted Graves's presentation several times with questions about specific points. He wondered first whether there was a problem with high accident rates in this particular mine. Graves responded that he did not know specifically about the accident rate at Mine 18 but went on to note that past cases had been arbitrated on the issue of accidents and fault. Through this line of inquiry, Hobgood explained later to me, he was trying to understand how much the situation in which Rosie worked contributed to her problem. In his later private meeting with the union, he got an earful on this score.

Hobgood then reviewed Rosie's accident record and asked both parties to explain it to him. According to her record, she averaged one accident every four months from the time of her employment ten years ago; the average for the entire company was one accident every twenty-four months. Looking at the descriptions of some of the strains and contusions Rosie said she suffered, Hobgood asked whether the company offered any training and rehabilitation programs. After an affirmative response with little detail, Hobgood turned to the company to present its case.

Harry Maines, the industrial relations representative at Mine 18, handed Hobgood a copy of the company work rules booklet and asked him to turn to work rule 4, which states that "employees with unsatisfactory injury records will face disciplinary action." According to Maines:

> We know from our statistics that, with an injury record like hers, it is very likely she will have a more serious injury. We provide counseling to all employees who have an unsatisfactory record—that is, where the employee has an accident rate that is greater than the mine average. In these cases, we set up an interview with the employee and the supervisor to discuss performance. The employee is made aware of the record,

and then the supervisor makes recommendations for improvements. If the record does not improve, then the employee gets a written warning and then a final warning. And if still there is no improvement, he or she will be discharged.

Rosie received her first warning in 1983 and the second in 1986. In 1987, she had four injuries, and she received the final warning in February 1988. Since she came to work in May 1979, she has had twenty-five injuries. The union's position is that only one of them was her fault. Our position is that we are justified in giving this final warning.

Buddy Edwards, the corporate office industrial relations manager, added, "There is another arbitration award that Pete didn't mention. An earlier decision upheld the company's right to warn employees about their accident record based on accident statistics, not fault. I also want to mention that the union did not file a grievance on any of the earlier warnings issued to Rosie." At this point, Pete Graves said the union had no objection to the company jogging the employee's mind about safety through warnings. However, he added, the earlier arbitration case ruling required the company to prove fault before it disciplined an employee.

Hobgood has, on more than one occasion, referred to a principle in the coal industry that "if you have a certain frequency of accidents over a certain period of time, it's almost a statistical certainty that, if you reach a certain point on that frequency rate, the next accident will possibly be fatal, either for you or somebody who works close to you." From Hobgood's perspective, this "principle" meant that both the union and management had a serious interest in settling the case, because he assumed that neither one wanted to take a chance that Rosie would really be hurt. As I watched Hobgood mediate over a period of time, I frequently saw him work to "expand the focus" of cases like Rosie's. In such cases—when he believes that neither side will "win" in arbitration and/or deems there is a serious problem to be solved—he works to include other issues in addition to the actual grievance under review. In Rosie's case, after the formal presentations of both union and management, he tried to shift their attention away from the question of whether fault must be proved, to a broader discussion of the safety issues. He asked about the counseling process, safety orientations in the mine, other training on alertness, principles of safe lifting, and so forth.

. . . .

Up to this point in the case, about a half hour, nobody had spoken to Rosie at all. Rosie just sat quietly until Hobgood began asking her about her job, the pressures she was under, and any other problems she might have. Rosie is very soft-spoken, and it was difficult at times to hear her. Hobgood then mentioned her accident record—on the average, one accident every four months—and asked whether she thought it was excessive and whether others seemed to have the same problem. She was not sure. Hobgood then wondered about her work environment, whether there were reasons that she seemed to have so many accidents. Rosie responded that she was not currently working on her usual or "bid" job, that she had been moving around a lot and did not the know the people or the jobs very well. Hobgood empathized with her on the problem of being shifted around from job to job, noting that this practice can even lead to more accidents.

Mike Downes, TCC's vice president for safety, interrupted to challenge this line of reasoning. He explained that the accident frequency statistics include people who are not working on their bid jobs so that this explanation would not account for Rosie's record. Hobgood, however, continued to try to give Rosie a chance to give her explanation of events. He asked her whether any other common factors might contribute to her accidents, other than the fact that she has changed jobs frequently.

At this point, in a broken voice, Rosie responded, "I am under a lot of pressure. People keep saying to me, 'Don't get hurt or you'll get fired.' Or they say, 'We have to baby-sit Rosie so she don't get fired.'"

Hobgood then asked her about the most recent accident. Although she claimed to be accident-free for a year, the company noted that she had been on sick leave for depression during most of that year. Now back at work for three weeks, the situation, said Rosie, was somewhat better. Although she is not on her bid job, people are no longer talking about having to "baby-sit Rosie." Hobgood speculated aloud on whether her mental state may have contributed to her accidents, that maybe she was not being as careful as she could be.

Pete Graves requested a break from the meeting so that Hobgood could caucus with the union. As we walked to another room in the hotel, Graves said Rosie is in "a terrible situation" at Mine 18. The mine manager often asks her to perform jobs that are too difficult for her—lifting heavy timber, for example.

Her situation was even more complicated. Apparently, Graves had recently learned, one of Rosie's supervisors had tried to rape her. She reported the attack to the mine superintendent, who took no action against the supervisor despite claims that he would. Then in the mine, her co-workers wrote graffiti about her on the walls. She handled it "all wrong," Graves said, because she never reported it to the union.

The caucus with the union committee began with Hobgood asking about the conditions in the mine. The male members of the committee said, among other things, that Mine 18 has the worst safety record in the company; the mine manager always puts production before safety; and the annual retraining is a "joke." The committee members continued to complain about management in the mine. They told a number of horror stories about people who lost limbs working in this mine. The mine manager, they said, has told them that he does not care who gets killed as long as the work gets done.

Rosie sat silently through these discussions, though Hobgood tried to bring her into the discussion. He suggested that they keep the discussion focused on Rosie and what they could do to help her situation. "What we have to figure out is to find something to deal with your problem," he said. "What are the underlying problems? You don't just want to wipe out the warning, because you could get hurt. Let's focus on what we can do."

Though safety in Mine 18 in general sounded like a problem for both union and management, Hobgood endeavored to keep the discussion focused on Rosie and her specific problem. When the local union president said that they needed to think about safety training more generally, Hobgood said, "We have to keep the focus on Rosie; we need to use her situation to find a way to handle similar cases. But we can't go for too broad a solution, and we can't come up with something that is unreasonable." Later, when members of the union committee suggested that the mediator should propose a joint company-union initiative on safety, Hobgood cautions them to think one step at a time: "Let's not worry about that now; let's keep it focused around Rosie and her safety issues, how we can help her," he said.

Hobgood then asked Rosie if she was having any problems in the mines because she is a woman. According to Rosie, although there are other women, generally the men do not like women in the mines. "Considering all things, your health and the environment, is this the right place for you?" Hobgood asks. "Will you have a fair chance? Are you treated in the same way as other women?"

Rosie responded that she likes her job, that sometimes the men help, but that "they don't like women in the mines." She said she was willing to be retrained and that she wanted people to stop talking about "baby-sitting her so she don't get hurt."

· · · · · · ·

A grievant retains the final decision in mediation; that is, it is up to her or him to decide whether to accept a particular settlement or insist on arbitration. As I observed Rosie Bracken's case, sometimes I thought Rosie seemed almost irrelevant to the proceedings. Hobgood had the union and company representatives present their case, then engaged in extensive discussions with them about Rosie's record before she was even part of the discussion. Indeed, they talked about her and her record as if she were not present.

I was disturbed about Rosie and questioned Hobgood about whether her interests were subordinated to those of the union. I wondered why he let her horrible situation—attempted rape and harassment—just stand. His adamant response, one that I do not find totally satisfactory, is to compare what happens when he mediates to the grievant's fate in arbitration.

> The client is the grievant. As a mediator, you have to look after the person's rights. I think that she benefits by the ability of the system to focus on her and her needs in the workplace. If it had gone to arbitration, the focus would be on the policy, not her needs. She could have had another accident before the arbitration—you just don't know. But with mediation, she might just get some help in her environment on her job.
>
> Of course, any time you move from an individual issue, which grievance mediation allows you to do, to broaden the issue, you run the risk of it looking like the individual issues are subordinated to the broader

issues. I don't believe that her interests were subordinated. I believe that she would have lost if she had gone to arbitration. I do think at that point that you do have to balance institutional needs with her needs.

After this discussion, I began to notice some of the ways that Hobgood brings the grievant into the process. First, in an effort to make the grievant comfortable, he speaks directly to the her when he explains the mediation process. Union and company representatives are already familiar with the mechanics, but it is likely to be a first time experience for a grievant; thus he makes a special effort to ensure that the grievant knows what the process is. Second, although Hobgood has the company and union representatives present the case, he typically engages the grievant in a discussion of the problem as a way to "get a handle on the precipitating circumstances" that gave rise to the complaint.

Throughout this first caucus with the union, Hobgood let the union committee talk generally about the safety in the mine but gave Rosie numerous opportunities to enter into the discussions. On several occasions, he tried to move the union committee away from its institutional agenda, to focus more on Rosie. From my perspective, he tries to balance the needs of the union with those of the grievant. But in so doing, he sometimes treats a grievant like a child who needs to have the situation explained clearly to her, and who also needs to be protected by him from union colleagues.

An earlier case he describes as his most successful had these kinds of characteristics.

It was a discipline case where a woman had been forced into early retirement because of performance issues. While we were mediating it, her husband was on his deathbed. The union committee was pushing her, saying you ought to go ahead and arbitrate this, you can win with arbitration. We weren't able to address that issue, but we were able to address her financial needs in terms of insurance and medical costs. She was under such enormous pressure because of her husband's health, because of the union committee, all of those things.

So, at one point I said to the union committee, leave her alone, let her take a walk, let her call her husband. She left and I saw her in the hall; there were tears running down her face and I put an arm around her and said, "Look, whatever decision you make has got to please you." I just put my arm around her and held her a moment and told her she should just do what she thought was right. She settled for $50,000 and agreed to drop her EEOC [Equal Employment Opportunity Commission] complaint. And because she settled, she was able to continue her health coverage. I remember this case because it was emotional, and I feel that I helped her with a difficult decision at a hard time in her life.

* * * * * * *

Grievance mediation, according to Hobgood, is a process that requires balancing the needs of the grievant with those of the institution of which she is a member. Hobgood's understanding of the politics of the situation is based both on a differential view of the union and the company and especially on the kinds of assistance that a union officer might need. First, Hobgood seems to act in ways that suggest that the company is in control; that is, the very fact that the company agrees to mediate indicates to him that it believes it has a potentially weak case for arbitration. This means that the company has an incentive to settle, and the outlines that the settlement takes will tend to be set by management. For this reason, Hobgood often caucuses first with the management committee to hear its version of the kind of settlement they envision.

In Rosie's case, however, the union had requested the first caucus break; that discussion helped shape Hobgood's first private talk with the company. He asked Harry Maines of Mine 18 and Buddy Edwards of the corporate office to join him in the hallway. Before Hobgood got the chance to speak, they informed him that the first arbitration case, in which the arbitrator said the company could warn an employee based solely on the record, also concerned Rosie (under her maiden name). She had received the written reprimand because she had one of the worst safety records in the company. The union, they said, never argued about it or mentioned that fault had anything to do with it.

Hobgood defended what in effect was an attack on Pete Graves. "Listen," he said, "you know Pete is a thoughtful person. He's not out for a winner in arbitration on this one. We talked to the union, and they have a serious concern about the safety record in this mine. I'm concerned about it too, so how should we proceed with this?"

If the company often has more control over the range of possible settlement, it is the union leader who, according to Hobgood, takes more of the risk. The union leadership present in this case were all elected, and support for grievance mediation is not universal among union members. The byplay in caucuses is often the expression of political challenges. Indeed, the bringing of a grievance itself may constitute a challenge by one group in the union to its leadership. This view about the politics of the union guides Hobgood's actions in several ways. As just noted, he is quick to defend a union leader like Graves, whom he once described as an "extraordinary individual who understands the process and knows how to use grievance mediation for the maximum benefit of his members. He sees it as an opportunity to achieve what is in the grievant's best interest."

Hobgood works with these representatives, on either the management or the labor side, by doing things that he believes will ease their job. For example, his parting words to the union at the end of the first caucus were to defend Graves's support of settling in mediation. "You can go to arbitration and be right; but there is a saying that you can be dead right. Arbitration will not solve this problem," says Hobgood. Further, he claims that one of the reasons he used the first half of the caucus with the union to let the members complain about safety conditions in the mine was that it "helps Pete if they get a hearing." As the case unfolded, Hobgood continued to lend support to Graves in his dealings with his own committee.

The political dynamics on the company side are viewed somewhat differently by Hobgood. At the table on the company side typically sit management from both corporate and local industrial relations departments. Hobgood knows these people well because, like the union representatives, they appear at most of his cases. From Hobgood's perspective, Buddy Edwards operates under a different set of constraints than Pete Graves, and with sometimes less than enthusiastic support from his management. "He [Buddy] was able to introduce this new concept [mediation] over the resistance of his management," Hobgood says. "Remember, he's responsible for the labor relations in several mines, and in some of the mines they have a much more conservative and traditional style of doing things. So, while he and the people who work under him in labor relations have taken to the process very well, they haven't always been as successful with the foremen in some of the mines."

There may be other members of management from industrial relations, line management, and other corporate officials present as well. Hobgood is always interested in how these company people whom he does not know will influence the proceedings. And just as he learns about the politics on the union side from acquaintances in management, so too he picks up information from the union about the company representatives. For example, in one case at another company, the union representative told Hobgood that the reason there were so many people from management (a situation the union resented) was because the company was worried that the industrial relations representative was making settlements that were too favorable to the union. A "give-away artist," he was called.

In Rosie's case, Hobgood expressed curiosity about Mike Downes, the new vice president for safety, during the caucus with the union when he asked about the relationships on the company side. "If we want changes in the safety program, we need to get practical," said Hobgood. "Who needs to be influenced in order for any changes to take place?" Graves responded by saying that the vice president for safety is new and that he knows that there are problems in 18.

When Hobgood met in the hall with Buddy Edwards and Harry Maines after his meeting with the union, Edwards suggested that he thought it would be a good idea for Downes to hear what Hobgood had to report about his meeting with the union. Hobgood agreed and convened a caucus with the full management team, to help Edwards and Maines deal with people they have trouble convincing.

· · · · · · · ·

Often Hobgood, after his first round of caucuses with the parties, talked to me about what kind of settlement he thought would eventually be reached. This is a kind of "fast forward" technique in which he invents a number of possible scenarios. He calls this practice "getting a fix on the case."

"Pretty early on," he explained, "I get a feel for what a settlement will look like. You get a 'fix' on things because you've been there before. That's why the parties want you. Anybody who says that mediation is a pure, free-form process, that mediation is not content-driven, is wrong. You have to begin forming a vision early on. That doesn't mean that everything is all mapped out, that you have the strategies and tactics all set. Or that you think that just because you have a fix on things, the parties will agree. You have to condition them—that's what the process is all about. The parties are buying more than a conference leader."

Hobgood's fix on the case means that he thinks he understands enough about the circumstances of the grievance to formulate the central themes in a possible settlement. These ideas then become the basis for the kinds of arguments he will make to the parties to try to bring them closer to his "fix" on the settlement. In Rosie's case, Hobgood described to me his fix on the case at the conclusion of his caucus with the union, ninety minutes into the case: "They obviously have safety problems at this mine," he said, "and their training and rehabilitation program is inadequate. She's obviously got problems, but she is willing to get training. You see, all that complaining we let the union do helps you get a fix on it. That's one of the reasons I let them complain so much."

At this stage, Hobgood said he believed that some kind of training and rehabilitation program for Rosie, worked out jointly by union and management, would make sense, coupled with the removal (or promise of the removal) of the warning from her file.

While Hobgood may have his own fix on the case, he is quite clear that directly suggesting this to either management or the union would be a mistake. The parties need time to get used to the kinds of ideas he has in mind. This is what he means by "conditioning" them. "The mediator," he explains, "is the *only* person devoted to settlement. He is not concerned with the best settlement, just a settlement the parties can live with. If you push them in one direction or another, you take on the burden of convincing them to do it the right way. That's when you lose the advantage you have. It's important not to let your own ideas about what ought to be get confused with what is. Once you start lecturing them, you can turn them off. You have to go slowly and condition them."

· · · · · · ·

Following the conversation in the hallway with Maines and Edwards, Hobgood began the caucus with the full management team by describing the safety concerns raised during his meeting with the union. "We had a lengthy discussion with them [about safety]," he said, "and it is clear that this is a problem for all of you. We need to change the mind-set. They want to work with you to find a solution. Pete Graves doesn't want another serious accident. But they contrast this mine with others at TCC, and think that the style of management at the mine is part of the problem. At this mine, there is a more aggressive stance on productivity and, although it may not be intentional, their sense is that safety does take a back seat."

He then began posing questions about management's willingness to broaden the issues from just the warning to Rosie to the problem of safety training in that mine. The purpose of these questions, he said, was to test whether his fix was correct and also to get management used to the idea of safety training as a possible outcome along with some compromise on the warning.

For example, Hobgood told the management representatives:

> I understand that you want to deal with this kind of problem by the warning letter. I see your objective; you don't want a serious injury. But is there some other way? Are you prepared to break the pattern to do something beyond the ordinary, to try to change attitudes? Can you hold the final warning in abeyance for say, six months, while you do some other things?
>
> We talked about a safety reorientation. I think that there is a good chance to modify behavior. She seems

willing. Could we do something on a trial basis for people with particularly serious safety problems? I don't want to overpsychoanalyze the situation, but is there something that can be done with her?

Later, Hobgood told me he "may have moved too soon by suggesting that they remove the warning letter as part of the agreement on retraining. It's common practice to do that, make a trade like that, but I may have moved too quickly on it." It is important, Hobgood feels, that people feel that they have time, that they are not rushed.

Indeed, Hobgood's fix was challenged almost immediately by Wayne Roberts, the vice president of industrial relations, who is also Harry Maine and Buddy Edwards's boss. Roberts picked up the accident record and began to talk about Rosie in a derogatory way, wondering how this woman could have so many accidents and saying that she clearly was unable to keep her mind on the job. Hobgood tried to refocus the discussion away from Rosie and the past; instead he encouraged them to consider the problem as a joint one that can be solved by looking toward the future.

"I am not excluding the possibility that she is accident-prone," said Hobgood. "That's a problem. But we can use this as an opportunity to do something constructive. You could go on as you have, along the disciplinary route and set the stage for getting rid of her. But I assume that your objective is to save her as a functioning employee."

Buddy Edwards supported his boss by questioning the motives of the union. They had to realize, he claimed, that there must be a drastic turnaround in Rosie's behavior. They could not use this grievance as a way to buy time for her and delay the inevitable. He refused to withdraw the warning from her file. Roberts, after some further comments about Rosie and her work habits, agreed to consider a rehabilitation and safety program for Rosie and other employees with similar accident records. The program they proposed was one in which a safety supervisor would analyze Rosie's record, observe her on the job, and design a program to help her work more safely.

Hobgood said he was concerned about the warning because he believed that its removal was important to the grievant; it would lessen the pressure on her by alleviating the fear of being fired. He asked the company to consider a time limit, such as six months, for the warning to be in effect, and, if Rosie had no accidents, to remove it from the record. "The purpose is to take the pressure off of her and not make her so nervous," said Hobgood. Roberts refused.

Hobgood then pressed on another part of the union's proposal—joint safety training—and asked if management would consider such a program with the union. "My point in raising the union's participation is not to challenge your training," said Hobgood, "but that it is a way to get them more involved. It would make it more of a problem-solving effort and move you away from an adversarial mode." The company refused.

It was quite clear, Hobgood later admitted, that his timing had been wrong in this caucus with the company. Ever patient, however, he remains optimistic that in such situations, given enough time and "conditioning," parties will come around to accepting either his fix on a settlement or some variation of it.

. . . .

Hobgood uses the word *conditioning* frequently when discussing his style of mediation. He summarizes conditioning as the variety of ways a mediator tries to develop "a settlement mentality" in the parties. The problem, from Hobgood's perspective, is that parties simply get into habits of doing things, and any change or new idea is interpreted as a possible threat.

He sees this reluctance to risk a change in terms that would be familiar to a behavioral psychologist: "People get into habits so that their reaction to things is automatic," he says. "That's where resistance comes. So, if you're going to make any headway in changing their behavior, you have to condition them to want to make a change. In contract mediation, one way you condition them is get them to commit to settling."

For example, he points out, "One of Bill Usery's [former U.S. secretary of labor] skills is that he keeps asking the parties if they really want to get a settlement, do they really want to make a deal. Then he'll say that he's not convinced they really do. If you go through that, and this is part of the conditioning process, and they keep saying honestly we really want a deal, then when you get down to the hard part and they dig in, he'll say, 'Now look, you told me you really wanted a deal.' So it's really setting the stage early on."

In some situations, the circumstances do the conditioning, as is the case when the company and union realize they both lose from a strike and they should focus on methods to avoid it.

> The behaviors of the parties are going to do the conditioning, and of course the mediator is also part of the conditioning. . . . In grievance mediation, you don't really ask if they want to settle. The conditioning you're trying to do is different. On the safety program here, I'm trying to condition them to think in terms of broader issues and to get them off of the sheer right and wrong of the situation. Now you may not be on the right track in raising the issue, but it's always relevant in the final analysis because, as part of the conditioning process, you are involving them and getting their thinking on the issue. Conditioning is like learning, it's always part of the process.

When TCC resisted his efforts to remove the warning and agree to a joint safety program, Hobgood took it as a signal that

he needed to do more conditioning. He felt he had to be persistent, to keep raising the issue of the warning and appealing to
them to help Rosie. He would raise the issues through questions
because he believes it is one of the best ways to get people
to change their minds. "I think some mediators have a tendency
to tell people what they ought to do," he says, "what's right or
wrong. The problem is that people have a natural tendency
to resist this kind of thing. When you use questions, they have to
answer. They have to tell themselves what they want to do,
to reach their own conclusions. Sometimes questions are guided
by what you don't know. But questions are powerful even when
you know the answer because it conditions them to think about
the answers they want."

In Rosie's case, Hobgood posed a series of questions to the company about the warning. The questions were linked with his own
ideas about how to handle it and were almost rhetorical in their
effect: "If you leave the warning in the record, would there be a
period of time when it could be dropped?" he asked. "Otherwise
what motivation does she have for her going through the training
and becoming more careful in her work? At what point will the
final written warning lose some of its impact? Is there some provision in your procedures when a warning loses its effect?"

Roberts again refused to move on the warning:

> We are not using the written warning to hurt her, or as
> part of an attempt to avoid discharging her directly.
> We are committed to doing all we can, but if it doesn't
> work, management has done all that it can and we will
> then suspend with intent. . . . Our experience with
> attendance problems is that they have good atten-
> dance until the period is up and then they start miss-
> ing again and we have to start the disciplinary proce-
> dure all over again. We do not want to tell her that we

will do something for her that we have not done for others.

Despite the continued negative response on the warning, Hobgood tried to create a connection between the warning and the safety program so that the company would come to see both as part of the settlement. He shifted the focus of discussion from the warning letter and reported on the union's complaints about safety in the mine. He did this, he later confided, both because he was frustrated at management's refusal to deal with the warning and because Edwards had told him that the safety people needed to hear about problems in Mine 18.

Wayne Roberts then opened fire on the union: "This committee and rep have beaten this issue to death," he charged. "They don't like the mine manager. The mine has the highest grievance and arbitration rate in the company. The union is trying to use that arbitration they have that says we have to prove fault as a way to make inroads there. It was a bad decision, and if we arbitrate this case, we will win. We have the right to issue a written warning."

Hobgood countered with a defense of mediation and a justification for expanding the problem to include the safety program. "What is troubling about the arbitration award is that it focuses on the wrong thing," he said. "Fault is a small part of the problem. Whose fault it is doesn't solve the safety problems. Let me say this: Pete Graves is concerned about going to arbitration. He says he doesn't just want to win; he's really concerned about what happens to Rosie."

Buddy Edwards agreed that the union did not want to risk another arbitral decision that might jeopardize the "fault" principle. But he said that the way things were going, all the movement was on management's side—"We are offering to teach her, and they want us to remove the warning too."

Mike Downes, the vice president of safety, then spoke for the first time. "This mine," he claimed, "has the worst safety record in the company, but that record is improving." It is improving, he said, because management is watching employees more closely, communicating better, singling out those in dangerous jobs, and scrutinizing those with bad histories. Although they are watching people like Rosie more carefully, they have not alerted the employees to this change in strategy.

Hobgood then cautioned the management representatives that the workers always know what is going on and will start to see themselves as targets.

• • • • • • •

As a result of the meeting with management, Hobgood changed his mind about the agreement that would be achievable. En route to the union caucus, he summarized his perception of the case and his strategy for meeting with the union. "This is a situation in which the company could win in arbitration. This is not a good case for Pete Graves," he said. "I will call him out and get a feeling from him privately about the strength of his position at this point, how much he's getting pushed into going to arbitration. He doesn't want to go to arbitration on this one. She's a real safety problem, and my guess is that she's probably been depressed for a long time."

When we talked about this case afterward, Hobgood said his thinking was influenced by the bind the union was in concerning their chances in arbitration. His fix on any case is heavily influenced by his assessment of how the parties will fare in arbitration. Although he objects to the description of mediation as "peek-a-boo" arbitration (see Feuille, 1992), he freely gives the parties a peek. I have seen Hobgood give an advisory opinion in only one case, but in each of the eleven cases that I attended with him, he informally evaluated parties' chances in arbitration. The threat of arbitration is a club that Hobgood uses to force parties to recon-sider their options in mediation.

I have seen him often begin a meeting with one of the parties, typically the union, by discussing its likely fate in arbitration. He is not always able to predict who will actually win but can usually remind the union of its uphill battle to prepare the kind of case it will have to make and the risks of doing so. In making these argu-ments he refers to a number of factors, including these:

- The uncertainty of an arbitration decision—"You never know which way an arbitration will go."
- Trends in arbitration awards relative to a given case—"On welding cases, it is always hard to figure out whether the contract has been violated."
- The quality of the union or management's case—"Unless you can show that the out-of-class assignment is a safety issue, you will have a tough time in arbitration."
- The kind of data that the union would need to provide and management's inherent record-keeping advantage in this regard—"On these kinds of cases it is always easier for manage-ment to argue the case because they have the job assignment data and you would have to find witnesses."
- Patterns in arbitral decision making—"Arbitrators are reluctant to rule on internal jurisdictional cases unless you can show that the union lost work."
- Arbitration would not deal with the "real" problem—"Even if the arbitrator decided that senior welders should be on the day shift, you [the grievant] wouldn't necessarily get your job back."
- His assessment that the union would likely lose the case (as in Rosie's situation).

Hobgood argues that arbitration is essential to grievance mediation, that it is a major part of the conditioning process. It is "the threat of arbitration that makes mediation work," he believes. If parties think that they will not win in arbitration, then they are forced to look at the mediation options more seriously. His predictions of how they will fare in arbitration help move the process along. In addition, he also points out that arbitration is costly in terms of both risk and money. "Arbitration is so unpredictable," he says. "One of the values of mediation is that you can find that out here. The beauty of this process is that you can anticipate what an arbitrator will say so that you don't waste money on arbitration."

Once Hobgood was convinced that the union would not want to go to arbitration on Rosie's case, he changed his fix on the final settlement: the warning letter would remain. He became even more convinced that the union should try very hard to settle in mediation. When he met in the hall with Pete Graves, Hobgood said, "This arbitration case is going to create problems for you. She's a horrible case. The arbitrator will look at it, and I think it's a tough call whether he would remove the warning letter. You'd take a risk because you might undermine a good decision. The decision makes it hard for you to deal with an unsafe employee. The best position for you is to have [the earlier arbitration award] in your hip pocket and not use it. They are willing to do special things for Rosie which are legitimate." The balance between concern for the grievant and for the institution has now shifted in favor of the latter.

Hobgood reported that the company was willing to set up a safety program but refused to change the warning in any way. Graves said that he did not trust the company and felt that Rosie would be fired at the first opportunity. "My experience is that once a worker gets a warning, the next step is that she's gone," he said. Hobgood said that he believed the company would not remove the warning from the file and added that, in all likelihood, neither would an arbitrator. "The arbitration case you've already won is a good one," he said. "But Rosie's case is a bad case to take to arbitration."

Graves then asked about union participation in a safety program. Hobgood replied that he raised the idea with the company
representatives but they were resistant at this point. As Graves
prepared to return to his committee, he said, "We have to handle
this girl with caring."

Once Graves concurred that the case was weak, Hobgood
abandoned his efforts to get the warning removed and concentrated on the joint safety program. He called Harry Maines and
Buddy Edwards out into the hall and told them he agreed with
their contention that Graves would have a problem if he took
this case to arbitration. But, Hobgood reiterated, Graves still was
under political pressures from his committee to take the case to
arbitration. He said that Pete needed to settle two issues in mediation: a safety program that really helps Rosie and an agreement
to involve the union in it. The three then returned to the management caucus.

Hobgood opened this session by stating:

> Pete is sincerely interested in getting away from win-
> ning this case and throwing it up in your face. This
> case creates problems for him. There are some [arbitra-
> tion] cases that you wish you hadn't won. On the
> strength of this case, his winner could be in jeopardy if
> he goes to arbitration. And even if you won, it would
> not be focusing on the real issue, which is how to deal
> with accident-prone employees. We need to deal with
> this case constructively and help him address his prob-
> lem.
>
> We're looking for a way to deal with safety prob-
> lems. Could you outline exactly what the program for
> her would do? I know you cringe when I say this, but
> would you be willing to bring the Local in on a consul-
> tative basis? I am not suggesting veto rights, but a col-
> laboration so that you could be less confrontational on

the safety issues. . . . Pete Graves is under political pressure to make it a confrontation between this mine and the workers. So there are two elements: the content of the program and the role you are willing to have the union play now or in subsequent stages. He needs to be able to say, "Rosie, this is a case we will lose." But he also needs to be able to tell the union that they will be consulted. It makes people feel good to be consulted.

. . . .

In grievance mediation, the parties are dealing with a single issue, so there is some creativity involved in trying to expand the scope not of the issues themselves but of the kinds of things that you might be able to pull in that would give you some trading material if you want to call it that. It also means that you have to expand people's thinking on the issues, what really is a part of this. . . . In collective bargaining, at least in the private sector, you're talking more of an element of power, whereas in grievance mediation you're talking about the next step being rights. So there may not be the motivation that power has to push people to make changes.

In some cases, it is difficult to expand the scope of the major issue in dispute. Most of the cases that I observed Hobgood mediate seem to be ones in which the union claims a contract violation in the assignment of work, or the allocation of overtime, or manning rules. Thus, the mediation process is largely a matter of trying to determine whether the contract and/or a consistent past practice has been violated. While Hobgood generally tries to question the disputants about what interests are at stake (why did the company do what it is accused of, and how does this impair the grievant and the union?) and whether some solution can be found to satisfy these interests, in the end, conditioning in these circumstances means convincing the parties (my observation was that this was typically the grievant or the union committee) that their arbitration case is weak and that it would be better for all concerned to settle in mediation.

In other cases, different issues were brought in and incorporated into the settlement. In Rosie's case, Hobgood was clearly pleased that it looked like he would be able to incorporate a better safety program into the settlement. After meeting with Edwards and Downes, he was optimistic about the outcome of the case: "I'm on a roll," he exulted. "We could have resolved this case by having the union withdraw the grievance without prejudice. The union's case is weak and they don't want to risk arbitration, so they might have withdrawn it. But because of this process, we now have a real opportunity to make a difference here. It's a chance to help Rosie and also to change the situation in that mine."

* * * * * * *

Edwards came out of the company caucus room and told Hobgood that if the union agrees to withdraw the grievance without prejudice, the company will institute the joint safety program and call it a settlement. Hobgood then went into the union caucus room and addressed his remarks primarily to Rosie. "What we have been trying to do here is get away from a win-lose solution and deal with your problem," he said. "This is not a good case from your point of view. . . . You would take a big risk in arbitration with this one. With your record, whether it is your fault or not, it would be a risky case. The company thinks that if they don't do something that you might jeopardize your life. They want to be constructive. They assure me that they do not want to fire you. Let's get away from the question of firing and create a situation where you can work safely and comfortably. Our task is to make sure that you are not hurt. Harry Maines is committed to this."

To the union committee as a whole, he said, "You also have a desire for local union involvement. What they are willing to do is to come up with a program. They want the union and their people to look at the safety record and together come up with a course of training. It's a small step to create a safe environment.

"When we started," he concluded, "we were talking about a good arbitration case here. Now we have used it to take a positive first step. They are not willing to take the letter out of the file, but they are willing to deal in a positive way."

Graves responded that the committee had a problem with the word *final* in the warning letter, that Rosie fears that the next time there is an accident, whether it is her fault or not, she will be fired. Hobgood said that he will see if the company will remove the word *final* with the understanding that, if the next accident is of sufficient gravity, she will be discharged.

. . . .

This kind of back-and-forth shuttle, between room and hall, by the company and the union, and the meetings in the hallway with spokespersons from both sides, is a hallmark of Hobgood's style of grievance mediation. There comes a point in the case, however, where the parties may be close to an agreement but are not quite there. This is the time where he says "more squeezing or conditioning" is required. Many of the things he has done previously are repeated or reiterated: the quality of the arbitration case or the need to solve a problem or keep a valued employee. He asks a question or asks for their ideas, or he brings the key players together in the hall and pose the questions to them, or he may bring the grievant face-to-face with the offending supervisor to see if they can work out a settlement that "both think is fair and equitable." At other times, he repeats arguments he has made earlier. As he likes to say, "If you don't have the law, pound on the facts; if you don't have the facts, pound on the law; and if you don't have either, pound on the table."

Finally, Hobgood often proposes a settlement that is meant to apply only in a specific case; maybe it will be a trial period for a system on overtime call-in, or maybe it will be an exception for this grievant in this case. He has proposed as a non-precedent-setting exception, for example, that an employee be given a chance to rebid a job that somebody else holds, or that a welder be given a job on the day shift when his classification has been reassigned to the "owl shift." This activity is what he means when he says that "you have to keep looking for alternatives; you have to find ways to keep conditioning the parties." And that process continues right to the end of a mediation.

* * * * * * *

In the final minutes of Rosie's case, Hobgood made one last attempt to squeeze out of the company a limitation on the warning. In a conversation in the hall with Edwards and Maines, he said, "We are on track, but we need some final squeezing. The word *final* bothers them. Let me ask you, but hear the whole reason before you say no."

Edwards explained that his boss, Wayne Roberts, and Mike Downes had instructed him that if he were pressed to take the *final* out of the warning, then the company would go to arbitration. Hobgood asked them whether the severity of a future accident would affect a possible discharge. Edwards responded that Rosie would only be discharged if the accident were her fault, resulted from egregious violations of the rules, or were very severe. She would not automatically be fired for the next accident.

Hobgood then suggested that they call Pete Graves out to discuss the issue. He told Graves that the company refuses to take the word *final* out but that the understanding would be that no action would be taken if a future accident were not her fault or were inconsequential. Edwards blamed Rosie; she has psychological problems. Graves blamed the mine superintendent; there are safety problems at the mine that could cause future accidents. Hobgood said that he is stymied, wondering what to do as he stood silently with his arms folded.

Graves asked Edwards if the company will clarify what *final* does *not* mean. Edwards said that he could agree to put some language in that said *final* does not mean that the next accident automatically results in discharge. They asked Graves to explain this to Rosie.

There was a final joint meeting. The provision detailing exactly what *final* means and does not mean is inserted. Hobgood complimented the parties and said that this agreement is a new start and tells Rosie that it gives her the opportunity to start fresh. Graves explained the program and provision to her, adding, "I would rather have you fired than dead."

• • • • • • •

Evaluations of grievance mediation experiments in coal and other industries have produced some impressive results (see Goldberg and Brett, 1983). About 90 percent of the cases brought to mediation settle prior to arbitration. Bill Hobgood has a high settlement rate in his practice. Of the eleven cases that I observed, eight settled in mediation. In some of the situations, a settlement was reached when the union withdrew the grievance. But withdrawing the grievance, as in Rosie's case, may also be the basis for a trade resulting in a settlement that is broader in scope than the initial complaint. Settlements may result in new programs, as in Rosie's case, or they may be agreements to refer the grievance back to an earlier step. Frequently, arrangements are made to take care of specific job assignments—an employee is reinstated at a lower-paying job and, in return, agrees to abandon two lawsuits against the company. Sometimes an agreement makes a special exception for an individual, or it may result in a letter in which management states its intent to clarify an action that stands.

Hobgood believes that most cases are amenable to settlement in mediation, at least as far as the issues raised in them are concerned. "I think that mediation is appropriate to any case," he says. "There are some that are harder. In certain cases, they are fact-based. Here the problem is who saw it, what's the evidence. These are harder but still they're amenable to the process. You always have some issues where a compelling principle is at stake, a contractual issue that needs to be established up or down. These have to be arbitrated."

It is not always easy to determine which of these cases fall into the need-to-be arbitrated category. But issues are not the reason that Hobgood feels that cases do not settle in mediation. From his perspective, failure to settle generally stems from political reasons. For instance, he says, "You get a situation where the business agent knows it's a bad case. But at least in mediation, it's more predictable. He has some control, so he may be willing to settle, but he may be being pushed by his members or the grievant. On the management side, he feels 'I have to back my supervisors and take it all the way.'"

While there are always reasons for failing to settle, Hobgood cites Rosie's case as an example of the benefits and success of grievance mediation. He speaks of it as the "Raincloud over Rosie" case, perhaps reflecting his belief that she was a victim at the mine or somehow jinxed. The case, he says, "is a good example of how mediation can deal with a broad range of issues if it chooses to. An arbitrator might make a correct decision based on the facts but not be able to deal with the broader safety issues.

Also, the case demonstrates how issues that really have nothing to do with the case, like the sexual assault, would not be dealt within arbitration, but become part of the situation that she's in. And then you can use mediation to try to solve the bigger problem."

Opportunities to broaden the issues as in Rosie's case are not that common. While Hobgood sees the potential of issue broadening, the parties are not always convinced. He often lacks the leverage to get them to consider the more systemic issues that he would like to address. There are also limits on how far systemic change can actually happen in grievance mediation. In a utility industry case, for example, Hobgood tried to design a settlement that would resolve a class of job jurisdiction cases where union members were performing work that was a violation under a strict reading of the contract. With a focus on the union's interests in protecting jobs and the power company's in getting flexibility, he proposed a process to investigate the issues. The company rejected his suggestions, which angered the union, and so what should have been a relatively easy case on apprentices failed to settle.

· · · · · · ·

Nowadays, Hobgood's professional practice seems to be shifting away from the actual practice of grievance mediation. He is an independent consultant in the labor management field, and his work increasingly involves more training and development. His dilemma is deciding whether to mediate or train, a choice that others in the field are often forced to make. Part of the attraction to the parties of grievance mediation is its low cost relative to arbitration. Inevitably, the low-cost advantage translates into lower fees relative to the other ways that Hobgood can spend his time. So he finds himself thinking about grievance mediation as part of a larger system, spending more time trying to convince companies and unions to sign on, and less time, about two days per month, actually mediating.

"Mediation is still probably the most attractive part of my work," he says. "I'm doing more work installing the system now than actually mediating, doing the training, making more speeches and presentations promoting it. I'm moving away somewhat from grievance mediation per se, but the value of my mediation skills is crucial to making this new system work. Instead of blithely saying that everyone in the world needs grievance mediation, I now think of it as only one element in a total approach."

* * * * * * *

At the end of her mediation, Rosie said she understood what would happen. She thanked Hobgood and got up to leave. Hobgood and Graves shook hands, and everybody agreed that the mediated settlement promised a new beginning at Mine 18. Five hours after he had begun, Hobgood adjourned the conference until the next morning, when there would be three more cases to mediate.

Two years after Rosie's case, she is still employed at Mine 18. She has not had a single accident since the agreement.

Deborah M. Kolb

References

Feuille, P. (1992). Why does grievance mediation resolve grievances? *Negotiation Journal, 8*, 131–145.

Goldberg, S. B., and Brett, J. M. (1983). Grievance mediation in the coal industry: A field experiment. *Industrial and Labor Relations Review, 37*, 49–70.

"Mediation is an educational device even more than
it is a problem-solving device. . . . It can help, so
long as it is done right, by assisting people to reach, to
illuminate what is at issue, and to highlight underlying
interests."

—Patrick Phear

5

Patrick Phear

Control, Commitment, and Minor Miracles in Family and Divorce Mediation

As I searched out the address of Patrick Phear, I found myself on one of those Boston streets that seem to ooze a respectability born from long association with the right kind of people, if not the right kind of architecture. Feeling a dull flutter of nervousness, I paid little heed to what would have, on some other occasion, appeared to be something almost forbidding about the street's respectability or off-putting about its architecture. I focused instead on those first few awkward minutes of half-glancing mutual appraisal and impression making. And I wondered whether Phear himself approaches his work as a divorce and family mediator with the same slightly vexing nervous anxiety.

I thought about ways to ease into my first conversation with a person who had been variously described to me as "intelligent, hard-working, and driven," "arrogant," and "very bright but difficult to get along with." These descriptions fueled my initial concerns; they also aroused my curiosity about the fit between such a person and a process like divorce mediation, in which the mediator's own calm, self-effacing, nonjudgmental demeanor is often said to be essential in cooling or cutting through intense emotions to reach rational solutions.

In Phear's field, mediation is used, although infrequently, within so-called "intact" families to deal with conflicts between

spouses, between parents and their young children, and sometimes between fully grown children and their aged parents. It is,
however, at the end of marriage, with all its attendant financial
concerns and need to provide for children, that divorce and family mediation has received its greatest play and seen its greatest
growth. Fueled by atrocity stories and allegedly widespread public
dissatisfaction with the legal process of divorce, mediation is
increasingly incorporated into the legal and judicial processes as a
helpful preliminary to the final, formal steps for dissolving mar-
riages, determining continuing support obligations, and arranging
child custody. Alternatively, some like Patrick Phear have
opened up private family and divorce mediation practices, hanging out the proverbial shingle and trying, for a fee, to soothe
human misery.

While the jury is still out as to whether family and divorce
mediation is better than traditional legal means of dealing with
those problems, whether public programs will be fully institutionalized, and whether private practice will enable mediators to
make enough of a living to survive, for Patrick Phear the jury has
long been in. He is a successful, widely respected family and
divorce mediator, the type whom other mediators seek out when
they have family problems, a "first-generation" mediator who
entered the field in 1976 before there was much of a field to
enter. A native of Zimbabwe, he had been trained in South
Africa as a zoologist. After migrating to the United States in
1965, his first job was as a researcher in cardiac physiology at
Boston City Hospital. Subsequently he did similar work at
Children's Hospital in Boston.

Phear describes the change from cardiac research to mediation as "one part boredom, one part personal experience, and one
part passion." He says that mediation looked especially good,
despite his deep uncertainties about what it actually was, to
someone who spent his days "moving hearts between dogs and
wondering how to protect sixty-year-old men from heart attacks."

The boredom of a well-settled professional routine, at about the same time, combined with a painful personal experience, a divorce accentuated by some very difficult custody questions. Concerned about the impact of the divorce process on his own children, he began to do some reading on children's postdivorce lives and was "appalled to discover that something like 100 percent of juvenile delinquents and teenage pregnancies occur amongst the children of divorced families."

Phear pulled together an informal study group to consider how Children's Hospital might respond to the rapidly increasing divorce rate and its consequences for children. It did not take long before the group's interest moved beyond what the hospital could or should do to what divorcing couples themselves could do to mitigate the consequences of divorce. By 1975 this group, inspired by the new Dorchester Urban Court Mediation Program, had become interested in devising judicial procedures that would pay special attention to the children of divorce. It established itself as the nonprofit Children's Judicial Resource Council (CJRC) and obtained foundation support to develop a model program for court-annexed divorce and family mediation. At that time, Phear took a sabbatical from his research position. He never went back.

In 1980, Phear, frustrated with the difficulties of trying to teach judges and other legal officials to embrace and institutionalize mediation, left the CJRC for private practice. He learned to mediate by hanging out in the Dorchester Urban Court, whose then relatively new program in community mediation was attracting considerable attention; talking to key people in the field, like Harvard law professor Frank Sander; and "just doing it," he says. His private practice began with a flurry of cases referred by lawyers, judges, and others whom he had come to know while working with CJRC. He now mediates over a hundred family cases a year, most of them divorce related. In addition, he mediates community cases, complex civil cases, intrabusiness and hospital disputes, and a small but growing number of cases between children and their elderly parents. He also helped Child Find, Inc., a successful, nationwide program, to mediate the return of parentally abducted children. He is in demand as a trainer and a program consultant and has written extensively.

• • • • • • •

Entering Phear's unpretentious, somewhat cramped three-room office suite, I was unceremoniously beckoned through to the adjacent office by a "Come in" more indicative of confident, almost neighborly, friendliness than of initial subject-meets-researcher anxiety. There I found Phear, a tall, angular man with the grayish appearance of someone in his late forties long afflicted by an uncontrolled passion for cigarettes and strong coffee. He was seated at a metal desk almost invisible under its burden of papers, files, and books, lighting what must have been, given the evidence of the ashtray perched on the papers beside him, another in a long line of quickly extinguished cigarettes. Hardly looking up, he nonetheless politely gestured me to a chair and seemed preoccupied enough that for a moment I imagined he might not really notice the introductions and preliminary politenesses.

Our conversation began as if in midsentence, as Phear vigorously nodded his agreement to participate in my research and somewhat impatiently pushed aside all further talk of what I would be doing. "See this?" he more disclaimed than asked, as he held aloft some loosely bound papers. Almost without pause he took off on a critical, stream-of-consciousness monologue about a brochure and set of training tapes put out by the Academy of Family Mediators. My initial worries quietly evaporated as he vividly denounced the tapes as a "farce ... an absolute farce."

He described, with a flair for detail sufficient to satisfy any appetite, one of the three mediations presented on the training tapes. The case of "Willie," he said, involved divorcing parents with a child custody dispute. He mused that cases like this were the source of his unremitting frustration with court-annexed family and divorce mediation. Eagerly announcing his continuing fidelity to what he called "the public arena" and his hope that some day family and divorce mediation would play an important role in changing the legal process of divorce, he vehemently denounced what he had heard as "abusive and unprofessional."

Struggling, Phear tried to find more neutral language to describe the mediation model being publicized by the Academy of Family Mediators. After a short pause, he proclaimed, with all the quiet confidence of a professional assuming that his listener already understands (or is willing to tolerate) insider jargon, "It's med-arb [a generally not-well-regarded mix of mediation and arbitration] in the strictest sense without any real acknowledgment of what the guidelines are. At least in arbitration you know what the rules are. Here, who knows?"

Satisfied with this and rediscovering his indignant tone, Phear turned his monologue away from jargon-like abstraction about dispute resolution techniques toward a more particularized critique.

> And this fellow [the person mediating the Willie case] says, "In mediating a court-ordered custody I start with the most suspicious view—that the parties are up to no good." And he goes on and on about how you've got to get them talking, which he didn't. He didn't let them talk at all! He kept telling these people how bad they were, and he endlessly attacks these people for thinking as they think and saying how wrong it is, and he believes that he can substitute his judgment endlessly. What he is trying to do is to get them into the position to agree with him and not to follow what they want at all. He sets himself up as the authority on

their lives and gives them a process in which he, not they, always comes out a winner. For him, he might as well be a judge. The couple is prohibited within his system from presenting evidence. And they are cut down for doing that. And he, the mediator, is drawing a sort of common judgment that he will give back to these people, and if they don't like it they are hostile.

This critique highlights questions of mediation technique: the mediator talks too much; the parties talk too little; he is judgmental and manipulative; they are acquiescent. But in the context of Willie's case, technique is not what most catches Phear's interest. There is something else bothering him, something that goes to what he calls "the profession."

For him, mediation is an autonomous, self-contained professional activity. Although it requires some of the skills of a therapist and the knowledge of a lawyer, it is neither therapy nor adjudication. Phear aggressively contends that mediation is sufficiently different from other kinds of dispute resolution that most prior training is irrelevant. He says, with barely concealed delight, "I consistently refuse to give my academic credentials when I'm asked to speak about mediation. When they want to know what my credentials and background are, I say that for your purposes I don't have any. I don't want a mediator's credibility to be based on training as a lawyer or a therapist."

When he talks about mediation as a profession, Phear refers to collective standards mediators ought to take seriously and enforce, standards that he has been instrumental in developing. Indeed, at almost every turn, his talk about mediation is full of "oughts." By his own account, he is so insistent about how mediators ought to practice because he is extremely jealous of what he views as his profession and worried that perhaps too many people are now doing "what *they* call mediation."

"If the truth be told," Phear says, "many of those people shouldn't be starting practices." He readily, indeed eagerly, characterizes his own attitude toward the profession as stubborn and dogged and calmly notes that his own rigid sense of the oughts of mediation, as well as his hard-nosed version of professional standards, "rubs people the wrong way."

Phear is as tough on himself as he is on others. Indeed, his passionate concern for the minute details of mediation practice and the process of mediating takes on meaning only in the context of his driven, almost compulsive, self-scrutinizing insistence that mediation be done right, that unrealizable promises not be made, and that mediation develop a professional ethos sufficiently strong to assure some measure of quality control. For himself, he is confident that he does mediation right; as he says with but a gentle touch of arrogance, "I think that I am good. I think that there are other mediators who are probably as good as I am. I don't think there are many who are better."

For Phear, questions of professionalism are embedded in concerns about fairness and deception, sensitivity to possible abuses of power, and concerns about rights. Here the man sitting at the metal desk is a moralist as well as a mediation technician. The forcefulness and unhesitating conviction of Phear's articulate denunciation of Willie's mediator suggested to me that those who had provided my imaginative introduction to Phear could not be far wrong. Here was judgment unhesitatingly and incisively delivered, judgment about fairness and unfairness to vulnerable persons.

Phear savages the mediator who, in Willie's case, presented himself without the guise of judicial authority but nonetheless acted more like a judge than a dispute resolution professional. He was too eager, in Phear's opinion, to suggest a solution, exercise authority, and guide the parties in such a way that they would eventually see his solution as the only alternative. As Phear views it, the tapes presented a mediation parody, authority imposed within a court setting, without the protections of due process of law. Scrupulously engaging the moral passion of the good person made witness to scandalous wrongdoing, he says, "I think he's giving people second-class justice by subtly denying them the due process they get in courtroom. These people are prohibited in his system from presenting evidence, but nonetheless he is making judgments that will have great weight in court. I mean, if you are going to subject yourself to someone else's authority and judgment, why do it outside the tried and true procedural guarantees that courts give you?"

A clear sense of what mediation is emerges from this critique. Mediation for Phear is, quite simply, "facilitated negotiation and nothing more." While it may differ when done in family and divorce disputes from the way it is done in labor, environmental, or community disputes, mediation has, when done right, "the same generic core." That core involves activities through which people can come to understand better the nature of their problems. Phear elaborated:

> Mediation is an educational device even more than it is a problem-solving device. Sure, it helps resolve problems, but even when it fails to do that it can help, so long as it is done right, by assisting people to reach, to illuminate what is at issue, and to highlight underlying interests.
>
> I think what my profession is, is the skills that enable or empower people or help people trust that there is in fact a process out there that will help. In a good mediation you would say to them, "Why are you here?" And they would say, "We are here because we can't agree on how best to proceed for Willie." And you would say to them "What help do you need?" And they would say, "We don't know." "Okay, so why don't we sit down and talk about it. Let me use my skills and

> training as a mediator to help you two identify the pri-
> mary issues. Once you've got these questions set, we
> will be in a position to get into and fully understand
> them. Let's go ahead, and at the end either you'll
> decide you don't want to make that decision [about
> custody for the child] and you'll give all your informa-
> tion to the judge, or you'll proceed, as most people do,
> to go along this [mediation] road. It won't be exactly
> what you want, but it won't be out of the cards either."

Here is a significant shift in the ideology of mediation accompanied by a series of somewhat immodest claims. For Phear, good
mediation may or may not be able to produce agreements and
lasting resolution of problems. But it can always help people
identify primary issues, fully understand their problems and get at
underlying interests.

Phear worries that mediation often promises too much and
delivers too little. He sees signs of this overpromising in the
Willie case. In that mediation, there is too much emphasis on
getting beyond the "so-called presenting problem, the proverbial
barking dog . . . to what is really bothering these people, which is
something deep in their past. Whatever precipitated the problem
[the barking dog] is going to be a real issue that has to be dealt
with." Some family and divorce mediators, Phear believes, like to
make things more interesting for themselves by getting at all the
"deep stuff." Family and divorce mediation of this type, he contends, simply encourages the parties to engage in the nearest possible imitation of the conflicts within their marriage, and it pre-
cludes being able to move beyond rhetoric and stated positions to
get to underlying interests. "How," Phear asks "are you going to
change the communication patterns of two forty-year-old adults
in four or five hours of mediation? They're going to have to solve
their problems within the context of their ongoing communication patterns." Mediation in which mediators impose solutions or

needlessly compound problems is, in Phear's view, "the antithesis of what many of us believe mediation should be." Thus, the mediator in the Willie case neither effectively resolved the custody dispute nor helped the parents educate themselves about their interests or disagreements.

Just as Phear's own verbal pace slowed a bit, signaling what I thought would be the impending end of a now almost breathless story of this mediator's failure, he summed up his feelings by saying that if the mediation presented on the Academy of Family Mediation tape were to catch on, it would be a "tragedy."

As our initial meeting wandered toward its conclusion, I asked what it is like for him, after more than a decade of building a successful private divorce and family practice, to do mediation. Phear slouched in his chair, lowered his eyes, and became quiet. Then without raising his eyes or righting his posture, he said, "It's a lonely and difficult life."

Surprised, I rather awkwardly pointed out, as if trying to recharge his batteries, that he is indeed one of the few people really making it in private practice. He responded:

> Look, I can do two mediations a day, each of about two hours. And that requires that I spend half an hour beforehand reading my notes, two hours with them, and probably an hour after for doing my notes. That's close to seven hours a day right there with almost no other human contact, just very clinical, very buttoned-down, very, very hard work. It's like a golf pro. I think of the finite number of golf swings; once you've seen them all three or four times, it would be hard not to get impatient. It is tempting to say this is a type B, subset III and pull the solution out of the drawer. It is a danger, you know, falling into formulas in any type of mediation. Really, it's hard work to mediate, to listen

to the subtleties and nuances of what people are saying, to hear all the emotional pieces. It's difficult, tir-
ing, and painful.

At this point, our initial conversation seemed to have called
itself to a halt, having provided a brief glimpse of Phear's intriguing combination of pride and concern, as well as his personal
investment and passionate belief, about the profession and practice of family and divorce mediation.

· · · · · · ·

Hazel and Alex could not have come to Phear's office with
anything like the nervousness or curiosity that had bracketed my
own initial encounter with him. Indeed, it is not clear that either
of them could have regarded their arrival with anything other
than the exasperated, dim hopes of a couple whose three-year-old
divorce ended a ten-year marriage but provided no more than a
brief respite in a continuing legal struggle, complete with numerous court appearances and efforts to modify or enforce previous
agreements. This postdivorce struggle focused on the emotional
and developmental problems of Robin, their extremely sensitive,
gifted five-year-old child, as well as the details of child support
and joint custody arrangements.

Phear had described Alex as a "big, balding, shaggy man in his
early forties . . . you know, he looks like an aging hippie with hair
everywhere and scruffy clothes," who had recently remarried.
Hazel, he said, was "petite, button-down, put-together with an
eager-to-please, easy smile," not yet remarried, and planning to
go back to school in psychology. They were both well off financially as a result of the recent sale of a company Alex founded.
They came to Phear on the advice of their lawyers after they
found themselves yet again in court, this time fighting over

Hazel's refusal to provide a financial assessment of a joint account that had been established to take care of expenses for Robin. This was what mediation professionals sometimes refer to as the "precipitating incident." Hazel's adamancy, and its particular contribution to the familiar escalating cycle of charge/countercharge, was a response to her ex-husband's demand that she include the value of Robin's old clothes in that accounting. When she refused, Alex filed a motion for contempt of court and Hazel a similar motion alleging nonsupport.

Phear told me, with a convincing genuineness, that he liked both Alex and Hazel and that they were "very easy clients, nice clients to deal with." When I inquired about what made them "easy clients," he responded:

> Alex came here with considerable reluctance. He claimed and seemed, at some level, to really believe that they had what he insisted was the "perfect agreement," even if it didn't keep them from fighting. He did not want to mediate at all. He initially agreed to participate in only one session. That seems typical of his cautious, careful outlook on things. He is very invested in his intelligence and being very smart. Hazel, though she's not as difficult as trained psychiatrists, who are often really impossible, is very invested in being "clinically appropriate." Yet she wouldn't listen to a word he said. And he, well, he had everything worked out. He sent me a "mediation agenda" before the first session. Typical. He's going to run his life, her life, the life of their child and tell me how to mediate.

If these were "easy clients," I wondered what difficult clients were like? Phear responded to my wondering by explaining:

> They [Alex and Hazel] say what they think. When

they are frustrated, they show frustration. They think about what is important to them and they are willing to say that. They correct me rather than let me go a long way down the wrong tracks. They are experienced negotiators, and they know what the alternatives are. In fact, they're here because the alternatives have failed. Even Alex, who was so reluctant at the start, quickly realized that mediation was better than another trip to court. Yeah, sometimes Hazel would call me for what seemed like an artificial crisis, and Alex would just outright sabotage things by not doing what he was supposed to, but, by and large, they were good.

With a chuckle, he added, "Most important of all, they show up on time and leave on time."

Still a little unconvinced by Phear's characterization, I asked, "How about the lawyers? Didn't that make Alex and Hazel somewhat difficult to deal with?" Phear answered, "No, in fact, just the opposite. They have terrific lawyers. Both of their attorneys know me. In fact, I encourage people to see lawyers. I recommend it from the get-go. They should see a lawyer or an accountant or any other professional they think they might need help from. This is a huge advantage for mediation. It is really helpful to have clients who are fully informed. Advice from lawyers is safer than the advice they'll get from friends and relatives. If you don't know what a judge might do in dividing assets, how will you make an intelligent choice?"

Phear's attitude toward what some divorce and family mediators call "lurking lawyers" sets him apart from those who say that lawyers stir up trouble, introduce unnecessary complications, and generally compound the difficulties of mediation. Indeed, Phear provides names of lawyers, tax consultants, and other professionals for those who need such help. He had even suggested, in a way he claims is typical, that Alex and Hazel consult and consider other mediators before deciding whether to use his services.

This openness, receptivity, and seemingly laid-back attitude turn out, perhaps paradoxically, to be an important part of Phear's strategy for getting and keeping clients. It is a way of projecting self-confidence about his professional prowess, the kind of "shop around, but you'll be back" assurance of a slick car salesman, but presented without the aggression or disdain so often encountered in that setting. It is an initial step in his effort to get people "committed" to mediation.

> I give them plenty of options right from the beginning. It is all part of the routine. I want them to feel that they can see anyone in the world, that they can talk with anyone. But I must say that it's all pretty self-serving. People always come back. They feel that they have really made a choice. Even if they don't call anyone else, they feel like they could. They feel empowered and choosy. I do it very, very purposefully because I want them to be in my room totally voluntarily. They have total freedom of choice. That way, when I ask them to think about something and one of them asks me why, I can ask them why they chose to come here.

Once clients decide to mediate, Phear begins to educate them about what mediation is and how it can and should be used. Thus he began the process of mediation with Alex and Hazel by getting both parties to sign a consent form. Then he said, "Actually, what I think we need to be doing is using this hour for me to find out exactly what help you want of me, and to clarify the issues we need to address and what you are in disagreement about. Secondly, we should develop some understanding of why you disagree in those areas. I want to help you think about what information you need to get in the ensuing weeks if you choose to come back. Then I would be able to tell you both whether I think mediation would make sense for you and whether it is something I want to do with you."

He went on to describe mediation in the slightly disengaged but not distant tone of a person for whom the reference to the hypothetical "barking dog" was part of a familiar, by now too-often repeated, introductory routine.

> I guess one of the easiest ways to think about media-tion is to compare it with some dilemmas for people, like being bothered by a barking dog. You could go to a lawyer, and the lawyer would ask you what times the dog barks; he'd be concerned about statutes and rights. Or you could go to a therapist who would be interested in your mental health. What is your human interest? When you go to a mediator, there isn't a right answer on whether the law should apply or mental health should apply. The truth is that both need to apply. Here we try to find ways you both can understand your problems, and try to help you figure out for yourselves what you want to do about them. Whether you end up agreeing or not, you should, in any case, end up with a clearer sense of what you have in common and what you disagree about.

He artfully avoided promising Alex and Hazel that they would resolve, in the end, the problems that have brought them to mediation and implied, without the slightest trace of doubt or resignation, that an agreement might not be as important as sim-ply achieving greater understanding and clarity. By turning atten-tion away from resolution and agreement as the ultimate products of mediation, he communicated a sense of priority spiced with clear-headed realism.

Phear generally talks about mediation as involving three different phases. The first deals with what he calls "issue clarification and definition." In this process, Phear says, the mediator helps the parties identify the issues or questions to be dealt with. This "framing" of the dispute leads to the second phase, "information gathering," in which the mediator's questions help inform the parties about their separate and joint interests and goals. In the first two phases, mediation focuses on the developmentof principles and criteria that might provide the basis for agreements.

The third phase is "resolution." Here the mediator tries to pull together, in a coherent fashion, the interests and principles that the parties share and to use those interests and principles to forge an agreement. Phear says that in this phase, the mediator ought to be trying not for compromise but for an "integrated solution that makes sense of what the parties have been negotiating."

The resolution phase, however, can only be reached if the parties achieve what Phear, borrowing an idea developed by others, rather evocatively labels "intimacy." When intimacy is achieved, the parties trust each other, the mediation process, and the mediator so much that the sentence "Why won't you take $50,000 to settle this?" is heard as just one more question, not as what the mediator thinks you should settle on. Phear claims he can tell when people reach the stage of intimacy because they are "open, receptive. . . . They start talking about other people's interests as well as their own, and about process needs as well as outcome needs." They have, in essence, internalized the ideology of mediation.

"The good mediator," Phear says, "refuses to give advice or suggest solutions; he refuses to substitute his judgment or his knowledge for the judgment or knowledge of the parties." His energy should be devoted to identifying principles and criteria from the parties themselves. At one point, however, in the five mediation sessions that Alex and Hazel had with Phear, he seemed to violate his own "no advice" principle. This occurred late in their third session, when Phear revisited the issue of their joint account, an issue that they had discussed several times before. He directed their attention to part of the latest draft memorandum of understanding that he had prepared from the previous meeting that said, "Each month, on day one, both parents will deposit a set amount, still to be agreed-on, into this account." This provision engendered a long discussion of the best way to manage the account, which concluded when Phear suggested a principle that might be used in thinking about the joint account. "For each of you to feel whole," he suggested, "the final arrangements need to be such that control is minimized along with the potential to be manipulated."

"Well, to put it more positively," Hazel said, "I would like to see this with more mutual participation in a number of different decisions, not just Alex's usual no, which is, I think, a distortion of what joint custody really is."

Ignoring the potentially provocative reference to Alex's "usual no" and Hazel's reference to joint custody, Phear suggested, "Let me just go through the purposes of the joint account. You agree, I think, on these purposes, and if that is right then the good pieces can be kept while we work to minimize the friction. But, I have a totally different proposal I'd like to make, not because I necessarily think its a good idea but because looking at an alternative sometimes helps clarify things."

The mediator who does not give advice seemed to be doing just that when he went on to propose that the joint account be dissolved, that each parent make expenditures for Robin independently and keep a record of what the expenses were. In his proposal, every six months there would be an accounting and necessary reimbursements to even out contributions to preserve the one-third, two-thirds formula prescribed by the divorce agreement.

Phear later told me that he had made his proposal just to "break the logjam" about the joint account. "I wanted to give them something new to chew on just to stop the rehashing of differences over the joint account," he said. When I asked Phear whether his proposal violated his own "no advice" principle, he laughed the gentle laugh of a teacher whose message still had not sunk in and said, "By this time, there was considerable trust. I was really an intimate in the sense that I could say to them 'Look, this perfect agreement you guys have is not do-able.' So I was and they were by this point recognizing the truth of that. As for the account, I accurately understood the problem and could join them in thinking about a solution without imposing anything on them. My analysis of the problem was sufficiently intimate that it made sense to them, which began to allow them to move."

Still unconvinced, I asked how he knew that intimacy had been reached. Without hesitation, he directed my attention to the place in the session where Hazel and Alex responded to his proposal.

"I could probably live with that," Hazel said, and Alex responded, "Yeah. Your idea is even better than you think. We wouldn't even have to sit down and say we'll now increase the amount from this to this. You are talking about a situation whenever bills come in that we pay them. Eventually I pay two-thirds, Hazel one-third, and all we do is take care of our own budgets and don't make deals with each other."

As Phear described it, at this point Alex and Hazel had stopped "taking jabs" at each other; there was, in his view, an openness and joining indicative of "intimacy." And eventually his proposal became part of Alex and Hazel's final agreement.

If clients are to clarify their problems, identify principles, and reach the stage of intimacy, Phear believes, they cannot be allowed to use mediation as a forum for seeking rhetorical vindication or blaming spouses for past or current problems. As a result, he overtly instructed and gently chided Alex and Hazel to avoid the strong temptation of focusing on the past and using mediation to ventilate personal grievances.

"Mediation really is hopeless at deciding past rights and past wrongs. It is excellent at looking forward to designing things in ways that make things better for people who have learned some lessons from the past. So it's used to move ahead, and I think that you shouldn't try to persuade me of any version of what the other is like. You should really try to understand each other," he explained to Hazel and Alex.

In most divorce cases, this is, of course, more easily said than done. No matter how often parties are reminded to avoid the "he said/she says," to limit assertions to themselves and their feelings and talk about what they are hearing from the other party, they nevertheless resist. They regularly bring in the past, make accusatory statements, and find ways to suggest that their spouse has been, or is, guilty of some misconduct.

In Alex and Hazel's case, Phear was artful in rephrasing assertions and accusations. Yet Alex and Hazel, like many other clients in family and divorce mediation, seemed intent on keeping the fight going. In their third session, almost six weeks after they first came to see Phear, he told them, "You are caught in this funny war. Neither of you wants to acknowledge what you really agree on. Alex, I don't think you have heard forthright from Hazel that she shares your view that the quality of your relationship is an important thing in Robin's life."

Replied Alex, "What Hazel has done is tell me many times that there is nothing we can do about our quarreling. It's as if she proposes to continue quarreling."

"You are hearing Hazel say she is not willing to invest much in your relationship, so that is one of your assumptions," said Phear. "That's what you have heard. So that's what you assume."

Phear tried to move Alex away from the "she saids" and instead toward talk about what he has heard and assumes. This was part of his ongoing effort to socialize Alex and Hazel into one of the rules of mediation—namely, talk only about oneself and one's own interests, not about the other party. But at first Hazel, then Alex would have no part of it.

Responding to Alex's comments about their quarreling, Hazel said, "Maybe I can clarify my position. I have experienced some of the most heinous things in this divorce. I never ever thought things could sink this low. Alex's behavior from time to time, is, to say the least, highly objectionable. I found it impossible over the years for Alex to take responsibility for his share of any problem. He just gets preoccupied with my share. I don't consider it highly likely that we will find a reasonable way to discuss things, so when problems arise I try to say to Alex, 'Why discuss things and get further involved?'"

"Again," Phear said patiently, "I am hearing from both of you that neither is enjoying the current relationship and both of you wish it were different. Both of you are really pessimistic about whether it can be improved. I should add to that, however, that I am also talking to two people who are really invested in doing things right for Robin. So I'm confused. Why are things different in this room that allows you two to talk? Why is it here that you and Hazel can talk?"

"I have a thought," said Alex. "I think it is that Hazel is self-indulgent about misbehaving with me, but she puts on a better behavior with other people. It used to be. . . ." At this point, Phear loudly cut him off, saying, "Let's not do used-to-be's."

Unfazed, Alex continued by saying, "If she could do it here, she could do it everywhere, but let's be truthful, we don't have a good relationship here, even though we are not loud and fighting."

Turning conversation away from the past and away from blame and recrimination was particularly difficult in this case because of Alex's continuing sense that they already had the "perfect agreement" and that everything would be all right if Hazel would just live up to it. "I think," he said, "that most of the provisions in our agreement were very carefully worked out. They are excellent provisions and the judge in fact complimented us on having put together such a very good agreement and having given it so much thought and care. I think we deserved the compliment. We aren't going to do much better. What we need to do is to implement what we agreed on, if Hazel is able to do that."

Phear proposed that the pair should nonetheless explore what in that agreement is not working and posed a hypothetical issue for them to discuss. "Suppose," he said, "that one of you has decided for a variety of reasons that Robin needs karate lessons. But you disagree about the value of the lessons compared to other things she might do. How do you proceed from there?"

Phear posed this hypothetical problem, he later said, as a way to shake them out of their already polarized positions. "It was a window for each of them to see how the other thought about a new problem, a way for them to consider and maybe discover new possibilities for communications."

Hazel, however, used the hypothetical question as another occasion to talk about past experiences rather than future possibilities. "You are kidding, right? This is a joke. Alex would immediately know what he thought. His ideas are pretty set and rigid about what he wants and doesn't want. There is never much room to open a door. To open a door involves so many bizarre interactions that we never get to substance. It would just invite more of Alex's disrespectful, psychologically abusive behavior. And in the end we might never really get to discuss it."

"So this feels hopeless to you, a brick wall," Phear said. "Well, how about if Alex comes to you with the idea?"

Raising her voice, Hazel replied, "It doesn't usually happen. Alex is generally content with the way things are. I have the new ideas, I find the resources, I ask the questions." And the cycle of accusations and arguments about the past began again.

At the conclusion of Alex and Hazel's case, I asked Phear whether he thought he had failed in his effort to educate them about mediation and get control of the blaming and accusations. I explained that, in my view, they had resisted at every turn and rather ingeniously found ways of introducing backward-looking narratives, as well as questions of guilt, into their conversations. Phear nodded and, in a typical fashion, rhetorically transformed what seemed like a flaw in his technique into a virtue. "To be a good mediator doesn't mean that one has to invest a lot in the effort to establish an elaborate set of ground rules for client behavior," he said. While he acknowledged that he tolerates a fair amount of the blaming and he said/she said rehashing of the past, he claimed that, in the end, it generally proved helpful:

> It is very useful to me to listen to characterizations of what went on before. Of course, I have to be attentive to how the other person reacts to this. If it's just more rain and they are sitting there calmly then it's one thing, but if they seem anxious I'll intervene. Good mediation theory says I should stop them and say, "Just talk about your needs, not about your spouse's needs or behavior." Truthfully, however, there is only so much energy that can be expended in mediation and it's a question of how we use it. As much as possible I need to know what their experience is so that I can find a way of fitting their communication within each's understanding of who each other is. While we want process without carnage, we do need catharsis somewhere along the line.

· · · · · · ·

To overcome, or at least counteract, Alex and Hazel's recurring fault finding and accusation making, Phear identified areas of agreement and consensus. He tried to cut through the forest of charges and countercharges and continually cultivated joint recognition of shared values, commitments, and concerns. Clients like Alex and Hazel are encouraged, almost badgered, to acknowledge points of agreement even if they are cast in the most abstract, general terms. In this way, Phear implies, even as he explicitly downplays the importance of reaching a final agreement, the agreement the parties seek is already, albeit implicitly, at least partially present.

The second session with Alex and Hazel provided a good example of Phear's strategy of constructing consensus around general principles where Alex and Hazel could only see conflict. This session, in which they could barely contain their anger and showed themselves to be adept at pulling each other's strings, was largely devoted to the question of Robin's emotional development. In particular, they focused on her difficulties in making friends at school and on whether there was sufficient information to figure out how to respond to her problems. As Alex and Hazel talked about these issues, Phear occasionally interrupted to elicit more information, but for the most part he just listened while first Hazel, then Alex talked. Eventually, Phear quietly suggested that they talk about how Robin was doing in school.

Alex responded by observing with audible impatience, "What we never get to talk about is where we ourselves fit into Robin's education. My sense has always been that Robin gets most of her academic education at home but that she has trouble fitting in at school."

In the almost civil conversation that ensued, both parents agreed that there was a problem. While Hazel talked about the need for them to "spend some time learning about education for kids who are bright," Alex led the talk back to the strife between himself and Hazel. "What we really need to do," he said with his voice rising, "is to have a friendlier, more polite divorce and give Robin better support. Just because Robin has a difficulty doesn't mean we have to buy a solution. We are the solution."

For Alex, the issue just beneath the surface was Hazel's continuing recalcitrance—her unwillingness to behave herself and
abide by the terms of their already "perfect" agreement. Hazel,
not Robin, became the problem as he tried to refocus the discussion of Robin's emotional needs. As Hazel began registering her
disagreement with her ex-husband's analysis, Phear said, "Let me
tell you what I am hearing. My hunch is that Alex hears Hazel
talking about a lot of rationalizations 'for buying solutions.'
Hazel, as you hear Alex talking you hear more ignorance than
maliciousness and believe that if only you could use the right
words the light bulb would click on. Ultimately what I need to
help you do is to both slow down and overlook your assumptions
about not being heard. You do, in fact, agree with each other
about a lot of things. I think I could put out some general principles that you both would agree on."

While Hazel reluctantly seemed to acknowledge that she and
Alex might share certain, as yet unarticulated, principles, Alex
chimed in with an "I told you so" kind of remark that threatened
to undo the consensus on principle that Phear was energetically
trying to create. Alex, almost in a whisper, said, "I can't think of
anything we disagree on," to which Hazel replied, "You just said
that Robin has been evaluated and that the therapist who did the
evaluation said there was nothing wrong with her."

Alex, now with a raised voice replied, "I didn't say that."
Phear then said, "No, no, Hazel, let me correct you. What I heard
Alex say was that she had an evaluation and that the conclusion
that came out of that for him was that the most important thing
for Robin would be for you to have a good divorce."

Phear refused to hear only disagreement. After restating what
he had "heard," the mediator reiterated, "If the question is how
to help Robin, you have several areas of agreement. First, the
more amicable your divorce the better for Robin. Second, you
both are troubled by things like Robin's lack of a satisfactory
social life and her persistent signs of a frustrating perfectionism. I

think you agree that given who Robin is you need to be careful how to help her."

By insistently hearing agreement where the parties express disagreement, Phear "sells" mediation. He gives the parties a reason to believe that something can be accomplished in mediation even if it involves no more than a recognition at the most general level—for example, that both Alex and Hazel need to be "careful" in dealing with their daughter. This kind of agreement is very far from a resolution of the dispute but constitutes instead an agreement on principles to guide the effort to reach a final resolution.

When I suggested that such constant rephrasing of disputes until the parties acknowledged agreements in principle seemed both transparent and banal, Phear rebutted, "I'm not embarrassed to say that often the points of agreement are stated in very broad, general terms. They are banal. I will start, if I have to, with the fact that we can all agree that we are human beings and that we are in this room. I've got to get them to start moving toward trust, seeing points of overlap in their interests. There is, of course, a lot of con in all this. But I need to get them to trust that at least one other person has heard that they want to be a good parent. And one person in the room will start to understand what being a good parent is. So when I frame points of agreement I'm talking to each one as an individual. You both want to be good parents. You see, I want them to trust me and to start trusting the process. And if they can't agree at the most general level that the other cares about their child, why would they ever agree on anything?"

As Phear sees it, he helps his clients move away from their negative postures toward a posture of cooperation. Whatever its meaning, Phear's use of the word *con*, gently placed in context rather than aggressively flaunted, endeared him to me; that sharing of a kind of inside "street smarts" helped solidify trust between mediator and social scientist in the kind of casual but skillful way that similar gestures might solidify trust between mediator and clients.

* * * * * * *

Trust the mediator who controls the process and commit to the process that he controls: these could be the mottos of Patrick Phear's professional life. "Mediation," Phear patiently explained to me, "is a process that really can help people resolve their own disputes. As a mediator, if you came to me, I would need to help you understand my process and commit to it. But you need to see that I am in control of it. . . . And then my skills would have to be to ask questions to help you define the overarching common goals and principles that you are looking for that make it worthwhile to truly negotiate around the specifics of your problems.

"In mediation, I am the orchestra leader, the orchestrator of the process. The parties decide the content of the process, but as for the process itself, they can choose whether they want to play violin or drum, but if they want to play in this orchestra they're going to have to play when I point at them." The control he seeks to establish is, in contrast to the mediation in Willie's case, control over the process, not the substantive agenda. Phear is quick to differentiate control over the process from the "exercise of authority" characteristic of the mediation he recounted in the dreaded Academy of Family Mediation material.

Phear uses three major tactics in his efforts to control the process: making himself a party, caucusing at strategic moments, and avoiding what he calls "premature closure." When he used the first tactic, in Alex and Hazel's case, he transformed their sessions from bilateral negotiations into what, in the literature on mediation, has been called a "community of three." Doing so required that Alex and Hazel respond to his interest in making the mediation process work and recognize that he had needs and interests separable from theirs. Thus, when Alex and Hazel seemed to be using the conversation about the best way to evaluate Robin's emotional needs to trash each other, Phear said, "What are you trying to achieve by trying to show that you have such different meanings about evaluation? Are you trying to educate Alex or me?"

When Hazel responded that Alex was "just not educable," Phear continued, "I should say that I am not educable either. It matters not a whit whether I understand or agree with you. If I turned to Alex and said, 'You have to get it through your thick head that Robin needs to be evaluated,' I don't think it would make a difference, and that's not the way I, as a professional, think that mediation can operate. I can't tell either of you what to do."

With this, Phear reminded Hazel about the nature of the mediation process and his role in it. He claimed that while he too was a party to the conversation, he was a special kind of party, one whose opinion should not matter, one without the power to command. Unlike Phear's nightmarish vision of the mediation in the Willie case, he tried to redirect energy away from efforts to educate or persuade him. He did so, however, by interjecting himself and his views as a professional.

Moreover, he used the discussion to focus Alex and Hazel on the process of mediation, gently insisting on the priority of that process. Though he may have been uneducable about the depths of their differences, he tried to educate them, believing that they were both educable about what he could and could not, would and would not do for them. He claimed ownership of the process while resisting what he took to be Hazel's effort to enlist him against Alex, and he set ground rules, not by instructing Hazel or Alex about their behavior but instead by focusing on his own behavior and what he was willing and able to do for them.

At two critical junctures in Alex and Hazel's mediation, when things seemed to be reaching a standstill, Phear used the second tactic. He tried to regain control by caucusing, that is, meeting separately with each of them. He told me that he uses caucuses for a variety of purposes, sometimes to do a little reality testing, sometimes because he needs to say something rather direct without appearing to take sides. Most often, though, a caucus serves to help him "regain control" and move the process along. He says he often has a target in mind when he caucuses—that in most instances, caucuses deal with an issue or a problem of greater concern to one party than the other.

In Alex and Hazel's case, the target of the first caucus was Alex, who had become quite frustrated during a long discussion of how Robin's clothes would be dealt with during her repeated movements between Hazel's and Alex's homes. While Alex insisted that there was no disagreement about the clothes, he continued to complain about the difficulties Hazel caused in figuring out which of Robin's clothes belonged where. He became more and more agitated about the amount of time that was being devoted to "such a trivial issue."

Phear reports that when he first started to mediate he was always surprised at how much energy went into the trivia, but now he realizes that resolving the "minor" issues that emerge in the course of the mediation provides a key to unraveling more substantial matters. "Most mediators," he claims, "say that you should pay attention to and even start with the easiest issue to resolve. That isn't my view. I try to pay attention to any issue that might illuminate the nature of the problems. Talking about clothes is no big issue for these people given their financial situation. But it gave me a way of seeing how they thought about their relation to Robin, how much they saw Robin as a tool in their own struggle. It was a very safe flashlight to use to get an understanding on what was really going on."

Thus Phear started his private meeting with Alex by talking about the clothes; however, he quickly changed the subject. Reminiscent of the first strategy for keeping control, he reminded

Alex of his own stake as a "professional" in their mediation and told him that he was frustrated by Alex's pattern of denial. At first, Alex did not seem to get the point—namely, that he was impeding the mediation process by acting as if things were all right or would be if only Hazel complied with their "perfect" agreement.

"I think that nothing is wrong except Hazel," Alex said. "Literally, every single one of the points we've come here to discuss have not, or should not have, presented difficulties for us. The only difficulties are caused because Hazel refuses to live up to our agreement. She is here to try to get some advantage rather than just living up to it."

Mediation, Phear told him, "isn't going to work unless you see that Hazel is not just refusing to go along to drive you crazy. If you really think that, you are wasting your time and mine. Maybe pieces of your system aren't working for her. Where I am frustrated is that I can help you identify general principles and some pretty trivial elements that would make life easier for both of you and for Robin, but every time we get close to something you say, 'No, that isn't a problem.'"

Reminding Phear that the couple's original agreement had won praise from the judge, Alex said, "I don't see what we'll get out of a new agreement, but maybe you are right. Maybe we'd be better off to have an agreement that required a great deal less of us to work things out ourselves."

This unexpected recognition and concession by Alex turned out to be a crucial turning point in the case. As Phear later explained, it was the first time Alex really acknowledged that he might get something useful from the mediation. Perhaps unintentionally, Alex had identified what Phear called a "principle of disengagement" that Phear would later use to pull all the pieces together. But the recognition of this breakthrough did not come instantly as Phear continued to appeal to Alex for an acknowledgment of the mediator's need for help.

I can help you achieve that. I am trying to help you recast small pieces of your agreement. I understand that the mountain looks tough, but we can only climb this mountain one step at a time. Yes, accounting for the clothes or photocopying financial statements might seem stupid. But if that will make Hazel more comfortable with your agreement, is that worth it to you? I can't help you reach agreements on the larger issues like Robin's emotional development unless you are willing to acknowledge the smaller problems and make what seem to be trivial accommodations. You have to realize that you can't do it better anywhere else. You are who you are and she is who she is. You can't change that.

Phear took control in a somewhat ironic way by asking Alex's "help" in dealing with major concerns by making "trivial accommodations." He seemed, in this caucus, to go along with Alex's basic contention about the existing agreement by emphasizing that what is at issue is Hazel's "comfort," and he used the caucus to forge a thinly veiled alliance and to strike a deal. When Alex agreed to that deal, Phear broke off their caucus and briefly met with Hazel alone to inform her of Alex's agreement. He then brought them back together to summarize the results of the caucusing, telling them, among other things, "I am not going to help you with the larger areas until I feel we can reach accommodations around the smaller ones. Until I can help you comfortably agree on what records you exchange, right or wrong, or what clothes, I don't think I can help you with Robin's emotional well-being. I would be doing a disservice to go for the larger questions, but if I'm wrong you should find someone who could do it differently. I can only do it my way. Professionally, I have something to do here."

Phear used both his professional status and professional

integrity to maintain his control of the process. At the same time that he warned that they may have to go elsewhere if they refused to cooperate, he held out the promise of a larger reward (getting to the question of Robin's emotional development) for coopera-tion. In essence he placed himself between them, asking each to cooperate with him rather than with each other, so that he could do his job. He also asked Alex and Hazel to help him so that he could help them. While he began this summary of the first caucus by acknowledging the frustrations of his clients, it was really his frustration that dominated. The clients had to cope with his problems before he was willing to help them cope with their own.

Far from the virtually invisible or voiceless neutral, Phear made his presence visible by making explicit demands on his clients. He "constructed" his clients, that is, constructed a way for them to behave in mediation, by getting Alex and Hazel to focus on him rather than each other. By the end of the third ses-sion, he had gotten them to agree to let him write a memoran-dum suggesting points of agreement concerning both Robin's clothes and the sharing of information about the joint account.

The third way in which Phear controls the process in family and divorce mediation is by preventing his clients from reaching what he calls premature closure on particular issues. Indeed, I noted many instances when Alex and Hazel seemed on the verge of tying down a particular resolution to some outstanding issue only to have Phear intervene, tell them to "hold" that piece, and try to change the subject. This was true, for example, in the dis-cussion of Robin's emotional needs during the second session when Alex said, "Robin is, in my view, emotionally fragile. She can get quite frustrated; she gets distraught when things don't go well. I would say we are in very, very close agreement on this." "The question," Phear reflected, "as I am hearing it, is who would be the best person to help Robin with the emotional aspects of divorce or of being such a bright kid. But let's come back to that."

Phear began to identify what he described to me as a "piece of the puzzle"—namely, the need for outside help in dealing with Robin's emotional development. But rather than driving to a conclusion where there was "very close agreement," Phear moved off in another direction. When Phear tried to change the subject, to explore another area of Alex and Hazel's problem, Hazel was reluctant. She wanted closure on the question of what to do about Robin's emotional development and especially the question of therapy. Indeed, throughout the mediation Hazel played the skeptic, frequently questioning Phear's rephrasing of things or his suggestions and desires to move ahead. In this instance, Phear held her off by telling her that he needed to hear about other things before reaching closure on Robin's needs and by promising a written memorandum that could be reviewed at the next meeting:

Hazel: Before we move, I feel the need to try to pin down this thing about Robin's....

Phear [interrupting]: What I am going to do is to write that out, send it to both of you, and get you to look at it in written words so you can think about the pieces that I'm hearing from you both and the principles. I think it will be very useful for you, like what Carter did with Begin and Sadat. We can then try to understand what those principles are. What we do with them will have to wait another week.

Hazel [quietly]: Okay.

Phear: I really need to understand more pieces before we can figure out what to do with Robin's needs at this point.

Hazel [barely audible]: Okay.

I was quite surprised by Phear's behavior at this point in Alex and Hazel's case. Given what seemed to me the difficulty Phear was having in managing Alex and Hazel's interaction and in identifying consensus in the midst of their disagreements, I was surprised he not take advantage of the opportunity to resolve what seemed like such an important and previously contentious issue. His explanation took the form of a quietly delivered, but obviously well-rehearsed, lecture contrasting his "systems" approach with the dominant, "linear" models in the field of divorce and family mediation.

"If you read the literature and you watch John Haynes's training tapes,[1] he tries to resolve issues sequentially. You look at the custody piece, then the visitation piece. But I really don't think it works that way. I think you resolve them all of a piece and the beauty of mediation is that you can, in fact, cross-weave custody, visitation, and support. To resolve custody first needlessly constrains every decision up the road. To give you custody is to give you the bulk of the time with the children, probably the house and the biggest chunk of the family finances," he said.

Drawing me a diagram, Phear went on:

> You don't have to do it that way if you think of mediation as being like moving around a circle. You need to understand all of the relationships among the issues. You can't resolve any issue until you understand all issues and have identified the principles which will frame the resolution. You are always simultaneously grinding the lens through which resolution can be crafted while eliciting the information necessary to make agreement possible. What this means is that you have to erect some firm barriers between understanding a problem and solving it. You have to run away from solutions. Every time someone proposes a solution, I ask why that solution seems attractive. I see any proposal as a source of new information and understanding. In the end, it is harder to mediate in this circular way because people are conflict-averse and want closure. It imposes greater demands on the mediator to

keep things open for longer, but it means that you don't prejudice issues unnecessarily or have to reopen what everyone thought was resolved.

This "running away" from solutions is aided by Phear's use of the so-called "single text negotiation" model, in which the mediator prepares and continually revises a memorandum of understanding, thereby providing the basis for all negotiations. Single-text negotiation is a way of keeping issues open while other issues are being explored. While it also provides a product that the parties can use along the way as they consult with their lawyers and other advisers, single-text negotiation keeps parties somewhat off-balance, without bearings, not exactly sure where they are or how close they are to agreement, until the mediator provides a summary formulating their understandings and agreements for them.

This continual open-endedness ensures that the parties are dependent on the mediator's version of where they are in the process. The mediator ultimately makes magic out of a complex series of explored but unresolved issues. In the meantime, the parties cannot trade off in any simple "split the difference" sense because nothing is resolved. For Phear, this is the only way to allow a full exploration of the issues and the only chance to produce a solution that honestly takes into account all the issues and concerns.

. . . .

Whenever the idea of control came up with Phear, it was almost inevitably accompanied by a conversation about "commitment to the process." This idea of commitment to mediation—spoken as if mediation was or should be capable of almost religious inspiration—was, in fact, a recurring theme. By contrast, one never hears lawyers or judges talking about commitment to litigation. Perhaps the need to mobilize and manage commitment is a response to the "voluntary" character of private family and divorce mediation. Perhaps it is an indication that mediation demands a greater investment of self than other forms of dispute processing. Perhaps it is a response to the fact that, like the ups and downs of marriage itself, the real payoffs of mediation are obtained only if people are willing to stick with it.

Alex and Hazel's commitment to mediation was managed and mobilized by reminding them of what would happen if they were unable to reach an agreement. With each reminder, Phear evoked the world outside his office—a world in which Alex and Hazel found communication difficult and painful, a world of lawyers and endless litigation. In so doing, he tried to get each of them to invest in the process, accommodate to its sometimes uncomfortable demands, and recognize that, whatever their reservations, mediation remained the best available alternative. Sometimes this effort was overt and direct; near the start of the fourth session, he asked Hazel, "You had said you felt like you were being beat up mentally. What makes it different here?"

Hazel responded, "Basically Alex isn't in charge of what is going on. He is not in a position to dictate, to try to dominate the conversation. Without the presence of a third party Alex is controlling, manipulative. He is very passive-aggressive. He is very . . . twisting what is going on. It is very hard to have a free conversation without being threatened, manipulated, without conversation being molded by someone who is trying to be in charge."

"What I hear," Phear said, "is that there is more freedom here to think thoughts without being pressured. And for you, Alex, Hazel is calmer, more in control of herself, and that might make it more productive for you. I am trying to figure out, you see, why you need me. Having just gotten through one piece where you clearly are in agreement, I want you to think about what made that possible."

Inviting or allowing the kind of blaming and finger pointing that is supposedly out of place in mediation, Phear has another agenda; he asks why things are different in mediation because he wants Alex and Hazel to compare what they can do in his office with what happens outside mediation. In this way, a situation that both might find hopeless appears hopeful. Mediation has value for them not only because it identifies areas of agreement that the parties themselves are not able to see but also because it enables them to communicate in a way that just does not seem possible outside the mediator's presence. Thus, Phear turns what looks like a conversation that ought to have little place in mediation into a conversation that increases Alex and Hazel's commitment to the process.

Occasionally, in the course of reminding Alex and Hazel about the "rules" of mediation, Phear threateningly suggested that maybe they were in the wrong place. "If you want to be right, then you are in the wrong forum. To be right, you are going to have to go back to court. Here we can try to understand why your agreement isn't working as it should," he said.

Again Phear was mobilizing commitment by reminding them of an already failed alternative waiting in the background. Here Phear played on a general assumption he makes about mediation, as well as a more specific assumption about Alex and Hazel. As he explained to me:

> I need to remind them about the alternative, to remind them of that to maintain their commitment to mediate. Just because they sign an agreement to mediate doesn't mean that I can ignore the need to maintain that as an active thing. Look, none of this would be a problem in this case or in any mediation if one of the parties had enough power to impose a solution. They have to realize, and really accept, that neither has enough power to get what they want. The problem

for me is to avoid saying things that would give one person enough power to impose. Well, if it was like in the academy training tapes, I would just come in and say what I think is best, it isn't a problem any more because given my added weight one of them becomes right. So I have to avoid that.

. . . .

Keeping clients committed to a process that tries their patience, that requires them to "behave" themselves, insists on finding agreement where they see only disagreement and, at the same time, endlessly resists closure even where agreement seems at hand is, of course, not simple. It is, however, a necessary prerequisite for mediation to work. In and of itself, mediation guarantees little. In fact, when I asked Phear about what made the process work, he showed me a well-worn comic strip, given to him by Frank Sander, in which two mediators agree that successful mediation is a "miracle." Like the characters in the cartoon, Phear readily concedes that there is no good or satisfactory explanation for what happens in the latter phases of mediation. Yet, explanation or not, I thought I had seen something approaching such a miracle in Alex and Hazel's case.

Midway through the fourth session, Phear brought up the subject of the joint account that they had established for Robin's expenses and asked how they wished to deal with it. When this led nowhere, he said, "Well, let's hold this piece and recognize that there are different ways of handling this, but the real problem here is communication. All the other pieces will fall into place, but we've got to understand the communication issues."

Phear's statement that communications issues had to be addressed met with considerable initial resistance from Alex, even though at earlier points this had seemed to be his position. Phear responded, "Let me say something about how it feels for me to be sitting on the fence, so to speak, looking down into each of your yards. I am sure that to get through this you are going to have to learn to celebrate your differences rather than letting them chew away at you. But it sounds to me like, if I wanted better communication, I'd try to design a system that would recognize that, from time to time, changes will have to be made. On those occasions you both need to feel like you can initiate communication and that the other will respond seriously. You might need a system for helping you get beyond your own inability to hear each other. Because I am struck that no matter how much agreement you have, you still focus on just the disagreements."

Alex impatiently interjected, "Well, we have had an agreement to try to handle all that. It is crystal clear and I think it is very, very workable." Phear responded, "It's no good trying to persuade me because I don't make decisions for you. It's important, very important, that you understand why you see things differently, but don't waste your time trying to persuade me."

Returning to the discussion of the joint account, Phear said, "On the question of the joint account, at least we can agree that, if the account is to really work, information needs to be exchanged and that information needs to be complete."

"Complete!" Hazel gasped. "For months and months, I've gotten no information at all."

When Alex protested that Hazel was not being truthful, Phear commented, "I think we all need to accept responsibility. I think we can all agree that you have sent Hazel a chunk of information but that information was for a variety of reasons not useful to her."

"It wasn't what I wanted and it wasn't when I wanted it," Hazel said.

"You are saying that it wasn't in a form that was useful to you?" asked Phear.

"That's right," said Hazel.

"Then I don't think you were meaning to belittle Alex or claim that he sent you no information," the mediator said.

Said Hazel, "I never said he didn't send me information."

At this point, Phear paused for a minute, as if gathering himself, then continued. "What it feels like to me," he told them, "is that when we start getting close to resolution, things disintegrate. What I want to do now is to spend a few minutes alone with each of you going through an array of things on which I think you are very close to agreement so I can get a better sense of what the critical pieces are."

This second, and last, caucus started with Hazel. Phear began as he had in the earlier caucus—dramatizing the prospect of failure and then offering to make agreements explicit.

"Look," he said, "I don't want to be pessimistic about this, but I really am beginning to feel that I'm not helping here. I'm not sure what I can do at this point. It seems that we get close to an agreement and then Alex does something that really reaches into your space in some way and then you need to sort of slam the doors not to be rocked by him."

"That's a very general statement," replied Hazel, "but my sense is that he is really enjoying his game in a demonic sort of way. And I don't know if he wants to or could give it up."

Phear said his intent was not to "characterize" Alex but to get Hazel's feelings on items on which he felt an agreement was possible.

He spelled out what he thought they could agree on, and Hazel indicated she was ready to strike the deal. As in the earlier caucus, the party "targeted" responded rather quickly to Phear's threat by inviting him to explain what agreements he thought they had reached or were capable of reaching. And in each caucus Phear ran through a series of understandings.

> What I wanted was to get them to respect the process, because it wasn't working for them and I thought it

could. We weren't going anywhere. We had a whole lot of agreements and principles all over the place. We each understood all the problems. Everything was there but they weren't allowing it to come together. Something had to change or I was just going to quit and I wanted them to know that and to focus on that. I thought I had a model for them, a model in which they would have to separate things out and build a system in which they relied on third parties for help. It was there all along, but whenever we'd get close one of them would do something to rile the other. I needed to get their attention and to tell them that they were at a point of decision. They could go on the same way, but without me. If they wanted me, then they'd have to pay attention to what I was hearing and reflecting back to them about what they were saying.

To ensure cooperation and commitment at this late and critical juncture, Phear visibly interjected himself into the mediation process. This time, however, he felt that the pieces could all be put together. At the end of the second caucus, after briefly meeting alone with Alex, he brought the parties together and proceeded to outline the pieces of the agreement that he had sketched out separately with each of them.

The key items in this agreement were as follows:

I.   Robin's clothes will continue to travel back and forth with her. To the extent necessary, Hazel and Alex's new wife, Sally, will decide what new clothes will be purchased for Robin. Alex will get all his information about Robin's clothes from Sally.

II. When either parent is concerned about Robin's development or behavior, he or she will do the following:

    A. Write the other detailing the concerns and asking for a formal meeting. The other will respond within a week.

    B. If they are unable to agree, they will seek the help of a relevant third party who is already involved in Robin's life—for example, a pediatrician or teacher.

    C. If they still cannot reach agreement, they will seek the help of an expert in the area they are concerned about and follow this expert's advice.

    D. If one parent is unable to follow that advice, they agree to seek the help of a mediator.

III. The joint account will be dissolved, with each party paying Robin's expenses from his or her own budget and giving a monthly accounting of what has been spent on Robin. Each January they will balance these accounts and insure a two-thirds, one-third allocation of costs.

IV. For the future they will each set up a trust fund for Robin—Hazel in the amount of $20,000, Alex in the amount of $40,000.

After a few questions and a brief general discussion, the session ended when Hazel and Alex concurred that these proposals could provide a workable basis for an agreement and that Phear should write up a final memorandum of understanding. He did so, and that memorandum was reviewed and approved at a relatively brief final session.

I was stunned by how quickly this mediation had moved from the brink of failure to an agreement. But Phear was not surprised. He explained that Hazel and Alex moved mercurially from the edge of breakdown to agreement because "they really had no options left. They knew that court wouldn't be the answer. They'd been there a dozen times, and they weren't interested in a battle for sole custody. So what choice did they have? They knew they needed a third party and I was it. They had a very high level of commitment to the process which I just relied on and pushed to the limit. The rest was the usual 'minor miracle.'"

Unlike the "tragedy" of mediation poorly done, the "miracle" of an agreement results from keeping the parties committed to the process long enough so that all the pieces can come together. To do this requires that the mediator be in control without being in authority, that he manage frustration and premature desires to find solutions, that he keep the parties focused on their underlying interests and their areas of principled agreement, and that he never promise more than he can produce.

For Phear, the miracle was "usual" in the sense that he had seen it happen many times before and "minor" because mediation does not magically cure all problems. When I asked him how the agreement Alex and Hazel reached in mediation altered and improved the "perfect" agreement with which they had started, he laughed:

> Quite candidly, not all that much. In a way, I think Alex was right that the agreement that they had was a perfectly logical agreement. All we did was to adjust it to accommodate the triviality of day-to-day interactions. It was what they were experiencing day-to-day that made them distrustful of each other. The original agreement did not accommodate their humanness. It was both too detailed and not detailed enough.
>
> What we did was to give them a way of making joint decisions that had worked for them in the past— a decision-tree process, a four-step process—so that each disagreement doesn't lead to a standoff. If they can agree, fine; if not, they aren't left on their own with the only choice being to continue to fight in the old destructive ways or to call in the lawyers. Really simple, huh?

Phear predicted that the "handiwork" of mediation would keep things relatively stable for "six months, nine months at best. Then," he continued, "there will be an eruption and they'll probably be back."

When I told him that seemed to me a sign that his efforts would have failed, he shook his head and said, "Only if you think mediation can, in the course of a few sessions, change people whose lives have been built around fighting and who are so very, very different. I don't. I don't even try. What I try to do, and think I did with Alex and Hazel, is help them find a way of living with who they are that doesn't lead to so much fighting and so much pain."

• • • • • • •

Limited promises, confidence in a process that regularly produces small but, nonetheless, consequential successes—it all seemed to make sense to me. I understood, or thought I did, the source of Patrick Phear's intense pride in his profession as well as what seemed, throughout my research, a sometimes unattractive insistence on the correctness of his way of practicing family and divorce mediation. I understood why the major issue in his practice was keeping people committed to a process they could not quite fathom.

Commitment, as Phear uses it, means many things. When he asks his clients for commitment, he asks them to invest in and to "trust" the process. He calls on them to act like members of a "community of three" and to participate actively in making that community work. He asks them to undertake obligations, to be willing to give something to make mediation work for them. Most of all, he asks for resolve, a willingness to go along with a process that, on the one hand, keeps some issues open long beyond the time when people themselves may feel ready to reach closure and, on the other, must go on even when it is not clear that any agreement can ever be reached. Fight hard, use tricks and guile, threats and cajolery to keep people mediating confident that minor miracles happen. Patrick Phear—mediator, minor miracle-maker. Who was I, who had never made a minor miracle, to question? It all seemed to make sense.

What had, over the fifteen months of my research, kept me committed to Patrick Phear was a rich curiosity about a person whose professional ideology and professional practice seemed so contradictory and (dare I say it?) somewhat mysterious. He is dogmatic, solid, up-front with his "rub people the wrong way" views of mediation. He is big, bold, and full of fiery idealism in his views on "the profession" and professional standards. Yet he is, at the same time, hard to pin down about the mediation process itself; open, yet elusive, about the way the "minor miracles" get made: ironic, somewhat cynical, and full of doubts about a process that seems, on occasion at least, to be so manipulative; and worried about how family and divorce mediation are being marketed and used.

These contradictions were vividly on display when he visited me in my office for a final debriefing on our work together. He came, thermos full of coffee in hand, generously returning the favor of my first anxious pilgrimage to Boston. As we settled in, I suspected that something was on his mind. However, we talked for more than an hour and were close to what seemed like the appropriate end of our conversation when, without warning and without waiting for a question, he sat back in his chair, smiled slightly in the boyish way of someone about to reveal a secret, and said:

> I actually have a theory about why I am a successful private mediator. You know, it's because I won't *own* people's cases. I don't give therapy and I don't do law. The therapists know and the lawyers know that I won't take over their cases, and the people know I'm

not going to try to solve all their problems. So when they talk about me they don't come expecting me to take over and tell them what to do. And I always deliver something, at least greater clarity and understanding.

Even if, for instance, Alex and Hazel had fallen apart they would have left with a better feel for their problems. So my clients always get a success and the people who refer cases to me always get their cases back. I set it up so that I can never fail; I can't fail because they can't fail. I control my product and the process that produces it. It's a sure thing.

Here I was facing Phear the entrepreneur, not Phear the moralist or the maker of minor miracles. Here he came dangerously close to embracing the very thing that he had so vehemently criticized in the mediation of Willie's case, namely practicing mediation in a way that ensures that the mediator, not the parties, always comes out a winner. Phear continued:

I am currently worried that a lot of the training I have done in mediation, particularly in courts, has led to a system of justice that I totally deplore. It is this calling in and training people to mediate knowing, when we all know that most of them will do it just the way it was done to poor Willie's parents. You know, all they are going to do is impose things. I'm not sure how many of the real skills of listening and assessment are teachable. I worry because it seems so sexy right now. I hear people whom I like a lot saying, "Let's let a thousand flowers bloom, and it doesn't matter too much what they all are, let's call them all mediation." It's all very self-serving. I don't want to be making a living out of something that I think is basically a scam.

Startled by Phear's choice of words, I asked whether his practice of making "minor miracles," which had been so opaque to
me, was now being described as a scam. "No, no," he said softly
through lips closed around a just-lighted cigarette. "Look, I have
skills, I am superaware of all the nuances around me. It is those
skills that are so very useful in mediation. The scam occurs when
people without those skills, without the life experience that
breeds them, mediate or, as frequently happens, arbitrate under
the guise of mediation."

There was no hint of boast in his comments but rather the
sound of some distant, unpleasant recollection now packaged,
though not fully contained, in another critique of his profession.

Phear went on to explain that all of the "good mediators" he
knows come from what he calls "complicated" childhoods in
which they grew up "desperately needing to make sense of a
world of conflict." He said he was now really worried because he
sees mediation as a "very middle-class, WASPy kind of problem
solving, you know, separate out the emoting, put it over to the
right and deal with logic over to the left. You translate your anger
into an interest and then move right here. That's just so wonder-
fully middle-class WASP."

I was surprised by this switch into ethnic stereotypes but
nonetheless made some oblique reference to my own working-
class, Jewish background and jokingly said that maybe I am in a
better position than he to appreciate the virtues of this separate-
the-emotions, stay-calm approach to problem solving. Phear
laughed and responded, "There's nothing wrong with it except if
it is taken too far. It's just too easy to impose it on people who
don't happen to behave that way.

"Mediation forgets that," he continued. "It forces things into
one way which, when it is done right, can and does produce
results. But it's not for everybody either to do or to have done to
them. The tragedy is that there may be just now both too much
doing and too much being done to."

So we ended where we began, back to Willie and tragedy. Here again a critique of imposition, of insensitivity, of the mass marketing of skills that can, in truth, only be acquired through one's own life experience. Now, at the end, Phear had, in his own intense self-scrutiny, perhaps done my job for me; perhaps Phear, family and divorce mediator, had done as good a social science critique as I would or could do. Here in my office was another "minor miracle."

Austin Sarat

Note

1.   John Haynes is among the most prominent family mediators in the United States and has written extensively on the topic. He is also the founding president of the Academy of Family Mediators.

PART TWO

• •

Builders of the Field

Not so long ago, when one mentioned mediation, people gave a quizzical look. Limited to certain fields, mediation was frequently confused with other, more common forms of dispute settlement like arbitration and adjudication. Although it would be hard to claim that mediation is now a household word, its visibility is considerably greater. In no small part, this visibility can be attributed to a number of people who, for a decade or more, have publicly advocated for the use of mediation in legal, public, family, and community disputes.

Many people have been active in spreading the word about mediation. In the legal arena, Linda Singer, Michael Lewis, Carrie Menkel-Meadow, Frank Sander, and Steve Goldberg, among many others, have written about the benefits of mediation as an alternative to litigation and arbitration. In the public sphere, practitioners and spokespersons like Gerald Cormick, the late Jim Laue, Phillip Harter, Gail Bingham, and Susan Carpenter have pushed the boundaries of mediation to resolve public sector disputes. In the community and family realm, John Haynes, Jay Folberg, Joan Kelly, Chris Moore, Ray Shonholtz, and many more have actively developed programs and practices that get mediation out into the community. More recently, some of these field builders have even taken their word to eastern Europe to help develop the capability to deal with the seemingly intractable disputes that are creating such hardships there. Many others, too numerous to mention, have made significant contributions to getting out the word on mediation.

People build the field in many ways. All generally have some firsthand experience as mediators. But then they choose different avenues to spread the word. Some do it through their writing. Many of those mentioned earlier have written popular and professional books that make the case for mediation, where and how it can be used, and then offer their advice on what mediators can do to assist parties in the resolution of their differences.

Others are known for the mediation experiments they have developed in communities, courts, prisons, and corporations. These programs are a means to connect mediators with parties who may need them. Some of the programs—neighborhood justice centers, state offices of mediation, multi-door courthouses, and so forth—have had considerable impact on drawing in prospective mediators and providing a forum for mediation to occur.

Training and conferences are other ways to build the field. Under any number of private and public auspices, practitioners and others offer skill-building programs that attract would-be mediators in all the fields in which practice is possible. As one of these trainer-mediators once remarked, if a professional's caseload is not sufficient, training is another way to make a living at mediation. Conferences and other professional activities attract those already in the field, as well as others who are curious to learn more about it. Field builders are always very prominent at the annual meetings of the Society of Professionals in Dispute Resolution, the Dispute Resolution Section of the American Bar Association, and the Academy of Family Mediators, as well as at more specialized conferences on topics like grievance mediation.

Obviously, many people whom we could have profiled have had a hand in building the field. The three we chose—Albie Davis, Eric Green, and Larry Susskind—exemplify the people who have built the field, and the kinds of activities that mark their practice. Davis is an early adherent of mediation, coming out of her community activist background. She has written extensively on mediation, been instrumental in developing court-based and community programs in Massachusetts, been involved in training, and been a highly visible presence in professional organizations. Green is probably best known for his design and implementation of innovative forms of alternative dispute resolution in business and for his founding of a private company to offer these services. From both an academic and a private institutional base, Green has been instrumental in converting corporations and attorneys to the virtues of mediation. Susskind is both a professor and a practitioner of mediation in public sector disputing. Coming out of his planning background, Susskind has worked on a number of fronts, through writing, program design, and teaching, to promote negotiation and mediation as viable means to resolve public disputes that cover the gamut of policy issues, including investment, low-cost housing, and siting, among many others.

These mediators are both in the field and yet separate from it. Their professional identities are not solely in their practice but also at the boundary between theory and practice. They do not practice full time, but split their activities among mediation, teaching, writing, and public advocacy. This approach has a number of consequences for their practice when they do mediate. They have considerable discretion in the cases they choose to mediate. While professional concerns figure in this decision, they are also motivated to experiment. In this way, they connect the various fields of practice and move mediation into new areas.

The boundary positions of the field builders—from labor relations to public policy, the family to business, and so forth—have an impact on how field builders mediate. This group of mediators self-consciously seeks to link theory and practice. They explicitly use theory to guide their interventions, then reflect on this experience in their writings and teaching. Not as closely tied to market forces as the full-time professionals, field builders have more leeway in how they are judged by others and how they judge themselves. Their reputations, from both their practice and their writings, can insulate them from the kinds of scrutiny others experience routinely. This may explain why this group, more than the others, can confidently make claims for mediation and so keep alive some of the myths that make practice difficult for others.

In the careers of the three individuals we profile, one can witness the development of the field, how and why people are attracted to it. They are among its most enthusiastic practitioners; thus, we get to see something of the promise in the field, what those who are committed to it see as its potential. Indeed, the three profilers—Sally Merry, Lavinia Hall, and John Forester—were attracted to Davis, Green, and Susskind because they saw in their work the possibilities of making sense of the directions in which mediation has developed in the three fields represented here. They are both the field's history and its future. As early adherents and spokespersons, they provide models for how to break in; in their current work, they suggest the issues that will engage the field as it develops further.

• • • • • • •

"*I have long been fascinated by power—What is it? Who has it? Who wants it? Who needs it? And how do you get it?*"

—Albie Davis

6

• •

Albie M. Davis
Community Mediation as
Community Organizing

In an increasingly established and politically centrist field, Albie Davis maintains a more rebellious, politically left slant than many other practitioners of mediation. She is concerned about community and the way ordinary people relate to the legal system. Unlike many high-profile mediators, Davis has a grass-roots vision of mediation and its possibilities. In fact, she is one of the most visible and articulate spokespeople for this position, both in Massachusetts, where she is director of mediation for the Massachusetts District Courts, and nationally, as a frequent guest speaker at conferences and other such events.

For the last eight years, Davis's formal job has centered on increasing and enhancing the use of mediation in the sixty-eight district courts of Massachusetts. She starts new mediation programs, seeks out funding for these programs, meets with funders to tell them about new initiatives, and facilitates (that is, "lobbies for") legislation relevant to community mediation (such as a recent bill to put a surcharge on the small claims court filing fee, to pay for community mediation). She nurtures and promotes mediation in the state by providing technical assistance and training programs, and she frequently speaks on the subject to local groups and at universities.

Davis has been active in several state and national organizations interested in mediation, such as the alternative dispute resolution (ADR) subcommittee of the Massachusetts Supreme Judicial Courts' Commission on the Future of the Courts, the committee developing training standards for the Massachusetts Association of Mediation Programs, and the Institute for Judicial Administration's project to create standards for court mediation programs. With colleagues in the Society of Professionals in Dispute Resolution (SPIDR), she has actively been involved in issues that are helping to form this new field—in particular, ethical standards, the dilemmas surrounding "credentialing," and the role of women in the field. Several years ago, she did an influential survey of mediation staff salaries, noting patterns such as generally low wage scales, gender stratification, and the economic consequences of affiliating with social service agencies. Her growing body of published work on mediation practice includes numerous, frequently cited articles and a book in progress on Mary Parker Follett, a turn-of-the-century scholar who, largely because of Davis's efforts, is now recognized as the "mother" of today's ADR movement.

The term *respect* crops up over and over when Albie Davis talks about mediation. With years of experience in community organizing predating her work in community mediation, Davis firmly believes in the dignity of people of all backgrounds, races, genders, and classes. Mediators must respect the parties, their opinions, and their situations if they are to be effective; they must honor their competence and their "ownership" of the conflict. In Davis's words, "a genuinely respectful attitude by the mediator most often elicits a positive response from the parties" and encourages them to draw on their natural problem-solving skills and creativity. "As important as it is that mediators be skillful," she cautions, "I'm uncomfortable when all the focus falls on the competence of the mediator at the expense of the parties' competence."

Thus, empowerment—encouraging people from all walks of life to *know* that their opinions are valuable and that they are creative human beings who can design solutions to their problems—is crucial to Albie Davis. When it works as it should, the mediation process not only is empowering, she says, but it also recognizes the interplay between emotions and intelligence. Davis credits her training in "reevaluation co-counseling"—a peer counseling method that evolved in the early 1970s—with giving her a perspective on the connection between the expression of emotions and the ability to use one's intelligence fully. "There are many closet co-counselors in the mediation field," she notes.

Characteristic of Albie Davis in mediation or community organizing is an "as if" strategy that flattens hierarchies and works to construct social situations based on equality—"as if" all parties were equal regardless of the power relationships outside the room. Long a feminist, she has become increasingly vocal about the issues surrounding gender, the silencing that women experience in conferences, academic life, their writing, policy decisions, and the courts. "I have faith in the fundamental competence and creativity of human beings," she says. "Each person who is silenced is harmed as an individual, but the loss is society's as well." In both her life and her mediation practice, mediation is subordinate to the goal of creating a society in which each individual can find full expression of his or her own talents.

Community mediation, she believes, is the "soul" of the ADR movement. It is here, she believes, that the potential to bring together people from all walks of life is at its ripest. Yet she can be skeptical about some community programs. For example, the early rhetoric of the San Francisco Community Boards espoused local neighborhoods' "ownership" of conflict and right to intervene. Such a stance, in Davis's view, smacked too much of community control and not enough of tolerance for individualism. Despite its anticourt, antigovernment rhetoric, Community Boards seemed too committed to establishing a new governance structure in the community. As Davis puts it, "I have been too socialized as an individualist" to buy into that world view. Furthermore, she asserts, "unchecked community intervention into the lives of individuals can be as troublesome as 'big brother' government."

Davis's experience as a community organizer and her current work within the court system combine to raise a number of personal contradictions that she struggles with on a daily basis. For example, she actively promotes mediation but, at the same time, worries that the ADR movement overall is becoming too careerist. She believes strongly that people from all walks of life can learn to play the role of mediator, and she does not want to see barriers placed in the way of learning and practicing mediation; yet she is concerned about people who insist they are "naturals" without demonstrating practice or skill. She seeks out funding for community mediation from public and private sources, while knowing that ownership of programs can easily drift to funders. "Form follows funding," she lamented in her 1986 assessment of community mediation in Massachusetts (Davis, 1986).

Mediation has a great deal of promise for developing multiethnic dialogue and collaboration, but in most communities it remains a white, middle-class enterprise. Davis believes in the "transformative" power of mediation but says, "As a child of the McCarthy era, I'm a great believer in due process and the sacredness of our civil rights. So I'm stressed when I see mediators fall into the trap of dismissing the legal system in their enthusiasm for mediation." In terms of the old distinction between community-based and court-based mediation programs, Davis generally supports the community programs, but she has also encouraged experimentation with court-community relationships. "Right now," she points out, "the courts have the cases. And furthermore, this is a democracy. Why shouldn't our justice system be first-class?"

No one's life or work can be summed up solely by a review of their past; this is particularly the case when dealing with a subject like Albie Davis, who is intellectually and professionally evolving and dynamic. She is now in her mid fifties and a grandmother, but Davis's intellectual curiosity and outlook on life are still vibrant. Today and throughout her past, several prominent themes keep repeating themselves: political and community organizing, empowerment, racial and gender equality, and anti-authoritarianism. She is increasingly intrigued by the largely overlooked work of early twentieth-century scholar and management consultant Mary Parker Follett. These leitmotifs of social consciousness have accompanied and influenced Davis thus far in her life's journey and, in particular, have helped bring her to mediation. It would be a great mistake to state that they are the only reasons she has become the mediator and person she is today, but they do help to explain her a bit.

From 1974 to 1981, Davis was the director of a state-funded program called Political Discovery. Every three or four weeks over a seven-year period, the program brought together between sixty and seventy city and suburban schoolchildren and their teachers for a five- to ten-day session in downtown Boston to explore various aspects of the city and to appreciate people of different races, ages, and communities. One of the programs was a course on law and justice. Here, teachers and students met with judges, sheriffs, prisoners, lawyers in big firms, and legal services lawyers during visits to courts, prisons, and city hall. The students questioned these people about the law, how the justice system worked, and whether it was fair. All of the speakers, from the attorney general to the prisoners, in one way or another stressed the failure of the legal system. The universal lament was that the justice system favors the rich over the poor, white people over people of color.

This common disenchantment with formal justice gave Davis pause, and then one day, she and the Political Discovery group met with the staff of the Dorchester Urban Court: Della Rice and Kathy Grant. Rice and Grant were involved with something new, a different model that seemed more promising in a world of criminal justice failures. Down the street from the courthouse, tucked into a storefront next to a Hispanic *grocería* and a used furniture outlet, a racially integrated group helped their neighbors solve their problems through a seemingly simple process called mediation. In contrast to the formal legal system, this "mediation" was very appealing to Davis and the others.

This initial exposure led Davis in the direction of promoting mediation in the schools. In the late 1970s, she wrote a successful grant proposal to train young people from several schools as mediators. This experience fueled her advocacy for teaching conflict resolution skills in the classroom. She later wrote several widely known articles on this topic and worked diligently on plans to bring together educators and mediators, including the first national conference on the topic of school mediation, which took place in 1984 on Cape Cod. At that watershed event, the fifty attendees agreed to found the National Association for Mediation in Education (NAME), which has become a well-known and influential force in the effort to encourage conflict resolution programs in schools.

Such concerns as respecting every individual, valuing racial, cultural, and other forms of diversity, and seeking collaborative work appear in Davis's earlier activities as well. She confesses she has long had an anti-authoritarian streak—resisting being told what to do—that turned her away from organized religion as a very young child. She remembers being concerned since childhood with social injustice, acquired in part from her mother's nonelitist principles and her father's left-wing progressive politics.

As a white child growing up in California during the Second World War, she watched in dismay as her Japanese-American friends were sent off to internment camps. During the McCarthy era, while she was in high school, she learned the importance of keeping the government from intervening too extensively into people's lives and the value of due process. She attended the University of California at Berkeley a few years before the free speech movement, but it was already a place with some radical interests. She lived in a student cooperative, Sherman Hall.

In the early 1960s, Davis (by now the mother of four) was living in Sacramento and became involved in helping house and feed the protesters working with the late Cesar Chavez and the grape pickers' strike. She describes the outpouring of support from families in Sacramento to feed and house two thousand marchers, and she found, with exhilaration, that she could help mobilize the community to provide for others. Chavez was a great organizer, and she learned an enormous amount from watching how he worked. At about the same time, she read and studied the work of Chavez's teacher, Saul Alinsky. After seeing how grass-roots organizing worked to feed and house the grape strikers, she realized that good organizing certainly involves a broad vision, but in the end is made up of little components, of attention to detail. She also recognized that it was important to stay connected to people, to get them involved at the start. During this period, Davis was also involved in Democratic politics in California, helping found a racially integrated Democratic Club. In 1966, she was asked to be the manager of the Sacramento County Democratic Headquarters to help reelect Governor Pat Brown, and later she was appointed to the statewide Democratic Central Committee.

As Davis only half-jokingly puts it, "When this upstart actor, Ronald Reagan, was elected governor of California, there was a mass exodus of active Democrats from the Golden State to Washington." Her then-husband, David Davis, went to work for the Johnson administration while Albie Davis found part-time work in the capital for a liberal member of Congress from California. An advocate of public education, she enrolled her children in the Washington public schools. She also joined with her neighbors to form D.C. Democrats for Peace and Freedom, a group promoting the end to the Vietnam War and home rule for the District. Later, David Davis took a job in the administration of former Boston mayor Kevin White, then served as director of the Massachusetts Port Authority, necessitating the family's move to Boston in the late 1960s.

Their new home was in an integrated, inner-city neighborhood, the South End—a poor, primarily African-American, Hispanic, and Asian neighborhood that was attracting liberal, city-minded white professionals. A friend of Davis's daughter lived in a nearby public housing project reputed to be fearfully victimized by crime. When her twelve-year-old daughter was invited to her friend's home, Davis paid a visit to the friend's mother in the project. The other mother, now a lifelong friend, pointed out that she knew Davis was nervous about her daughter coming into the project. "Don't you think I am nervous too when my daughter goes all the way over to your house?" she asked. Davis says that question served as a "wake-up call," and she began to rethink her assumptions.

In the South End, Davis again sent her children to the public schools, although she was aware that public education in Boston at that time was considered a disaster. Gathering together a group of other parents, she helped start a new public school with open classrooms, ungraded learning, and integrated classes. At one point, when school administrators reneged on their promise to expand the ungraded program to the middle school, Davis and a group of mothers from the housing project took over a classroom; they unbolted the desks and threw them out in the street, then rolled out a rug onto the classroom floor. The group of mothers insisted on teaching their children in this alternative classroom. For two weeks, they continued with instruction in this school until the city finally appointed a teacher acceptable to both parents and students. The school takeover is described in detail in

Common Ground, a best-selling book about public education and the school busing crisis in Boston (Lukas, 1985).

"I'm proud of all my children," says Davis. "They've all graduated from college, and they're all doing interesting and important work. My only regret about our civil disobedience from those earlier days is that we should have kept those old desks and sold them!"

• • • • • • •

In 1978, when the South End became too expensive for her (she divorced in 1972 and became a working, single mother), Davis moved to Dorchester, a racially mixed neighborhood within the Boston city limits where housing was still affordable, and gentrification and deterioration were and still are being experienced. She remembered the Urban Court Program, and when a mediation training was announced in 1980, she and her sixteen-year-old daughter Carol, twenty-year-old son Matthew, and partner John Chandler all signed up. They were trained by Kathy Grant, Della Rice, and the Urban Court volunteers.

As the years have gone by, Davis has been exposed to many different mediation models and theories and has developed her own view of the subject. Nevertheless, she acknowledges the significant influence of the Urban Court on her philosophy and approach. "Today," she says, "I realize how deeply our model, with its heavy emphasis on private caucuses and instructions to find out the parties' 'shopping lists' and 'bottom lines,' was a child of the labor mediation experience. The Urban Court can be traced to the Institute for Mediation and Conflict Resolution (IMCR) in New York, and IMCR's training was developed by George Nicolau, a labor mediator."

She notes that people associated with the Dorchester program trained "most of the people in the other early mediation programs in Massachusetts, and they, in turn, trained the next generation.

As a consequence, the entire state's style is premised on the IMCR model." The approach has not proved to be universally effective; according to Davis, Urban Community Mediators and its sister programs have adjusted in response to varying applications of mediation, particularly in cases involving parents and their children or students and fellow students. "Nevertheless," she says, "the fundamental philosophy of respecting the parties—their competence and their ownership of the conflict and its solution—and the basic premise of listening carefully and nonjudgmentally still hold us in good stead."

Today, after several reincarnations—abandonment by the court, affiliation with a youth agency, a dramatic mediators' strike and walkout, and the eventual formation of a free-standing program—the original Urban Court Program lives on under the banner of Urban Community Mediators (UCM). The current membership of UCM, which now numbers seventy-five, includes some who have been with the Dorchester Urban Court since the 1970s, many newer members, and some who are active and prominent in mediation work statewide. Among these mediators are Kathy Grant, who coordinates mediation services for the Consumer Protection Division of the Massachusetts Attorney General's Office, and Davis herself.

To better understand UCM, I attended a business meeting some three years ago, not long after the walkout from the youth agency. At that time, a racially mixed group of eight men and women gathered around a table in a community center near the heart of the black community in Boston to discuss finding a permanent office and providing the mediation services and training programs for which they had received small grants. Much of the discussion reflected the initial inspiration of the group: where to locate an office so that people of all races could feel comfortable going there; how to provide mediation training to deserving groups (such as local schools) at limited costs; how to hire a creative, dedicated, and experienced person to run the program on a shoestring, with no clear prospects for further money up ahead.

There is enthusiasm for the skills of mediation. The group discusses holding another training session to accommodate all the people who want to be trained to mediate, and several talk about the number of calls they have received from people eager to learn. Most of the small grants they have received are to train others in mediation skills rather than to provide the service themselves. Even though the prices charged for training are low, many of the volunteers are willing to provide the training free to deserving clients.

Without staff and without an office (and dependent on the answering machine of a new member), the group has been handling mediation cases referred individually and from the Roxbury and Dorchester courts. In order to facilitate referrals, volunteers would sit in each court for several hours a week, at times with the agreement of judges and court clerks. Some of the problems facing the program seem the same as those preoccupying community mediation programs over the last fifteen years. How can the program find enough cases so that people who want to mediate have a chance? How does the program address the frustration of volunteers who want to mediate and too rarely get the chance? (Since the program has traditionally "mirrored" the disputants when assigning mediators, and since most parties referred to mediation by these two courts are people of color, it is primarily white mediators who lack cases.) What can be done about clerks who refuse to send cases to mediators sitting in the courthouse because the clerks feel they are doing the job adequately themselves?

During the transition period between UCM's break from the youth agency and the time when it received sufficient funding to hire its own staff, Davis spent a few hours a week at the Roxbury District Court doing mediation intake work. I accompanied her for two of these days.

The scene embodied the frantic pace of any busy city court-house—people waiting in the corridors, names called brusquely over loudspeakers, police coming and going, attorneys conferring anxiously with their clients. We sat in the room used for clerk's "show cause" hearings, judicial proceedings supposedly designed to determine whether there is sufficient evidence to charge some-one formally with a crime. The clerk referred two cases to media-tion: one involved a fight between a man and a woman who had been drinking, during which the man was arrested (the police officer making the complaint failed to show up), and the other a complaint by a woman that her neighbor played loud Spanish music, fixed his car on her property, and dumped his trash into her yard.

Neither set of parties wanted to schedule a full mediation for a later date. So, in a matter of a few minutes, Davis worked to shape some settlements that she believed were "inadequate but, given the circumstances, better than nothing."

Davis was concerned about mediating cases like the one between the man and the woman. "The case highlighted for me the need for a 'living policy' on the types of cases that should be referred to mediation, in particular those involving domestic vio-lence," she said. "By this I mean a policy that is constantly assessed by court personnel and program staff. Since our break-away from our former sponsoring agency, UCM has enjoyed strong support from its all-volunteer staff. But it is difficult to see patterns and develop and enforce viable policies when we keep shifting intake workers each day." In this case, Davis called the court clerk to make sure the mediation program had a policy on domestic violence before any such cases were referred in the future, as well as to double-check on the case. She called the absent arresting officer as well.

Many changes have occurred in UCM since my attendance at that business meeting and observation of Davis doing intake three years ago. As a consequence of their experience handling cases during the transition, UCM has adopted a policy of not conducting mediations in the courthouse. The frantic atmosphere, UCM leaders feel, spills over into the mediation session and mitigates against the more calm and reasoned approach necessary for reaching an agreement that will last over time.

While the membership showed no interest in doing mediation to make money three years ago, now, in keeping with the dramatic changes in the field, the dynamics are changing. A few UCM members have formed their own mediation firms, and others have begun working part time or full time, either as staff or consultant trainers. Yet, even these more entrepreneurial mediators remain loyal members of UCM, volunteering their time to mediate and help govern the organization.

UCM has become well known for its training expertise, having conducted training programs for insurance companies, universities, elementary and high schools, neighborhood agencies, youth groups, and statewide housing authorities, among other organizations. At present, the group receives more inquiries about service than it can fulfill. Of its seventy-five active members, at least thirty are involved in mediation training.

One long-standing dream of Davis and her UCM colleagues has been fulfilled: UCM has found a home of its own at a busy intersection by a subway station. Grants have been written and sufficient funds raised to hire a half-time director, plus a half-time school mediation coordinator. However, nearly twenty years later, the original 1975 Urban Court budget of $140,000 and staff of six seem like an unreachable fantasy in this era of a shrinking economy.

• • • • • • •

The themes shaping Albie Davis's early community organizing are echoed in her approach to mediation: a concern with racial integration and difference, a respect for people of all kinds, an interest in enhancing the power of people who are typically seen as powerless, and an emphasis on the value of communication and collaboration across the boundaries that normally separate people. Underneath these interests is a skill in political organizing, in getting people together and figuring out how to listen to them, coordinate them, and make a splash.

After listening to Davis's account of the road that led her to mediation, I asked, "Did mediation live up to its expectations for you?" I could see how she was enticed to the Dorchester Urban Court but suspected that she might now feel homeless in the contemporary world of mediation. Davis responded that the experience of mediation in Dorchester still "feels good. . . . Each time I mediate, I am reminded of how well the process works, and how rewarding it is to help people help themselves." She acknowledges the attractiveness of mediation and applauds the interest in performing mediation professionally. But she worries about people who do not bring social consciousness to the project and just look for the "mediator's high." In her present job as director of mediation for the District Courts of Massachusetts, people call her for all kinds of information about alternative dispute resolution. But most are seeking a career in mediation.

. . . .

In talking about her mediation practice and the way she became interested in it, Davis stresses her interest in power. "I have long been fascinated by power—What is it? Who has it? Who wants it? Who needs it? And how do you get it? I admit that my views on power are in flux. In the sixties and seventies, I was influenced by the Saul Alinksy maxim, 'Power is not only what you have, but what the enemy thinks you have.' I was involved in numerous confrontational and adversarial activities then—us versus them. But, since my involvement with mediation, I have begun questioning the necessity of the 'enemy' orientation."

Mary Parker Follett is part of the reason Davis's views on problem solving and power have shifted. It was in 1989 that Davis first encountered the work of the brilliant but today largely uncelebrated theorist, and she has become a leader among the growing number of Follett fans in the U.S. conflict resolution community. Davis says she was "attracted to Follett's notions of 'power with' instead of 'power over.' The biggest challenge is exploring the possibilities for cooperation and collaboration without being naive. I'm committed to pushing the boundaries for mediation, but I always have one eye out for cooptation. Racism, sexism, and other forms of oppression are a reality. Abuses of power abound. Cynical uses of mediation can flourish easily in a society which refuses to address its own inequities."

In fact, Davis says, it was the "men-on-deck, women-below-deck" phenomenon—a distinct power imbalance—that "motivated me to do everything I could to bring the ideas of Mary Parker Follett to the fore. In the 1920s, Follett put forward all the essential elements of constructive conflict resolution—the potential of conflict, the limitations of domination and compromise, the promise of integrated solutions, the circular nature of relations, and more. Women, young and old, need to know that it was a woman who did the early pioneering work around integrative bargaining. I am obsessed with learning more about Follett and promoting her ideas."

In the summer of 1989, Davis wrote the first of two articles about Follett for *Negotiation Journal*. The interview format she used in that oft-cited first article on Follett sparked the idea of having Follett appear "live" before audiences. "An Evening with Mary Parker Follett," starring Eileen Stewart (a college administrator, mediator, and actress), with a backup slide show by Davis, was a highlight of the annual 1989 Society of Professionals in Dispute Resolution (SPIDR) conference and the kickoff plenary for the 1990 Academy of Family Mediators' annual conference.

In 1992, Davis convinced SPIDR to institute an annual Mary

Parker Follett Award to honor a person or organization who, "in the spirit of risk taking" and collaboration, makes a significant contribution to the field of conflict resolution. Davis herself has received a small grant to allow her to continue her research and writing on Follett, whom she describes as "the mentor I never had."

Davis's interest in Follett ties in with her feminist instincts. She notes she has become more and more interested in the way feminism contributes to mediation practice, and increasingly vocal about the issues surrounding gender and the field of conflict resolution.

> Gender expresses itself in several ways, one being the profession itself. Our newly emerging field, which owes so much to the experience of women, is becoming stratified, with women at the lower-paying and less prestigious end of the spectrum and men at the higher-paid and more glamorous end. Each day I receive phone calls from women who are attracted to this work. Because men have received most of the credit for being the "founding philosophers," they assume they must look to men for the answers.
>
> I am delighted that by bringing Mary Follett's brilliant ideas to the forefront, I may encourage women—young, middle-aged, and older—to express their own views with confidence. To my joy, Follett is attracting as many male admirers as female, which certainly makes sense, since she teaches so profoundly on universal themes.

· · · · · · ·

When Davis discusses how she mediates cases, she speaks as

both a veteran trainer and mediator. She has run dozens of train-ing sessions over the past nine years, trained hundreds of media-tors, and mediated hundreds of cases herself. Her cases have mostly involved people in Dorchester and Roxbury, but she has also mediated in other cities and towns in Massachusetts, at the University of Massachusetts at Amherst, and, currently, among employees and managers within the District Court.

How do her philosophy, her politics, and her organizing skill affect the way Davis mediates cases? It seems clear that she became involved with a particular image of mediation: its social justice, promises of empowerment, and potential for neighbor-hood connection. She saw the version of mediation that was a logical extension of Chavez and Alinsky and neighborhood organizing, not that which promised to make the courts more efficient.

Davis thinks of mediation as a time in which people can make something together. She tries to focus not on getting an agree-ment but on the process of working together: "I try to tame my own ego and give the people themselves the opportunity to reach an agreement," she says. The process should not be too agree-ment focused and manipulative because, as she puts it, "the seductive nature of mediation must be held in check."

As a consequence, when she uses strategies others call "stroking" or "transmitting the positives," Davis tries to explain what she is doing and why it will work. "I value being up-front about the mediation process and the theory behind it," she says. "I'm a strong believer in genuine 'informed consent.'"

Though not denying that the mediator manipulates the inter-action between the parties, she often describes mediation as "consensual manipulation." Her ultimate test of an ethically sound mediation would be to show a videotape of the private ses-sions to both sides and have them conclude that what she did and said with the other person was okay. Of course, given the confidential nature of mediation, this is not possible; but she tries to conduct the private sessions in such a way that the absent party, if he or she were watching, would feel "respected."

Davis believes mediators must both exercise their native intelligence and honor their intuition. They must be able to absorb information at many levels simultaneously. When mediators work in pairs, each must consider how he or she is relating to the other mediator and to the parties, taking in this information in very different ways. At the same time, the mediator must be planning ahead, assessing information and feelings. As Davis puts it, the mediator should be analogous to a living cell: simple and transparent so that one can easily see everything going on inside, but at the same time, very busy inside. She urges mediators: be transparent to the parties when you mediate. If you have a theory about what is happening, share it with the parties. Tell them that it is common for people in mediation to get stuck, that there are always ups and downs during the process, that emotional outbursts are natural, that creative resolutions are possible.

When she is training would-be mediators, Davis encourages her students to be "thinking mediators—to think about the theory and the process." She urges them not to focus on reaching an agreement and tries to prevent trainees from conceptualizing their role as mediators as "getting them [parties] to see it this way." Instead, they should think about where they are in the process at this point and take their cues from the parties about how to move ahead. At the end of the process, the parties may have created a solution that no one could conceptualize at the beginning.

But "holding back" in this way can create a sense of ambiguity that is hard for people to manage and a tendency to want to look for solutions. When a mediation seems to be stuck, Davis believes the mediators should ask themselves a series of questions: should this case be in mediation in the first place? Were the parties forced to come by a judge? Are they negotiating in good faith? Or is one party using mediation as a form of discovery? Do they trust me and the process enough for it to succeed?

Davis objects to talking about tricks for "dealing with difficult people," arguing that defining a person as difficult reveals a lack of respect for the person. In general, she does not like the idea of "tricks." The interest in techniques of mediation rather than its general philosophy is, in her view, a trap, not a creative approach.

Davis has summed up her approach in an article in which she likens the process of mediation to the birth of her granddaughter: "This doctor handled the birth like a good mediator. She was there for the parties. They felt her competence. But they did the work, and it was their agreement" (Davis, 1989, p. 17). In her training materials, she describes the process as a series of logical steps:

> Mediation moves through several natural stages. First, the parties are set at ease, the process is explained, and questions about the process are answered. Then, each party tells his or her "story." Next, the mediators help the parties define issues, identify interests, and sort them. When issues and interests are clear, the task becomes to draw on the parties' creative talents and develop mutually agreeable options for settlement. In the final stage, an agreement considered satisfactory to the people involved is reached (and often written).

The process Davis uses downplays the importance of accuser and accused. She urges mediators not to call people complainant and respondent, suggesting instead that one person be identified as the person who brought the problem to the attention of the program. The decision about which person to invite to speak first and with whom to have the first private caucus depends on the parties and the problem. Who goes first is important because that person is often able to shape the story, unless, Davis says, "media-tors make a special effort to give the second party a fresh start." Sometimes, Davis says, she tries to have the most confident per-son go second, using the chance to go first to bring in the less engaged person. However, even that approach has its limits, since the more reticent person may not feel comfortable going first. Separate opening sessions to avoid the "who goes first" issue can backfire as well. Davis speaks of "earning" trust and notes that the level of trust fluctuates throughout the process "but hopefully builds over time."

· · · · · · ·

From my perspective as an observer and an interviewer, eight different themes constitute the core of Davis's practice as a medi-ator. These themes emerge in training, on her training tape, and in her mediation sessions, and they reflect in many respects her IMCR roots. Following is a description of those common themes in Albie Davis's training sessions and in her practice.

Rituals of Respect. Each participant in the mediation session is greeted politely with a shake of the hand and a statement of wel-come. The mediator stands for the greeting, then asks the parties to sit down. Each is addressed by surname. If less formal names are used, permission is sought from each party. Davis then explains that the session is confidential, that the agreement is theirs to craft, and that her role is to facilitate the discussion. She makes an effort to look at each person and speak to him or her directly. This first part of the session must establish some kind of trust for the process to move ahead. Trust is also produced by allowing each person to speak without interruption from the other side.

Repeating Back the Story. After each person tells his or her story in the initial joint session, Davis then repeats the story back to the person. In training sessions and demonstrations, Davis begins by saying, "What I heard you say is ..." After summarizing each person's account, she asks whether she has captured his or her understanding of the problem and what the person would like, using questions such as "How would you like to see this resolved?" and "What is it you want?" As she puts it, "You are trying to build a picture of how the parties are connected to one another—how their lives came to mesh."

Talking in Private. After each person has presented his or her side of the problem and established the particular issues of concern, Davis sometimes moves to private sessions, talking to each person individually. The choice of whom she will talk with first depends on the situation and whom she thinks needs the attention first. The other person is invited to wait outside. When comediating, the mediators typically spend a few minutes together before the private sessions deciding whom they would like to talk to first and planning out the details of their strategy. In these private sessions, parties are encouraged to expand on their definition of the problem and raise concrete issues and concerns. In the private sessions, Davis says, it is easier to show empathy for each person.

Withholding Judgments. In response to a question about what a mediator does when she has a solution in her mind, Davis says that the idea is not to provide her own answer but to let the parties come up with one themselves. The skills of mediation listed in the training session—patience, objectivity, neutrality, analytical skills, communication skills, asking the right questions, and having empathy—focus on the capacity to listen but not take sides. Davis emphasizes the importance of letting the parties make up their own agreement rather than imposing her own ideas on them.

In a mediation awareness session I visited, participants questioned whether this stance was possible. Several wanted to know how mediators handle situations involving injustices. Davis responded that this is a complex question, but in general the mediator has to let go of his or her own ideas and let the parties decide for themselves. The agreements must reflect the parties' sense of justice, not the mediator's. The process builds on each person's individual sense of justice. One trainee asked whether the mediator's role is to make sure the outcome is "fair." Davis answered that this is a very common question and that it points to a gray area between the competing values of letting people make their own decisions and recognizing larger societal values and principles. These are seemingly contradictory and conflicting principles, and there is no easy solution. They have been debated extensively in the mediation field for some time, and they will continue to be a source of controversy in the future.

Searching for Themes. As she listens to the parties, Davis says she is also searching for broad themes—for example, respect, communication, trust, privacy, or the meaning of being a good neighbor. Often supposedly contradictory complaints, such as "My mother never listens to me!" by a son and "He never talks to me!" by a mother, can be merged into the theme of communication. The theme can then be stated in a positive manner by the mediator: "Both mother and son wish to improve communication." Once Davis has grasped the major themes, she presents them to the parties for approval or modification. Once the parties settle on the themes, the agenda is set and the session moves on to a problem-solving stage.

Sustaining Momentum and Morale. Several people at the training session asked what happens when the mediator and the parties reach an impasse, a complex and not readily answered question. Davis says she tries not to use the word *impasse*, which she feels places emphasis on "stuckness." Instead, she encourages new mediators to be relentless analysts, asking questions: what is going on? Why does it appear that motion has stopped? Is the escalation of emotions or withdrawal of the parties a natural stage of negotiation? Have I lost trust? Have the parties lost faith in the process? Why? Is this case inappropriate for mediation?

She credits the work of Phillip Gulliver (1979) with providing "invaluable insights" into the natural stages of negotiation, and she often uses his research to illustrates that mediation sessions move into and out of moments of coordination and antagonism and that these swings are healthy signs of progress. "Some mediators confuse increased antagonism with an impending breakdown of the process," she says. "And, if you see it that way, it may well happen." She also cites Follett's concepts about the continually evolving nature of any set of relationships, including her insight that any analysis of the past is merely a snapshot of what was, not what *is*. "Stay fluid and learn to look for the movement," Davis urges new mediators. "If the parties learn by trying the process that they do not want to agree, and they conclude that they will be better served by other approaches, that is their prerogative. And perhaps that's a successful outcome," she says.

Formulating Integrative Agreements. When asked if the purpose of mediation was to reach compromise agreements, Davis said no. Since she has been reading the work of Mary Parker Follett on the potential for integrative agreements and the pitfalls of compromise, she is less fond of compromises. It seems that both parties lose something. She prefers integrative agreements, by which she means the crafting of solutions with some new features that benefit everyone. The search for an integrative agreement means that people must understand well their own and others' interests. Once they have achieved that level of understanding, they must then tap into their creative abilities. If handled well, this period of a mediation can actually have elements of playfulness and fun, she notes.

Handling Power Imbalances. Davis is acutely sensitive to the difficulty of this issue and the difficulty of discussing it effectively. When one trainee asked, "If one person is getting less than the other, what is the mediator to do?" Davis responded that assessing power imbalances is itself very complex: there are many ways to measure power, and there will always be power imbalances fluctuating between any two people. "But," she continued, "the power issue is incredibly important." The process should make sure that both sides are listened to equally. One can help to equalize parties by giving them equal time and trying to "help them think through what they might gain through mediation or whether they should consider other approaches." Private sessions can give weaker parties more of a chance to talk. Davis emphasizes that if the parties are not forced to go to mediation the difficulties are less. It is important to look at the outcomes over time to make sure they are fair and internally at the process to see if it is fair. However, in some contexts—such as most domestic violence cases, for example—the power imbalances are systemic, and mediation cannot deal with them.

. . . .

These themes are all evident in a mediation case Davis role-played for a 1989 promotional and training videotape. The neighborhood case involved a complaint of harassment lodged by an older woman against a young neighbor she accused of painting graffiti on her door, driving over her lawn and leaving tire tracks, and being rude and noisy in general. The impetus for the complaint was a particularly loud party during which the graffiti and the tire track incidents took place. She had repeatedly called the police to come to the home of the young man, which annoyed him a great deal.

Davis began the process with a session with both parties present in which she introduced herself and the process. She addressed each person by his or her last name and title (Mr., Mrs.) and said that she would listen to each one. She started with the complainant, the older woman. This woman began her story by announcing that she was a widow. She described how the neighborhood was changing, that her friends had moved away, and how she felt a generation gap between herself and this young man. As she described the graffiti and the tire tracks, Davis prompted her to expand on what the incident was and how she felt about it.

I asked Davis what she was thinking during this initial discussion as we watched the videotape together. She said that during this part of a discussion, she is thinking on many levels. She is aware of the nonspeaking person who must listen and has not yet had a chance to speak. She is concerned with the need to develop trust with him and is aware that she cannot allow the discussion with the first person to continue too long. "At this early stage," she said, "I am most concerned with earning the trust of both parties by listening carefully to what each has to say and letting each know I understand both the conflict and the significance of their comments." She looks for areas of agreement and tries to establish trust. Her style is to allow each person to talk without interruption as much as possible.

As the disputants talked, she was alert for positive statements toward the other person and indications of a willingness to communicate. She noted, for example, these statements by the older woman: "I would be happy if I could call him about the noise," and "He seems to be a basically nice person, although I don't know him very well." As each party talked, she also looked for any areas of consensus and points for negotiation. For example, the young man said that he would not mind if the neighbor called him if he is making noise. Davis picked up on this as a possible point of agreement.

Davis does not focus on presenting incidents unless the parties indicate that is a priority. For example, she did not ask the older woman what the graffiti said, deciding that it was discreet in this instance not to; she asked only for the details of the incidents that seemed significant to her. Asking about the substance of the graffiti seemed to her to risk heating up feelings. She decided to stop asking each party to expand on his or her story when she sensed she had a full picture of the individual and collective stories. A clue that people are finished is when she begins to hear the same thing or type of thing over and over.

Davis also considers whether there are any important parties who are not present. This is part of ascertaining the cast of characters. In this case, for example, the young man said that his friends, rather than he, were responsible for the graffiti and the tire tracks.

A key technique in Davis's practice is the use of summaries of each person's story. In this case, after the older woman paused, Davis summarized her story with an introduction, "What I have heard you say is ..." She stated that the woman was disturbed about the noise, the tire tracks, and the graffiti on her door. This technique provides, Davis thinks, "a way of checking to see if I got it and to let them know I am listening." It also lets her fashion a story that makes sense to both parties. People come into mediation with vague ideas about what the problem is and who the cast of characters is, and she helps them construct a story together.

When she turned to the young man, she also asked him to describe what was on his mind. He provided a briefer account of the situation and, although Davis asked for further information, the account remained clearly shorter. While he was presenting his side of the situation, Davis was careful not to accuse him of wrongdoing. He acknowledged that he did have a wild party and that his friends had been disruptive. But he was unhappy that she called the police all the time. Davis concluded this discussion also by summarizing his story and his concerns.

At this point, the summary provides a way to move from the phase of gathering information to a phase of negotiating. The summary here benefits the mediator by allowing her to check that her perception of the situation squares with that of the people—"to see if I have it right"—and helps the mediator conceptualize the situation and humanize it. It is also a benefit to the parties, helping them see the connections between the events. Davis believes that if she can construct a story that both parties accept concerning the incident, it will be possible to reach an agreement and focus on what to do next. They do not have to agree on every point, but Davis generally helps them agree to some kind of simple story that both parties consider accurate.

She decided to hold the first private session with the young man, since she was afraid that he was the more alienated and the less comfortable of the two and that he'd had less time in the public session. She was also sensitive to the fact that he, a young man, was facing two women, as complaining party and mediator. His neighbor was accusing him of illegal behavior, while he was only accusing her of not being a good neighbor. Consequently, Davis concluded that it was most important to build trust with the young man and that the caucus would help her to do that. She was again conscious of not pressuring him to admit to the accusations, particularly since they were illegal actions.

In the private caucus, she began by asking him how long he had lived in the neighborhood (eighteen months) and whether he was planning to stay. She considered this information critical, since if he was planning to move out, the problem clearly would be different. If he was planning to stay, long-term solutions were needed. He said he liked the apartment and the neighborhood and had no plans to leave. He expressed other grievances about the situation, as well as his annoyance about the frequent calls to the police. Once his parents came to visit him, and the neighbor was rude to them. Davis picked up on this as an important issue to discuss with the other side. He acknowledged that the people who came to the party were wild, but claimed that they were not really his friends. He said he was attending Alcoholics Anonymous meetings and trying to get his drinking under control. Using questions, Davis made several oblique suggestions. She asked him what he would do if the neighbor rather than the police had called about the noise. Then she asked again what should be done about the graffiti. He said that he supposed he could repaint the door.

At the end of the private session, Davis asked whether there was anything he would like her to hold back and not tell his neighbor. He said he would like to keep his attendance at AA meetings private. Davis says she prefers this strategy rather than making a blanket promise of confidentiality, because such promises are often difficult to keep. Instead, she asks for specifics that must be held in confidence. (According to the Dorchester model, a mediator can share some things from the private session as long as they are not specifically ruled out. This approach keeps more information in the hands of the mediator.)

Davis began the second private session by asking the older woman several probing questions: "What would you like the neighborhood to be like? How do you think this could be a good neighborhood to live in for both of you?" In her replies, the woman cited the problem as "his friends" and claimed that young people are "different." Davis recognized that the older woman did not want to be afraid. Pursuing the suggestion that the young man would give her his phone number, Davis asked if she would call him first instead of the police if he gave her the number. She readily agreed.

As Davis watches this session on videotape, she notes that at this point she was searching for the concrete things that the woman wanted corrected and, at the same time, was trying to find out what the woman really cared about. Her reason for searching for concrete problems is not that she thinks these points will resolve the problem but that she believes that small acts can produce a broader understanding. When she told the woman that the young man had offered to repaint the graffiti-covered door, the woman sighed. Davis interpreted this sigh as a signal of relief that the young man was willing to take this first step and that the repainting was a symbolic concession.

In the private session with the woman, having presented the young man's offers, Davis then raised the young man's complaint about his neighbor's treatment of his parents with the statement: "You are both concerned about respectful treatment." Then she pointed out that the older couple visiting him, to whom he felt she was rude, were the young man's parents. The older woman was surprised, embarrassed, and apologetic when she learned this. Davis concluded the session by asking whether there was any information she wished held private.

Davis then called both parties back for a final public session. In this brief concluding discussion, Davis summarized the situation, saying that the older woman had spent a great deal of time in the neighborhood and that the young man, though a more recent arrival, also liked the neighborhood and wanted to stay. He would give her his phone number, and she agreed to call him if there was a problem. The older woman was interested in getting to know him better. The woman apologized for the insult to his parents and said that she would call him instead of the police if there were problems with noise—a more personal approach. The young man apologized for the party and his friends. Davis asked what could be done about the door, and the young man offered to repaint it. Then Davis asked who would supply the paint. The older woman offered to provide it. Davis summarized that the young man agreed to paint the door and supply his phone number and the older woman agreed to call about noise. The written agreement, which both signed, repeated this discussion. After they signed the agreement, Davis congratulated both parties, telling them that they had worked hard and were very creative about searching for a solution.

As we viewed this tape together, Davis and I discussed whether the agreement addressed the underlying issues of neighborhood change and generational frictions. She replied that she does not feel that mediation is meant to solve *all* of life's problems, but she thinks an agreement of this kind helps neighbors to work out a few things together. Both parties brought many other problems to the situation—her recent widowhood, his history of drinking—and they lived in a changing neighborhood that left the older woman feeling scared. The issue of neighborhood change is a "contextual" issue, one that must be recognized but may not be changed within the scope of the mediation session unless the parties agree to undertake such a task.

Did this agreement resolve the problem? Davis answers this question with the following interpretation: the woman was a widow, vulnerable, and scared, a person who had recently lost her friends and was living in a changing neighborhood. The party and the incident with the graffiti and the tire tracks frightened her, making her even more afraid. Through mediation, she got to know the young man better, as a person with parents, with a phone number, a person she could talk to. So the neighborhood became a little less scary for her than before, and she now had a way to reach him. This would not change the whole neighborhood, but it showed, in a symbolic way, that the young man was willing to do something for her, and that was important to her. Furthermore, if the case had gone to court, the judge probably would have denied the woman's complaint or, even before that, the clerk would have talked her out of going to trial and simply continued the complaint—a procedure Davis refers to as "clerk's probation." For the young man, this woman was probably a minor irritation, so the improvement for him was relatively minor. His life seemed full with his school, his job, and his friends. On the other hand, he faced a possible court record, which this mediation session eliminated. So, whether or not it resolved the problem, mediation led to a reconceptualization of the problem and, therefore, a kind of solution.

Yet, there is some ambiguity in Davis's position. On the one hand, she argues that the parties themselves are responsible for the story they construct together, the terms of the agreement, the extent to which it addresses root problems, and the people who are included and excluded. It is generally fair if both parties think it is fair. In response to each of my questions, she says that she simply takes what they give her. On the other hand, she also talks about her central role in collaboratively constructing a story: the way she helps parties put the loose pieces together, identify the actors, focus on the issues. She talks about the power a mediator has in summarizing the story and in conveying information back and forth between caucuses.

Respect involves treating each person in his or her own terms, allowing each to define the frame of the problem, not imposing agreements, and being transparent to the parties rather than "stroking" or "tricking" them. Yet this sometimes forces Davis to accept agreements that do not necessarily conform with her own understanding of respectful treatment between the parties themselves. Also, allowing parties a free hand in constructing agreements does not necessarily produce results that conform to her conception of social justice.

· · · · · · ·

The way Albie Davis practices mediation combines liberal legalism, in its insistence on individual freedom of choice, autonomy, tolerance, and equal procedural rights, with grass-roots community organizing, in its concern with people who are, in practice, often denied such forms and measures of equality. As the community mediation movement changes, she seeks to navigate between the sometimes contradictory positions into which this commitment has thrust her. She retains individualism and liberal legalism while allying herself with the interests of those for whom such autonomy and respect have historically been denied in American society. She neither expects community mediation to rebuild communities, nor is she simply interested in providing faster and more efficient services for those who bring their problems to court. But she firmly believes that community

mediation can make a difference, can help to improve the lives of
individuals.

Albie Davis has staked out a distinctive space in the community mediation movement, one that draws on the dominant ideological themes of American culture—individualism and self-
reliance—but also espouses a grass-roots source of authority for
mediation practice. Other branches of the movement have
become more concerned with providing better dispute resolution
services or enhancing personal growth. Consequently, she focuses
on the empowerment of the individual in mediation, not on the
conversion of interpersonal problems into political ones. Her
work seeks to promote what has been labeled the personal
growth, rather than the community empowerment, ideological
project of the ADR movement (Harrington and Merry, 1988).

The grass-roots mediation that Albie Davis practices and promotes is different from mediation in many other domains. The
differences lie primarily in philosophy rather than in the details
of technique, however. Unlike many other mediators, Davis sees
the process as a form of community empowerment and as a politics of respecting the authenticity of every person. This orientation reflects her background in community organizing.

But do community organizing and community mediation go
together? Community organizing tends to involve powerful advocacy and confrontation; community mediation requires a more
accepting stance. As a recent *Negotiation Journal* article (Barsky,
1993) points out, obvious and often impossible strains persist
between mediators and advocates; some have left mediation
while others, like Davis, try to balance activism and mediation,
seeking to retain some of its philosophy in the increasingly institutionalized world of contemporary ADR.

Perhaps Davis answers this question in her assertion that she
is not a conflict avoider or even a compromiser. Instead, she says,
she is a forceful person with some collaborative skills who, as in
her community organizing days, is still willing to be a party to a

conflict and to do battle over an issue, and there are many such issues in her field.

Sally Engle Merry

Note

I am grateful to Deborah Kolb and Austin Sarat for their careful reading of the manuscript, as well as to other members of the research team who offered insightful help throughout the writing of the profile. I am particularly appreciative of Albie Davis's openness, cooperation, and willingness to share her knowledge of mediation with me.

References

Barsky, A. E. (1993). When advocates and mediators negotiate. *Negotiation Journal, 9*, 115–122.

Davis, A. M. (1986). *Community mediation in Massachusetts: A decade of development, 1975–1985.* Salem, Mass.: Massachusetts District Court.

Davis, A. M. (1989). The logic behind the magic of mediation. *Negotiation Journal, 5*, 17–24.

Gulliver, P. (1979). *Disputes and negotiations: A cross-cultural perspective.* New York: Academic Press.

Harrington, C., and Merry, S. E. (1988). Ideological production and the making of community mediation. *Law and Society Review, 22*, 709–737.

Lukas, J. A. (1985). *Common ground.* New York: Knopf.

"*Being able to create options and float them as you go along, creating options, and helping parties save face are major skills of the mediator.*"

—Eric Green

7

. . . .

Eric Green
Finding Alternatives to Litigation
in Business Disputes

Entering into mediation is something that lawyers do, often long after litigation has begun and much time and money has been spent. Sometimes it is they who have convinced their clients that mediation offers a nonbinding chance to see what they can get, and a way to reduce the uncertainty and risks of a trial and possible appeal. Sometimes it is the judge who pressures the lawyers to try mediation, often because the case is likely to consume numerous trial days and is in all likelihood to be appealed by the losing side no matter what its outcome. Even ten years ago, the use of mediation as an option in business disputes barely existed.

Eric Green graduated in 1972 from Harvard Law School, where he was an executive editor of the *Law Review*. He clerked for Judge Benjamin Kaplan in Boston and then became a litigator with Munger, Tolles, & Olson in Los Angeles for three years. It was during his tenure as a corporate litigator that he became involved in corporate mediation. As Green tells the story, he was working on the *Telecredit Inc. v. TRW* patent infringement case when the discovery process became financially and personally onerous for all the parties. When relations had become so acrimonious that junior lawyers and paralegals researching documents in opposing counsels' offices were no longer even allowed coffee from the firms' coffee pots, lawyers calculated that hundreds of thousands of dollars had been spent by each side to prepare for a complex trial involving great uncertainty for everyone.

Agreeing there had to be a better way, they decided to create a nonbinding "information exchange" that would take place in front of high-level corporate management and a neutral adviser to be paid by both sides. The process was designed to overcome the parties' objections to arbitration, including arbitration's tendency toward compromise, the parties' lack of control over the outcome, the complexity of the case in relation to the type of case arbitration is usually used to resolve, and the unsettled question of whether an arbitrated decision would be enforceable in a patent case such as this.

The information exchange was completely private—that is, completely outside the judicial system. Each side's lawyers presented the case in the presence of the chief executive officers of both companies, and a former judge served as the neutral adviser. Each then had time to respond to the other's initial presentation. Following those presentations, which took only two days, the chief executive officers of both companies met. Based on what they had heard and on their business judgments, they reached a settlement in principle within one hour.

The defendant, TRW, agreed to pay Telecredit for a license, with credits to be granted based on TRW's legal fees in the case, which exactly matched the license figure. One side estimated that the procedure, which cost about $25,000, had saved them more than $1 million in lawyers' fees that would have been incurred through trial. The agreement, Green notes, marked the end of a long, bitter, expensive, and uncertain lawsuit and the significant beginning of an alternative dispute resolution process that was dubbed a "mini-trial" by the *New York Times*.

Mini-trial is a misnomer, however, because the process is not a trial but a form of mediation in which the parties themselves are the decision makers. While the attorneys still make the presentations, it is the executives or principals who decide when and how to settle and for how much. In terms of dynamics, the process of litigation has been transformed into a business decision. Rather than playing out the arguments of questions of law and fact, liability, and damages lawyer to lawyer and lawyers to judge, the situation is transformed into a cost-benefit business decision judged by the executives themselves.

Green says that one of the keys to the successful use of his alternative dispute resolution (ADR) practice is that "attorneys and parties have to prepare just enough to make economic decisions in a minimal-risk setting." Among its advantages, ADR can facilitate decisions that courts are powerless to hand down and keep future business relationships intact by reorienting them in a nonadversarial way.

As Green sees it, "Some of the biggest problems in the use of ADR are that cases settle too late, take too long to settle, and settle after too many dollars have been spent. Joint gains are often left on the table." This latter remark refers to the work of negotiation theorist Howard Raiffa of Harvard Business School, who emphasizes the aspect of efficiency in negotiations and the possibility of avoiding waste and minimally acceptable outcomes by analyzing the array of possibly acceptable decisions and consciously maximizing joint gains.

A full-time law professor at Boston University Law School since 1977, Green currently teaches evidence, dispute resolution, and professional responsibility, and chairs the school's placement committee. He has co-written an evidence casebook and is co-author of *Dispute Resolution*, the first dispute resolution textbook for law students. Wearing another hat, he is a principal and founder of Endispute, Inc., a dispute resolution consulting firm with offices in five cities. Begun in 1981 with his old classmate and law firm colleague Jonathan Marks, Endispute was initially a small business venture of two successful litigators-turned-mediators and legal management consultants. For Green, what began as

a part-time avocation assisting attorneys with difficult and interesting cases has grown into a firm that now demands all of his
nonacademic time and ensures that his average work week, at
least during the academic year, exceeds seventy hours. Green
headed up the private disputes section of the firm as senior vice
president, until it outgrew his availability, and he had input on
virtually every major case that passed through the office.

By early 1988, when I began profiling Green, I had known
him for several years as a colleague and had worked with him on
a number of cases as a mediator. As someone brought into the
Endispute firm by him, I was initially hesitant even to try to
assume the stance of observer. But, as it turned out, the questions
and perspectives of my fellow researchers challenged me to try to
balance distance and stance while maintaining close, firsthand
observation of Green, whose office was two doors from mine. I
saw him almost daily as a fellow colleague and, in the more formal research sense, observed him for more than 150 hours. I am
aware that but for the fact that we were in the same organization,
he would have been impossible to interview extensively. I was
able to ask him questions between mediation sessions, over coffee
or lunch, or between his conversations with clients on his car
phone while going to and from meetings.

Green is a man in almost perpetual motion. Even seated at a
desk, he is at the eye of a hurricane. There is a continual swirl of
clients, two secretaries, phone calls, and, most noticeably, seemingly unmanaged and precarious stacks of paper. The lawyer's fat
accordion files, correspondence, and thick piles of phone messages cover his desk, line the floor along the walls, and spill over
onto his couch, creating an obstacle course. He is constantly
interrupted by calls and people. He is almost always affable, but
harassed, behind schedule, intensely preoccupied with a series of
projects long overdue, and pressed by the cases at hand.

When asked why he personally maintains so much control
over every detail of his cases, Green says that, like any private-

practice lawyer, he is "client driven and obsessed with client satisfaction." What distinguishes him from the average private lawyer, though, is that the people he thinks of as his primary clients are not just the parties themselves but also the lawyers representing them and the judges dealing with them. The lawyers and judges are the chief sources of cases referred to him and to Endispute. Even though the parties pay, their cases are often referred to by the name of the judge or attorney who has sent them over—"Judge X's case," he will call one, or a "construction case from Attorney Y." Green is a lawyer's lawyer, with his main source of repeat clients the professionals in charge of the case. It is the judges or attorneys who will think of Green the next time a certain type of case comes around.

One such real estate/construction lawyer uses only Green as a mediator and cites Green's expertise in such cases. "These cases," this attorney says, "often involve threshold questions about whether there is liability and, if so, what the damages are. Usually an insurance policy is where the money to pay for the claim will come from. Green knows that you probably don't want the insurer there, because the strongest claims may well be outside the limits of the policy. He stays in touch with the insurer by phone and keeps him informed, gets his authorization to settle up to a certain limit, but keeps him out of the actual sessions." In other words, Green is able to be inclusive and yet have at the table only the parties who will move his process forward.

Green markets his services as a way of reducing the time, energy, and dollar costs of litigation through hand-tailored dispute resolution processes. Writing to the attorneys involved in a trademark litigation to try to break through the impasse that seems to have developed over the idea of voluntary mediation of the dispute, Green said, "Based on my private conversations with each side and my experience in these matters, it is my belief that a favorable environment for mediation exists at this time, and that there is a readiness to consider all resolution options. I am satisfied that there is a sufficient likelihood of success to make the effort worthwhile. . . . The parties seem to be blocked from taking this step, perhaps by positions and beliefs that flow from prior failed settlement efforts."

In this dispute, one party was demanding a major concession from the other as a precondition to mediation. The other side refused, prior to what it saw as a comprehensive negotiation process that might well include discussions over whether, and under what conditions, it would meet such a condition. The result was a stalemate.

"Based on my experience in resolving intercorporate disputes, including disputes over intellectual property, my suggestion is that both sides engage in a quick, voluntary, and risk-free mediation without any preconditions," Green wrote to the attorney involved.

> So long as a careful effort has been made to determine that a favorable environment exists for mediation (such as by identifying the needs, interests, demands, and attitudes of both sides and determining that there is a substantial possibility of reaching a mutually acceptable accommodation through good-faith bargaining), it is generally counterproductive for the parties to maneuver for advantage prior to the mediation by insisting on concessions on key bargaining issues as preconditions to mediation. Requiring explicit concessions in advance of mediation sometimes has the effect of creating an impasse where one would not otherwise exist. No one wants to start the game on their own twenty-yard line.
>
> The kind of mediation I have in mind would involve the four of you . . . and take less than a day to complete. Since the case is fully discovered, the mediation could be held without delay. The case would

either be resolved quickly, or you would know that you were headed to trial in June. Both the defendant's product name and the plaintiff's trademark would be the subjects of mediation, and the parties would come to the mediation prepared to listen, negotiate, and discuss modification of the defendant's name and the validity or invalidity of the plaintiff's mark and related issues. Preparation steps to maximize the chances of success would be completed by counsel.

In his role as mediator, Green gathers information in a series of "snapshots" from lawyers and sometimes judges even before the parties have committed themselves to the process. He then composes his own early assessment of prospects for settlement, including issues and values. Dealing directly with both the attorneys and the parties themselves, he gets a more complete picture of the parties' chief concerns and particular interests in settling the dispute. Unlike the adversarial dynamics of litigation, Green is bent right from the beginning on getting the parties to look to the future and resolve the case at the lowest cost. He is willing to persuade the parties to come to the table, and, once there, a priority for him is to find out whether there are aspects of the case that his legal information has not given him. These surprises may range from learning that there are very high attorneys' fees accrued (which may make achieving a reasonable settlement difficult) or that there are some face-saving issues of reputation that will need to be addressed if any agreement is to be reached.

A typical case involves an independent sales representative for a manufacturer, who is suing his former employer, the manufacturer, for breach of contract and willful infliction of emotional distress. The case has been sent to Green by a federal judge, who says that, after two settlement meetings, the parties are still considerably far apart.

The parties appear to be at the point where the company would offer $350,000, while the plaintiff/salesman's attorney has mentioned $750,000 during the settlement conference. The salesman has alleged damages as high as $7 million. The judge tells Green that "heavy discovery" has already been done. The case cannot be calendared for trial for three months, but a firm trial date can be set then if it will create the right incentives to encourage the defendant to settle. It is the judge's understanding that the plaintiff is hurting for cash. An expensive trial in three months, with the prospect of an appeal by the losing party (which in all likelihood will take another year), will result in the plaintiff losing his house. The plaintiff has strong incentives to settle. Finally, the judge notes that the plaintiff's attorney, a bright junior partner in a big firm, seems very invested in the case and has spent a lot of time on it.

Armed with this information, Green puts in calls to both the plaintiff's and defendant's attorneys. He explains that he is call-ing at the suggestion of the judge, who thought that he might be able to help, and that the case might profit by some mediation. Both sides are receptive, and an early-morning meeting is arranged for the next day at the plaintiff's law firm.

Green says the third-party neutral "adds knowledge, commu-nication, and belief that a settlement is possible to help resolve a dispute. Basically, the third party is a new force in a dispute who works to help the parties." By taking some of the heat the parties might otherwise project at each other and generally serving as another focus for the parties, he adds, the third-party neutral can also serve as a scapegoat or pest-advocate for settlement.

"Being able to create options and float them fast as you go along, creating options, and helping parties save face are major skills of the mediator," he says.

Sometimes having one lawyer call the other to float the idea of mediation is enough to get the parties to the table. If the relationship between the lawyers is poor, however, Green prefers to call both attorneys himself.

Green thinks that "until you have your foot firmly in the door, the mediator should not lay out too much of the process." The risk of the process for the parties is some time plus a fee. Green's list of the important factors in determining the success of mediation includes information transfer, the involvement of people who are above the fray and have the authority to settle, and good timing. Finally, Green says statutes such as the Massachusetts Mediator's Confidentiality Statute help to lay the ground rules and context for mediation. He always has the parties sign a mediation agreement before they begin the process. For Green, mediation is a separate, second chance to resolve a dispute. Green says that there are only two difficult, mysterious, and intangible "arts" in mediating: "one, getting the parties to the table and two, getting the rabbit out of the hat—finding the solution to an impasse."

At 8:15 the next morning, the attorneys meet with Green in a large conference room overlooking Boston Harbor. His mediation of this case, Green tells them, will "probably require more quantified analysis, given all the discovery that has taken place to date, than a more open, creative mediation approach." The latter requires somewhat less preparation and can often be used successfully where discovery has not begun, but as Green is noting, the parties here are way past that point.

In presenting things this way, Green is taking a bow to the expertise and hard work of the lawyers. He is letting them know that they are not being displaced but rather are integral to the success of the process. Since he has never worked with the attorneys before, he also lays out how he works. The cases are not "run through a mill" but dealt with in a hand-tailored manner, each unique from all others. These are elite lawyers, and Green, a former elite litigator himself, clearly understands their concerns.

While some who observe and analyze the ADR movement would say that the idea that practitioners in the movement have "invented" new processes is an exaggeration of their originality and an expression of ego, no one seems to doubt that Eric Green has succeeded in marketing alternative dispute resolution techniques to a conservative, litigation-minded, turf- and fees-protecting part of the population (that is, trial attorneys) more effectively than many competitors.

The quantified analysis approach to mediation Green proposes will allow each party's complete theory of the case to be presented. He estimates that a personally designed "mini-trial" will take ten to twelve hours, at the end of which the parties will know whether a settlement is possible. There will be "no long, drawn-out process, and nothing that will delay the parties' moving to trial," he says. Green notes that the judge will assign a firm trial date for April and will brook no delays should trial be necessary.

After outlining how the mini-trial process might work, Green allows for a presentation by the lead attorneys on their approaches to the case, and then a scheduling of telephone conferences and face-to-face meetings to prepare for the mini-trial.

Green explains that after this initial face-to-face meeting, he will speak with the parties privately by telephone to determine their questions, issues, and the ranges that could make settlement possible. Approximately two weeks from now, a one-and-a-half-day mini-trial will take place. Between now and then, he will work on questions of law and fact with counsel and clients for each side separately.

He outlines the format of the mini-trial for the attorneys: "Each side will get to present its case for up to one-and-one-half hours. After a short break, each side will get a half-hour rebuttal time, to be followed by a half-hour question period, during which time both parties can ask questions of each other. After another break, I will meet with each side privately and then allot up to four hours or so for parties to talk with me or each other, as needed. If necessary, the session could continue into the next day. If no agreement is reached by then, I will report to the judge that the parties will proceed to trial." Green adds that confidentiality will be absolutely respected and that he will be perfectly frank with the parties about the possibilities of settlement so as not to waste anyone's time, especially if preparation for trial is needed.

The push for unembroiled, senior decision makers who can look at the case in business terms, rather than being sidetracked by the rococo details of litigation moves, is perhaps the crucial element of the mini-trial. Changing a battle to a problem-solving, cost-benefit, and risk analysis process requires participants with fresh eyes. In this case, hearing each side's story as relayed by the attorney in charge, Green feels the only hope for settlement is a fresh, clear-eyed look.

The plaintiff's attorney outlines the case as he sees it, presenting both the facts and the theory of law he has prepared to use at trial. The defendant's lawyer then responds with his version of the events, noting several pivotal points on which his client and the plaintiff differ. During these presentations, Green listens, occasionally asking, "What do you think your chances of prevailing on that will be?" or "What cases are you relying on there?"

When the presentations are over, Green asks each attorney to send him those documents they think are key to the case. When one says his notebooks run to six feet lined up against the wall, Green says he does not want to review six feet of documents. "I'd like the key three to six documents that support your case. I'll review both sides' documents and then we'll talk about them before your mini-trial presentations," he offers.

Green asks the attorneys to discuss their clients' availability and to get back to him that afternoon. Since the CEO of the manufacturing company will be coming from overseas, Green offers to meet with him on the morning of the mini-trial. Prior to that, he will meet with the attorney and the plaintiff and

probably will be speaking with both attorneys several times
between now and then, he says. The parties agree on his fee and
that they will split it. Contracts dealing with the confidentiality
and fee agreements will be sent out to the attorneys for their sig-
nature within the day.

Green then speaks privately with each side, giving each attorney the chance to say anything in confidence he has not wished
to say in front of the other. The defendant's counsel say that they
are worried about the plaintiff counsel's "lack of judgment
and . . . his excess investment in the case." Questioned further,
they explain it is their understanding that the fees for the counsel
services might be bordering on $150,000 and that this would, in
turn, drive the settlement costs beyond what the defense could
consider.

Green then meets with the plaintiff's counsel and confirms
the fears of the defense counsel regarding the time already spent.
He realizes that getting another senior player in on their side
would be important. "This young partner might well be too
invested in the case to have a clear perspective on its worth. He
may be identifying too much with his client's interests and not
have enough distance to judge what a good settlement would be,"
he explains. He urges the attorney to consider bringing to the
mini-trial a senior partner who can assist him by offering another
perspective on the value of settlement. He explained again that
one of the most important aspects of a mini-trial is for the principals to hear and judge the case from a business point of view, not
just a legal one. The plaintiff is an independent sales representative, without any senior people to help him think about the business aspects of settlement, unlike the situation on the defense
side, where the CEO has remained relatively above the fray.

The plaintiff's counsel makes clear that whatever happens, his
chief concern is to settle as soon as possible, since his client has
had no income for over six months. Green now has it from the
judge, the defense counsel, and his own observations that the

junior partner might really be too intent on the idea of "winning big" in litigation to help his client reach a good settlement. Having agreed with the plaintiff's lawyer that they will speak that afternoon, Green rushes off to teach his class.

Later that day, Green prepares a memo outlining some incentives for a defendant to settle in a timely fashion. "Time is often an important factor in settling disputes. Usually, time favors one side more often than the other—generally, the party with the stakes. Most often, this is the defendant. A common question posed by the stakeholders contemplating ADR is why they should want to settle more quickly than they would otherwise settle if the case were left to traditional processes."

There are a variety of reasons for parties to choose ADR to resolve their dispute, depending on the individual situation and circumstances, as Green points out:

- Law or standards may be changing adversely for the defendant.
- Evidence may be disappearing because witnesses are dying or disappearing, or documents are becoming difficult or impossible to locate.
- Damages may be accumulating (that is, interest may exceed the original investment value, medical condition of the plaintiff may deteriorate, or wastes may be becoming more toxic or more difficult to clean up).
- Issues of tactical advantage may arise (such as in a case where the opponent is less prepared and knowledgeable about the case than the defendant now is).
- Continuation of the dispute may be causing bad public relations for a company.
- The dispute may be casting a shadow on business marketing or new product development, mergers, and acquisitions or causing a problem with disclosure requirements.
- Litigation is expensive.

- The possibility surfaces of getting a discount now because of factors affecting the plaintiff's need for settlement.
- Litigation may be creating fatigue or boredom.
- Sometimes, ADR is simply the right thing to do.

· · · · · · ·

Several days later, a five-hour meeting takes place, this time with the plaintiff and his attorney. The first part is taken up with the salesman/plaintiff presenting his version of the facts. He describes his current emotional and financial situation and prospects (or lack thereof) for employment.

He says that just after he changed jobs within the company and was moving his family halfway across the country—literally while they were driving to their new location—he learned that his company had acquired a major competitor firm in his new region. He was assured by his boss, a senior vice president, that he should continue east to Massachusetts. Over the course of six months, the "potential" that he had seen in the new sales territory vanished. His predecessor in the new territory was taking clients with him, and the firm with which his had merged had an in-house sales force rather than his firm's independent sales force.

Over time, despite initial assurances from the firm that all would be well and lucrative for him as a salesman, it became evident that the two sales forces were in competition and that, in the long run, it would be cheaper for the firm to convert most sales forces to in-house, salaried staff rather than independent salesmen like himself who were paid on a percentage commission basis. He painted himself as an effective salesman caught in a difficult situation.

Six months after the acquisition, his firm made an offer to terminate his contract. During a ten-day period, he negotiated the terms of this agreement by phone and letter, with the offer eventually tripling from $345,000 to over $1 million. The final offer was made by telephone, and, according to the plaintiff, he verbally accepted it and asked for interest on the money, which would be paid in stages. The company then took the position that its offer had, in effect, been rejected when the plaintiff attempted to change its terms by asking for interest payments, and took the offer off the table.

Green listens to the story and says, "I know how you feel, and I sympathize with you completely. Let's see how we can make you whole again. I agree you may never be the same. My advice would be to drop the claim for 'willful infliction of emotional distress.' In my opinion, that claim could be extremely messy. The defense will bring in details about your and your wife's psychological counseling, marital problems, and sex life. It can be invasive and damaging. My interest is in helping you put this behind you, so you can get on with your life."

The language of "making you whole" and "not opening the door" to certain legal issues is legal language that signals the attorney about what Green thinks should be pursued and what will be fruitless and dangerous to the plaintiff's case. He is letting the plaintiff know that while he is empathetic to what has happened, he is not here to right all the wrongs of the past. He agrees that the plaintiff "will never be the same." That is not his job; his job is to help get the parties looking forward and moving toward the future.

At times, Green shows skepticism and even annoyance with the high numbers the plaintiff continues to float. When he seems stuck around the $1 million-plus-interest figure, Green asks, "Do you really think a court would award you damages of that order? My expectation is that a court will want to know how you will mitigate. You're a young man. Surely you don't expect the court to pay your expected wages for the next twenty-five years." Here he is beginning to set the stage for getting the plaintiff to stand in the defendant's shoes, to imagine what might be the defendant's considerations in making an offer. The $7 million demand in the complaint is never even discussed at the table.

Green then suggests that he, the plaintiff, and the plaintiff's attorney work through the scenario of preparing for trial together. They agree, and he begins by summing up the issues on which it will be necessary to prevail. They concur quickly and then move on to the question of damages and how those are to be assessed.

It is at this point that Green uses "litigation decision analysis" to help calculate what he believes is the accurate settlement range. By this he means not the pie-in-the-sky amount of money that the plaintiff would like or his attorney would like to get for him, but rather the point at which settlement is worth more than the risks of litigation.

He begins by getting the parties to calculate the costs to date, the so-called "sunk" costs of the attorneys. They estimate $150,000 (and estimate the defense has probably spent $50,000 so far). They then spend substantial time discussing the likelihood of their prevailing at the highest settlement discussed, $1 million, and decide that the chances are fifty-fifty. The final part of the calculation involves estimating what their legal costs will be through trial, about $50,000. From this they calculate:

$$\begin{array}{l} \$500,000 \ (\$1,000,000 \times 0.50) \\ \underline{-\ 50,000} \ (\text{further legal costs}) \\ 450,000 \\ \underline{+150,000} \ (\text{legal costs thus far}) \\ \$600,000 \end{array}$$

From a litigation decision analysis perspective, any settlement that equals or betters this figure would be better than the risks of going to trial.

This is a business, cost-benefit perspective on litigation. Although it is everyday stuff for senior executives, Green knows that initially it is a very foreign way of thinking for attorneys, who have been trained in the fine details. The idea of reducing their legal arguments to weak and strong issues at trial is second nature, but going further and making rough estimates of percentages and calculating those out is foreign.

Green tells both sides privately that, in his opinion, $600,000—not the $750,000 settlement figure or the $7 million demand—is the settlement value of the case. The other figures are drawn from the air, while the former represents a sum that would compensate without the downside risk of losing in litigation. He reminds the parties that if litigated, the outcome would almost certainly be appealed, which would take another year; by then the plaintiff will have lost his house, and he and his family will no doubt have suffered further psychological stress.

He then moves the parties back to a discussion of what they have agreed are the three key questions that could be the subject of litigation or mediation: Was the contract terminable at will or not? Was there willful infliction of emotional distress? And, in the event that there is liability, what is the measure of damages?

The plaintiff claims that the contract was not terminable at will, but rather that as an independent representative with the exclusive right to sell the company's product within a geographic region, he has a contract for life. The defendant corporation has sought a declaratory judgment that the contract was at will and therefore terminable or, alternatively, that the plaintiff's termination was for cause. They review the case law together and discuss what will need to be prepared for the mini-trial to address these issues.

Before adjourning for the day, Green asks how the lawyer is progressing with finding a senior attorney to attend the mini-trial. He emphasizes that this person will need to have the confidence of the plaintiff to help reach a settlement, just as the CEO from the other side, who would be coming from abroad, had authority from his corporate board.

. . . .

The next day, Green speaks by conference call with the defense counsel in California and Boston. They paint a different picture of the plaintiff, his work history, and the contract negotiations. From the defendant's point of view, the plaintiff was only a fair-to-middling salesman who had only gotten the job because the first- and second-choice candidates had not panned out. The defendants claim they had no idea that a competitor company would become available when the plaintiff was hired and that all the negotiations to acquire it had occurred precipitously, over a three-week period.

As to the history of settlement offers, these had been presented by the business vice president of the company, with the overseas director being informed only after the offers were made. When the number reached $1 million, the director "felt he had to involve the board because the numbers were getting so high." In retrospect, it was their view that the "American vice president had exceeded his authority."

One attorney says that after the offers had gotten "out of hand," the overseas director came over to try to wrap up the negotiation himself. With the authority of the board, the attorney says, he negotiated directly with the plaintiff at a September 15 session and presented a final, take-it-or-leave-it deal calling for payments over three years of 6 percent in the first year, 5 percent in the second year, and 4 percent in the third year of the two merged U.S. companies' gross revenues for the plaintiff's New England region.

According to them, the plaintiff did not respond at the time but called the director three days later to say he wished to accept the offer. The defendant, however, contends that the offer was terminated when the plaintiff left the meeting without accepting it. Following this telephone conversation, the plaintiff was sent a letter terminating his contract for failure to meet his sales quota.

After the conference call is over, Green says he feels "quite certain that this idea of a termination-for-cause contract had never been the company's intention until after the September 15 meeting." Presuming this is true, this development is damaging to the defense's case because a jury might see this action as a retaliatory one, not as one based on the merits of the salesman's performance.

Over the next several days, Green talks with attorneys for each side, asking questions about how they see the strengths and weaknesses of their case at trial. In these private conversations he asks questions that convey his own views on aspects of the case— for example, "Do you *really* think the court will exclude that evidence? I disagree."

He reviews the documents he has requested and questions each side on the inconsistencies in the other's stories, sometimes indirectly. Among the documents he reviews are the complaint and answer, specific cites and relevant cases, the employment contract in question, and "smoking gun" internal memos for business plans that alluded to how the two companies' merger would be managed.

The smoking gun documents are ones that the defendant's attorney has claimed will not be admitted into evidence; the plaintiff's attorney has argued that they will be admitted and will be damaging to the defense's contention that there was no intent to handle parts of the merger in certain ways. Green thinks that the documents can get in at trial under an evidentiary exception, and, prior to the mini-trial, he gives both sides his opinion.

· · · · · · ·

At 8 A.M. on the day of the mini-trial, Green meets for two hours with the manufacturing corporation's president, whom he has not met before, and with his three attorneys. He goes over much of the material again and gets the CEO's version of the facts directly.

During a break while the parties are caucusing, Green tells me that he thinks the settlement range is now more like $500,000 to $600,000 based on the "series of snapshots" he now has. He believes that there is liability on the part of the company for breach of contract and in the way they attempted to terminate the plaintiff's contract as a retaliatory gesture. He believes that the overseas holding company's executives and the American executives in their subsidiary failed to communicate and keep each other informed during the period when the offers were being made. He reiterates that this is a case that should settle. Shortly after noon, the mini-trial begins with all the parties present. It goes nonstop until after 1 A.M.

As laid out by Green at the initial meeting, lawyers for each side present their case with the plaintiff and the overseas CEO present. The plaintiff's counsel has brought along a senior partner from the firm as a "reality tester" and business decision maker. Green, in an aside, tells me that the choice is a bit of luck. The senior partner, who is the junior partner's mentor, is one of Boston's best-known, tremendously successful litigators, and as a senior partner is also a successful businessman.

Both sides make their presentations, and then each has an additional thirty to forty-five minutes to ask questions. A short break follows. There have been no surprises in the presentations. The parties are each put in separate conference rooms, and Green begins meeting with each, shuttling back and forth between the two rooms. Although it is now dinner time, he does not "release" one side for dinner while he is talking to the other.

Green begins to press hard on each side. He tells the defendant that the judge will calendar the case as soon as possible if it is not settled, and he should know that the judge has no desire to hear this case. He says, "It was your corporation's responsibility to live up to its moral obligations." To the plaintiff, who is still demanding more than the $600,000 that the litigation decision analysis had reached, Green is terse: "How greedy can you get? . . . I know you're hurting, but what good does it do you?" To the defendant, who expresses a concern about setting precedent for other sales representatives' claims, Green says that the settlement can include an agreement to keep the terms confidential.

Green presses the parties toward settlement. He is selective about what he reveals at what point in the process, trying to present as offers that show progress even what he knows is still unacceptable to the other side. When he brings an offer of $500,000 from the defendant to the plaintiff, he knows it is too low. He works with the plaintiff's counsel to structure a counterproposal of $550,000 that, from a tax point of view regarding tort settlements, is worth more than the $600,000 Green thinks the plaintiff will need to close the deal.

When he returns to the defendant and explains that he thinks he can get an agreement at $550,000, the defendant resists. Green shows real emotion for the first time, saying, "Hours ago in this room, $550,000 was not out of the question. What happened?" The defendant wishes to structure the deal around a percentage of gross revenues so that the plaintiff will assume some risk. If the business does well, the plaintiff will do well; but if it does not, he will get less. The defendant does not think the plaintiff should get everything so easily.

Green takes the percentage concept back to the plaintiff, and the plaintiff resists. He needs cash in hand to pay his mortgage, other debts, and current living expenses while he works out what to do with his life.

It is now 11 P.M., and plaintiff and counsel are suggesting that they break and start the next day. Green says he wants to finish tonight. In confidence, Green says, "I know this case ought to settle, but I don't know whether it will. I want to keep the heat on and settle tonight, while all the details are clear and on the table. If they break until morning, the parties will lose momen-tum. Their desire to go home may be the fuel needed for final settlement."

Moving between the two rooms, Green reminds each party of the downside of going to trial. To the plaintiff, he says, "The jury will find the idea of a contract for life incredible. You have a duty to mitigate." To the defendant, he presses his view that "the jury can find you acted in bad faith, bringing a sales representative east and then trying to dump him."

After a private caucus, the defendant offers $550,000 to be paid in three payments over two years, the first payment to be paid in thirty days. Green delivers the offer to the plaintiff, who accepts.

The parties are now brought together for the first time in seven hours, and a handwritten draft agreement is drawn up and signed. Each party receives a photocopy, and the lawyers agree to speak the next day about final draft language that will be drawn up by the defendant's lawyer. Any problems will be mediated by Green.

Among the terms, the plaintiff promises not to compete in old or new sales areas and agrees that this settlement extinguishes all claims he may have against the company. He further agrees to keep the settlement private. Any disputes on the implementation of the agreement will be arbitrated by Green.

· · · · · · ·

It is 1 A.M., sixteen hours after the first meeting began. The parties shake hands and prepare to leave. Everyone is quiet. In the lobby of the building, the plaintiff offers Green a ride to where his car is parked. Green asks the plaintiff during the ride what has puzzled him all along: why did he not accept the better offers early on?

The plaintiff says that since the company had more than tripled its offer over a ten-day period during the negotiations, he saw no reason to stop and was surprised when the rug was pulled out. "Wouldn't you play it out to see how much you could get?" he asks. He also tells Green that it was the senior partner, brought in to add a business-decision dimension to settlement offers, who advised him and the junior partner to "settle the case for $550,000 if you can get it." "Otherwise," the plaintiff says, he feels "sure that my lawyer would have advised me not to accept."

Green says he is certain that "having the senior partner act as a principal, as business executives do in mini-trials, was the key to making the process a success." Despite Green's exercise in litigation decision analysis with the plaintiff and the rational process of mapping out alternatives and risk factors, it seems that it was the leadership of the senior partner and mentor of the junior partner who convinced him and the plaintiff that $550,000 was "a good deal." Without Green's getting the plaintiff and his counsel out of the "win big" and "grave wrong" mentality of legal arguments, this case could be going to trial. Green says that, in his opinion, the single most important factor in getting agreement was the senior partner's valuation of the worth of the case after he had heard both sides' presentations.

Green has thought from the outset that it was in the junior partner's interest to get his client to settle and not take any further risks at trial. Green feels that the senior partner, with his trial experience, knew the risks involved and the problems of appeal. Not least, he was aware that the junior partner had probably over-valued this case and run up legal fees working on the "win big" theory for trial, rather than pursuing the less risky strategy of settlement. His ability to "look at the big picture" has gotten them reoriented toward settling things and "getting on with it."

• • • • • • •

Green is most often hired as the privately retained neutral by all the parties to a well-contained dispute or as a consultant to one party in a massive dispute involving many parties. In the past, even when his role was limited to advising one party behind the scenes, he was able to help minimize transaction costs, rationalize compensation payments, and limit their exposure to related cases. In what he calls decreasing level of effectiveness but increasing ease of entry, some of the different dispute resolution roles that Green has played in settling cases are as follows.

First, Green has served as a court-appointed settlement special master in federal court asbestos cases in Ohio, Connecticut, and Massachusetts, and also in state court in Massachusetts. In Ohio, he designed and mediated acceptance among plaintiffs' counsel and many defense counsels of a case management plan and case evaluation and apportionment process. This plan was used to settle every asbestos case filed in the Ohio court without trial and with substantial bottom-line savings for all parties. He describes his role in Ohio as an "ADR process designer and mediator with clout."

In Massachusetts, some six years later, the climate for asbestos litigation had changed drastically. Many defendants were now bankrupt, and increasing numbers of plaintiffs' claims were being filed. Green acknowledges that this is "a tougher climate to get settlements in" and that the success at trial by defense counsel in Massachusetts has required him to play a lighter hand in mediating than he was able to have in Ohio. At this time, he says, "there is no such thing as objective value in an asbestos case. A case is worth what the plaintiff's lawyer can get for it, and what the defendant's lawyer is willing to give."

To date, in the work that Green and other mediators have done in this area, one of the keys to settlement has been reaching lump-sum agreements that the plaintiff's firm may take and allocate among the plaintiffs as he or she sees fit. This raises the ethical question of who is the best person to allocate who shares among plaintiffs in a clustered, lump-sum settlement. Is it the court or a special master? In some situations, it is the plaintiff's lawyer with approval by Green.

The judge has utter confidence in him and has said he is the only one "indispensable to this litigation," but the changing circumstances and future assets available for settlement have diminished to the point where comparably ill plaintiffs are getting a small percentage of what plaintiffs with the same level of illness got several years ago. This is part of the big, national picture of which Green's mediation is a small part.

Second, Green's role as private mediator is the one he is most frequently asked to play. As shown in the employment termination dispute described in this chapter, he is hired to help the parties reduce unnecessary transaction costs and explore ways to resolve cases fairly, efficiently, and consistently. This role is similar to that of a special master, but lacks the clout and constraints that come from being court appointed, says Green.

Third, Green works in private case management as a settlement adviser. If a single defendant decides that it is better to attempt to work out an individual settlement of the claims against it rather than coordinate with co-defendants who may have different attitudes and interests regarding early settlement, Green may serve as a mediator between that defendant and the plaintiffs. While this role is similar to Green's mediator role, it raises many of the complexities of the multiparty case, he explains, such as good-faith settlement issues.

A fourth role has been that of case manager and ADR coordinator for all the defendants in a dispute. In Superfund and toxic tort cases, for instance, it is not unusual for the defendants to agree to retain a consultant to coordinate case management and negotiations with the government or plaintiffs' counsel. This coordinator deals with the intradefendant conflicts so that they do not "end up doing most of the salvaging for the plaintiff," Green explains, adding, "There is generally a benefit to having someone other than one of the trial attorneys designated to have settlement responsibility." Again, Green was advocating for perspective on and distance from litigation.

Finally, sometimes Green has sometimes worked with trial counsel and in-house counsel as a single defendant's adviser on ADR, either completely behind the scenes or in some strategic discussions with all defense parties. Occasionally he has negotiated with plaintiffs on behalf of his client. Usually this role comes about because the defendants themselves had "different attitudes about fighting or talking," he says. Some parties or their counsels have a negative attitude toward this kind of litigation, at least until the legal bills reach a high enough level or the first seven-figure jury verdict comes in, he says.

In the first three roles, Green is a neutral, with contractual fiduciary and mediation responsibilities to both plaintiffs and defendants. He helps parties design and agree on a case management and evaluation process that will allow them to prepare, examine, and resolve all pending cases and establish procedures for future cases. In the fourth role, he was an agent for those defendants who retained him, under the joint defense aspect of the attorney-client privilege. In the last role, he had a solitary attorney-client relationship, which is why Green decided to limit his work to neutral roles where he had a fiduciary relationship with the parties.

• • • • • • •

When Green and his colleagues Steve Goldberg and Frank Sander co-wrote the casebook *Dispute Resolution*, anthropologist Sally Merry criticized it for presenting a crystalized, positivist, marketing approach to dispute resolution. Merry (1987, p. 2058) writes that it "presents a superficialized, uncritical view of the [ADR] movement, concentrating on techniques and glossing over problems." Titled "Disputing Without Culture," Merry's review sees the authors as interested chiefly in the fit between disputes and the processes that resolve them most effectively, a taxonomy-typology approach of matching problems to processes, in a book that presented alternatives statically as "cubbyholes" into which disputes could be fit rather than stages through which they pass. Merry views the book as a how-to text in its concern with describing each potential dispute resolution process, analyzing its strengths and weaknesses, and offering some guidelines for evaluating effectiveness largely in terms of efficiency in cost and speed and of satisfaction of participants. The book "produces a technocratic preoccupation with appropriate forums . . . with a tool kit of techniques along with rules about when each tool should be employed" (Merry, 1987, pp. 2059–2060).

Interestingly, this criticism of the book outlines some of the criticisms leveled at elitist lawyers said to be "practicing law on the head of a pin" or "missing the forest for the trees." It is those elitist practitioners who are the main source of Green's clients, and it is he who helps match up their particular problem with an ADR process. His is very much a legalistically oriented and pragmatic litigation-alternative view of mediation, and its narrowness is well suited to the area that he mines for clients. Not surprisingly, Green regards Merry's criticisms of *Dispute Resolution* as "recognition of what we set out to accomplish in the book."

Lawyers and their thinking are the focus of Green's business and his work. Even his own view that he is client driven and obsessed with the need to satisfy the client is part of the definition of most successful lawyers in private practice. While in some respects in his approach to mediation Green is responsible for taking some control out of attorneys' hands and transforming legal machinations into business decisions, the lawyers are still the requisite experts, presenting the facts. Similarly, the judges who assign cases to him are maintaining control over their own dockets. The cases they send him are cases they believe can be resolved without the need for trial days. Often they deal with questions that they would rather not have juries answer, and they are certainly not interested in seeing their decisions appealed.

Green, as he himself has assessed, likes the role of "power mediator" or "mediator with clout." He is intimately familiar with the problems of time, money, and the risk of jury outcomes that lawyers and their clients think about. The elite legal culture is home territory for him: it is where he was trained, where he has practiced, and the arena in which he markets his version of ADR.

Lavinia E. Hall

Reference

Merry, S. E. (1987). Disputing without culture. *Harvard Law Review, 100,* 2057–2073.

• • • • • • •

"Accountability for the quality of the outcome—
providing training for everybody and helping them
maximize joint gains—is the focus of my activism."

—Lawrence Susskind

8

• •

Lawrence Susskind
Activist Mediation
and Public Disputes

Lawrence Susskind fits no stereotype of a typical university professor. He teaches urban and environmental studies at the Massachusetts Institute of Technology, and he complements his steady stream of publications with an even more active professional life as a mediator who works to resolve massively complex public disputes. In any given year, Susskind literally is in the middle of a half dozen multi-party, multi-issue disputes—for example, the siting of hazardous waste facilities, designing controversial regional public housing plans, crafting city-suburb cost-sharing schemes to assure regional water quality, or devising toxic waste clean-up strategies involving industry, government, and community members.

Susskind's vision of public dispute mediation and his successful practice have made him a controversial figure in the dispute resolution community. Both his vision and practice pose a challenge to the popular wisdom of the field, which regards "neutrality" as sacred. Many mediators concern themselves with process alone, leaving the substance of agreements to the parties themselves. The demands of neutrality, according to most public dispute mediators, prevent them from focusing on power imbalances among negotiating parties. Other mediators working in the public eye wonder whether mediation can be a viable strategy when participants number thirty or more, when the process is

highly political, and when parties vary enormously in their expertise, resources, and political experience.

Susskind rejects mediator claims to pure neutrality. He suggests, instead, a stricter notion of nonpartisanship and the
provocative idea of activist mediation. He has argued that mediators must address power imbalances among the parties to public
disputes by, for example, providing premediation negotiation
training to all parties.

The profile that follows presents Susskind's responses to a
series of questions I raised to learn more about his views and practice of mediation. I guided our lengthy interview sessions with
three primary goals in mind. First, I wanted to learn how his work
had developed. Somehow Susskind's dispute resolution practice
had grown from his earlier work on public participation in urban
planning and policy-making processes. How did this happen?
Second, I wanted to explore the controversial positions Susskind
has taken regarding the ethical responsibilities of mediators
working on public issues. If "being neutral," for example, was an
inadequate, if not altogether deceptive, characterization of the
responsibilities of public dispute mediators, just what alternative
did Susskind have in mind? Third, I wanted to press him about
actual cases and how he handled them. In the heat of practice,
faced with angry, skeptical, politically contentious parties, what
did Susskind find most challenging, most perplexing? What did
he find most satisfying, most difficult?

The remainder of this profile presents Larry Susskind's story in
his own words. For purposes of transition, however, I make a few
observations in italicized type.

. . . .

*I knew that Susskind had long been interested in the promises of active
citizen participation in government, and I knew he had taught, written,*

consulted, and practiced widely. But I did not know much about how these pieces of his professional life had developed, complementing or tugging at one another. So I began by asking Susskind about his roots, professionally speaking, and the subsequent development of his practice:

Let me describe what I do as public dispute mediation, and not environmental mediation. What I did in the late 1970s was environmental mediation, but I've tried to broaden it since then to be the mediation—the resolution or the management—of disputes in the public sector. I work on three types of public disputes: first, disputes over the allocation of scarce resources—like a piece of land or a body of water; second, disputes over policy priorities—Should we emphasize environmental protection in this context, or economic development? Should we emphasize meeting the needs of this group or that group?; and third, disputes over quality-of-life standards, environmental standards, human service standards—disagreements over the standards that ought to be set within a policy that has been made or is being made. I don't view the last grouping as primarily environmental any longer, though I did at one time.

When I was an undergraduate at Columbia, I majored in sociology and English literature. I was interested in studying drama and poetry. But I didn't act; I wrote and produced plays. If you look at my work on role-play exercises and simulations now, it traces directly back to my work in drama, particularly in stagecraft. I think this probably has a lot to do with the way I manage events within the context of dispute resolution. It has something to do with writing and producing plays too, as a matter of fact.

The work in sociology led me into urban planning. I went to the School of Design at Harvard, and I thought I was going to become a city planner. I thought that had to do with design, which I had to learn, so I went to what was called the Design School. Little did I know that I was hitting the place at a moment in time when nobody knew what the hell they were doing or what city planning was. At least that's the way it looked to me.

That first year in planning school I got involved in advocacy planning with Chester Hartman, who was my first instructor. We worked on a grass-roots project to try to get a rent control bill passed in Cambridge. I thought, "This makes sense to me." But the Harvard hierarchy was telling Chester, "You're not getting tenure; you can't stay here. What you're teaching is not going to count for credit." And I'm thinking: "Oh no, this is not right. What you guys are doing doesn't make any sense at all."

I transferred in the middle of the Harvard program and finished my master's degree at MIT the next year. My sense of planning, when I transferred, was confused. Having studied with Charlie Abrams at Columbia, I thought planning was going to be about how you develop cities—particularly in developing countries, and particularly neighborhoods within cities—in ways that respect both the politics and technical expertise that planners ought to be able to bring to things. I got to Harvard and they weren't talking about that at all. They had a notion that it had something to do with land use, and they had *rules* about land use.

I applied to the master's and Ph.D. programs at MIT at the same time. I said very clearly on my Ph.D. application that I wanted to teach urban studies. I wanted to work some in the university, and I wanted to get involved in how change happens in cities. But I also wanted to move back and forth between a scholarly role, a consulting role, and an activist role. I think I've done that, in my own way.

I wrote my master's thesis about the problems of planning new towns. I'd looked at the programs to build new cities, both in the U.S. and elsewhere. The problem was you couldn't *talk* to the people who were going to live in the place to find out what they wanted. You couldn't talk to them because you didn't know who they were. So you turned it over to some "experts," and the planning process just didn't work.

By the time I was doing my doctoral work, the Nixon administration had passed the revenue-sharing legislation of the early
1970s. I was primarily interested in a couple of questions: what
level of authority should reside with whom? And what level of
authority should match what spatial level?

These questions actually emerged from the "new towns" work
that was going on then at MIT. In the planning of new towns,
one reason that the damn thing didn't work was that you had too
much of a centralized plan and you didn't have neighborhoods
having control over how they evolve and grow. "Oh, but if you
give them complete control, then the advantage of planning the
new town, the economy of scale, would be lost," the argument
went. My question was, when you switch the level of authority of
the allocation of the block grant, do you increase or decrease the
responsiveness, in the use of money, to the needs of different
groups? That's a participation question. In other words, people
knew how to lobby city hall under the old program because they
could sort of play off the city and the feds. With this new program of revenue sharing, it wasn't clear whether low-income and
poor people were going to be better off or worse off. I studied the
gains and losses that the block grant programs meant for the poor.
That was what my dissertation was about.

Because of that work, I was hired by groups on all sides of the
question—the League of Women Voters, the Brookings Institute,
Arthur D. Little, the Center for Community Change—who
wanted to monitor what actually happened with these general
revenue sharing and block grant funds. Everybody thought it was
going to be either good or bad to make this change, and here I
had written about it, and people said, "What would you look at,
what would you watch?" Dick Nathan had put together these
monitoring studies at the Brookings Institute, and then the citizen activist groups said, "We want to have our own *citizen* monitoring study." So I got hired by a lot of the grass-roots groups to

design citizen monitoring studies. For a while it seemed like I was working on every monitoring study everywhere.

I tried to design these monitoring studies in a way that would leave people empowered to continue tracking and monitoring this stuff on their own. It wouldn't just be data gathering; it would be education in a way that would leave people with an ability to follow what was going on in their own communities on an ongoing basis. This was a very different approach to the issues from that of many economists. I wasn't interested in equity-efficiency trade-offs. I was interested in *power*. Do you get better allocation decisions—more accountable to the people that really know what they need—when you switch the locus of power from the federal level to the local level? All of this got me tagged as a citizen participation type.

Then I got invited into a small town on the north shore of Boston, where I knew the town and I knew a lot of the people, to help the citizens there do a plan for the town, since the town government wouldn't do one. This was in Rockport, and we did something called "Planning for the Future of Rockport," which was a completely citizen-based process for growth management and planning for the town. For me, that project was motivated entirely by the desire to find a new model of how to teach planning. I liked what I'd done as a student with Chet Hartman. So I brought in students from MIT as the staff from beginning to end. We had a community-based laboratory, with a real client. We had real political restraints; we had time pressures. And the students were the staff; I had undergraduates and doctoral students all working together.

That led to the town of Arlington, a Boston suburb that borders Cambridge. The town government invited us in, saying, "Look, you did this thing up in Rockport. We're interested in having citizens involved here too." What I learned from Rockport was that we hadn't left behind any institutionalized organization, because we were, in a sense, fighting city hall the whole time. We weren't really working for the town government in Rockport; we were working for an ad hoc citizens' group. The group of folks who had been on the planning board, citizen members, had invited us. They said, "Look, the city government isn't going to do this. We want to get citizens from the whole town doing it."

In Arlington, we worked to create the Citizen Involvement Committee, and that's a group that still exists today.

About that time, something called the Citizen Involvement Network was created by the Rockefeller Foundation. They wanted to pick the twenty-five best examples of citizen involvement in the country, support them for several years, and document how citizen participation really works. Arlington's Citizen Involvement Committee was chosen as one of the twenty-five, and I got hooked up with the national Citizen Involvement Network. I started advising them, based on the work of the monitoring studies, about how they could have citizens monitoring this rather than having some evaluator come in and write it up. I felt the citizens could learn themselves by looking not just at their own community but at the other twenty-four, and they could pass ideas around. That was the key to the Citizen's Involvement Network.

In Arlington at that time we didn't have an "outside professor" problem. There wasn't a racial issue. There wasn't a problem, in moderate-size towns like Arlington, with outsiders coming in. They had no model cities history; nothing like that at all. There was this feeling of, "The university is agreeing to help us. Isn't that wonderful!" And there was tremendous respect for the university resources that were coming in. And we brought the money. We didn't ask them for a penny. I raised the money for all those projects and said that we would pay for them. And we actually provided money to the citizens' group.

The problem came in the next project, which is really where my mediation work begins. The Red Line, the subway, was about to be extended out from the inner city, from Boston, to Route 128, with a major stop near the Alewife Brook Parkway in Arlington. The Citizen's Involvement Committee said, "You just can't do this. There has to be citizen involvement in this decision." And they went and lobbied the governor, and they had very strong state legislative representation from Arlington at the time. And out of that came a request that we create a regional citizen involvement process for the detailed planning of the Red Line extension.

It helped that I had been a gubernatorial appointee for the six years before that. The regional agency was put in charge of the planning process. Since I had good contacts in Arlington and with the state, when they said, "Let's do this," I turned it into another student involvement project.

The governor appointed me to chair the regional Citizen Advisory Committee for this process, with the concurrence of the four communities that were involved in the subway extension: Arlington, Cambridge, Somerville, and Belmont.

"Well, we need staff," I said.

"We have professional staff," various officials responded.

"I know," I said, "those are engineers. We need people to really work to help the citizens' group gather the information it needs to have some real input into this."

Fifty, maybe sixty people were appointed by the four towns, the governor, the regional park authority, all the ad hoc environmental groups, the watershed association, the business community. It seemed like everyone had a chance to appoint someone to be on this committee. We had this huge crowd turn out. The meetings went on for twelve or thirteen months, every Wednesday night. I will remember it for the rest of my life. From six to midnight, with preparatory stuff between meetings. It was an incredibly elaborate process.

What I kept trying to do in the meetings was to say, "Let's pick some topics; let's gather the information we need; let's understand the assumptions, and then let's try to reach some type of agreement on what we want to recommend here." But then, halfway through the process, it dawned on me that the real problem wasn't getting everybody heard. The real problem was how to avoid having the whole citizen advice-giving process undercut by the fact that the citizen types couldn't agree on anything. So I tried to say then, "The real issue here for all of us is to get consensus." And I announced that to the group. Otherwise, the whole process was going to end up having no effect on what the engineers were telling the state to do. So I had to try to get an agreement among the people with different views.

I thought, "Geez, I've worked on all of this participation stuff starting back with getting rent control in an advocacy mode, and then I watched rent control erode in Cambridge a piece at a time. It's there on paper, sure, but it's not what it was intended to be in the beginning. There was really no way to hold it in place given the constant battle that was taking place politically." So the goal here was really to get some agreement on what was the smartest thing to do.

The Citizen Involvement Committee's main job was the environmental impact assessment, which for that project had to be done under federal and state law. The assessment rested on the choice of alternatives that the various people involved would consider. So we spent a lot of time trying to tell the engineers about new alternatives, like, "Don't extend the subway at all" or "Have buses down the same right-of-way instead of a fixed rail." And the engineers were saying "No, no, no. That's not a realistic option." The initial battle was over what alternatives to consider. And that's where I discovered the power of the impact assessment process as a way of structuring citizen participation.

The assessment process requires citizen participation. It requires that you scope out options. It requires that people have a chance to be heard and write their comments down and get reactions to their comments. So I then decided to try something that was an absolute shot in the dark. I remember the issue got very hot and heavy about the size of the parking garage that was going to go with the subway station. The engineers projected that we needed to house ten thousand cars. The citizens' group wanted no parking, because that wasn't their idea of promoting mass transit. And the engineers wanted to pave over a sensitive environmental area too.

So I said, "Let's have a slide show showing us images of parking garages of everything from ten thousand down to nothing." The engineers who were working for us at the time, and paid by the state, said, "Where are we going to get slides like that?" I said, "I don't know. Call around the country, the world, and get pictures other engineering firms have worked on."

And so we had a slide show: "Well, here's a picture of a parking garage of ten thousand spaces: Logan Airport." People said, "There's no way you're going to put that many cars here." And the engineers said, "You know, that's probably right."

We had these images of different garages, and I then started using straw polls at the end of each meeting, and said, "This is not binding on anybody, but let's just see. Here are some ranges now. Could we get an agreement that the garage should not be more than twenty-five hundred cars?" Ninety percent of the people agreed after the slide show. So when we really had a sense of what this was about—and it wasn't just a symbolic debate—it was a lot easier to get agreement. That became the key turning point in the process.

The engineers backed off. Everybody backed off. It was fascinating. I hadn't expected anything in particular. I was trying to promote good discussion, an informed discussion.

The same thing happened with the discussion of the forecasting models. When you get behind the statement of what is and what isn't acceptable from the technical people to the assumptions they're making, you open the black box. You bring everybody with you. You test the assumptions. You jointly generate the data. You jointly make the forecasts. You jointly *imagine* the image. . . .

But the project ended on a very sour note. By the end, we'd reached an accord on a new option for what should go where. And the option included a set of trade-offs that no one had envisioned in the first place, which was, could you *improve* the environment in exchange for allowing this development to go ahead—all the watershed improvements that you've always wanted, the bikeways you've always wanted?

And we reached an accord in which we had a new option to study in the impact statement. Everyone said that's the option, that's what we should do. Everyone, the whole committee, agreed.... So we took our recommendation to the state. And they picked an option without all of the promised compensation in the form of bikeways and the waterway improvements. The state included some of the ideas, but not all. So we said, "What's going on here? We put all this time and energy in." We called in the Massachusetts secretary of transportation. He said, "It's beyond the scope of this group to tell us to do this."

And then, acting on behalf of the group, I said, "We're going to file legislation to formalize this group as the ongoing manager of this process." The group wanted to do it, but the city manager of Cambridge, who had worked out this deal with the state for the option he wanted, wrote a letter asking that I no longer be chair of the group and saying that he didn't want some new ad hoc authority that would take away the power of the cities. He didn't mind an advisory group, but not an organization with power.

I thought the only way the group was going to get what it wanted was to get some institutionalized standing. So we drafted legislation that challenged the authority of those in power. And those in power unappointed me, declared the task force's work over, and thanked us for our work. But we had the agreement.

The Alewife project went ahead pretty close to our option, but without a lot of things that had been promised—embittering a lot of people who'd worked very hard to generate this new option, and who had thought they had given away a huge amount to agree to not litigate against the whole thing. That's the only reason the Alewife station on the Cambridge-Arlington town line got built; otherwise it would still be in court today.

There was a lesson here: you needed to have a clear mandate. I'd started with Chet Hartman, with the advocacy work, completely on the outside of the establishment. Then I moved to the monitoring studies, and then to institutionalized citizen participation; so the next step was to move completely within the circle. I started completely out of the circle, got closer and closer, and now I'm in it, but I want to change what goes on in terms of the understandings in the circle. I want to be in a relationship that clearly establishes who has what authority to make what decision, and where we are going to get those in power, in the beginning, to say, "Rather than have gridlock, rather than be in conflict forever, we are going to try to work this out."

Now, I didn't know you called that mediation. Nobody did. It wasn't called that; it didn't exist as mediation. When I wrote about this experience, I called it consensus building in the land-use planning process. But, having done that, having seen that you could convert citizen participation, I then said, "Look, I want to look at some other models of citizen participation."

That led to the European study, reported in my book *Paternalism, Conflict and Co-Production* that I edited with Michael Elliot. The model of co-production was, I realized, what I had created in the Alewife station case, but there were all these European antecedents of it. So we did all these case studies, we discovered these antecedents, and I said, "Co-production—that's what I'm going to call it." But nobody knew what co-production was; it was too awkward a term. But the European study did convince me that this idea wasn't crazy. What I learned from

Rockport, Arlington, Alewife, and the monitoring work was that you can stand on the outside being an advocate throwing bombs . . . and you can win some victories. But those victories will probably be short-lived, and they won't really redistribute power.

Then I got a call from the Kettering Foundation, saying they had this experiment they want to try called a negotiated invest-ment strategy (NIS). They were going to have a federal team, a state team, and a local team in three different cities trying to come up with a long-term development plan. Kettering had had me out several times to talk about my work on citizen participa-tion. They had come up with this idea of the negotiated invest-ment strategy, and they had gone to the Carter administration and asked for support. . . . Marshall Kaplan in HUD suggested maybe they should get one urban planner in one of the three cities. Bill Usery, the former secretary of labor, was the mediator for St. Paul. Jim Laue was the mediator for Gary, Indiana, and I was the mediator for Columbus, Ohio. They called us facilitators. Frank Keefe (former Massachusetts secretary of administration and finance) and I did that together, and it worked. . . .

What we did was help the federal, state, and local teams, each with twenty to twenty-five people, to agree on long-term public and private actions to promote development in the cities, includ-ing ways to coordinate all the federal programs. These three groups met in a big room, with three big tables and a little table for the facilitator. Our job was to get an agreement on a five- to ten-year public and private investment package for each city. I wanted Frank there because I felt I didn't know the inside opera-tion of government well enough. Because this was really involv-ing the details: the nitty-gritty of federal contracts, with letters going to the state, "Could the state do this?" The policy debate was incredibly elaborate. It was unbelievable, just unbelievable.

We negotiated the agenda. We negotiated the ground rules. That's where it occurred to me that these people were not going to let someone decide what the agenda was going to be. We're talking about having the most senior people that you could have in that situation.

We said, "Frank and I will meet privately with each group and ask them what the issues are that they're concerned about." We'd write a summary of that and hand it out at the next meeting to see if we could get an agreement on it with everybody. The next meeting would come, and everybody would have rearranged it, and so we negotiated the agenda.

Then we asked each group to prepare a position paper on each issue on the agenda. We divided the next several meetings into periods for discussing the collection of those papers.

We met and people presented their papers. Frank and I then tried to look for the points of agreement and disagreement, sharpened the agreements and disagreements another time, and then said, "Look, here is what we agree and disagree on, but don't close on this issue until we look at the next issue."

We went through all of that and began to develop a single text. Then we looked for trades across issues, and then we developed one overall document. Then those groups all took it back for ratification. Basically, we went through the set of steps we now go through—prenegotiation preparations, then negotiation, then postnegotiation follow-up.

Nobody "walked," because huge amounts of federal money were contingent on the consensus. HUD's Kaplan had good connections to Eisenstadt (in Carter's office), who said, "You guys reach an accord and you're going to be first in line. You're going to free up a lot of discretionary funds. We want to demonstrate that this can work." So there was a very clear incentive.

I wrote a report that summarized the agreement that went into effect. I then wrote a report about the process, which was the first thing ever written about the negotiated investment strategy process. I was reflecting on this, thinking, "This is different from Alewife—all these groups accepted the fact that the product was going to be the thing that got implemented."

It was the natural next step. I thought, "The agreement is going to hold, the agreement is going to be, because we have all the powers that be here, and we also have representatives of citizen groups and others. What we come up with is going to be the agreement, and my job is to help them get an agreement."

· · · · · · · ·

I also wanted to explore how and why Susskind had come to be a controversial figure in the world of public dispute mediation. I knew he had challenged the virtue of "neutrality" as the essence of mediators' practice. I knew he had also touched off a flurry of debates when he argued that public dispute mediators should be held accountable for their work. So I probed to learn more about both Susskind's claims and his efforts to shape the evolving field of public dispute resolution. If neutrality was an unworkable or even misleading ideal for mediators to aspire to, what alternative did Susskind have in mind? Susskind had written about "activist" mediation. Was that a contradiction in terms? What could activist mediation mean? Susskind began by characterizing the central controversies in the field:

Four debates permeate the practice of environmental, or more broadly, public dispute resolution. The first has to do with the timing and mode of entry. The second has to do with the activism of the neutral. The third concerns the expertise of the neutral about the subject matter and the institutional terrain, not just the subject matter. And a fourth involves the ongoing responsibilities and accountability of the mediator for the quality of the outcome. These are the dimensions along which there are substantial ideological and practical differences in the field.

I can describe my own practice to illustrate the issues. With regard to entry, my interest has been in creating some sort of first-order neutral auspices to market the notion of dispute resolution—the State Offices of Mediation, or legislation creating legitimacy around the use of mediation in the siting process, or the Administrative Conference of the United States legislatively having the authority to say, "Now it's time for negotiated rulemaking." In other words, creating an institutional legitimacy for the use of mediation and auspices that will not *do* the mediation but that will alert people to the possibility and the advantages of it and get it started. I think that's absolutely crucial.

Someone calls you and says, "I've got a dispute. Can you help be the mediator?" That's how most private dispute resolution has worked. Most dispute resolvers wait to be called by one of the parties. But it's too hard to create legitimacy when you're invited in by only one side. I wanted to solve that problem, and that is why I pushed the concept of state offices of mediation. That is why I think we need rosters of mediators, preapproved. That's why I worked with the EPA and the Administrative Conference on the federal legislation creating negotiated rulemaking.

I had this idea of the state offices on the plane out to a meeting in Colorado, and so in my talk there I said: "Look, I'll give you an illustration of what I mean by institutionalizing a demand." And I proposed something called "governors' offices of mediation." I wrote about the idea, and started talking it up to various groups, including the National Institute for Dispute Resolution. NIDR, which was just getting started at the time, decided to take the idea and run with it, and so they offered grants to the first four or five states that would put in proposals. I worked with the state of Hawaii, the state of Massachusetts, the state of Minnesota. The only early ones I didn't work with were Wisconsin and Alaska. Gerry Cormick worked with Alaska, and Howard Bellman worked with Wisconsin, and most of these states put in proposals and got the money from NIDR to create the state offices. Those were the seeds.

Back then, I was also working with Massachusetts and other states to get siting legislation, and I was working with the EPA to

get negotiated rulemaking, and now I'm trying to work with public utility commissions to get negotiated rate setting around the
country. It's institutionalizing the demand to solve the entry
problem.

Of course, there are clearly cases that shouldn't be mediated,
and that is where these state offices also help; they save the time.
Len and Suzann Buckle [professors at Northeastern University]
wrote a wonderful report on the New England Environmental
Mediation Center before it went out of business, showing that it
had to go sniff out twelve to twenty cases before it found one that
you could actually get. And it used up all of its resources looking
into cases, meeting with the parties, trying to get this side to
accept mediation even though they got called by the other side.
That's what is killing these centers: no one is paying for that
overhead. That really struck home.

So the first issue is, What is your theory about entry? It's not
that I wouldn't come in if one side called me. But that's not my
view about how we ought to organize the field, and it is not my
view of what's going to make it possible to be successful more
often.

But institutionalizing demand doesn't mean that mediation is
a panacea or the cure-all for everything. What a state office can
do is look at fifteen cases to find the one you ought to mediate. It
has the institutionalized support to pay for that.

My metaphor . . . for the state offices is that they match up
dispute "have-ers" with dispute resolvers when it is appropriate.
They have a roster of the resolvers; they get a call from the have-
ers, or they go find them, because it's legitimate. It's in the state's
interest to go snoop around. When they see a situation where it
might work, they tell the parties all about it. The mediator isn't
there selling a service, so it's a lot more legitimate; you're not a
consultant selling your wares.

I need to say, categorically, that at the local, state, and federal
levels there are disputes over scarce resources, over policy, and

over standards that are not handled fairly, efficiently, wisely; nor do they produce stable results when you use the conventional approaches to handling them legislatively, administratively, or judicially. I can document it; I can demonstrate it. There is no question that that is true.

We just don't do as well as we could on those four standards of effectiveness. I know it. Fairer, wiser, more efficient, more stable outcomes: that's the logic of it.

I am not prepared to abandon dispute resolution because it doesn't achieve the ideal. Especially when I can demonstrate that it does *better*, for those that the critics say they're most concerned about, than all of the other options currently available to those groups, including direct action and the law. If we care about relatively powerless groups, we have to recognize when they're going to do better compared to what they're likely to get from court or from direct action. The "as compared to what" argument is a pragmatic one.

I'm not making any argument in principle against courts or against direct action. Not at all. I'm not prepared to say that in every situation dispute resolution will do better. I'm prepared to describe the attributes of situations when we shouldn't use it. But many times, it *is* better. I do try to be sensitive to the issues of power, precedent, and the vulnerability of the powerless, and I tried in the last chapter of my 1987 book, *Breaking the Impasse*, to address the issue. I'm still in the same groove on this one, though maybe it's a rut. It's the "as compared to what?" point of view.

It's true that some practitioners have made statements which have damaged the credibility of the dispute resolution profession. Some have made understated claims about mediator activism, for example—that mediators have no business being concerned with power imbalances or unrepresented parties.

But in my view, mediator activism is appropriate. First, it is appropriate for a potential neutral, a neutral who may potentially be acceptable to all parties, to go out and recruit parties. To go out and recruit representatives of interests who the parties already at the table feel should be present but aren't. I think it's appropriate for a neutral to go out and round up representatives, or even help groups coalesce, to become enough of a group to name a representative, to know that their interest is at stake. That's activism on recruitment.

There's a second kind of activism. The parties are there. They've framed the agenda narrowly. They don't see a potential linkage. It is, I think, appropriate for a neutral to ask in the form of a question whether they might want to expand the scope of the agenda, because other cases or other experiences might suggest possible trades. That's activism.

It is appropriate, third, for the neutral to provide skill-building training to parties who need it, as long as the offer is made to *all* parties, to enhance the prospect of maximizing joint gains. That's activism.

It is appropriate in my view, too, for the neutral, when meeting with the parties privately, to push them to consider their best alternatives to a negotiated agreement, their BATNAs, and the ways of improving their BATNAs and thus to clarify their attitudes toward what the option of no agreement really means to them.

It is appropriate to question people, to cross-examine them in private. "Do you really know what you're going to get if you don't accept this? Have you thought about that? Is there anything you can do to improve your walkaway if you get no agreement?" To push them hard, to cross-examine them, to help them understand whether and when they should agree or not agree to certain packages. That's activism. It's appropriate to suggest items to put on the table that the parties themselves haven't suggested— things to trade.

It's appropriate to do this either in caucus or together, by asking questions, adding possibilities, to open up new options: not to advocate any one, but to raise possibilities, to broaden what's available to work with, and to be the initiator of that and not to pretend that you're not. That's activism.

You ask questions: "Have you thought of this? Have you considered this? What about that? Have you taken these three steps down the line and thought about what this will mean to you? Did you know about this thing over here? Might that be relevant?" I'm not pretending that by asking it as a question, you're not being activist. Quite the contrary. I'm saying that's the form of activism that I would personally prescribe, and I would say that I would be an advocate for the agreement back with the constituents of the parties. So, we work together at the table, and one guy says, "Well, I see why this is reasonable. Will you come and help me sell it back to my people?" You bet I'll go and represent the interests of the whole group, if told by the whole group it's okay—back with the constituents of one group, or with the press. That's activism.

So there's activism in recruiting parties, in raising other issues, in asking about the issues, in providing skill building, in cross-examining parties about their alternatives, even in suggesting items to explore that no one has yet brought up. The rest of the environmental mediation or public dispute resolution community are scattered along the continuum of views on activism, starting from, "Don't do any of those things at all, because the parties won't own the agreement. . . . It will fall apart, they'll disavow it, they'll think it's yours," or "Who the hell are you to interfere? It's their dispute, not yours."

This kind of criticism sometimes comes from scholars with a labor orientation. But the most experienced labor mediators I know say, "That's wrong. I do all the things you said." It's a myth about the labor realm that you don't meddle because the parties won't own the outcome, that they won't feel it's theirs, that you'll be injecting your values inappropriately, that it's unethical.

I'm not neutral with regard to the outcome. I'm *nonpartisan*. That's a big difference. I refuse to adopt the interest of one side as being more important than the interest of any others. I will not side with any party, including the least powerful. If only for pragmatic reasons—I wouldn't be able to maintain my role in a dispute if I'm viewed as partisan.

But I'm not neutral with regard to the quality of the outcome. I want an outcome that maximizes mutual gain, that doesn't leave joint gains unclaimed. I want an outcome that takes the least amount of time and that saves the most money for the parties. Maximizing joint gains means that you haven't left something on the table that would have been better for both sides, even if the parties didn't propose it.

In any event, the rest of the dispute resolution community arrays itself along this continuum of activism and there are little markers that move up and down on bringing parties in. Some people are with me on that. On generating options, no way. On generating data, on bringing your experience to them from other cases, no way. On offering to be an advocate for the thing, out there in the public and the press—no way: "Hey, you don't want to get identified with any one proposal. Then you won't be viewed as neutral by other people who might not like it later, and you might hurt your reputation. You're just a process person. No substantive involvement." That's their view.

But the patronizing tone of some of the critics gets to me: "These dispute resolvers are coming up with stuff that's just cooling off these people who would get more if only they would go to court."

Wait a minute: Who decides this? The people can't decide for themselves whether this is okay? Only you, the great paternal observer, knows? I have a lot more confidence in people's ability to know their own interests, to make comparisons, or to make risk assessments for themselves than the critics do. So when anyone objects to my activism, I want to remind them about the voluntary nature of the agreement. Also, because some people have relatively few resources and may be there because they don't have a better alternative, I want to remind the critics that activism can also mean training.

That's why I want another piece of activism—bringing resources to the table—to ensure that nobody is disadvantaged. We create the resource kitty in negotiated rulemaking cases, in which any group that can't pay the fare to come to Washington can dip into that fund.... We do it with the concurrence of the parties already in. Everybody has to agree to every move. You have to have a resource kitty; you've got to have an equal playing field.

The people who bring up the issue of cooptation suggest that a resource kitty and training may look attractive in the short run, but they coopt weaker parties. But what they're really saying is, "These dumb people." You have to follow the logic here, that "these dumb people" are being conned into accepting something that they don't realize isn't as good for them as something else.

You can't believe in cooptation without being patronizing. That's it in a nutshell. Because then you're saying that you see it, and they don't—that they're giving something away, that they're being fooled, tricked, sold a bill of goods. That's what cooptation means. But people know their own interests. Even if they begin with insufficient information, expertise, or organizational capacity, they're likely to do better in a public dispute resolution process than if they go through the normal process.

Bringing people into a process, giving people a feeling of participation, and then not empowering them to have any say was the problem with citizen participation; it didn't really promise anything. But in dispute resolution, participants have a veto. They can always step out. They can take whatever position they want. They can go back and use the other options available to them. I don't think the critics are paying enough attention to that, as compared to every other option available.

Another dimension of activism involves expertise. There are people who believe that neutrals sell process. They go in and don't need to have ever worked in that institutional context. They don't need to know the system of rules, laws, and informal understandings. They don't need to know the technical language; they can learn it. Only the parties need to know; it's their agreement. The neutral is not supposed to know the issues well enough to contribute substantively. You're only a process person.

But first, you're a drag on the inventing process if you don't know what they're talking about. They can't stop to educate you. You've got to know at least what they're talking about. Second, you're less than a helpful advocate of a good outcome if you can't bring to them the experience of others that they don't know, with regard to the range of solutions they might invent. I got involved in a land use case, for example, where the people never understood that you could have property value insurance as part of a siting process. I said, "Well, here's a case, here's a case, and here's a case of property value insurance." And they said, "You mean we can do that? Wow, that solves a big problem for us."

It's perfectly appropriate, even necessary, for a mediator to do this kind of thing. It is, certainly, if we care about the efficiency of the outcome, meaning maximizing joint gains, stability of the outcome, and the wisdom of the outcome, as measures of whether we did a good job. The wisdom of the outcome, here, simply means that, in retrospect, the parties did not forgo available technical knowledge with regard to the options they considered. In retrospect, the parties won't say, "Oh God, are we dumb. We didn't even know that possibility existed."

So the notion that the mediator or facilitator shouldn't have any expertise doesn't make any sense. It's only if you say, "My job is to help the parties reach an agreement amongst themselves. I don't care about the agreement; I have no responsibility for the agreement. I'm neutral! I'm neutral with regard to the quality to the outcome. I don't care about the outcome; I'm a process person." Only if you say that do you then argue, "I don't need any expertise except process expertise." That's nuts.

This leads to the issues of responsibility and accountability, which are terribly confusing. I got myself in a lot of trouble with a *Vermont Law Review* piece on the accountability of mediators. People said, "Oh, you mean you're *so* concerned about the quality of the outcome that you would *advocate* the interests of those least able to advocate their own interest? Well, then you're clearly not neutral, and you're not a mediator."

I said, "Now look. When I say I'm committed to the best possible outcome, it means several things. It means the outcome's viewed as fair by all parties; it means I ask questions; it means I help put more options on the table; it means I help train people to advocate their own interest, but I offer the same training to everybody. It *doesn't* mean I take sides."

It's very hard to find a way of saying that the interventions that you make, while offered equally to everyone, help some disproportionately, particularly those least able to help themselves. So you *are* having a disproportionate effect on those people's abilities to pursue their interests, but what you're doing, you're doing equally for all, except that it has a more beneficial effect for some. That is a very hard point to get across.

So, when I say I'm accountable for the quality of a mediated outcome, people say, "Well, then you're not neutral, because then you're trying to steer the outcome toward a particular outcome *you* think is good." And I say, "No."

Accountability for the quality of the outcome—providing training for everybody and helping them maximize joint gains—is the focus of my activism. It's all in the phrase "maximize joint gains."

Efficiency is a function of not leaving potential joint gains on the table. That means that the mediator must have an absolute concern about the quality of the outcome, the substance of the outcome. You can say, "Oh my God, they're not maximizing joint gains. I have to say something to help them squeeze out all possible mutual advantage." I'm accountable for helping to manage a process that will produce those gains for the parties.

I'm partly to blame if it doesn't work out. If the agreement doesn't get implemented later, because we didn't anticipate a boulder in the road, I'm partly to blame. I had a responsibility to help them think clearly about the prospects for implementation. But many of my colleagues will take no blame—"I'm not responsible for implementation. That's the whole point," they'll say. "It's the parties' agreement. It's not mine."

This is a very hard point to get across, particularly within the community of mediators, because it's such a sensitive issue. You say words like *accountable* or *responsible*, and they explode before they hear the rest of the sentence.

• • • • • • •

My conversation with Susskind next turned to the issues I most wanted to explore: his "feel" for his own practice—the difficulties and challenges, the satisfaction or worry, his own emotional and reflective response to the complexity and movement of mediation practice. How, I wondered, would Susskind feel about dealing with angry and doubting parties, with the irrationalities of politically charged public conflicts? How would Susskind make sense of the real messiness of practice?

The work itself is enormously satisfying—to work out a resolution in some contentious public dispute—because it basically achieves what I organize my life around trying to do. I set out to stay involved with issues on the ground in everyday life, people's struggles in their everyday life, to find a way, by working at the intersections between theory and practice, of doing that while still keeping my eye on the bigger picture, and still remaining primarily an educator. No small chore. I want it all. I want to stay in the university; I want the satisfaction of being an educator. I want to be a theory builder, but I want my theory to come from practice; and I want my practical intervention to solve problems in the world. Then I'll be happy. And I think I'm getting that. That's what's satisfying.

So, for example, I get a call in the Hartford case: "We've never tried this before, but we're trying to get all these communities in the Hartford region to agree on an allocation of affordable housing responsibilities. What do we do? Are you interested?"

The first exciting part for me is trying to construct an image of what the process would be like, costing it out, putting a team together, and selling it to the people involved. In this case, they had a review committee that had eight, ten, maybe twelve practitioners and companies invited to come and make presentations. So I knew I was one among many, and I thought, "Look, I'm going to tell them," as I always do, realistically, "this is what it is going to take. This is one model of the process. These are the choices you'll have to make. This is why the team I can put together can do the job. These are the issues that are going to come up. This is what I've worked on that's like this that is helpful. These are the problems that I don't think you've addressed yet. Are you sure you want to do this?" I don't pull any punches when I come and do those interviews. In a way, we're back to stagecraft....

It's a challenge to convince people that there's a right way, based on experience so far, to think about the questions they need to ask themselves, and I try to turn those occasions into a situation in which, even if I don't get the job, they'll know a lot better what they need to get and why and how they need to do what they need to do.

I really relish those occasions; I'm never the least bit nervous about them. I look forward to them; I enjoy them. I've never walked into a situation where I've had any stagefright at all having to do with dispute resolution. I'm nervous about lots of other things, but not about this. In just about any situation now, I really believe I'm going to have a sense of what I ought to do, based on a lot of experience at this point.

The frustrations and satisfactions emerge in different kinds of ways. In this Connecticut case, for instance, we get the contract, we agree to do it, I put the team together, I go down, and we meet with all the parties, and it's a high. I'm doing what I want to be doing. I see the possibilities; I know this can work. I'm excited to meet a brand new set of people, all of whom have strong views. All of whom are very able, who have never heard of dispute resolution before, for the most part, who don't see what's coming and I do—what the process is going to lead to, the problems that are going to come. But I can't tell them about it all at the beginning because it won't mean anything.

We start, and then there's six, eight, ten, twelve, twenty-four months of exhaustion, and many let-downs, because I see very clearly the steps we have to go through, the problems we're going to have to resolve, the confrontations we're going to have to have, the learning that has to go on, and they don't.

I may not know anything about the particulars; I just know there's a set of dynamics that are going to have to work themselves out. Some people are going to emerge as strong speakers and others aren't. Someone is going to throw a bomb somewhere along the way. Someone is going to have a bright light turned on and decide that dispute resolution is the greatest thing that ever happened. There are going to be moments of real anger; there are going to be moments when someone is going to leave, and we're going to have to fight to get them to come back, because they think leaving is the only choice they have. I know that all that is going to happen.

It's like having this ability to predict the future and trying to figure out what to tell another person. You come down from another planet. You know their whole history, and you know where it's going to go, and you come from the future, you come back. You can't tell them what's going to happen! It isn't going to have any meaning. After a while, it's very much like being a time traveler, if you do enough of this stuff.

I can see what we have to resolve. It's grueling. It's absolutely grueling, sitting in a room with twenty, fifty, one hundred, two hundred people. They're all just paying attention to what they're concerned about; I'm trying to pay attention to what all of them are concerned about.

I'm watching all the nonverbal stuff. I'm trying to keep a script in my head; I'm trying to be responsive; I'm trying to watch every face; I'm trying to watch the relationships between the people; I'm trying to keep tabs on the clock; I'm trying to worry about how I'm being perceived. And in the end I'm exhausted; I'm sweaty; I'm tired; I come home and I go into a deep sleep. It's an incredible outlay of energy. . . .

And doing it, week after week after week, when you *know* that you could consolidate it if you could just fast-forward. But then you know that you can't. You want to, but you can't. They have to live it; it's theirs. It's their dispute; they have to live it. But it's *frustrating* a lot of the time. And you can't let on any of the frustration. You can't *share* it with any of the people in the group, which makes it even more frustrating.

Even when you think something is going to a dead end, you have to let it go. Unless they know it's a dead end, it isn't a dead end. So, there's great frustration because of the commitment of the time and energy, yours and theirs, that in one respect you know might be shortened but in another you know can't be.

You're constantly trying to keep it moving, but you have to be very deft at those interventions. I'm constantly editing what I'm saying; I'm on a delay loop. I have to think about how it will be perceived, if it will help or hurt.

I make mistakes all the time; I still do. I guess my thinking outdistances my ability to talk, and my ability to talk outpaces my ability to listen. So I'm constantly thinking ahead; I'm half listening, and I'm then trying to speak. Sometimes I'm talking too fast for them to get it, or I'm trying to run the whole thing on slow motion for them, when I want to speed it fast forward for me. It's very crazy.

I try to use humor more than anything else to deal with mistakes. Say I said something, someone's getting angry, and I realize that it's because they thought I said something that I didn't mean. But they *think* I said it, and they're just going to get angrier. So I stop and I say, "Maybe this is a good time for us to run this back and start over again. Could I be allowed to edit out what I just said, because obviously I just screwed up." Or I'll say, "Maybe I ought to ask this person to come here, and I'll go over there and sit down and listen, because obviously I'm not hearing how I sound very well."

A lot of the time I use sarcasm as a form of humor, because it's the easiest form of humor for me; I'm not much good at punch lines, so it's sarcasm—but with myself as the butt of the joke. I'll try to make light of what is going on, to ease the tension in the room. If there's going to be anger, I want it aimed at me if it's going to be aimed at anybody, rather than at the process. I want to be able to soak it up, absorb it like a pillow; I don't ever hit back.

If someone is angry at what is going on, I want them to get angry in a way that doesn't hurt their relationship with another person in the room. Getting angry's okay, but getting angry and out of control isn't. People often get out of control in these circumstances, and so I have to try to find a way to wrap some humor around it and let the person save face and not have them walk or ruin the relationship.

They might stand up and make a speech, and everybody will start their eyes rolling, and they're saying, "Get this jerk out of here," and I know that that person is going to have a hard time gaining any respect from the rest of the group, and yet I work for that person as well as the rest of the group, and I want this person to be able to recoup their respect from the rest of the folks there.

So when they're done, I'll say, "Gee, I really agree there's a concern that you have about this, this, this, and this," and I will try, as best I can, in a pithy way to take the most legitimate part of what they said and say it again to the rest of the group on their behalf so the rest of the group will see, "Gee, there was really some important meaning in that."

I'm trying to keep everybody working on the problem rather than going at each other. It's not easy—it's hard. A lot of these situations involve incredible stakes for a lot of people, and they're very highly charged.

But it's not the meetings part that's hard; it's the part that's between the meetings, after the meetings, writing it up, organizing the staff. The drag for me is managing the administration of it. A lot of stuff happens between meetings. All the phone calls, all the follow-up review of the material, writing the press releases, making sure that arrangements are all set for the next time. I used to do all of that, but I don't anymore. I now have staff to do all that. But fatigue is a big issue.

In the meeting—getting it to work, dealing with the flow of things—I'm not worried; I assume it's all going to work out fine, and I'm going to know the right thing to do. I'm prepared; I've thought about this stuff.

But I do get very frustrated when somebody can't express their own views well to the rest of the group and the rest of the group is pouncing on them. I know that if I intervene, the person would take it as an insult, and yet I know I could express that person's view in a succinct way that would help them. Then I have to call a caucus or call a break, and during coffee, go over and talk with the person and try to say, "God, I know if I were where you are, I would have been really upset with this group. Maybe you could try it this way, or that way." You can't do it publicly, and then it takes more time, and so you're constantly fighting the clock.

The clock is the worst enemy because you know people want more time to talk about things, but you also know that they don't know that the last item on the agenda needs a half an hour, and there's only twenty minutes left. If you cut it off, they're going to be angry, but if you don't take the last item up, you're going to mess up the whole process. So you say, "Hey look, guys, I really think we've got to go on to the next issue," and you start to talk like you've gone on to it, and wait to see if you can get away with it. There is always an immense amount of adrenalin flowing because I'm fighting the clock.

I'm operating on some other plane when the mediation starts. It's like I'm having a conversation with each person simultaneously. Partly I'm teaching. But how do you teach without being pedantic? How do you teach without being explicitly Socratic? How do you teach without giving lectures? How do you teach without appearing to teach?

I do it by saying, "If I were in that situation . . ." or "Might you . . . ?" or "Imagine if . . ." "What if . . . ?" "Could that be construed as . . . ?" Everything is questions. It's all questions. It's not questions in the Socratic sense, where I'm manipulating what comes next, because the parties often tell me to shut up, and that's it, and they're going to go ahead and do this.

I'm not fishing for anything. I'm just saying, "God, have you thought about this?" I'm just talking about it as I'm thinking about it, and I'm trying to reveal a thought process that I'm going through. That's the teaching. I'm trying to let my thought process come out loud with them. Some people will say that a lot of this is the force of personality, that I'm underestimating the extent to which the individual mediator's personality has a lot to do with how this process works. But I'm not underestimating it—I know it's important. But I can't do anything about it. I may as well just be who I am.

There are a lot of issues here about general trust building. Take the Maine low-level waste siting process, a case I worked on through Endispute. After the first meeting of the stakeholders, there were a bunch of letters to the editor saying, "This group of

professional manipulators from Endispute, Inc., has been hired by
the Authority to coopt the members. . . . People should refuse to
join the advisory group, they should boycott the process." And
the press showed up at the next meeting with television cameras
and everything else, and I had to figure out a way to start off the
meeting in a way that would build trust.

So I said, "Before we begin today, I want to make a statement.
I want to respond to some of the letters that have been published
this week in the newspapers, and to some of the concerns that
have been raised. If *anybody* in this group at *any* point in this
process thinks that I am trying to steer this toward a particular
outcome, call me on it. Point it out. Interrupt. Say that you think
it's the case. If I don't make an adjustment in response that satis-
fies you that I'm not partisan, I'm out of here. I don't need this.
You don't need me."

And the headline the next day was "Mediator Promises to
Withdraw if Bias Detected." All the rest of the discussion—all
the substantive stuff that we thought was going to be the
debate—they picked up, and after that I didn't have any problems. I said, "I work for you. Hold me accountable."

I did have a private go-to with the most obnoxious, difficult
person up there last time, and I said, "You know, I'd like to help
you."

And he says, "Sure you would."

"I'd like to help you get your interest in this process," I said. "I
know you don't believe that. You think I'm working for the
power authority or the nuclear plant or something, but *try me!*
Call me during the week. Tell me something that you want on
the agenda. Tell me something before the meeting, *before* you
write a broadside to the paper. Give me a chance. Test me on it.
Give me one opportunity to demonstrate that I mean what I say.
If I mess up, then don't believe me any more. *I work for you.*"

He toned down the rhetoric dramatically. He's still writing his
letters, because he uses it as an organizing tool, and I said to him,

"I know you need to do this to keep visibility, you have to keep your members abreast of what you're doing, and you want to raise money. I understand that, that's fine. I don't have a problem with that. I don't take it personally. I'd just like to see you get more of what you want; I think I can help you do it." And I said, "And I'm making the same statement to everybody here, and I know that doesn't fit your model of how things get done. *Try me.*"

In the Hartford case, a guy who was very important to the process came but said nothing for the first two meetings. Finally I tried to move an item off the agenda, and I said I thought we had an agreement on something, and he said, "We don't have any agreement on that. What do you think, this is *your* agenda? I thought that was going to be the case. I don't need to be here if you think you know what the answer to this whole thing is." And I said, "Hey, look. I thought we had an agreement on that." I took a magic marker and put a big X through the page where I had written the agreement. I took off the page, crumpled it up, and threw it in the garbage can, and I said, "Here, come up and write what you think you agreed to. I missed it. I'm sorry, I missed it."

He came up and said what it should be, and he became one of the key supporters of the process for the rest of the time. It was a very crucial moment. I misconstrued what the group had agreed to. I thought I heard one thing—he heard it right, I heard it wrong. And he took my writing it wrong as an effort to say that that's what they had agreed to when they hadn't. The group said that he had it right, and I had it wrong. After I made the corrections, I didn't have a problem dealing with him the whole rest of the time. In fact, he became an activist for the process. He said, "This process is really and effectively accountable to people. We have a chance here to shape this policy. Let's do it."

A lot of people have become almost embarrassingly supportive of a process that they only partly understand. "Oh, we should do everything by consensus. We should always have processes like this. We need neutrals for all of our public meetings." They do this because they feel a sense of efficacy. It's not like going to a hearing where you say your piece, you leave, and you have no idea whether there is any take, or you know it's getting done behind closed doors.

They see the embodiment of an ideal they have, which is that people can sit, reason together in the political world, and an intelligent outcome that takes account of everybody's concerns will emerge. I think most people in the public sector would like to believe that's possible.

People know what's happening. They come in to the public policy mediation process skeptical. They come in realists, not cynics: realists, with skepticism and cynicism floating around, and they wait to see what happens. And, if they get an agreement and feel they've been heard, and they've watched something that works to get everybody involved, and the strongest didn't neces-sarily prevail—logic prevailed, interests were served, politics weren't ignored, the thing has a chance of being implemented—it's enormously positive. Why wouldn't they become advocates of mediation?

There are two light bulbs that come on. You can see them flashing around the table at key moments. One is, if you don't like what someone just suggested, don't just say you don't like it, try to suggest an alternative that meets their concerns but that's also better for you too. They stop saying, "That's crazy! We're not going to do that. I'm opposed to that." They realize that the way to get what they want is to offer the others something that, in fact, responds to their needs but also responds to the speaker's own needs, whereas what they heard didn't.

The first couple of meetings, and for some of the people most of the time, it's, "No, no way! We'll never go for that." That's all they say. To get past that attitude, I try to say, "Well, what if that person had said this and this and this, would that be better?"

They'll respond, "Yeah, that would be better, but it's still not there." Then I say, "What would you add to it to make it better?"

That's the question-asking process. I am modeling the process that I'm hoping they're going to use in dealing with each other. I'm taking this person's side when he says "No," and I'm saying, "You're saying 'No' to him. I can see why you're saying, 'No,' but what else could he have said that would have satisfied you?" I'm getting him into the mode of making proposals in response to things that he doesn't like rather than negative statements, and the participants see that that's the way to deal with others they disagree with in this kind of process.

At some point I see the light bulb go on. The next time something comes up that this person doesn't like, he or she says, "I don't like that as much as this and this. Could you live with that?" and the person looks over and smiles at me. You can just see it; it is a very obvious event. They get it, and it's very intriguing.

And then you'll get a lot of people along the way saying, "You know we had a thing at home last week, and I tried doing this process, and it really worked with my kid." I get it all the time in the sidebar conversations—people taking the same approach to consensus building and trying to apply it in their personal lives or at work.

The essence of the process is acknowledging the other's needs as well as your own, and making proposals that respond to both. Arguing that you don't like what the others want, and you want something else instead (which is the old model of bargaining), doesn't produce agreement. Remember, we're trying to get an agreement. We're not done until we get agreement.

When people stay in the mode of "no, no, no," I have to act on their behalf with the rest of the group, as if they were getting it. I say, "Well, John said, 'No.' I think we can all understand why he's not completely enthralled by Jane's idea, but perhaps, John, what if Jane had said this and this and this? Would that have been better?"

He'll grudgingly say, "Yeah, it's better."

I'll say, "Could you live with it?"

He says, "No, I can't live with it."

"What would it take for you to live with it?" I ask. "You don't have to commit to anything, but just help us understand what's bothering you about it." Those are the kinds of interventions a mediator makes.

John either moves or he doesn't. If he doesn't, I say, "Well, John, if I were you, my God, I might suggest this and this and this. Would that be moving in the right direction?"

He says, "Yeah."

I say, "We're not committing John to anything but let's work with this for the moment. What about the rest of you, if John had said this?"

It's all "If this, if that, what if . . . ?"; "Could you . . . ?" I don't think I ever make declarative statements about what the group should or shouldn't do, or has or hasn't done.

We take breaks when people can't sit anymore. One of things I'm bad at, I know, is releasing people soon enough for breaks. I could sit for the whole day. I don't need breaks. It's part of being impatient. I don't want to waste the time.

But people need more time, just to get up and walk around and socialize. So, every break I turn into caucuses between me and someone, or I just motion a few people over and say, "That was great, what you did. That was a super proposal; that really broke the logjam. Can the two of you add anything to what she has been saying that will get those guys over there who won't budge on this to . . . ?" I don't call it a caucus—it's a mini-mediation within a mediation.

The time to deal with just one party is between meetings. We don't do it at meetings. We distribute a lot of written proposals and summaries. I will put a draft together and send it to everybody and ask them to send their individual comments back. This way, I'll know where everybody is on every proposal beforehand.

I get back completely contradictory comments, but at least I know where everybody stands. Then I try to formulate something, or to lay out two poles, and say to the group, "We got all your comments back, and we got a bunch of you here and a bunch of you here. I don't see that it makes sense to just put one of these up. We have to do something about this. Who's got a suggestion?"

The parties are there for lots of reasons. They're in the process because someone from their organization told them to come. They're in because they don't want the embarrassment of having to explain why they didn't come in. They don't want to get hassled by someone above them or at the same level. They're in just out of curiosity. They're in for a thousand different reasons. And some aren't in at the beginning, and some drop out during. We have to go and get them back, or decide to go ahead without them. . . .

You can sometimes look ahead and know that somebody is going to threaten to walk. It's a source of power, they think. I can make a list of tactics that someone is going to use with almost 90 percent certainty in every dispute. I know what they're going to do; I know how people will respond. There are always surprises, but basically I know what to expect.

There's the person who goes to the press and announces that the group did this or did that, and it's not true. And then the next meeting they don't want to come; they don't show. So the others are really angry.

I ask, "What do you think we should do, group, about John and the article in the paper?" Someone will respond, "That wasn't true. We had an understanding, we had a ground rule: No negotiating through the press. He broke the ground rule."

And I say, "What should we do?"

"Oh, screw him, who needs him?" is the response.

"Well, I think we really need him," I'll say. "We need him back."

"Well, you call him," a participant will say. "You get him to come. I'm not calling him."

"You want the mediation team to call him? Okay, we'll call him," I'll say. "What should we tell him?"

It's the subject of negotiation, with the group, what to do. Everything is negotiated.

Now, anyone can go to the press any time they want. They can say anything they want as long as they don't attribute something to the rest of the group or to someone else. You can't tell political people that they can't talk to the press. But you can have a ground rule: Don't attribute something to someone else. You can say anything you want for yourself.

We do a press release after every meeting. Even if we meet for ten months, we do a press release after every meeting. We always give a public notice of every meeting. Every meeting is open. You can't have a meeting like this and not have it open to the public or the press. There is no secrecy.

What about between meetings? I don't announce my phone calls to the press. We do a lot between meetings. But I want to know, by what comparison is this process secretive? Compared to what?

I do have a sense of the limits of this model and my own style. I am an inappropriate person for many disputes. I'm an inappropriate guy for disputes in which the parties are looking for therapy, personal therapy. I'm just not good at that kind of endless sidebar conversation about how you feel and how I feel. I'm focused on solving the problem. I'm not in the therapeutic mode; I'm in the problem-solving mode, to use Sally Merry and Susan Silbey's distinctions about mediator styles.

I'm probably guilty of not listening carefully enough to the possibility that there's no solution. I just work and work and work on the assumption that there is one. I keep pushing and struggling. The other thing is that some people are truly put off by the pace at which I go. For instance, I'll ask them a question, then another question. I'll say, "Okay, I hear you," and before they finish the sentence, I say, "Yeah, yeah, I know you're going to say this, and then they're going to say that. But if you do that, then they'll do this, and then what are you going to do about that?" I can be too fast, and people are put off by it.

The closer we get to a solution, the greater propensity I have to say, "You're going to say this, and they're going to say that, and this one will say that, and the only choice you'll have is this, because you're concerned about that." And people don't want to hear all that. They want to live it. They don't want me to live it for them. They want to live it. And I'm probably wrong some of the time, which is even worse.

So the pace has to be controlled, but for those that want a much slower pace and a personal touch along the way, I'm the wrong guy. I don't have the time. I'm probably the wrong guy when the parties know each other really well, and they're rehashing all this old stuff—they're reliving all these old battles. I just don't have a lot of patience for that. When I say that I don't have a lot of patience, basically I opt out. I try not to stay with disputes or get involved with disputes where I don't feel that I'm the right person, and I try to recommend other mediators.

I'm very, very selective, and I can afford to be, because I don't have to make my living doing this. But I imagine if I were to try to make my living at this, and I had to take assignments that I thought were boring, I'd be really awful. My mind would be on other things.

There are times in the process when we try to keep people from rehashing history. The point is not to interpret what happened but to get an agreement on what to do. So I'll say, "Why don't we give each person a few minutes to give their account of what happened, and there will probably be real differences. You'll probably disagree. But we'll understand more about what people are proposing if we understand where they're coming from, so let's listen. But once we hear it, let's not try to get agreement about what happened. We want an agreement about what's to be done."

People start this process with needs, desires, wants, concerns, ideology, uncertainty, and interests. All of them. And I expect people to change—to alter their sense of what they would or wouldn't like to have happen by listening to what other people say. Mediation is not a question of plugging answers to questionnaires into the computer and printing out the optimal joint gain resolution. Learning and inventing goes on, reconsideration goes on, and argument matters.

People discover something about their own interests along the way. That's why you encourage disclosure, as opposed to just connecting the microphone into the computer. People are not just collections of preset interests; they also have all kinds of tacit wants and needs that come into play.

As a negotiator, you know that if you're representing a community, there's a diversity of views within that community, not just a single hierarchy of weighted interests. There's what's spoken and what's unspoken; things you would like to admit, things you won't admit; there are things you realize and things you don't yet realize; there are a lot of inchoate concerns.

You listen; you hear what other people say; you identify with that; you're informed by argument and debate; and you could never predict at the beginning where you are going to come out on the issue of your community's responsibilities by the end.

All interests are not knowable at the beginning of a mediation, or even at the end. I mean, when confronted with a package or choice, when we have come as far as we have, when we don't have any more time or money, when we've explored and plumbed and probed, and when the mediator asks, "Do you want this package or the alternative, which is no agreement?" then parties know what is in their best interest, relative to what the options are, better than anyone else can know them at that time.

That's what I mean when I talk about interests. I don't think of interests as completely known quantities from beginning to end. If I were to use the economists' multi-attribute decision analytic frame, I'd say that between the beginning and the end, we've added a large number of attributes, we've changed the rank ordering, and we've changed the rationale for the weightings and the rank orderings along the way. The list of what is known changes because of the conversation. The conversation *matters*.

There is a danger if a mediator walks in thinking, "You have your interests, you over here have your interests, you over there have your interests, and now we're going to talk." If you don't presume that people are going to learn anything from the conversation, you won't promote useful dialogue. If you don't presume that people will alter and adjust their calculus as they go, then you won't honor and value the learning that needs to go on: the clarity of communication, the usefulness of bringing new information. That's a big danger.

Arguments about bringing knowledge and expertise and being activist and so on all honor the fact that people don't know everything that they want and need and can't be explicit about it at the beginning of a dispute. Otherwise, we wouldn't go through all this inventing.

I don't assume some perfect rationality from everybody in the room. I assume, first, that emotion will overcome logic during the course of the process. Almost everybody will often do things that, if they thought about them beforehand and were asked, "Would you do that?" they'd say, "No." But they—we—will do it anyway, because emotion dominates logic.

I expect it to happen. I expect someone to blow up, even though blowing up at their ally is stupid, but they'll do it anyway. I expect it. Which means we have to give people room in the process, that we have to give them a chance to save face. The mediator has to absorb a lot of that, and deflect it. The person will be glad you did it, because they'll be the first to tell you that emotion overwhelmed logic at the time. They won't say it that way, but that's what happens. They'll say, "The guy just ticked me off." I expect that.

Second, I expect people to say, "Option one is better than option two, option two is better than option three, but I don't believe one is better than three."

"Wait a minute!" I'll say. "One is better than two; two is better than three, but you don't think one's better than three?"

I expect that because certain things have symbolic meaning, we don't understand. So I try to remember, "There's something in option three that means something to you that I don't understand, which means that it's better for you than option one, even though one is better than two, you agree, and two is better than three, you agree—but if you had a choice between three and one, you would choose three."

I try to remember this. I expect people not to be able or willing to communicate lots of value overlays I don't understand. I expect "illogical" statements, but "illogical" for good reasons.

I try to respond not by convincing people that they're wrong but by taking what they've said at face value and trying to understand what it is about option three that makes it better than number one. I cross-examine people to make sure their priorities are clear.

Third, people let personal likes and dislikes outweigh their strategic advantage. I might say, "It'd be great if you had that guy as your ally."

"No way!" is the response I might get.

"But if the two of you were in agreement, it would clearly carry the day," I'll say.

"I don't like the guy. Period," they'll say. "I'm not having a private meeting with him; I don't like him." Or they'll say,

"You're right, it would probably help. But I'm not doing it." This is more of a personality thing than anything else.

I also expect people to have a bad day—they've had a fight with their spouse the night before; they didn't get enough sleep, they're cranky; they're worried about something. I expect as much.

Anyone who doesn't expect problems like this hasn't tried to mediate. So much of what is written about mediation is written by people who haven't tried to do it, who haven't looked at it closely. It drives me crazy!

Now, think for a minute about the definition of democracy that most people have. The definition that theorists have has to do with rights and freedoms and not responsibilities. But if you *really* look at democratic theory, at least in the way I think it ought to be looked at, it's about the balance between rights and obligations, or rights and responsibilities. You have a *right* to express your own views; you don't have a right to get everything you want. You have a *responsibility* to behave in ways that respect the needs of other people and doesn't infringe upon their rights.

And what are the mechanisms of democracy we use to balance rights and responsibilities? There aren't very many. Voting? Voting's a big thing. You vote. Are you balancing rights and responsibilities? Not really. Especially with referenda. You pick one side and take no responsibility for the downside. How should we work on this balancing? By participating in the processes of government? That doesn't look to me like many people sharing much responsibility. They are complaining, they're lobbying, they're going to a public meeting, they're saying what's good for them.

The mediation of public disputes is the *only* mechanism I can see which allows, indeed encourages, people to balance their rights and responsibilities as citizens.

And why? Because there's no agreement unless you listen, hear, and respond to the concerns of others. There's no action unless we all accept the responsibility for accommodating the needs and interests of everybody else.

Where's there another forum, another mechanism of democracy that does that? I don't see one. Maybe that's too extreme, but I don't see one. You go to court—are you balancing anything?

The need of parties to respond to each other brings out a sense of responsibility. It recalibrates what I think was the initial notion, the Jeffersonian notion, of democracy. People come in with, "I want this, I want that," and leave with, "We need to do this," in every case I've worked on.

When you see someone, starting with the mediator, attempting to accommodate your concerns, it behooves you to seek to accommodate other people's concerns, if only to get what you want. It is too hard, face-to-face, to say, "Well, now that you're doing what I want, that's great; I don't have to do anything for you." It comes down to that. It's too hard. I don't care how tough-minded you are. You can't encounter another person face-to-face, have them demonstrate that they want to help you get what you want, and then not accept responsibility for helping them get what they want. People can't do it. But you don't have to do that in a public hearing; you don't have to do that when you vote; you don't have to do that in court.

As a mediator, I create a context in which that is what happens, a setting which is protected enough, and where there are rules and rewards and encouragement for behaving in that way, and the usual impediments are taken away, and the burdens are made clear. Is there any other setting in which responsibilities are balanced with rights in this way?

The mediation process is the epitome of what I think democracy is really supposed to be like. It's not that people are no longer concerned about what they need. It's that they now realize that the only way to meet their needs is to respond to what others need as well, and therefore to come up with something they can do together that meets their needs. And this doesn't happen for altruistic reasons. The "we" here is special. This "we" can help each of us get what each of us wants and needs. There's no loss of "I," but there is recognition of others, of differences.

Participating in politics usually involves three things: lobby, vote, or stand for office. What else is there? Those don't promote the kind of balancing of obligation and responsibility that face-to-face, joint problem solving creates.

I wouldn't argue that my model of direct democracy is best and we should abandon all the conventional mechanisms. I'm in favor of representative democracy. But I do think we can supplement it on occasion in the ways that I've described, and I think that it does produce "we" decisions in an informed way. What's interesting to me is, What is our option?

Finally, of course, there are public disputes that shouldn't be mediated at all. I don't think disputes concerning rights—constitutional rights, human rights, basic rights—should be mediated, even if you could meet the interests of all sides. We have certain basic constitutional, human rights that are decided and legislated in a different way. I don't think that those ought to be compromised in any way by negotiations.

While I wouldn't mediate conflicts over rights, I think there are skills and tools of dispute resolution that can help us have much better public, or even private, debate and discussion, so that we can learn to live with our differences. I don't think we are going to resolve differences through mediation when rights—fundamental rights, constitutional rights—are at stake. So if someone came to me and said, "We would like you to mediate the state policy on abortion," I'd say that there's no point in reaching a negotiated policy agreement on abortion. It's a constitutional matter.

• • • • • • •

Susskind's views are likely to be welcomed by some, but greeted skeptically by others. For some practitioners, for example, Susskind is a gadfly, a stinging and disturbing political reminder of issues that seem intractable; he risks asking far too much of mediators of public disputes. For some more academic observers, though, Susskind does not challenge public dispute mediation fundamentally enough; his concerns with case-specific practice and even with the institutional delivery of public dispute resolution services threaten to distract attention from broader, underlying conditions of power and powerlessness, affluence and vulnerability. Thus where Susskind finds possibilities and opportunities, others may share his aspirations but nevertheless be less sanguine about their realization in everyday practice.

Larry Susskind nevertheless champions an alert pragmatism concerned with issues of power and exclusion, learning and deliberation, rights and responsibilities. His recommendation of an activist mediation style deserves widespread debate and criticism, for it cogently challenges the illusions of neutrality held not only by many mediators but also by many public-serving professionals who work in the face of conflict every day. And those who find activist mediation troublesome, Susskind reminds us, have a persistent practical question to answer: compared to what?

John Forester

PART THREE

. . . .

Extending the Reach of Mediation

In communities, at the workplace, in families, and on the world stage, mediation is a daily activity. People do it all the time. Yet their professional identity is not that of mediator. Rather, they are policemen, employees, mothers, diplomats, judges, social workers, bosses, neighbors, teachers. In ongoing situations of conflict and dispute, people get involved and try to help parties deal with their differences. These people are mediating, even though they do not necessarily align themselves with the profession.

Early on in our project, we decided that this part of the field was important because it represented probably the most extensive application of mediation. While these informal practitioners might lack the training and professional experience of the other two groups, they may have more of an impact. Further, interest is increasing on the part of other professionals—such as police, managers, teachers, and physicians, among others—to incorporate the techniques of mediation into their work. Understanding something about what happens when people mediate outside the profession complements the other portraits in the book.

Selecting people to profile for this category of practice, which has few boundaries, was complicated. In choosing the field builders, we had a more-or-less defined population. While we might quibble about a few people, there is enough consensus to define the population. There is also a distinct, although considerably larger, population of private-practice professionals, most of whom belong to one professional association or another, depending on their area of specialization. The universe of government mediators is larger still, comprising mediators who are employed by a host of federal, state, and local agencies. Choosing people outside the profession presents an even greater challenge, because the potential pool of people is truly limitless. Everyone, in one way or another, can claim to act as a mediator at some point in time. What we wanted to do was select people who had either national or local reputations as people who mediate as part of a larger social or economic agenda. That is, we wanted to understand not just what these people do when they claim to be mediating, but how these activities fit into other parts of their work.

Jimmy Carter and Joseph Elder use mediation as part of a larger agenda to pursue peace in the world. Profilers Eileen Babbitt and Tom Princen had studied more traditional forms of mediation, so they viewed these two men as part of different traditions in the international sphere. Juju Atkinson and Linda Colburn represent a group of people who operate in traditional organizations and use mediation as a supplement to other forms of influence that they have. Atkinson does so in the courts and Colburn in running a public housing project. Their profilers, William O'Barr and Neal Milner, knew these women from the mediation work they did in communities and were interested in how the use of mediation fits into their full-time occupations as judge and manager, respectively.

Outsiders are different from the other groups of mediators. First, they lack an institutional base of mediation to support their activities. They are really out on their own using their other positions and the force of their personalities and energy to pursue their agenda. And these agendas are quite different from those of the field builders and professionals. Outsiders have specific ends in mind and see mediation as a means to pursue them. As a result, they get involved in cases that fit these criteria. That is, they choose cases in which they think they can make a difference. They are not professionals. They lack the systematic approaches of the professionals and the commitment to bridging theory and practice that field builders have. Outsiders are more likely to improvise based on what they find; their approach is ad hoc, relying on their personalities, their relationships with the parties, and their positions.

For the many who try to use mediation in the context of work, these profiles demonstrate some of the dilemmas as well as some of the possibilities that using mediation can provide.

"Many times, once they strip away all the he said/she said kind of thing and I can get the other party to focus on the issue, we can start talking about the issue and get it resolved."

—Juju Atkinson

9

Juju Atkinson
Blurring the Distinction Between
Mediation and Adjudication

On the wall of Magistrate Juju Atkinson's office in the Durham County, North Carolina, courthouse hangs a sign that reads, "This Is a Court of Law. You Will Conduct Yourself Accordingly." This sign would perhaps be unnecessary if the offices assigned to the county's two small claims magistrates were more imposing or if the magistrates wore robes or sat on raised platforms. As it is, only the U.S. and North Carolina flags in two corners suggest that her office is, in fact, a courtroom.

Five days a week, fifty weeks a year, except for state and national holidays, Juju Atkinson hears small claims cases in a room that sometimes cannot even accommodate the parties and witnesses in one case, much less those assembling for another.

I first met Atkinson in the summer of 1984. I had asked the chief magistrate for permission to study the small claims courts in Durham as an initial step in my study of informal courts in four states. He granted permission and referred me to the presiding magistrates. At that point, I had no way to assess whether what I found was typical. Was Atkinson's approach to the administration of justice unique, or just one instance of more general patterns? Did her judgments reflect underlying legal principles, some personal sense of how to operate, or perhaps nothing more than what she had for breakfast?

Consider the judgment Atkinson rendered in the trial that took place in the 3:30 to 4:00 block on a June afternoon in 1984. The case concerns a woman's efforts to obtain possession of some household furnishings following separation from her husband of four years. Atkinson begins by asking the plaintiff to state the reasons she has brought the lawsuit. After listening patiently to a long and rambling narrative that details not only how the property in question was obtained but also the ups and downs of the couple's relationship, Atkinson turns to the defendant and asks him to respond. Again she listens while the defendant airs his version of the couple's problems. After both parties have spoken their pieces, she moves toward a solution:

Atkinson: Okay. So, Mr. Baker, you say that you're willing to return the furniture to Janice Oliver Baker. Since you are not communicating, how is this best going to be handled? Through the sheriff's department or ...

Plaintiff: I would prefer it like that if I could get it that way.

Atkinson does not respond immediately. Then, she speaks again:

Atkinson: Is there any other way?

Plaintiff: Well, I could get someone to go over there and pick the furniture up, but I'm just afraid that it's going to lead to more and more confusion, and I don't want to deal with that.

Atkinson pauses again. I learned in subsequent research in the California, Pennsylvania, Colorado, and other North Carolina courts that this is a point where many judges proceed to render authoritative decisions. The plaintiff has expressed her clear preference to have a straightforward decision that involves no further communication with the defendant. Atkinson thinks that a decision in the plaintiff's favor will not return her furniture. There are many places where things could fail between a favorable judgment and possession of the household furnishings. Before the magistrate speaks again, the defendant breaks the silence:

Defendant: Uh, she doesn't have to appear, um, when the furniture is picked up. . . .

Plaintiff: No, I, I . . .

Defendant: All she has to do is send whoever she wants to pick up the furniture. . . .

Plaintiff: . . . if that was to happen. Yeah, definitely that would, if we do it like that, you know, I would just, you know, whoever comes to get it let them get it and just make sure everything is there.

Atkinson: Okay, what will she need to do? Have someone call you to make sure you'll be home, or should we set a time?

Defendant: Well, right now at this time I'm working [pause]. Right now I would not be there until three o'clock in the afternoon. Um, she can get in contact with my parents. They'd be more than happy to . . . [he pauses again].

Atkinson: Okay. Okay. What I will do is continue this matter until Monday at 3. Of course, if the furniture has been returned or if you've picked it up by that time, then we will dismiss this action. If it has not, the next step would be just to . . . [There is a brief but audible pause before she continues.] . . . a judgment would be entered. And from there, execution, which means the sheriff will go out and pick the furniture up.

Plaintiff: Okay.

Atkinson: But hopefully you can arrange some time to have someone pick it up. And if you would just give us a call here, then we'll dismiss it as of Monday. If you have the furniture.

Plaintiff: Okay.

Atkinson: Okay?

Plaintiff: Thank you.

Atkinson: Here's my number in case.

One might well ask why, if it was the magistrate's decision
that furnishings in question belonged to the plaintiff, she did not
render a simple decision to that effect. Instead, she became
entangled in the development of an agreement by which the
plaintiff would arrange to pick up the furniture and no judgment
would be rendered against the defendant. Many judges would not
consider such involvement a part of their role. They would see
such behavior as attempts to devise and suggest a strategy that
both parties find agreeable to be appropriate in mediation, but
not in the courtroom. Off the bench, many say they worry about
such matters but do not view it as an appropriate part of their
judicial role to get involved.

But Atkinson has a different understanding of her judicial
role as a small claims magistrate. She considers that the legal system allows her some latitude in her approach to decision making.
Only after I had observed many other judges at work did I come
to understand the degree to which she blurs the distinction
between mediation and adjudication.

Atkinson's description of her courtroom philosophy might be
mistaken for an effort to describe some of the essential characteristics of mediation. She explained, "I would like to feel that when
people leave, they have communicated and have mediated the
situation. It is not that Party A or the plaintiff may not get 100
percent of what they came in for and Party B may not get 100
percent of what they came in for, but both parties are really okay
with the final decision, both parties go out with something."

I asked Atkinson how what she practiced in her courtroom
differed from mediation. The question seemed to surprise her at
first, but then she responded directly:

It really isn't that different, because I try to run this
court very much like mediation, to some extent.
Except I have more leverage, in the sense that I'm the
bottom line when it comes down to a decision. I try to

get parties to come to an agreement, but if it's not forthcoming, or if they're not into that mode—which many times they're not—I make the decision and they walk out. One may like it; one may not. Neither one may like it. But in mediation, you really haven't reached anything until both parties can walk out and feel that they've gained something.

Atkinson claims to have practiced her role as a small claims magistrate like this for the fifteen years she has been on the bench. She knows that not all small claims magistrates view their role this way, but she is comfortable and confident with what she considers to be the way she would like to have things done if she were one of the parties in a small claims proceeding. It is that reason, not some abstract theory or principle, that guides her in her work.

In fact, she said, it was not until some years after becoming a magistrate that she even had a name for "mediation." She learned about it when a community mediation center was established in Durham as an alternative to court. Both she and her husband found the idea appealing. They attended training sessions and became community mediators in the spirit of community service. What she discovered there, she says, struck her as the way things ought to be done.

I asked Atkinson how often she uses a mediational approach in the courtroom. She answered:

I've tried it on all kinds of cases. You can't always do it, because the parties have to be somewhat amenable. You can kind of feel it after listening to the parties for a short time if they are amenable. Perhaps it's a situation where the plaintiff is suing for $1,500 and the other party feels that there are some legitimate reasons not to pay that much. The plaintiff might listen to

that and say, "Well, you know, I really feel that I'm
entitled to my $1,500, but if you feel the way that you
feel about my services, then I will be willing to accept
$1,100." I may even ask the defendant, "What do you
feel the services are worth?" or "What do you feel you
shouldn't have to pay for?" And we might come up
with a figure, and I might say to the plaintiff, "Are you
willing to accept $1,100?" Many times the plaintiff
might say, "Well, not really." But after talking, he or
she might come down and say, "Yeah, $1,100 is fine."

When Atkinson talks about adjudication and mediation, her
orientation is decidedly practical. Though she is unaccustomed to
talking much about what she does every day, her reflections on
strategy and technique provide insight into her philosophy of
problem solving and dispute settlement.

She explained the steps she uses in reaching a solution to a
case. First, she asks the plaintiff to state the reason for bringing
the case, then asks the defendant to state a position with regard
to what has been said. Second, she attempts to separate the issues
from the emotions, a process that continues through all phases of
the trial. Third, she works with the parties to derive a solution.
Fourth, she seeks closure.

I think that what I try to do is get the position of the
plaintiff laid out, instead of focusing on all the emotion. I try to just get it down to "What is your position? Is it the money or is it that you don't like the
people standing here? What is it you don't like about
the situation?" To get down to a basis from which you
can negotiate. And once I get that from the plaintiff,
then I'll listen to the other party's position. "What is
your position with regard to the other party?" Many
times, I can strip away the heat. "I don't like the way

he talked to me," or "He told me this," or "He said this to me," and "I'm not that kind of person. You don't talk to me that way."

Once we get beyond that, and get down to the issue, then I'll say, "Well, Mr. So-and-So feels that you have too many people living there," or "Mr. So-and-So feels that you're not keeping up the yard. What's your position on that?" And many times, once they strip away all the he said/she said kind of thing and I can get the other party to focus on the issue, we can start talking about the issue and get it resolved.

What Atkinson has described here is her effort to open up communication between parties who have been unable to talk with one another. In the role of judge or mediator, she enters a dispute as a third party to administer and facilitate conversation between the parties. Once channels are open to talk, the parties suggest the solutions. She merely moves on to help articulate the solution she sees emerging from their reestablished communication.

Not all her courtroom behavior has this quality. Sometimes Atkinson declares one party victorious and tells the other that he or she has lost. My observations suggest that such occasions occur when documents and other evidence clearly show that one party owes money to the other. Even in such circumstances, she rarely renders judgment and leaves it at that. She tends to ask when the loser might pay and to suggest a payment schedule. This additional negotiation on her part is motivated by the desire to help people who, in her opinion, are owed money to collect it and to help those who owe it avoid the additional problems that will come from nonpayment.

Atkinson explained the difference between court and mediation as having to do not with the role of the judge or mediator but rather with what the parties seek when they choose between the two. "For dispute settlement to work, or for dispute resolution to work, you have to have two parties who consent to the mediation process and want to have input into a resolution. And, of course, I think you have a certain mind-set that would be amenable to that type of forum. People who just want a third party to tell the opponent he or she is wrong are more likely to end up in court, instead of mediation. Mediation doesn't have that big fist, the threat that court imposes."

In her experience, first-time plaintiffs expect that the courts will deliver results more swiftly than a community mediation program. The stark reality that the court issues judgments, not payments of damages, comes as a real surprise to many. As she expressed it, "So many times, people come to court and after I tell them they have a judgment, they say, 'Is that all I get? I want my money.' And I say, 'Well, unfortunately, we can't enter a judgment and pay you at the same time. You have a judgment.' 'What good is court?' they say. 'This is no good to me.'"

It is this understanding of the limitations of the courts that prompts Atkinson to talk with potential litigants about their options. She takes it upon herself to give them filing instructions and provide information about the small claims system, but as often as not she asks whether they know about the Dispute Settlement Center. A stack of brochures describing the center and its work are on the bookshelf near her desk, and she often gives them to people for whom she thinks mediation might represent a better alternative.

"I think that if they understood the principles of small claims court and what they get in mediation, more people might be inclined to use the mediation process. But I think the attitude still prevails that you must go to court to get relief you can't get anywhere else," she said.

One of the areas of her work as a small claims magistrate and a community mediator that Atkinson most eloquently articulates is the necessity of separating emotions and issues in order to reach a solution. The inability of parties to do this on their own is one of the main reasons people turn to the courts and to mediation centers, she thinks.

"Many times you need a third party to help keep things moving. The parties sometimes are so emotionally into the situation that they are not able to stand back as the third party would be able to and define the issues more clearly. That is where I see the mediator being able to be outside of the emotional realm guiding things along and moving the parties in a positive direction," she said.

Both in court and in community mediation, Atkinson thinks, emotional issues are entangled with property disputes, calling the police, swearing out warrants, and so on. She is quite specific about her effort to separate emotions from other issues.

> I am sure there are a lot of different types of cases, but most of the cases that I heard when I was a mediator were dealing with assault; neighbors, relatives, friends, or ex-friends—the issues were always very emotional. Assaults usually are precipitated by some type of emotional outburst, and once things have calmed down, then many times they wished they had not taken out the warrant. Usually the reason mediation was an alternative arose from the fact that some of these cases were between family members, neighbors, friends, relatives, and other parties with some type of relationship. By the time we came into mediation, things had often calmed down and the atmosphere was very different. Many times the parties would still be angry but generally more willing to listen and communicate.

This effort to separate emotion from issue leads Atkinson to spend considerable time in both mediation sessions and small claims cases airing the emotions. Once the parties have expressed their emotions, then she believes they can move on to deal with assault and other offenses. Emotional issues seem to Atkinson to cloud the real issues.

. . . .

Some personal details help explain why Atkinson is so interested in her role as helper and facilitator in mediation and in court, as well as showing where her views about separating emotions and issues come from. She insists that she is not modeling herself after one particular person or some philosophy articulated by someone else. She sees her beliefs and their realization in practice as emerging from her own life circumstances and personal experiences.

In childhood, Atkinson said, she did not have any clear idea of careers. She did not have her eyes set on being a lawyer, doctor, or judge. Her own words tell us how she assesses both early experience and the satisfaction of her current work: "I always knew that I wanted to work with people where I felt I had some impact, and I knew I enjoyed work that was challenging and interesting," she said. "This job is perfect for me. Each day brings about new challenges of having to deal with new people and situations. This job is never boring because there are always new developments to keep it interesting. I feel very lucky to be in a job that I enjoy. My experiences on other jobs was not as satisfying. So far after fifteen years as a magistrate I am still being challenged."

In North Carolina, it is not necessary for a small claims magistrate to be a member of the bar or even to have studied law. The only formal training is a two-week course at the Institute of Government in Chapel Hill. Magistrates are guided by reference books and often attend continuing education courses. Atkinson's own story of how she became magistrate lacks any formal training in the law.

"When I was working at North Carolina Central University," she explained, "the year was 1976, a friend who was the chairman of the Committee on the Affairs of Black People at the time was working to place blacks in the clerk's office. He asked if I might be interested in such a position, and I stated yes. I later applied for a position and was hired in the fall of 1976. After working as a deputy clerk, I was asked to apply for a magistrate's position that had become vacant. I became a magistrate in 1977."

The absence of a legal education may be an important reason why Atkinson interprets her role as magistrate so flexibly. Her story of how she became a mediator is equally telling.

"When the Dispute Settlement Center first started in Durham County," she said, "I thought that there should be some avenue other than court for different types of resolution of problems. It was a great idea. The court system alone does not give people many options. Mediation is a nice alternative.... When I learned about the Dispute Settlement Center, I said, 'Wow, this is great,' and I wanted to know more about the process, and of course, I learned about the role of a mediator. I said, 'This would be a nice way to volunteer time to the community.'"

After Atkinson got married, her husband also became a mediator. During the first couple of years of their marriage, they often mediated on the same evenings, sometimes as co-mediators.

Until our very last meeting, Atkinson never brought up the issue of gender and the degree to which her being a woman might influence her outlook in some way. But once I had broken the ice, her words began to flow. Perhaps they would have come quicker had I, too, been a woman.

Some men, she said, get into power issues in their role as judges. Her experience had shown her that some men who sit on the bench want to be seen as strong and in control. A man wants everybody in the courtroom to be clear on who the judge is, where authority rests, and who makes decisions. For women,

Atkinson said, it is different. It is not as important to be seen as strong.

As she talked, she elaborated on her perceptions of the differ-ent emphases of men and women as judges: "I guess it's societal, but women tend to be more into relationships. In small claims court, we're talking about a relationship between two parties. They had to have some kind of relationship, even if it was just customer to retailer. I think that women are more interested in salvaging relationships than handing down some ruling."

I asked what male judges were interested in. She answered without hesitation: "solutions." The gender difference that Atkinson talked about was the practical, everyday version of many themes in modern feminist theory.

As I listened to Atkinson, I realized how much our personal histories and positions in society influence our approaches to life. For her, it was clear her views were a product of a complex set of factors: a caring and compassionate approach to others, an inter-est in getting things done rather than exercising authority, the absence of a formal legal education, an intuitive sense of the appropriateness of mediated solutions, and a genuine ability to empathize with the plights of others.

Exploring the personal circumstances that led Atkinson to her career as a small claims magistrate may exaggerate the dis-tinctive and idiosyncratic nature of her approach. Indeed, this may happen whenever we deepen our understanding of who someone is and what beliefs orient his or her actions. However distinctive the childhood, career path, and outlook, the fact remains that some other small claims judges in other jurisdictions share Atkinson's interest in seeking workable solutions rather than handing down authoritative decisions without regard to their practical application.

In many ways, her behavior on the bench suggests that she shares with many of her judicial colleagues in different kinds of courts a disposition toward settling cases whenever possible. But the approach of these judges who bring a mediational frame of mind to the cases they hear is aimed more toward fostering agreements between parties than toward settling cases.

The distinction between settlements and agreements may seem a fine one, and it is not one Atkinson herself articulated. It can, however, be understood by comparing her approach to that of other judges whose goal is characterized more by the phrase "disposing of cases." In actuality, settling a case might mean merely that the plaintiff agrees to drop the case against the defendant. This is a victory for the legal system, but it may not be a victory for the individuals. Only the case is settled. No consideration is given as to whether the underlying problem is itself settled. By contrast, agreement—a term much more at home in community mediation centers than in courtrooms—is a set of terms that both parties find acceptable and assert their willingness to abide by.

Atkinson thinks mediation is more limited by people's attitudes and misconceptions than by any inappropriateness of the process to situations or institutions. In thinking about broader applications beyond the small claims court and the community mediation center, she spoke excitedly about the schools: "Everything I'm reading about mediation says it's spreading widely. I see it in school. I mean, they have children in junior high and high school forming their own mediation centers to settle disputes between students, or between students and teachers.

"I don't know how it's set up, but it was good just hearing that the schools are moving into that area. Arbitration is also moving into many bold areas. Of course, I think it's wonderful."

In addition to this broadening of mediation and the increased uses of other settlement procedures like arbitration, Atkinson sees a greater role for mediation in family conflicts. Divorce mediation particularly gets her attention. "Many people," she observed, "look at each other and say, 'This marriage is not working,' but they're not really angry. They're really not trying to punish one another; they are not saying, 'I'm gonna take you to court and get everything you have.' I think mediation is for those individuals. So in mediation they get to go in and work through their problems, and many times you come out with a resolution that both parties are happy with."

Finally, I asked her whether there are people for whom mediation just will not work. She had this to say: "It won't work for vindictive people. Angry parties in divorces, people who feel that because of their position or power or influence, or because they are female, or because they are a doctor, or because of whatever they feel is their position, they can persuade the court to give them more or make the other person pay more to punish them in some way."

Whether Atkinson's approach fits academic models of mediation or judicial decision making, one thing is clear: an integrity in her beliefs and practice is evident. Nurturing, helpful, facilitative—these qualities guide her interpretation of her roles of mediator and small claims magistrate and of the sign that hangs on her office wall. It is a court of law, but it is she who interprets those laws and the behavior appropriate in it.

William M. O'Barr

♦ ♦ ♦ ♦ ♦ ♦ ♦

"[My] leverage at Camp David, Ethiopia, and
Nicaragua was the same—the ability to arouse public
and worldwide attention to the party that is guilty of
standing in the way of peace or believes they can act
with impunity."

—Jimmy Carter

10

. . . .

Jimmy Carter
The Power of Moral Suasion in
International Mediation

I was excited about my interview with Jimmy Carter. For several years, I had been following the development of the Carter Center[1] in Atlanta, Georgia, and its energetic commitment to the ideals and work of the former U.S. president. From my interest in mediation, I had read many accounts of the Camp David negotiations, and I was fascinated to learn that Carter was once again trying his hand at settling seemingly intractable conflicts. I also had heard from many who work with him of his intensity, intelligence, and warmth. Now I would finally get to meet this almost legendary man.

My interview took place at the Carter Center on a rainy spring morning in March 1990. The center is in a residential section of Atlanta on thirty acres of beautifully landscaped grounds. The four pavilions that then made up the center contained the Jimmy Carter Library and Museum; numerous nonprofit, international programs focusing on health, human rights, hunger, and conflict resolution; and conference and meeting facilities. Each pavilion has floor-to-ceiling windows that look out on the grounds and a beautiful Japanese garden. The interior spaces are decorated with presidential memorabilia and comfortably furnished for use as meeting and reception areas.

Carter's office is on the second level of one of the pavilions. As I reached the doorway and tentatively looked in, he looked up from his desk and walked over to greet me. He looked older than I remembered (I had not seen him since he left office ten years earlier), but he projected energy and strength as he smiled warmly, shook my hand, and said how happy he was to speak with me. We sat in comfortable chairs at the opposite end of the office from his large desk. The atmosphere in the room was very soothing, with classical music playing softly and the large windows bringing the lush gardens into full view.

During the interview, I was struck first by Carter's attentiveness and focus. He keyed in immediately to my questions, and his concentration never wavered throughout our talk. My second impression was of the former president's obvious immersion in and commitment to the work of the center. He explained that intranational conflicts are the focus of his conflict resolution work; no international organization, he pointed out, has the jurisdiction to intervene and no national governments can negotiate with insurgency groups. He thus feels an "obligation" to work in these disputes, because of his access to the important actors and his unique, extra-governmental status. He is, in effect, building an institution from which to conduct private diplomacy.

Carter's current conflict resolution work is based in large part on his experience at Camp David—his "first love," as one associate framed it. To understand Carter's approach to mediation, one must first understand that historic 1978 meeting of Egypt's Anwar Sadat, Israel's Menachem Begin, and President Jimmy Carter, the mediator. That mediation has been well chronicled by scores of analysts and by Carter himself in his autobiographical work, *Keeping Faith*. My review of the history of events leading to the Camp David Accords and the Middle East peace process will be brief.

· · · · · · ·

After months of Carter's cajoling, bargaining, pleading, and worrying, the Egyptian and Israeli negotiating teams arrived at Camp David on September 4, 1978. Carter's preparation for his mediation role at Camp David had included immersion in personal profiles of Begin and Sadat.

> This negotiation was highly personal for me, perhaps more than any of the others in which I was involved. Before I went to Camp David, I took a three- or four-day trip down the middle fork of the Salmon River and made a brief visit to Lake Jackson. As I typically did, I took along with me two thick briefing books that had been prepared for me by the psychologists in the intelligence agencies describing the two men with whom I would be negotiating. . . . The psychological profiles described these men, their characters, political origins, family backgrounds, obligations, allies, and enemies, and every possible consequence of a successful negotiation. By the time I got to Camp David, I knew a lot more about Begin and Sadat than they dreamed that I knew. Perhaps I knew some things that very few people knew. This gave me a chance to enmesh two highly diverse men in a successful negotiation. (Carter, 1987, pp. 6–7).

Carter met separately with Begin and then with Sadat, pushing each to be as flexible as possible and think creatively about solutions to longstanding problems. Sadat's primary concerns were the return of Egyptian territory, the sovereignty of the Palestinians, and the future relations of Israel with the other Arab nations. He was responsive to Carter's plan for aiming to negotiate a total settlement. Begin's primary interest was Israeli security, and he believed that the details of an agreement could be worked out by the foreign ministers if the leaders could draw up general principles.

On the second and third days of the summit, Begin and Sadat met together with Carter. Contrary to Carter's hopes, the two men did not get along, and they did not meet together again for the remainder of the negotiation.

At Camp David, Carter continued to play the same role he had played in the months preceding the meeting in the Maryland hill country. He negotiated vigorously with each leader separately, focusing on both the general principles and difficult details of possible agreements. He took the lead in drafting comprehensive proposals, shuttling back and forth between Begin and Sadat to get their comments and changes. In all, Carter and his team drafted twenty-three versions of an agreement before the negotiations concluded.

Carter's most dramatic and effective approach to these two men was on the personal level. He consistently reminded them of the consequences of failing to reach an agreement, framed in the terms that mattered most to each. He appealed to what he believed to be both men's real desire for peace. He reminded each of the constraints that the other faced and of the compromises that the other had made to date, as well as assuring each of the other's good faith efforts. He used his position as U.S. president to underscore the importance of an agreement to relations between each country and the United States. And he let them know how far out on a limb he was, personally and politically, and how disastrous it would be for him as well as for them if no agreement was reached.

Two specific incidents warrant description, as they are striking examples of Carter's powerful style. The first occurred on the eleventh day of the summit: Sadat announced that he was leaving after having an unsatisfactory meeting with Israeli Defense Minister Moshe Dayan. Carter asked to meet with Sadat alone.

"I explained to him," Carter wrote in *Keeping Faith*, "the extremely serious consequences of his unilaterally breaking off the negotiations: that his action would harm the relationship between Egypt and the United States, he would be violating his personal promise to me, and the onus for failure would be on him. I described the possible future progress of Egypt's friendships and alliances—from us to the moderate and then radical Arabs, thence to the Soviet Union. I told him it would damage one of my most precious possessions—his friendship and our mutual trust" (Carter, 1982, p. 392).

The second incident took place on the thirteenth day: the Israelis insisted that the language about Jerusalem was unsatisfactory and that the prospects for agreement were bleak.

> Earlier, my secretary, Susan Clough, had brought me some photographs of Begin, Sadat, and me. They had already been signed by President Sadat, and Prime Minister Begin had requested that I autograph them for his grandchildren. Knowing the trouble we were in with the Israelis, Susan suggested that she go and get the actual names of the grandchildren, so that I could personalize each picture. I did this, and walked over to Begin's cabin with them. He was sitting on the front porch, very distraught and nervous because the talks had finally broken down at the last minute.
>
> I handed him the photographs. He took them and thanked me. Then he happened to look down and saw that his granddaughter's name was on the top one. He spoke it aloud, and then looked at each photograph individually, repeating the name of the grandchild I had written on it. His lips trembled, and tears welled up in his eyes. He told me a little about each child, and especially about the one who seemed to be his favorite. We were both emotional as we talked quietly

for a few minutes about grandchildren and about war.
(Carter, 1982, p. 399)

After each of these very personal, very emotional sessions, the
stridency of both Sadat and Begin softened. Carter's willingness
to address the difficult emotions of these situations paid off.

A tremendous amount of dialogue also went on between the
other members of the respective negotiating teams. Carter, Begin,
and Sadat had each brought a small number of top aides with
them to Camp David, which proved to be extremely important.
At particular points, when the leaders became intransigent, the
aides and advisers continued to meet and discuss alternatives. In
the final hours of the summit, the results of these meetings saved
the negotiations from breaking down.

The agreements reached at Camp David were not as comprehensive as Carter had wanted them to be but, by all accounts,
were the best that could be attained. Some issues, such as the
withdrawal of Israel from the Sinai, were deferred to later negotiation. Other issues, like the jurisdiction of Jerusalem, were to be
clarified by letters between Carter, Begin, and Sadat, spelling out
the details of their resolution. On September 17, 1978, in
Washington, Sadat and Begin signed the Camp David Accords,
with Jimmy Carter as witness.

. . . .

After leaving the White House, Jimmy Carter returned to
Georgia and, in 1982, founded the Carter Center, the goal of
which was to focus on "issues of public policy through nonpartisan study and research, conferences, and special publications."
The center's Program on Conflict Resolution took as its main
activity the formation of an "international negotiation network"
(INN). The INN was to be an informal affiliation of individuals,

universities, and organizations from around the world, whose objectives included the coordination of conflict resolution efforts in intranational conflicts.

During the Reagan years, Carter's international mediation efforts were discouraged by Washington. As Reagan was preparing to leave the White House, in October 1988, the INN held a working session at the Carter Center to identify and discuss "hot spots" around the world that were not getting attention where the INN might have an impact. In attendance were people from the United Nations and other international and regional organizations involved in monitoring conflicts. According to one of the participants in this meeting, the group adopted several criteria on which to "rank" this list of hot spots. These included loss of life, potential to involve the superpowers, flawed or failed past negotiation efforts, degree of human need (such as significant health and welfare problems), and potential for successful intervention.

The conflicts in the Horn of Africa, involving Ethiopia and the Sudan, reportedly scored high in all criteria. According to Dayle Spencer, director of the center's Conflict Resolution Program, Carter's decision to move first to investigate involvement in the Horn of Africa was based on his concern for the suffering there, due both to war and famine. With the deaths of over one million people, Carter felt the Horn had the greatest need for INN services, so that was where they must begin. (In Ethiopia, the conflict was between the government of the People's Democratic Republic of Ethiopia [PDRE] and the Eritrean People's Liberation Front [EPLF]. For twenty-eight years, these two groups have been fighting over Eritrea's demands for self-determination. In the Sudan, the disputing parties are the Sudanese government and the Sudanese People's Liberation Army [SPLA].)

In April 1989, Carter led an INN fact-finding team to Ethiopia and the Sudan to explore possibilities for mediation of

the disputes in these countries. Carter enjoyed a better relationship with the Bush administration than he had with the Reagan
administration, and he was given access to briefings from the
U.S. State Department before departing. Carter and his team also
met with former officials of the Ethiopian and Sudanese governments and liberation movements who reside in the United
States, as well as with the leaders of private voluntary organizations working in the Horn. In these meetings, Carter's approach
was to explain his concerns about the conflicts and ask for the
perspective of these people because of their considerable
experience in the region.

Carter received State Department assistance in setting up the
initial in-country meetings. The disputing parties knew that
Carter was trying to talk with everyone involved in the disputes,
a difference from past mediation efforts in which some parties
were excluded from the dialogue. The team for this first trip
included Rosalynn Carter, Dayle Spencer, and William Spencer
and William Ury, both professionals in conflict resolution who
serve as members of the INN staff.

Carter was received by government and rebel leaders in both
countries, including President Mengistu Haile Mariam of
Ethiopia and General Secretary Isaias Afwerki of the Eritrean
rebels. From descriptions of the exchanges on this trip, Carter's
goal in these initial meetings was to gather information about the
conflict and the leadership and persuade them to give mediation
a try. According to members of his team, he would explain that
he was concerned about the suffering of the people in the region
and was there to "try to help them work out their differences." As
he listened to each person's account of the conflict and what he
felt they needed in order to negotiate, he consistently assured the
leaders in these first meetings that he understood their position
and plight.

Carter's reputation and previous experience in international
conflict appeared to have an impact even before any negotiations

began. In the Sudan, for example, the U.S. ambassador gave a party for Carter and invited all of the people from both sides of the conflict with whom Carter had met separately. One can imagine that, in the midst of a civil war, these people did not usually socialize with each other. However, they all attended the party. Carter, it seemed, had been the draw that overcame the political barriers. During the course of the evening, Carter reportedly regaled a table of the most influential guests with his stories of Camp David. The success of that social event lends credence to claims that a successful international mediator must be influential and must have stature—qualities that the former U.S. president has in abundance.

The Carter team prepared for each meeting on the days following by drawing up an agenda and a set of desired outcomes. Sometimes they would split up and meet separately with different officials. Even though the expectations on this first trip were low and the group was aware that caution was needed, a "real sense of excitement" still prevailed, according to Bill Spencer, about the possibility of helping move toward resolution of the dispute.

Carter began assuming a mediator role even before he had been asked to do so. He and his team developed a strategy as to the order in which to visit cities and schedule appointments. In this way, he began to carry "messages" from one group to another as he made his rounds. According to Spencer, he even confronted the Sudanese government officials as to why they were not delivering messages to the rebels themselves. In subtle and not-so-subtle ways, he began to create communication between the parties in these disputes.

Carter ended each meeting with an invitation to visit the Carter Center, considered a flattering proposal by many and one that several of the principal parties later accepted. In the months following this trip, Carter met separately in Atlanta with Afwerki of the EPLF and with the Secretary General of the Sudanese People's Liberation Army. In July 1989, Carter returned to the

Horn of Africa to meet again with government leaders in the two countries. According to one member of the mediation team, Carter used his powers of persuasion with Mengistu by asking the Ethiopian president to consider how much better he would be viewed in the eyes of the world, both now and in coming generations, if he were to be responsible for ending the civil war. Reportedly, Carter drew on his various identities as former president, farmer, engineer, Navy man, father, grandfather, and religious man to establish a "connection" with each person involved in the negotiation process. Making such connections helped him to frame persuasive arguments for taking steps toward peace.

These efforts apparently worked with Mengistu and Afwerki, for they agreed to either come themselves or send representatives to Atlanta and begin building an agenda for negotiations. Carter and the INN staff convened these talks at the Carter Center on September 7, 1989. It was the first time that the PDRE and the EPLF had agreed to talk without preconditions and with the knowledge of the international public. Carter himself made an announcement of the upcoming meeting in the August 18, 1989, *New York Times*. In the *Times* article, the representative of the EPLF to the United States and Canada was quoted as saying, "From our meetings with President Carter—and there were a series of meetings in Atlanta and in Khartoum—we were convinced of his concern for peace and human rights. That is why we decided to continue with his initiative."

Carter is quoted in this same article as attributing the lack of success of previous peace talks to preconditions and the absence of third-party observers. He referred to himself as a "mediator or observer at the talks." He also underscored the importance of publicly announcing the Atlanta meetings, to "force both sides to put forth their most attractive and reasonable proposals and demonstrate a degree of good faith to prevent failure."

Descriptions of the Atlanta meetings show Carter as wanting to set an informal, personal tone in the negotiations. The delegations did not sit at a table but opposite each other in plush, comfortable chairs and couches in one of the elegant meeting rooms at the center. Carter and his wife, Rosalynn, sat together at the front of the room, with the INN staff close at their side. The staff did not participate in the discussions but communicated suggestions and observations via notes to Carter during the proceedings. Carter and Mrs. Carter, however, talked openly with each other during these meetings, sometimes as if the others were not present. One staff member remarked that this openness had a positive effect on the parties—they could *see* how diligently Carter was working to assist them.

The first day was devoted to setting a preliminary agenda. The talks were recorded, and Carter asked each side to make an initial presentation to the entire group; thereafter, in both joint meetings and private caucuses, Carter and his team pushed hard on getting through the agenda. During breaks, the mediation team convened to brainstorm and prioritize for the next session.

In the joint sessions, Carter reportedly often took the role of a very strong negotiator, "beating up" on one side and then the other, a process the parties apparently did not like. One staff member characterized it as making the parties negotiate with him rather than with each other. In these bilateral exchanges, Carter would often intimate that there were ways in which he could possibly "help" each party, because of his access to the U.S. government and other world leaders. According to one staff member, Carter could have delivered "about 80 percent" of what he offered.

Between the joint sessions, Dayle and Bill Spencer often met with the delegations at their hotels. According to Bill Spencer, this gave the parties more access to the mediation team, as it was easier for the delegates to approach the staff with information or questions than it was for them to confront Carter himself. It also allowed the mediation team to bring the EPLF "up to speed" on the negotiation process, as they were not as experienced as their counterparts in the PDRE. Afwerki, the EPLF leader, was staying at the hotel with his team but not participating as a delegate to the talks. This created some confusion about who had the decision-making power for the EPLF, and it reportedly took the mediation team some time to sort this out.

After ten days of negotiations, on September 17, 1989, the leaders of the PDRE and EPLF, with Carter as witness, signed an agreement outlining the parameters for future talks. The next round was scheduled for November in Nairobi. While not constituting a settlement of their differences, it was a beginning—and far more than the parties had ever accomplished before.

Carter and his team met with many experts in the field of conflict resolution in preparation for the Nairobi meeting. One participant in these meetings described the Carter group as seeking advice on their mediation role and the structure of this next session. As a result of these consultations and the mediation team's experience in the Atlanta meeting, the Nairobi session was set up a bit differently.

Carter chaired the joint meetings, as before, but many more separate caucuses were held. In these private sessions, Carter and his staff reportedly worked vigorously with the parties to hammer out the language of an agreement, using computer equipment that they had brought with them. Carter himself manned a laptop, testing out phrases, printing out drafts, and presenting them to the parties. This was clearly a repeat of the exhaustive drafting process that had taken place at Camp David.

According to Spencer, the Nairobi meetings exposed the true agenda of the parties. Neither side was really negotiating sincerely. The PDRE was interested in "good press" about their handling of threats to the government; the EPLF wanted international exposure of their plight. Carter therefore "played more hardball" than at previous meetings. At one point, he reportedly threatened to break off the negotiations and "go public" with the insincerity of the parties' negotiation efforts.

This threat worked after a fashion. The delegations did reach a tentative agreement concerning the format and structure of actual negotiations. However, at the final press conference announcing their agreement, both sides became abusive and attacked Carter, as well as one another. These preliminary talks had held the parties in a de facto ceasefire for several months, but the EPLF resumed military activity before subsequent talks could be convened. Carter and his staff continued to meet with the Ethiopian parties separately throughout 1990, trying to rekindle the negotiations. As of May 1991, the conflict was moving toward resolution. Mengistu had fled to Zimbabwe, leaving his vice president in control of the government. Eritrean militia were marching on the capitol city, Addis Ababa, and U.S.-sponsored talks between the government and the rebel leaders were scheduled to begin in London.

• • • • • • •

Even though the Camp David meetings resulted in an agreement and the Ethiopian talks did not, Carter feels he has more potential to settle disputes now than he did as president. The flexibility he now enjoys as a former head of state is a definite advantage. He told me he now has the "total freedom to meet whom I choose. . . . The U.S. government and international organizations are barred from meeting with revolutionary forces, and international organizations can't intervene in the internal affairs of a country." Carter, on the other hand, can pick up the phone and make contact with movers and shakers in the United Nations, the U.S. government, and foreign nations. He is not bound by interest group pressures, the constitutional constraints placed on a head of state, or previous agreements entered into by the U.S. government. This flexibility, he believes, gives him more power as a mediator than he had at Camp David.

Carter's leverage in his present role comes from several sources. The most significant is his highly personal and moral approach to mediation. In his own words, he "feels an obligation to work in these [intranational civil] disputes" because official parties are forbidden from intervening and because these disputes are often deeply rooted and result in prolonged suffering for the communities involved.

As a mediator, Carter speaks as the "conscience" of the international community. His appeal to world leaders is to do what is right and just for their people. He invoked these themes at Camp David and again with the Ethiopian and Eritrean leaders. His words carry weight because Carter himself is known as a person of high personal integrity and spiritual belief. In Dayle Spencer's words, Carter has the "ability to let the world know if parties are not acting in good faith. [Leaders know that he] deals fairly and honestly and [that he] expects others to do the same."

Carter can use this status to apply pressure in a given dispute. His staff talked of his willingness to "put himself and his own reputation at risk." At Camp David, for example, Carter knew he was running a risk, against the counsel of his advisers, in continuing to push Begin and Sadat. He let these leaders each know that if they did not reach an agreement, it would "look bad" for him (domestically and internationally) as well as for them.

In his more recent intervention in Ethiopia, Carter took that same risk, with the stakes being a bit different. He did not stand to lose political capital if the talks failed, as when he was president, but he did run the risk of being considered ineffective or, even worse, detrimental to a resolution. This would not look good on his first try as a citizen diplomat. Carter also would look foolish if he called on his domestic and international connections in the service of an agreement without the parties negotiating in good faith, a fact he no doubt used to pressure Mengistu and Afwerki.

Carter's visibility and his willingness to use the media to mobilize national and international public opinion is another way in which he acts as a voice of morality. As one staff member put it, "when Carter gets involved [in a dispute], the stakes [for the parties] go up." Carter himself believes that his "leverage at Camp David, Ethiopia, and Nicaragua was the same—the ability to arouse public and worldwide attention to the party that is guilty of standing in the way of peace or believes they can act with impunity." (Carter was an observer during the 1990 elections in Nicaragua to verify that the process was "free and fair.")

There are two caveats to the effectiveness of this type of leverage. First, the leadership of the parties in dispute may not care significantly about their or Carter's international reputation. In that case, holding them up to public "shaming" will not affect their behavior in the least. Second, the strategy can backfire. As with the PDRE and the EPLF, the parties may be more interested in using this increased visibility to focus world attention on their separate agendas rather than on settling their dispute.

Carter uses the force of his personality and intellect when he mediates. As shown in both the Camp David and Ethiopian examples, he moves back and forth between mediating and negotiating directly with the parties. He immerses himself in the substance of the negotiations and strongly advocates for particular outcomes. He is, according to Dayle Spencer, a "very, very strong negotiator, one who imposes himself upon the parties to try and get them to agree."

What does Carter think is the most difficult task in mediation? Getting parties to the table. "The most difficult single problem is the first step—getting parties to recognize the status, legitimacy, integrity of the other side. . . . [This is] very difficult in a revolutionary situation. . . . [Parties must ask themselves], 'Are we willing to sit down with the scoundrels, criminals, terrorists whom we've denounced for twenty years?'"

Reflecting on his mediation experiences, Carter outlines three elements he feels are essential for bringing parties together for negotiation. First, the "politicians have to see a *significant* difference between the costs of continuing with the status quo and the benefits of sitting down with the other side. A modest difference isn't enough." Second, a "stalemate is necessary. [Parties must know that they] cannot win on the battlefield." Finally, a "mediator is necessary to handle the proceedings. Begin and Sadat did not meet for the last ten days at Camp David. They needed someone who could go back and forth, knew the details, could work with the associates on both sides."

Some in the field of mediation say that the Carter approach is doomed to fail because any real resolution process depends on working in a region for a long time, building relationships, and establishing trust. Carter's team, some say, "parachutes in" with offers of assistance, raising expectations and then possibly leaving people more discouraged if the negotiations fail. In my opinion, such criticism is a bit harsh. Not having interviewed the PDRE or the EPLF, I would hazard a guess that relations at the end of the negotiations were not worse off than before the talking started. During the ten-month effort, the violence abated. And the parties were able to agree on some procedural issues that may have laid the groundwork for later U.S.-brokered negotiations.

One senior practitioner of international dispute resolution has remarked that Carter has a significant contribution to make in helping communities in conflict, but his challenge is to find the most effective way to make that contribution. Carter shared with me his hope that ensuring free and fair election processes would provide greater stability in the developing nations. His monitoring of such elections, as in Nicaragua, is widely praised. Of course, the rival parties within a state must agree in the first instance to allow such elections, and herein often lies the insurmountable source of conflict.

Carter, however, has proven his ability to bring people together, at the Carter Center and elsewhere. International leaders are prone to trust him because his motivation is not political or monetary gain. He has established a reputation as someone truly interested in using his resources in promoting peace and improving the quality of life in all regions of the world. As previously mentioned, the programs of the Carter Center focus on health, human rights, democratic governance, agricultural development, and hunger relief in addition to conflict resolution. Many newspaper articles in the U.S. press have praised Carter for being the "best ex-president" and for regaining stature after his crushing political defeat by dedicating his ongoing work to public service. It would be hard for a sitting head of state to refuse help from such an individual.

Carter is also continuing to build a track record. As every mediator knows, this is critical in establishing credibility and securing future work. Even though the Ethiopian talks did not produce an agreement, they demonstrated Carter's determination to build on his Camp David experience and his willingness to take risks in highly visible, seemingly intractable disputes. Of late, he seems to have decided, after the Ethiopian experience, to work with less visibility as a mediator.

When Carter concluded the Israeli-Egyptian peace treaty (a process that took many weeks of work after Camp David), he returned from a grueling trip to the Middle East and wrote in his diary, "I resolved to do everything possible to get out of the negotiating business!" Fortunately, that decision was short-lived. Each time Carter intervenes in a complex international dispute, he gains more experience in the mediation role. With the number of disputes now raging in the world, such experience is sorely needed.

• • • • • • •

A postscript: The military regime of Mengistu Haile-Mariam was toppled in May 1991 by the forces of the Ethiopian People's Revolutionary Democratic Front (EPRDF), ending a decades-long civil war between the central government and the rebel movement based in the Ethiopian province of Tigray. The Eritrean People's Liberation Front (EPLF), having successfully dislodged Mengistu's forces from Eritrea prior to his fall, declared independence in May 1993 after a nationwide referendum. The Transitional Government of Ethiopia, led by EPRDF leader Meles Zenawi, is preparing for national elections, planned for 1995, that will put in place a democratic government.

Sudan today is still ravaged by civil war between the northern government of Khartoum and the southern rebel forces of the Sudanese People's Liberation Army (SPLA). The situation has been complicated even more by the fragmentation of the SPLA, with one faction fighting for self-determination and the others calling for secession from the north. The war has dislocated thousands, and some experts report that the humanitarian situation in the south is worse than that of Somalia prior to international intervention in that country in 1992. Since President Carter's initiative in 1989, there have been several unsuccessful attempts to bring lasting peace to Sudan. The most recent talks, convened by the Nigerian government, were in Abuja in May 1993.

Eileen F. Babbitt

Note

1. The Carter Center includes two separate entities: the Jimmy Carter Library and Museum, which houses the records of Carter's presidential administration, and the nonprofit Carter Center, a consortium of international and domestic programs focused on the promotion of democracy, resolving conflict, preserving human rights, improving health, and fighting hunger.

References

Carter, J. (1982). *Keeping faith*. New York: Bantam Books.

Carter, J. (1987). Principles of negotiation. *Stanford Journal of International Law, 23*, 1–12.

"I think there is a sort of a Zen, if you will, to dealing with violent conflict, and it has to do with getting back to your own center and quickly determining what really matters."

—Linda Colburn

11

. . . .

Linda Colburn
On-the-Spot Mediation in
a Public Housing Project

While both rhetoric and training in the field of mediation typically stress the informality and flexibility of the process, what most mediators do, in fact, is usually quite structured, formal, and inflexible. Although students of mediation learn procedures that presumably could be used in a variety of settings, mediation settings do not vary that much. Most of the work takes place in a room with a table and some chairs. "The parties" (itself a formal, legalistic way to describe people in disputes) have some idea of what to expect, and they know something of what is about to happen to them.

The process is typically quite civilized. The disputants stay in their chairs or get up at mutually agreed-on times. The mediator, who has been chosen because of his or her distance from the parties, talks about the need for mediator "neutrality." The mediator is not supposed to take sides and is there to make a process work. If someone throws a punch or the language gets nasty, the mediator simply has to stop the hearing and send everyone home.

Mediators' involvement with the lives of the disputing parties is indirect and fleeting. When I was working with a group of people trying to get better mental health services, I felt very sympathetic toward the mentally ill clients and I empathized with their frustrations. Yet their problems were only indirectly my problems. My job did not depend on making things work out. I make my living as a college professor, and my life would stay about the same whether or not these people got what they wanted.

The life of contemporary North American mediators is typically that simple. We do not have to work very hard to establish our authority. The people who come to us may not get along, they may even hate each other, but they will behave reasonably well in the mediation room. Often they believe they must cooperate because the court has sent them. We follow a set of standard procedures to work out the issue. Then, after the mediation is done, we wish the parties luck and head on home, probably never to see them again.

What happens when a mediator ventures away from this sheltered model? What happens when he or she tries to take seriously the idea that mediation can work in very violent situations and in situations in which it is hard to remain distant and neutral? What happens when the mediator has coercive power over the parties and yet wants to act as a peacemaker?

Linda Colburn's early experience is grounded in the kind of calm and predictable settings I have described. She began working in alternative dispute resolution (ADR) through training by the local Neighborhood Justice Center (NJC) and still does cases (another formal, legalistic word) for them as a volunteer. She is considered one of their best mediators in Hawaii. Colburn's mediation activities have increasingly ranged far beyond the justice center. She is known statewide as someone to call if a problem is novel or difficult. In her words, "I tend to get opportunities to work with people who are very difficult, or on the kind of conflicts that make people say, 'No, no, no, I don't want to do that one. Let Linda do it.'" As a result, she has used ADR skills in situations most mediators never encounter. She faced her biggest challenge during a two-year stint as the project manager at Maili Land, a housing project for the homeless, constructed and run cooperatively by the city and county of Honolulu and the Honolulu Catholic diocese.

As Colburn sees it, there are two sides to her life and practice as a mediator. One is what she calls "generic mediation," the process she learned at the local mediation center. It considers techniques and rules to be foundational and to need little adjustment as the setting or nature of the dispute changes. When she talks of her other mediation work, she frequently uses the term *peacemaking*. Peacemaking is far less formulaic, far more fluid, and far less frequently taught than generic mediation. There are more things to consider and more risks in peacemaking.

In the lawyer's office or the local mediation center where she volunteers, Colburn notes, she can take for granted the legitimacy of her being there. The parties know that their dispute will be mediated and start with an acceptance that she belongs. She uses the term *standing* to describe this authority: "When you have standing, and when there is some sort of professional obligation that comes with the territory, then your entry is very different. I wouldn't presume to go to my neighbors' house when I hear them arguing upstairs and say, 'Gee, would it help you to have someone clarify the issues?'"

She prepares for such a session by assuming that it will unfold in a calm and predictable way. It is not necessary to resolve the dispute immediately. She can afford to take the time to let a man's and wife's stories unfold.

"One of the things that I try to remind myself," she says, "is to walk in as though I have no previous understanding of that particular dispute, to set aside what the attorneys have told me and really try to hear the story as it's being related by the disputants, from their vantage point. I guess that brings me to another ground rule, which is to keep checking with them."

The lack of immediate pressure to resolve things gives Colburn time to test her hunches. As the mediation session proceeds, she is likely to caucus with each of the parties. Her "generic mediation" training emphasizes the use of caucuses. In the caucus, she tests her "intuition" about what is going on.

"I think that a rule for me is to pay homage to my intuition. If I sense that one party has a reservation about discussing the matter fully or lacks confidence in his or her position, then nine times out of ten that is one of the first things I try to surface in caucus," she explains.

Her language with the parties is polite, deferential, and therapeutic. If child custody is involved, she says to the parties, "It sounds like you don't really want to compromise your child's safety and you really recognize that this is something you may not be able to deal with independently. What are your thoughts about that?"

If things get a bit out of hand and one or both of the parties is being verbally abusive in the mediation, she might say, "I think you each have some good ideas, and the problem here appears to be in conveying those in a way that the richness and all the nuances are really appreciated."

If they refuse to recognize the verbally abusive behavior, she will say, "Gee, I am wondering if terms like *asshole* and *stupid* might have anything to do with how willing this person is to value your statement."

When I asked her what she would do if during the session she discovered that spouse or child abuse had taken place, she responded that she might call off the mediation, or she might continue in a nonjudgmental way, particularly when both parties acknowledge the abuse. She might talk to the abuser about his or her "confusion" in the relationship with the child, saying, for example, "By your own admissions, you have made decisions about your relationship with your child that you have regretted later. What are some of your thoughts now that you are not in the presence of the temptation, or what are the elements to keep in mind as we start looking at this whole business of custody?"

The assumption that it is not necessary to make an immediate decision is also apparent in the remarks she makes to the parties as they close out their discussions.

"Usually," she says, "I have two questions that I ask: What are you going to think of on the way home that you wish you'd said? And is there anything else you want to put on the table today?"

The lack of imminence and the parties' acceptance of her authority makes it possible for Colburn to remain neutral in the way that generic mediation training uses that term. She does not advocate any particular substantive solution. Instead, she concentrates on what she calls "advocating for the process."

As Colburn puts it, "I'm describing what happens under ideal circumstances. People want to be there, they've agreed on the time and place, and they've agreed on an agenda." For her, as for most mediators, such generic mediation is charted territory.

♦ ♦ ♦ ♦ ♦ ♦ ♦

Maili Land, which typifies Colburn's "other" mediation practice, is where her fear, excitement, and disappointment most clearly play themselves out. When she compares peacemaking to generic mediation, Colburn frequently talks about what she calls the "pizza incident" at Maili Land. When she relates this story, she becomes more intense and funny at the same time. Her language becomes much earthier.

The pizza incident began at 10 o'clock one night. Colburn was making the rounds at Maili Land, walking through the project to make sure things were okay before she left for the night. As she walked, she heard shouting from inside one of the units across the street on the far side of the complex. Even from that distance, she recognized the male and female voices, and from the sound, she judged that physical violence was pretty close at hand. As Colburn described it, using the pidgin dialect commonly spoken by non-Caucasians in the area, "I walked up to the door of their house, knocked, and said, 'Excuse me.' The yelling and screaming ceased. The man who had been shouting said 'What?' and I say, 'I am delivering pizza. You guys went order one pizza?'"

Colburn stood in the open doorway as both the man and woman looked at her as if she were crazy. They know she is the project manager, not a pizza delivery person, and of course, there was no pizza in Colburn's hands. She was an uninvited guest and, at least for the man, an unpleasant surprise:

> The guy said, "What the fuck! I nevah order one fuckin' pizza. I goin bash your . . . "
>
> I said, "No, no, no. I could not tell if you wen ordered one pizza or not. I was down the street and I heard all dis racket, and you know, it's kinda late, brah. You guys can cool it? What's the deal?"
>
> The guy says, "Fuck you," and slams the door.
>
> I knocked again and said, "Excuse me, you wanted pepperoni on top da pizza or what?"
>
> The guy says, "Wha'? I no want no fuckin' pizza!"

For Colburn, the pizza incident shows how "compressed" the conflicts at Maili Land were compared to the "ideal, generic" divorce mediation. The couple in the housing project did not ask her to intervene, nor had they prepared for the intervention of any third party. She had to use what she described as a "fake venue" to make her way into the apartment. "In this shelter setting, I was doing forced intervention," she said. "I would not presume to go to my neighbors' house if I heard them arguing upstairs," but in Maili Land she did something pretty close to that. Except, of course (and this is a big exception), the Maili Land disputants are not her neighbors.

In Colburn's opinion, Maili Land put her skills and beliefs to the ultimate test of what it is like to try to manifest peacemaking beliefs and skills outside of the mediation room with a group of people who often had no interest in making peace either with her or with one another. Peacemaking merged and conflicted with the other parts of her Maili Land tasks. Her work there took place in a setting where trouble and violence were always close to the surface and where resources to reduce them were scarce.

To understand this story, one must know something about the politics of culture in Hawaii and about Colburn's place in that culture. Half Hawaiian, by her own description she "looks like she just got off the plane from Nebraska." Colburn calls herself a mixture of two cultures, with a mother born on the mainland and a Hawaiian father born in Honolulu. Her education, work experience, and community involvement reflect this mixture.

"My father was part Hawaiian, and he had stereotypical Hawaiian characteristics. He was sort of a global thinker and was musically inclined and easy-going. My mother, who was from Kansas, was pretty task oriented and driven and was always tending to the details to make sure that everything occurred in the way it was supposed to," she says.

Colburn came to appreciate this mixture of characteristics, and her language skills and education reflect her interest in keeping this mixture intact. Colburn can speak English with an accent that sounds as if she did indeed just arrive from Omaha. But, as the pizza incident indicated, she also fluently speaks the pidgin English that is common in non-Caucasian Hawaii. She initially went to public school, and then transferred to the Kamehameha Schools, a private school for Hawaiian and part-Hawaiian students only. She went to Lewis and Clark College in Oregon, receiving a bachelor's degree in business administration and communication.

After working a short time in Portland, she returned to Honolulu to work as a sales representative for IBM. As part of this new job, she had to make contacts with politicians in Hawaii. Since she did not look "local," she found it necessary to establish in subtle ways that she was not an outsider. That was nothing new to her. She did this mainly by asking customers about their friends and relatives and by talking in the pidgin dialect when appropriate.

Colburn's pattern of moving in and out of cultures and work settings continued. She started her own security investigative consulting business, which she continued on a part-time basis after beginning work at Alu Like, a private social assistance and advocacy organization for Hawaiians. She was hired for her business skills; her primary task was to provide business-related technical assistance to Hawaiian entrepreneurs. While working at Alu Like, Colburn was tremendously impressed by the ability of her boss, a Hawaiian woman, to operate in two cultural worlds. According to Colburn, this woman had a remarkable combination of spontaneity, creativity, caring, and empathy, which Colburn considered "Hawaiian," along with the focus and task-oriented approach that she associated more with "mainland" style. This was the balance the mediator would come to seek in her own professional life, a way to combine order with spontaneity and goal direction with creativity.

While working at Alu Like, she took the mediation training offered by the newly emerging neighborhood justice center (NJC) in Honolulu. There was little particularly "Hawaiian" or "local" about her cases at NJC. But on her own, she began to get involved with issues that highlighted the politics of cultural identity and allowed her to test the possibilities for peacemaking in a broader sense.

Colburn and a Samoan woman were awarded a small grant to develop a small experimental trial mediation program in the state men's prison. Many of the prisoners incarcerated there were Hawaiian, and she found it necessary to establish herself as a Hawaiian as one means of gaining the confidence of the inmates. She also began to discover what it was like to move generic mediation skills to a setting where violence and coercion were close at hand and where rules, hierarchy, and manipulation could never be forgotten, set aside, or suspended. The first day, she reports, she and her partner were "thoroughly searched."

Everything we brought in was carefully scrutinized. We were told not to bring markers that were alcohol based, no permanent markers if we used markers at all. I was not going to sit and talk to some guy who was doing fifteen years for manslaughter and say, "Hey, you," so we brought little name tags and handed out the acceptable, nonalcoholic markers for them to use to write their names. The first thing the guy who took the first marker did was to unscrew the cap, stick the felt tip near his nose, and take a deep breath, hoping to get a buzz off the marker. These were those Mr. Sketch markers, fruit scented, and the guy's face got all contorted and wrinkled and he said, "What da fuck dis, dis smell like licorice." And another guy had this thing up his nose and he said, "Eh, dis ting raspberry."

Colburn and her colleague began to sense that this group would be different from the other workshop participants in many respects.

The inmates immediately tried to take advantage of Colburn in other ways. One of the things that was first on the inmates' agenda was a complaint that they could not get spray, aerosol deodorants in the prison store. The mediators thought this would be a simple matter to negotiate with prison officials. In a subsequent caucus with a prison unit manager, Colburn was told that bulletproof windows melt when they are exposed to extreme heat or flame. If you shake a can of deodorant and then light it, a little blow torch is created that melts the windows. What seemed an unreasonable restriction and a readily resolvable issue took on very different characteristics once the "opposing view" had been explored.

In addition, Colburn felt an element of peril. As she explains, "It's really spooky to be in a room full of men, who are there for reasons you really don't want to know, with your back against the door and only one tiny way out. And that way out requires the assistance of a guard who was initially suspicious as to our motives for being there. Especially when they're getting really upset and you suspect that their frustration is traditionally played out in ways that are dangerous."

Despite these early experiences, Colburn came to find the prison work tremendously stimulating and moving as both the inmates and the guards developed an interest in and a loyalty to the mediation process.

"When they started seeing that they could each get something out of this alternative nonviolent process, and we didn't as mediators take anybody's side—that it was up to them to formulate their position statement and put it out there in a way that wasn't offensive to the other party—then they began to feel like it was their forum," she reports.

Colburn and her colleague were able to remain "advocates for the process" as the inmates and staff moved from cynicism and disinterest to understanding and acceptance, and as participants began talking one at a time and not interrupting each other, being respectful in their behavior, focusing on group concerns rather than name calling. "They were doing the same kind of things that characterize the opening statements of a mediation at the neighborhood justice center," she says.

The prison work gave Colburn experience in a setting where violence was often imminent and where someone in authority could decide to disregard agreements or positions that parties had worked hard together to develop. She began to think of herself more as a peacemaker. She was attempting to go beyond the settings and assumptions that were part of her early NJC training and take on a broader mission, one that involved modeling conflict resolution skills in ways that encouraged disputing people to use these peaceful processes in their everyday lives, too. Colburn hoped that, by her own actions, she would show how one can be peaceful in emotionally charged situations. The mediator, she holds, can achieve the peace by being peaceful. "You can affect the other person's tendency to be peaceful, and then, when that occurs, you can begin to move toward resolution or reconciliation," she says.

Reconciliation involves more than just resolving the dispute at hand. It also enables the parties to develop insights into how they can avoid problems with each other in the future. This peacemaking process, which Colburn associates with Zen and Gandhi, required Colburn to take "the higher and sometimes harder road." These basic principles became the guide for all of her dispute resolution work, from the lawyer's office to the NJC from the crowded and badly lit room in the prison to complex, multi-party community disputes. She incorporates these principles into all of her professional and volunteer activities and has developed confidence about taking peacemaking into different cultures and situations.

It is, of course, much easier to evaluate one's efforts at modeling peaceful behavior in situations where people are hitting or shooting at each other. Colburn's work in the housing project became an important test of this agenda.

. . . .

The opportunity to work at Maili Land came along after Colburn completed her prison project work. Her initial involvement was not as a peacemaker, but as a policy and rule maker. The Catholic diocesan office hired her as a consultant to develop and negotiate an agreement between the city and the church's new nonprofit board, which was to oversee the housing development. She was also supposed to develop a management plan, some budgets, and a set of tenant rules and procedures. After she had worked on these tasks for a few months, the head of the church's peace and justice commission offered her the Maili Land project manager's job. She had not sought this position, nor was she all that comfortable about taking it. The head of the office's peace and justice program convinced her by emphasizing how much Colburn now knew about the project and how useful her conflict resolution skills would be.

In the course of her interview, she recalls there was recognition that the kind of "survival judgment" and compromise skills that she had acquired in diverse settings might come in handy at Maili Land.

The Maili Land situation offered an opportunity to Colburn to test her beliefs that peacemaking and management could go hand in hand and that her peacemaking skills could be used in situations and settings that were vastly different from those usually emphasized in the traditional mediation movement.

Still, she was a bit worried about the job—with good reason. The project had been trouble right from its start in 1986. It had been constructed primarily to meet the need of homeless families and individuals living on the beaches; but, as the church officials soon discovered, the homeless category included very diverse types of people. Some were intact families that moved into the project because nowhere else could they find the space they needed at a price they could afford. Some were loners who had not lived in a conventional housing situation for a long time, while others included drug users, criminals, ex-convicts, and the medicated and nonmedicated mentally ill.

Colburn describes the project's ethnic and racial mix as a "bizarre mixed bag. You can't get a whole lot more eclectic than we got out there," she says. "We had Pacific Islanders who did not speak English, and people who did not have their green cards. We had ex-offenders, felons from San Quentin, people shipped to Hawaii via one-way tickets courtesy of the state of Utah, California, Washington, Arizona. We had just about everything you could imagine."

According to Colburn, only three of the sixty-six households had any earned income when she began to work at Maili Land,

and half of the population was under eighteen. Most of the families had been evicted from where they lived before.

The serious troublemakers, especially the drug addicts/dealers, had been living in crude shelters on the leeward coast beaches for some time, and criminals gained control of the project early on. "Tenants were freaking out; they were leaving in droves. The criminals were extorting; they were threatening people, pimping, ripping people off, just beefing for the hell of it, blowing up cars, carrying knives, and robbing people of their prescription medication. There were a lot of recently deinstitutionalized mental patients living there. Family violence was not uncommon, and substance abuse was widespread," she says.

In the early days of Colburn's tenure, the police seldom responded to calls for assistance from Maili Land in a timely manner. Sometimes they responded but did nothing. There was no safe place for families to gather outside their homes.

Colburn's first visit to the project gave her a good taste of the immediate potential for violence. She arrived there with a camera, planning to accompany a crew to make a list of needed project repairs. She was conversing with Maili Land's maintenance manager in the parking lot when she saw a large man coming from the other end of the project. "He was yelling and screaming and gesturing. I had no idea what was up and sort of froze in my tracks," she says. The engineer, who was accustomed to this behavior, did not pay any particular attention to him as he came very close yelling and swearing. As it turned out, Colburn later learned, the sight of a stranger with a camera persuaded the tenant that the engineer had turned him in to narcotics officers and that Colburn was there to take pictures of him dealing drugs.

Maili Land's problems were magnified by the fact that the complex was operating without an effective landlord-tenant code. According to the deal that the church had negotiated with the city and county of Honolulu, church officials would develop a code that would take into consideration the difference between

Maili Land, a traditional homeless shelter, and more conventional rental situations. Colburn was supposed to develop the code as
part of her consultant's task.

This lack of rules created chaos because there was no way to
get bad tenants to leave even if they were not paying their rent.
No one was getting evicted, and there was no way to enforce
Maili Land's fourteen-month maximum tenancy term as short-
term housing. Indeed, the situation was so bad that the project
management did not want the well-behaved tenants to leave
even if they had lived there past the allotted time.

Maili Land was too new, too transient, and too chaotic to be
considered a community in anything other than a geographic
sense. There was little shared history, and informal social ordering was not working well. The church and city officials, as well as
many of the tenants, would have liked to see such a community
develop, but for the moment the dominant issue was establishing
a semblance of order in a much narrower and immediate sense.

From the start, Colburn tried to emphasize the maintenance
of order. One of her most important tasks as manager, she felt,
would be to quiet the place down and get rid of the dangerous
people. She wanted to reclaim safe territory for the cooperative
and motivated residents. There was no doubt in her mind that
making rules and policing them would dominate her initial
activities.

She was no indigenous healer; the church had brought her in
as an outsider without consulting anyone at Maili Land. In fact,
during her first few weeks there, some tenants would not believe
she was the new manager because they had heard a rumor that a
local television anchorperson with a name very similar to
Colburn's was the new manager. Her first task on the day she
started the job was to perform the first evictions of several families who had not paid rent for many months.

Stories about maintaining order and removing undesirables
dominate accounts of her early work there. For example, one of

her employees was severely beaten by a visitor to the complex. The police, as was so often the case, did nothing. She organized a very tense meeting with police, church, and city officials. As a result of this meeting, she had to deal with police officials in her neighborhood who were angry that she "went over their heads." Another time she had to tell outsiders with criminal records regarding weapons in their possession to stay off the premises. She confronted a man who had just fired a shot in his house and who then pointed the gun at her face. She also had to transport people having psychotic episodes to the nearest medical and mental health facilities to negotiate emergency services for them.

These stories make no distinctions among mediation, negotiation, and other forms of order maintenance. Such differences are not important to Colburn. The common thread involved violence, the potential for violence, or situations that could easily get out of hand. In each case, Colburn had few formal resources to rely on. She was not a police officer, carried no weapon, and was not a psychologist or a social worker. In addition, there was no enforceable rulebook to consult. These situations were seldom handled around a table but rather wherever they occurred, on the spot.

Colburn's recollections sound like those of a soldier rather than a peacemaker. Like war stories, her anecdotes tell of fear, adventure, uncertainty, pride, gallows humor, and danger. She stresses reclaiming territory, operating by her wits under extreme pressure, and facing up to violence as a test of character.

One "war story" tells of her assistance with the police undercover surveillance of a suspected drug dealer at Maili Land. The person under surveillance had thrown a chair through Colburn's office window a day or two before, and she was concerned that his violence was escalating. The police had a warrant for his arrest, but they had been unable to apprehend him. Recalls Colburn, "I arranged to go out to Maili Land at 4 A.M. and meet the undercover guys. We surrounded his place. I knocked on the door and I said, 'I'm going to use the key to come in the room. I'm concerned that we haven't seen you, and I want to make sure that you are okay. It's my job to make sure there is no problem here.' I had the key in the door and was turning it, and I looked behind me. There were the police, with their guns drawn in the hall. This was a very narrow hall."

Colburn talked repeatedly about people who threatened or tried to kill her and how little she could rely on others to protect her. For instance, when someone who had made a death threat set fire to her office door, she felt officials did not respond sufficiently. "I came to work and found the door all charred and smoke coming out of it. The fire department had left, and the police had left. A gasoline can with fingerprints of the person who probably ignited the door was sitting there, right by the door, left behind by both enforcement agencies."

Yet she did not see the people at the project as enemies, nor was her only task to defeat bad people. Her main emphasis was always on peacemaking, and she describes her work at Maili Land as "social development." Her techniques and rules of thumb were dominated by a need to accommodate twin agenda—peacemaking and social development—to settings and situations that were so colored by violence, order maintenance, and coercion.

• • • • • • •

Typically, peacemaking required what Colburn calls "mediation on the spot." As the pizza incident revealed, on-the-spot mediations were frequently proactive, so methods of getting involved were a very significant issue for Colburn. There were times when she used rules as the basis of her authority. She reminded people that she ran the place, that she wanted the dispute stopped, and that, if the parties were not cooperative, they could face consequences.

At the same time, she was not dealing with a group of people who had much faith in either the fairness or efficiency of outsiders. People in Maili Land saw themselves as victims of the same system whose rules she tried to use as the basis for entry. In addition, Colburn often found herself wrestling with culture conflict. The Maili Land tenants had what she describes as "a bizarre sense of what is appropriate." This assessment refers not so much to what she identifies as an ethnically based culture but rather to the cultural peculiarities particular to the project, especially "a culture that was used to duking everything out."

She learned to accept some of this sometimes bizarre behavior, or at least to let it pass, because there were more important and urgent life-threatening matters that required immediate response. "It's repugnant to me that anybody would call someone under seven years old a 'fucking asshole,' but in terms of the ethics of the community, that was not a really important issue. As a mediator, you just have to go through a different triage process to decide which issues are worth engaging," she says.

At Maili Land, she concentrated on disputes that had health and safety consequences. Colburn was not willing to tolerate immediate threats to someone's safety, whatever the cultural norms. Again family violence is an example. Many times the parties involved thought there was nothing wrong with hitting their children or their spouses, and they continued to do so in front of Colburn, telling her it was none of her business. They did not see the violence as a problem and, in fact, thought Colburn was the one with the bizarre sense of what was appropriate.

When someone accused her of being insensitive to the local culture and told her to go back to America, she said, "Okay, I can go back to America, and they could put one Hawaiian in this job, and you know what's gonna happen? The Hawaiian gonna do the same thing. The job is the job. . . . It's not a matter of where you are from. It's just not right to hurt people."

Perhaps the most serious obstacle to peacemaking was the condition of the people involved at the scene of the on-the-spot mediations. They were often at the height of their anger and not at all interested in cooling off and sitting down.

The pizza incident shows what Colburn faced and how she responded. It took place at the end of a typically long and difficult day. The day's activities reminded her, if she needed reminding, that she could not take on everyone's problems even if she was personally offended by their activities. Nonetheless, she would not tolerate immediate threats to a person's safety. At the moment she heard the shouting from the apartment, she had to decide very quickly whether to get involved. If she did get involved, she knew that she would have to convince others— those with a different ideas about appropriate behavior—that there was a problem and that she and they should do something about it.

Her job did not offer the luxury of setting aside time solely for mediation or developing written criteria to determine whether a conflict was ripe for mediation. Sometimes the clues that guided her on-the-spot judgments were quite clear. The people involved may be in too much danger or too irrational to make even the minimal connection needed for on-the-spot mediation. In the pizza case, she suspected someone might be getting hurt, and she knew enough about the people involved to think they might listen to her.

In contrast, Colburn felt she could not mediate in another situation where a man was breaking windows and beating his girlfriend. "The guy seemed to be posturing for his friends. He was bleeding profusely and refusing medical attention, but being very theatrical about it," she recalls. "He was just not rational with the blood loss and the shock of injury, plus he had an established history of drug use. There was no way for me to make a connection with him and say things like, 'Do you really care about this person? How do you feel about this person? What is this person to you?' There was too much stuff that had higher priority for him at the moment."

Most times, the choices were less clear. In such situations, Colburn typically asked herself how attached the disputants were to the ways they were handling the issue and how essential the intervention was for Maili Land.

Sometimes she describes her techniques as intuition or the ability to "read the bubbles above a person's head," as if he or she were a character in a comic strip. The intuition is based on using nonverbal, psychological, and spiritual cues to decide whether her style of peacemaking was appropriate. Note how in the following response to questions about her Maili Land work, Colburn moves from rather straightforward cues based on appearance to more subtle and reflexive mechanisms:

> There's an inventory that goes through my mind. Are they under the influence of any kind of a substance? Can I make eye contact with this person and connect on some abstract, unspoken level, and basically halt the momentum toward violence? What is this person's problem? What does he or she need most at this very moment? Is it to be listened to, respected, understood? Should I be directive and forceful because they are confused and deranged? Do they need to be confronted? To be appeased? Nine times out of ten, they just want to vent their feelings. I think there is a sort of a Zen, if you will, to dealing with violent conflict, and it has to do with getting back to your own center and quickly determining what really matters.

This is a rich inventory and juxtaposition of cues, a combination of straightforward reality checking and quick judgments about much less definable and more spiritual things like the ability to "connect." What makes this mixture even richer and more

complicated is that, as an administrator, Colburn also had to consider the goals of the organization for which she worked. Her job
required that she tend to health and safety issues. Any dispute
that threatened Maili Land's order or threatened residents' safety
got a high priority. These included battles that took place behind
closed doors.

In the pizza case, Colburn employed what she calls "disorientation," a technique she often used to get involved when she was
not invited. She believes that "people are the most genuine and
revealing when they are disoriented." Colburn totally surprised
the man and woman when she knocked on the door to say she
was delivering pizza. After the man slammed the door in her face,
she knocked again and used the same line about ordering pizza
even though both the man and his wife knew who she was. The
incongruity of her presentation interrupted the rhythm of the
violent argument and the life-threatening battering. "By then,
the guy was saying 'What is this broad's problem?' But while he
was saying it, he was not beating anyone up, and he had lost the
physical momentum of the assault," she explains.

Colburn's strategy was not so much to develop a case for her
legitimacy as it was to "cut the cycle," as she puts it. She had two
immediate and crucial objectives: to get the husband to quit hitting his wife and to get them to stop and think. The entire process depended on this disorientation to buy enough time for
movement to the resolution stage.

In another example, her disorientation strategy was less calculated, more dangerous, but nonetheless important. A man had
taken a shot at someone he thought was "fooling around" with
his wife. Colburn had heard them arguing and was heading
toward their unit when she heard the shot.

"I broke into a run toward their rental unit, which I realized
later was pretty stupid. When I got there the guy backed out of
the door turned around and put the gun in my face," she said. "I
called him by name, and said, 'What are you doing there? I mean,

what do you think you are doing?' And the guy was so stunned. I said, 'Put that thing down.' And he said, 'You want me to blow your fucking face off?' I said, 'You put that thing down, I like talk to you.' He said, 'I no like talk to you.' He put the gun in his pants, and I said, 'I hope that thing goes off and turn you into one soprano.' He says, 'Ah, fuck you.'"

The man then began to walk away. After checking in the house to see that no one was hurt, Colburn followed him.

> I said, "I am not through talking to you," feigning indignation to cover my fear. I'm thinking, "This is crazy, can't quit now." I followed him across the street to another complex, and I saw him throw the gun in the bushes. I confronted him in the courtyard and said, "I want to talk to you now. What the fuck you think you doing with that stupid thing over there? You are not even supposed to have a gun. You're a felon, and they can put you in jail for this." So pretty soon he kind of squatted down, and here we were, eyeball to eyeball, talking. He was crying because his wife had been fooling around and feeling bad because I had turned him down for a housing application earlier in the month. I said, "No, that is not the whole story, Frank . . ." and began to explain other aspects of the issue to him.

The initial disorientation arising from the confrontation stopped the momentum and created a new momentum of its own, one in which Colburn could be variously assertive, threatening, and even supportive of someone who could have done her great harm. Her language was initially provocative when it interrupted the rhythm, but after the initial confrontation, their language became shared.

She disoriented people in other ways. Outsiders who were dealing with her for the first time were surprised that someone with her Caucasian looks could speak pidgin and know all about the important family connections. Discussions of mediation tend to see these as ways of establishing rapport, but the situations Colburn dealt with were really at a pre-rapport stage. They depended more on surprise than on trust. As the pizza ploy indicated, she could go a long way on surprise alone.

. . . .

Some of Colburn's techniques for resolving on-the-spot disputes were very much like generic mediation, while others were quite different. Even if she had walked in on a dispute in progress, she tried to begin by asking each person to state without interruption what he or she thought the problem was. She attempted to give each the opportunity to vent anger and tried to elicit both parties' feelings on the matter. Then she tried to get people to anticipate feelings and situations that will lead to trouble, asking, "What do you notice when you start getting upset? What do you feel? What goes on in your body when you notice that you are starting to get upset? At what point do you feel you are about ready to go at it?

"When I mediate on the spot, I often say, 'You know what? It sounds like you feeling really bad about how you guys is fighting right now and all you want is peace, right? You don't trust her for go away cause you think she goin' fool around with somebody.' And then I get them to agree not to beat each other up for the rest of the night, and I get them to agree that whenever they start feeling the things—'you know how you feel when you get pissed off'—they will stop and think about taking a time out," she says.

One difference from generic mediation is in the speed of the events and the peacemaker's involvement in these events. In Colburn's situations, typically very little time was available to do what she wanted because the parties were in the midst of the conflict. There was no time to cool off and go to a mediation center.

A second difference had to do with the limited resources available to people living in Maili Land. Like the larger community around it, Maili Land lacks many of the support services that could reduce the incidence of conflicts or make them less serious. The police would not investigate an incident in which one of her staff members was assaulted. They botched the investigation following the gun shot in the home. There was no nearby place to keep a suicidal mentally ill person. There were few opportunities for couples to get respite from their problems. Anger management programs were not available, and the closest mediation center was in downtown Honolulu, about thirty miles away.

As a result of such limitations, Colburn encouraged agreements that she admitted would not be acceptable in other settings—for instance, getting the parties in the pizza delivery incident only to agree not to hit each other for the rest of the night. "Clearly this would be a totally unacceptable agreement for the neighborhood justice center, but that's the kind of stuff you have to do in the moment. Then the next day, you can try to get them referred to someone who is relatively competent," she says.

Such agreements can be risky. Voluntary compliance is a pretty fragile reed, so Colburn also used other resources at her disposal. She suggested further assistance as a means of reducing this risk. In the pizza dispute, she told the parties that if the initial agreement not to hit one another worked for them, it might be helpful to talk to people who know more about this kind of problem. "They have the time to spend with you, and they understand what it is like and can give you the support you need," she assured them.

And if they were not willing to take this additional step and if trouble began again? Then she would resort to threats or discussion of consequences. Colburn said to the man and woman involved, "You can beat each other up if you want, but if it comes to my attention, I'm not going to ignore it, and I am going to take actions either to have you removed from the premises or I am going to support you in trying to figure out alternatives for dealing with the problems. So it would be in your best interest to consider seeing somebody who can help you deal with these feelings."

In another incident, in which she was trying to head off a fight between two men, she asked one man what he could tell the other to make him feel safe. When that man answered, "Hey, I no give a fuck," Colburn said to him, "Would you give a fuck if your rental agreement depended on it?" In such incidents, mediation and management merged. She was perfectly willing to allow people to work out solutions on their own, yet at the same time she was willing to threaten them if they did not work out one that was acceptable to her. She made it very clear that the consequences of the pizza dispute impacted the housing project as a whole and her objectives in managing it.

The potential for danger, combined with her manager status, made Colburn less apt to respond as she would in places where she used generic mediation. In Maili Land, she had to intervene more quickly, be more directive, and sometimes make up rules on the spot, she says. When she told a couple that they could not remain in Maili Land if they continued to beat their child, she was, in her words, "making a capricious decision about a criterion for residency in the project."

Though in the pizza incident Colburn made the initial "forced intervention" on the basis of a contrived story, and though her demeanor was initially informal and tentative, she and they knew that she was not a neutral third party in the generic mediation sense. She could not focus on being "an advocate for the process," the role she described for herself in the prison and in the generic divorce mediations discussed earlier. For her, the key issues were violence and threats to public order. The first priority was to stop the violence immediately. In her opinion, forced intervention was necessary in the pizza incident because the situation raised "life safety issues that were immediate and compelling." There were legal, as well as moral and ethical, liability issues that involved allowing someone to participate in a fight to the point where someone got hurt or killed.

Colburn's description of on-the-spot rulemaking suggests that she had much latitude, but this combination of mediation and management also carried a risk that she would lose the delicate balance between outsider manager and insider peacemaker. She recognized both the strength and vulnerability of her management position.

People sometimes challenged her involvement by telling her, "You don't know what it's like to be homeless" or "You don't know what it is not to have money." Her response to one such accusation shows this mix of peacemaking and rulemaking: "I may not fully understand how it is for you, and I know that it is really hard, but I can't be sympathetic to your problem or want to help you if you are breaking the rules, and you are making life miserable for a lot of people, including me. If you need help, you need to make allies with the people here."

At times when she responded that way, people accused her of being an insensitive Caucasian. Her background and her experiences in operating in a variety of cultures helped her here. According to Colburn, sometimes someone would support her by reminding her accuser that she was local: "Eh, da buggar, she from here, you know."

To mitigate the outsider problem, she developed a storehouse of cultural knowledge about what she calls "the psyche of the Waianae Coast," which is the broader area around Maili Land. She especially sought out information about linkages to extended families. Who was related to whom? Who might come into the picture from the outside either to help or to hinder the resolution of a problem?

The families are important because their involvement usually made things worse. Colburn describes them as "the uncontrolled third parties not present." She usually tries to keep them out of the picture. If parties involved in a dispute are from the same ethnic background and appear to share a language, she infers that they shared other important feelings and background. If not, she tries to ask some quick questions about their families. In one situation where she was unfamiliar with the families of two antagonists, each of whom had threatened to bring in family members from the outside, she said, "So, what? You guys, you said you was goin' call your family. You stay real close to your family? What? You was goin' call your family, too? You must feel close to them, too. If they ready beef for you, den they must be real concerned about how it is for you."

After establishing that they had common concern for and support from their families, she encouraged them to keep their relatives away by suggesting to the two men that, no matter how well meaning the relatives were, the families could make things worse for both of them if more people ended up fighting than focusing on ways to fix the problem.

· · · · · · ·

Along with the threats, cajoling, and disorientation—in fact often at the same time—Colburn tried to act like the peacemaker of her aspirations, striving for what she describes as a Zen-like notion of being centered and peaceful in times when rancorous conflict is going on around you. At Maili Land, she saw herself as working in a culture that excessively validated anger and that lacked the economic or social welfare resources that could reduce the incidence of anger and the reliance on it. Part of her role was to "model" peace for people who lacked the skills and resources.

She saw her own response to an ensuing conflict as a crucial source of modeling, particularly because many of these conflicts took place where everyone in the project could see them. This peace modeling was not always so apparent in the earlier, disorientation stage. Colburn was not exactly Gandhian when she told the man that she hoped the gun he had tucked in his belt would turn him into a soprano, though that comment lessened the tension among bystanders at the time. At other times, modeling peace was important even at this early stage. Compared to pretending to be a pizza delivery person, there were many heavy-handed ways that she might have used to get entry. By using her humor, she showed them that a person can take an issue seriously but still be gentle and light-hearted about it.

Sometimes, her use of modeling was more dramatic. If people tried to hit her, she never struck back. In one case, a woman knocked her down in front of a crowd of project residents. Though she was very tempted to do so, she did not fight back. She got up and turned her back on the woman, who then knocked her down again. Size or strength was not the issue here: Colburn is close to six feet tall and has a strong physical presence. Her choice was based on her belief that disputes are situations where the peacemaker's behavior is sometimes the best educational resource.

Colburn's two years at Maili Land were an emotional experience, yet she thought that she had made important strides at the project. Evictions had taken place. Rent collection had increased fourfold. The police patrolled the grounds regularly, and violent tenants had been removed. Tenants now felt safe enough to gather outside at night. School attendance was up. Tenant turnover increased in a positive way because some of the families were able to get better housing in the community.

"They're so happy when they get out," she says. "You see them a few months later, and they are dressed differently; they have a job, and they are driving a car for the first time in years, and it is licensed and has a safety check. You see people really putting their lives together."

In addition, Colburn believes she helped resolve many small but important disputes between friends and neighbors, the kind that can make an important difference in the quality of one's everyday life. She is proud of the fact that her resident manager and other staff developed some peacemaking skills.

Colburn had grown to love the authenticity of the people at Maili Land. They were always willing to tell her exactly how they felt about something. They were "raw, earthy, and powerful," she notes, adding that things happened to them in "living color with Dolby." Being on the edge was exciting, too.

"You get people yelling, and they're throwing stuff and you're holding one person back, and they're shouting 'You fucker . . . don't call me a fucker.' It's like conducting Rimsky-Korsakov on a hot night. It's a cacophony of stuff, but it's all so vital and real. They are really right out there with their hurt and with their anger," she recalls, wistfully comparing this authenticity to the indirection and passive-aggressiveness that is often so much a part of her more conventional mediations.

During the first few months after her resignation, she continued to keep regular contacts with the Maili Land staff. Sometimes the staff members asked that she come out to make the rounds because, in their opinion, some of the tenants were acting up now that she was gone. Nonetheless, the job had been emotionally taxing to an extraordinary degree, probably more than she had ever imagined it would.

"It's painful," she says, "to feel so inadequate, and it's hard to remember that it is not inadequacy as much as the enormity of the task. A very capable person, when confronted with an enormous task, he or she may end up feeling anything but capable just because they are dwarfed by the complexity of the issues."

She did not feel that this emotional drain had much to do with her being an outsider. When I asked her if she had ever thought of living in Maili Land, she said that there was "no way" she could have done that and survived. Nor was she particularly troubled by the cultural complications. She seemed to have as much skill in moving through Hawaii's complicated cultural terrain and as much confidence about doing so as anyone I have ever encountered. Neither this skill nor this confidence was diminished by her stint with the homeless.

What ultimately got to her was the experience of so often fearing for her safety. She recalls, "On maybe four or five occasions, I thought I was going to die either because the person I was trying to deal with was on drugs or because he or she had a reputation for hurting or killing people, or was just so angry or out of control. And to have been assaulted once, you know, that's a real steep price to pay. There were a couple of men who have threatened me in a very specific way. I still watch my rear-view mirror when I go home."

The Maili Land violence threatened her beliefs as well as her body. Modeling peacemaking in that setting had high psychic costs. It was very hard for her to be centered, calm, and restrained with all the violence surrounding her. She experienced enormous temptations to violate her beliefs by, as one adviser suggested, "punching someone's lights out."

"I was constantly refraining from acting on my instinct and constantly repackaging my response. That made a difference; it was very comforting for some people. They knew that whether they had good news or bad news they were not going be judged and they weren't going to get yelled at. Toward the end, I did not have the energy to keep doing that and I began yelling at people. I was surprised at the power I felt when I succumbed to my anger," she says.

Even Colburn's dreams have changed as a result of her experiences. Before she got involved with mediation, she used to have dreams in which clear conflicts emerged. After she began to mediate, the conflicts in her dreams appeared less clear, with more emphasis on peripheral issues. Many of these dreams would be about how the pieces of the conflict fit together. She much

preferred these postmediation dreams, which she associated with
developing a more sophisticated sense of what conflict is about.
Her dreams about conflict became more confrontational and less
subtle when she worked at Maili Land. To Colburn, this was an
additional sign that her ability to conduct herself in accordance
with her beliefs was threatened.

Besides violence, what was the "enormity of the task" that
ultimately made Linda Colburn feel so inadequate? In Maili Land
on-the-spot mediation typically took place in a very fluid setting
where there were few incentives to work things out. By contrast,
her prison work was much easier.

> There are limits in prison. You go in there with an
> agenda, and you're out at a certain time. In the prison,
> there is security and back-up. In Maili Land, there's no
> security and no back-up. In prison, the guys have
> incentives not to act up too much because the ones
> allowed to participate in the mediation program are
> almost on their way out. At Maili Land, there are no
> incentives because they're on their way in.
>
> Because it is more elastic and open in Maili Land,
> there is no incentive to get down to business. In
> prison, the people can focus on solving their problems;
> you know they really don't want to use all of their time
> to bitch about the problems. In Maili Land, people
> weren't interested in solving their problems. They
> were still at their bitching and venting stage. I've had
> guys in Maili Land who would be perfectly reasonable
> in private conversation but tell me that if people are
> around, "Hey, you gotta understand, I mean I gotta act
> da kine in front of my friends, right?"

Her most enormous task was the one requiring her to reconcile her critique of Maili Land's openness with her love of the

authenticity of its people. How will she reconcile the earthiness she so admired with the acting out and posturing that often accompanied this earthiness? How will she reconcile the project's on-the-edge atmosphere with her fear for the safety of herself and others? No one should expect her to resolve these questions, but having to work with them created a great deal of pain and frustration and continues to do so.

Colburn continues to believe in her concept of peacemaking and on-the-spot mediation, but in her new job as an economic development officer for the Office of Hawaiian Affairs, these activities are less important than they were for survival at Maili Land. She hopes to use her skills to reduce some of the conflicts within that organization and the Hawaiian community. These conflicts will no doubt lack quite the energy and passion that gets the adrenalin surging the way it did in Maili Land. Passive aggressiveness, quiet avoidance, and long, formal meetings with ambiguous results will more than likely be the order of the day.

She still has broad aspirations for herself and for peacemaking. She would like to develop her skills so that she could become, in her words, a "Red Adair" of peacemakers. (Red Adair is the famous firefighter who is called to battle dangerous oil rig blowouts all over the world.) She would similarly like to be a troubleshooter who would be trusted to deal with the most difficult cases in a variety of settings. Her experiences at Maili Land suggest that some disputes are less predictable and more dangerous to the troubleshooter than the fires that Red Adair fights.

Neal Milner

"To be effective, we have to be unseen. . . . We can't become a part of the politically active situation."

—Joseph Elder

12

Joseph Elder
Quiet Peacemaking
in a Civil War

Mediators often create high drama in their attempts to manage international conflicts. One thinks of Henry Kissinger shuttling about the Middle East to secure a disengagement agreement, or Jimmy Carter grinding out an unexpected deal at Camp David. Or, more recently, former U.N. Secretary-General Javier Perez de Cuellar mediating a ceasefire in the bloody Iran-Iraq War; or Chester Crocker securing troop withdrawals and Namibian independence in southern Africa. Or, lesser known but no less dramatic, a papal envoy stepping into a territorial dispute between Argentina and Chile and diverting an imminent war.

This is the kind of heady stuff that commands headlines. Lives are at stake as territory and vital resources are being allocated and geopolitical alliances formed. Money and weapons usually accompany—or lie tacitly behind—this kind of mediating. But not all mediating is of this sort. Another brand of international mediation, often termed unofficial or "track two" diplomacy, also makes its mark in lesser-known ways around the world. It usually involves international actors other than nation-states or international organizations. Their resources are limited, but they often perform a function the major powers cannot. Some of them are religious groups with a peacemaking mission. The Society of Friends, the Quakers, is one such group.

The Quakers have long been involved in "reconciliation," providing crisis relief, holding seminars, and sponsoring conferences. Only in the last couple of decades have they engaged regularly and somewhat systematically in active mediation. Joseph Elder, professor of sociology and South Asian studies at the University of Wisconsin, helped define this more active role as a member of a joint U.K.-U.S. Quaker team in India and Pakistan after the 1965 war. Since the 1980s, he has mediated between separatist forces and government leaders in the strife-torn country of Sri Lanka.

This profile relates Elder's experiences and thoughts in the effort in Sri Lanka. It is the story of one person's often irregular attempt to facilitate communication and help bring an element of understanding to a society at war with itself.

· · · · · · ·

As a Quaker mediator of international (or in this case, intersocietal) conflict, Joe Elder has no army to nudge reluctant disputants toward agreement and no largesse to sweeten a deal. He has no jet, ready at a moment's notice, to take him to the next trouble spot. He does not even have a staff to book him a flight. Nevertheless, he still faces some of the same problems all international mediators face.

First, he must decide when and how to enter the dispute. Recognizing that what he does at the beginning and how he does it can affect future activity, he must find an appropriate access point and gain acceptance by the parties to the conflict. Second, he must define a role. Unlike in adjudication, arbitration, or administration, the role of an international mediator is not defined by law or even practice. The mediator must work with the disputants to determine exactly what that role will be. For any party to ignore this aspect of the intervention, or to presume that everyone understands what a mediator does, is to invite misunderstanding and, ultimately, mistrust and failure. And third, to make a difference, an international mediator, even a "powerless" religious person, must do more than just relay messages. A mediator must find ways to influence the parties. And the mediator must do this to meet the *mediator's* objectives.

As in their mediation efforts elsewhere, in Sri Lanka the Quakers' objective is to secure a durable state of peace. As will be seen, the Quakers have adopted procedures and conditions of mediation that carve out an unambiguous "neutral" role. In this role, the mediator places demands on the parties that, in some circumstances, can counteract the usual, self-perpetuating patterns of belligerent, often violent interaction.

I explore three features of international mediation in Joe Elder's work on the Sri Lanka conflict—entry, role definition, and influence building—by relating his practice and understanding of that practice, as well as my interpretation of that practice. As it turned out, however, this study was more than an analytic exercise.

I spent a full day with Elder in his modest home in Madison, Wisconsin. Initially, I had difficulty reconciling the encounter with my previous interviews of international mediators. This was not a plush suite in New York City or a stately office in the Vatican. As we sat at the kitchen table, sipping coffee, it became apparent that this was not going to be the usual just-the-facts telling. Nor was it going to be a "Here's how I achieved world peace" proclamation. Elder was not merely a less famous or less significant Henry Kissinger.

Elder engages in a brand of diplomacy quite unlike that covered by the media or portrayed in memoirs and diplomatic histories. Elder's "citizen diplomacy" is a natural extension of religious convictions and professional academic interests. Elder chose his home for our interview because it was convenient and comfortable and, possibly, because he did not have a statement to make.

As in his mediating practice itself, his goal is not to change the world or gain a place in history, but to find consonance between belief and practice. So, in a sense, the choice of his home did make a statement. It conveyed the modest, self-limiting nature of his practice. Moreover, I suspect that my reactions to his presence were not unlike that of many leaders he sees: initially, who is this man who flies off to far-flung places to "mediate" others' conflicts? And, then, this man may be useful. And, finally, this man may have figured out through conviction, thought, and practice what some in the peacemaking community, official and unofficial, have only begun to understand, let alone appreciate or practice.

Because the mediation work is ongoing as of this writing and very sensitive, the narrative has been reviewed and cleared by Elder. While this screening necessarily limits the telling, a slip here or there does not merely result in someone's personal embarrassment. Death squads on both sides have been rampant in Sri Lanka. Favorite victims are the "conciliators," those who indicate a willingness to talk. This is precisely Elder's business. And while he will downplay the danger, it is there—for him, for his fellow Quakers (those in residence and those visiting Sri Lanka), and for his many contacts inside and outside the disputing parties.

Finally, those readers looking for a happy ending, or any ending at all, will be disappointed. There is no closure in this case. There may never be, at least from the perspective of the Quaker role. What is more, I only relate a small piece of the total effort, dwelling, for the reasons already noted, on the Quakers' entry into this conflict and their definition of this particular kind of international mediation.

· · · · · · · ·

Sri Lanka is an island nation of sixteen million people just off the southeastern coast of India. It has been long troubled by tension between the majority and largely Buddhist Sinhalese (about 74 percent of the population), and the minority and largely Hindu Tamils (about 18 percent). Since it gained independence in 1948, Sri Lanka (formerly Ceylon) has been a democratically ruled country with a fast-growing economy.

In the early 1980s, however, things changed radically. A nationalist Sinhalese government passed laws concerning the national language, university admission rules, and ethnic composition in government jobs that favored the Sinhalese majority and discriminated against the Tamil minority. While the older generation Tamils fought these laws in Parliament and the courts, many younger Tamils sought Tamil autonomy or even a separate Tamil state. Many joined guerilla organizations, including the Liberation Tigers of Tamil Eelam, on the northern Jaffna peninsula, a predominantly Tamil region.

A major turning point came in mid 1983 when guerrillas in northern Sri Lanka attacked an army convoy and killed thirteen soldiers. Sinhalese mobs in Colombo and other southern cities went on a five-day rampage that resulted in hundreds of Tamil civilian deaths and left perhaps as many as a hundred thousand Tamils homeless. During the rioting, the government effectively looked the other way. It not only failed to quell the killing but did virtually nothing to punish the perpetrators. Some high officials even publicly condoned the killings; with few exceptions, no high officials condemned them.

As a result, Tamil guerrilla ranks swelled, and more units of the Sri Lanka army were moved to the north to suppress them. The government required all members of Parliament to swear allegiance to a unitary state. Many Tamil members refused and were expelled from Parliament. This drove the Tamil movement even further underground, leaving the government with no one to negotiate. The Tamil militant groups set up headquarters and, despite official denials by the Indian government, received training and weapons in Madras, India, in the state of Tamil Nadu, where fifty-five million Indian Tamils live.

As conditions deteriorated rapidly, an India-born, British Quaker of Tamil extraction traveled to Sri Lanka in early 1984 to assess the situation. He reported to the London Quaker office that the situation was serious and could easily get much worse. He suggested that the Quakers could provide civilian relief and medical support, a Quaker tradition that goes back at least a century. Another possibility was to promote reconciliation by sponsoring meetings or conferences with representatives of the disputing parties. The London office agreed to send out a fact-finding team and chose an international team of two members, including Joseph Elder. Elder had gained considerable experience in South Asia both as a scholar and as a mediator after the 1965 India-Pakistan dispute. Like the other team member, however, he was not familiar with the Sri Lankan situation at that time.

The team's mission was to determine whether Quaker involvement was feasible. Unlike the India-Pakistan effort, where Quakers had easy access to the likes of Indira Gandhi and Jayaprakash Narain, here the Quaker team had virtually no official contacts. Before leaving, they did generate a list of concerned people. Most of these were religious people—Christian (Catholic and Protestant, but no Quakers), Buddhist, Hindu—but also ex-government officials of Sri Lanka, India, the United Kingdom, and the United States, a few of whom had attended Quaker-sponsored conferences or seminars in Asia.

Upon arriving in Colombo, the two began by telephoning people on their list, adding new names, and making appointments. People were eager to talk and, in some cases, openly grateful that someone from outside the region was concerned about the situation in Sri Lanka. Since few people knew about the Quakers, Elder and his colleague usually would begin each meeting by describing the Society of Friends and their history of providing relief and of facilitating reconciliation in trouble spots around the world. They would also give brief personal histories. Elder would describe his involvement in India and Pakistan after the 1965 war, as well as other recounting trips, including several to Vietnam in the late 1960s.

In each meeting, the Quakers explained that they had come with three concerns. First, they wanted to inform themselves of the situation. On this, everyone was eager to help. Second, they wanted to locate some undertaking, such as a rural development project, to which they could make a contribution. Throughout their discussions, this possibility for Quaker involvement was generally ignored; apparently, money was not the problem. Third, they wanted to explore how Quaker experiences in other conflicts could be beneficial here. This third possibility aroused great interest and discussion, although the reaction was of two sorts.

For many of the laypeople, it was clear the government was not seeking a negotiated settlement. Sinhalese politicians found it untenable to support the Tamil cause in any way. And among Tamils, the older Tamil politicians had been discredited and rendered obsolete. The younger and much more militant Tamils (such as the Tigers) saw that accommodation led only to further discrimination and repression. For the extreme militants, a military victory and a separate Tamil state were the only feasible objectives. For the government, normalcy would return once the few hundred "extremists" were driven out or exterminated. No government official could countenance the dismemberment of Sri Lanka, a predominantly Buddhist society existing for twenty-five centuries on this small island and harboring a sense of special mission assigned by Buddha himself.

From this view, then, the increasing polarization and ever-hardening stance of both the government and the militants meant that negotiations, even discussions, were almost out of the question. With so much killing and so much mutual hatred and distrust, only a military solution for one side or the other was likely to bring the strife to an end.

Among a second group of interviewees, mostly religious people, the assessment of the situation was similarly bleak. At the same time, however, they felt it was essential to maintain a dialogue at some level, even if its outcome and immediate usefulness were unclear. As facilitators of such a dialogue, the Quakers, being impartial outsiders, might be more acceptable than Sri Lankans. In addition, they could travel where Sri Lankans could not, particularly to Madras, India, headquarters for many of the Tamil resistance groups. And they could draw from their experiences elsewhere to advise parties of nonviolent alternatives.

The Quakers believed that they could be one element in the process of change, not as providers of relief or development but as mediators. Moreover, some of those interviewed had reason to believe that some government leaders known publicly for their implacable hard line were, in their private conversations, in favor of a dialogue. Since no one else was doing it, maybe the Quakers could get a dialogue started. One approach would be to sponsor meetings in the Quaker tradition of conferences and seminars, bringing together Sinhalese and Tamils living in Europe and North America. Many expatriate Sinhalese and Tamils were significant actors in the conflict who regularly stirred up communal passions. Another approach would be to bring together leaders of the various opposing groups for secret talks. These options, by effecting changes in attitudes and increasing understanding, could provide openings for active mediation or other forms of peacemaking. For the Quakers, the uncertainties would be considerable. But, as Elder says, "we have never gone into a conflict situation knowing what opportunities (or difficulties) will emerge, nor how our role will evolve. It is enough to have a starting point."[1] The work in Sri Lanka, the Quakers were soon to discover, would be no different.

The second view was, of course, encouraging. But the Quakers realized that if they were to have any impact, they would need the cooperation of those responsible for settling the conflict.

Such contacts they did not have. For the government, the president was, of course, the one ultimately responsible. But, as the Quakers were to find out even on that first trip, the president had delegated much of the responsibility for settling the Tamil problem to hardliners. The official position of these hardliners was that only a few hundred Tamil "extremists" were causing all the trouble and that once they were driven out or killed, order would be restored.

Elder and his colleague became convinced that they needed to meet the hardliners. If they could not win their consent, let alone cooperation, in initiating a dialogue, Elder and his colleague at least needed their assurance that they would not thwart their efforts. The Quakers had neither the resources nor the inclination to operate clandestinely. In fact, the Quaker tradition of openness in meetings also applies to mediation efforts: each side knows the Quakers are visiting the other. However, sensitive information is passed on only with prior approval.

In their remaining few days in Sri Lanka, the question was how to reach the hardliners. Several religious people offered to help. One priest was a friend of one of the hardliner families. The family connection ultimately proved successful. On their last day in Colombo, the Quaker team landed an appointment with one of the hardliners.

Elder and his colleague were pleasantly surprised to discover that the hardliner was already somewhat familiar with the Quakers and their faith, having attended several Quaker international conferences in Asia over the years.

Turning to the question of a possible Quaker involvement in Sri Lanka, the hardliner said he and other Sri Lankan government officials were prepared to enter into a dialogue with anybody, but only when the killing stopped. A government cannot talk to people at the same time they are killing its public servants, he averred. He claimed the militants could not win. But he acknowledged that neither could the government extinguish the

militants. Serious, possibly irreversible changes were occurring in
Sri Lankan society because of the turmoil in certain areas. He felt
the hardliner policies were working, to some extent, since they
were leading to disillusionment with the separatist cause among
many Tamils. He said that, at the time, there were six major
Tamil militant groups and they could all be reached at their
headquarters in Madras. If the Quakers wanted to talk with them,
they could get their addresses at the Tamil Information Center in
Madras.

According to Elder, the hardliner "seemed to be looking for
alternative strategies, along with the very tough military strategy,
which . . . was to wipe out the militants, if possible." He encouraged the Quakers to pursue meetings or seminars outside Sri
Lanka. He suggested Rangoon, Burma, or the Maldives as possible sites. Including militants or their supporters would be all the
better. He wanted the militants to realize the futility of their
political objective of a separate Tamil state and their military
objective of acquiring territory through force.

The hardliner's statements took Elder and his colleague by
surprise. While his stance was ambivalent—he was seeking alternatives while at the same time pursuing a concerted effort to
crush the militants—this meeting proved to be pivotal. If the
home office in London approved a Quaker mission, then it
appeared that a legitimate and much needed role could be played,
albeit with great uncertainty and, possibly, some risk.

They returned to Friends House in London to report that,
despite the very real obstacles to reconciliation and the low prob-
ability of success of a mission, the Quakers could play a useful
"message-carrying" role and a conference might be possible. Later
that year, the London office approved and funded the mission.
Elder and others would make trips either together or separately
when they could. Since this would be an unofficial, ad hoc effort
with minimal resources, the timing of visits would depend more

on the members' own schedules than on events in Sri Lanka. If this was to be a form of mediation, it would have to be sporadic.

In January 1985, Elder and one other Quaker set off on a three-week trip to Colombo, Madras, and Delhi in hopes of meeting key people in Sri Lanka, including the hardliners, and initiating contact with the Tamil militant leadership. Meanwhile, the divisions between the Tamil and Sinhalese societies had only grown deeper. Killings and recriminations continued unabated.

Upon arriving in Colombo, Joe Elder and his colleagues contacted the hardliners and were accorded an appointment within four days. The spokesperson for the hardliners was very friendly and appeared eager to see them. "So we talked with him and said that the mission is on. We are prepared to find the Tamils and prepared to say anything constructive you want us to say," Elder explains.

The spokesperson instructed the Quakers to tell the Tamil militants that the Sri Lankan army could not beat the militants. But the militants could not beat the Sri Lankan army, either. The two sides could continue killing each other for years, as could their children and grandchildren. And nothing would be accomplished except great loss of life. Or the two sides could jointly identify their differences and work out point-by-point resolutions to those differences. And he, the spokesperson for the hardliners, was prepared to meet with the Tamil militants any time, any place to talk about the possible resolution.

For the Quakers, that was even more of a bombshell than the first meeting. The official position of the Sri Lankan government at that time was that there were only four or five hundred militants engaged in the violence. They were crazed young men with no jobs and with no sense of civilization. The Sri Lanka army had a far superior striking force that was steadily exterminating the Tamil militants. Indeed, in a few more months, the few surviving militants might be driven off the island, and the whole war might end.

The official government position was entirely at odds with the statement by the hardliner that the Sri Lankan army could not beat the militants any time in the foreseeable future. The explanation for this apparent paradox, according to Elder, is this: "When one gets involved in this sort of discourse, time and again one realizes the usefulness of having two lines of communication. [If a Sri Lankan government official] wanted to convey to someone on the other side the information that the extermination campaign could not succeed, that official would be destroyed politically [by his own side]. He could not say this to *anybody* except his most confidential listeners on his own side."

The spokesperson for the hardliners went on to say that the militants would have to meet two conditions. One, the killing would have to stop. Two, the militants would have to be willing to enter the Sri Lankan political processes then in place. In return, security force patrols would be reduced and amnesty could be arranged. The militants should drop their call for a separate state since Sri Lankans, including many Tamils, as well as the Indian government, did not support secession.

Negotiations with the militants had been tried before, explained the hardliner, but the militants proceeded to kill some security personnel, thus aggravating rather than reversing the escalating violence. Part of the difficulty may have been a lack of coordination among the different militant factions. An essential function of the Quakers, therefore, would be to get such coordination. Finally, the spokesperson noted that others had tried to serve as intermediaries between the militants and the Sri Lankan government. They had all failed.[2]

The spokesperson for the hardliners assured Elder and his colleague that while he could not speak for members of parliament, as far as the people he dealt with were concerned, the Quakers were the current go-betweens who could carry messages back and forth between the Tamil militants and the Sri Lankan government. In his opinion, this was a good time for a Quaker-sponsored dialogue since a lull in the violence was expected. He explained that the level of violence fluctuated rather predictably: in the northern section of Sri Lanka, a Sri Lankan soldier or a few government civilians would be killed by Tamil militants; a Sri Lankan security force would follow up with a major attack on some suspected nearby location, resulting in many Tamil civilian and militants' deaths; and finally, there would be an extended lull in the violence. At present, the Sri Lankan security forces were conducting a major attack on a suspected location, so one could predict that a lull in the violence would begin in a few days.

• • • • • • •

Two days later, Elder and his colleague went directly to Madras to establish contact with the militants and relay the hardliner's message. In Madras they met the Indian Quaker, and the three of them worked as a team. From discussions with a professor and an editor, they determined that five major Tamil militant groups had headquarters in Madras. It was fairly easy to find them or contact their representatives. Over a ten-day period, the Quaker team was able to meet with representatives of all five groups.

The militant group holding most of the cards, both militarily and in terms of popular support, were the Tamil Tigers. They were also the most violent group. The Quaker team met with the Tigers' representative on their second day in Madras. The Quakers began by explaining who they were and what their objective was in carrying messages. They relayed the hardliner's message. The Tiger representative disagreed with the hardliner's assessment that neither side could win. He believed the militants could—and would—win. He then laid out his conditions for agreeing to a ceasefire: government troops would return to the barracks; the government practice of arming Sinhalese civilians in Tamil areas would stop; political prisoners would be released;

the naval blockade between Sri Lanka and India would be halted; and negotiations would be conducted directly with the militant groups, not with the older, discredited Tamil politicians. As for a specific message to be relayed back to the government, the other groups would have to discuss it in the groups' ongoing unity talks. He believed this could be done in a week's time.

So a week later, the Quaker team again met with the Tiger representative, but he had not yet secured a set of proposals. In fact, he asked the Quakers what they had learned from the other groups. Clearly, despite the rhetoric, little unity existed among the Tamil militant factions. In fact, a couple of years earlier, when a militant victory seemed imminent and consolidation among groups was deemed crucial, the Tigers launched an attack against a smaller Tamil group called TELO. Hundreds were killed in gun fights in Jaffna, the predominantly Tamil city of northern Sri Lanka.

The Tiger representative asked that the Quakers return two days later. In this third meeting, he said that he had talked with all the groups. They wanted to know the intentions of the Sri Lankan government and what the government really meant by a ceasefire. The Quakers suggested that both sides establish some kind of regular and speedy communication between Madras and Colombo. Shuttling back and forth by Quakers or others was too slow for many essential messages. For example, when the Tigers wanted to reduce operations as a signal of good faith, rapid communication would help prevent the move from being seen as a sign of weakness. Finally, the Tiger representative said greater unity among the various factions would have to be achieved first before such a communication system could be established between Madras and Colombo. Moreover, he was extremely suspicious of the hardliners, who, he stated, had been trying to get the Indian government to expel the militants from India.

* * * * * * *

Even though the Quaker team was not able to obtain a unified message from the militants, Elder's colleague did return to Colombo to get in touch with the hardliners and summarize the views of the Tamil militants as the Quakers interpreted them. In the meantime, Elder and another colleague went to New Delhi for talks with high-level officials of the Indian government.

The main points of the Quakers' summary of the militant position were as follows:

- All militant groups sincerely desire peace, but not through weakness.
- At various times the militants have reduced operations to promote a peace process, but the signal was not adequately conveyed, and the reduction in operations was too often interpreted as a sign of weakness.
- The growing unity among the different militant groups will put them in a stronger position for future negotiations.
- Many militants do *not* want a separate state.
- The militants are suspicious of a ceasefire since they feel it would allow the government time to regroup for ever greater attacks in the future.
- The militants want a gesture of good faith from the government. It could be as simple, and as nonmilitary, as allowing fishing to resume in the straits between India and Sri Lanka.
- If there was a ceasefire, the government would have to halt all military operations and related activities such as arming Sinhalese settlers in largely Tamil areas.

The Quakers felt that the emerging unification of the Tamil militant factions would likely improve the chances for ultimately negotiating a peace. Furthermore, unless some kind of response were forthcoming within a reasonable period of time from the Sri Lankan government, attitudes would likely harden, the violence

might intensify, and future negotiations could be even more difficult to conduct.

In subsequent conversations in Colombo, the spokesperson for
the hardliners responded to each of the seven points, explaining
the government's position and identifying the actions the government had already taken to address some of the militants' points.
For example, fishing rights had been partially restored but not in
areas where gun running from India continued. He believed that
the government program of arming Sinhalese civilians in northern Sri Lanka was hurting the Tamil militants and that this was
one reason why the militants were expressing a willingness to
negotiate. He also said that Sri Lanka was ready to send a representative to a Quaker-sponsored meeting. He suggested that
Quaker House in Geneva might be a suitable site. And he agreed
that if such a meeting were held, the talks would center on ceasefire arrangements and not, presumably, on political issues.

· · · · · · ·

Several months passed before a Quaker team returned to
South Asia. After arriving in Madras, India, the Quaker team
reported to all five Tamil militant groups. The militant groups
were most surprised that the Sri Lankan government was interested in discussing a ceasefire. Most of them thought the Sri
Lankan government believed what it so frequently announced—
that is, that within a few months it would achieve a final military
victory over the militants.

The Tiger representative listened carefully to the Quakers but
doubted that the militants, as a united front, would have anything to gain from a ceasefire. He said he would discuss with the
other militant groups the Sri Lankan government's proposal to
meet abroad. Throughout the discussion, the Tiger representative
alternated between talking seriously about the meeting proposal

and about winning an independent Tamil state. The spokesperson for the hardliners had exhibited the same ambivalence.

Overall, the Quakers concluded that the militants favored a ceasefire and were genuinely interested in negotiations. At the same time, the militants' profound distrust of the Sri Lankan government made them extremely cautious. The Tamil militants regularly stressed that they were not fighting the Sinhalese but the Sri Lankan army, which they felt was waging a war against their people. This perception, based on the confusing and tragic events of their recent history, was universal among the most diverse of the Tamil militants and was a powerful motivating force. The cycle of violence could be broken, the Quakers felt, if a period of de-escalation could take hold. And a settlement could be reached (all the elements were already well discussed in various draft documents) if the mutual anger and suspicion could be overcome. An early step toward that end could be a conference held on neutral territory.

. . . .

Over these many months, the idea of a formally convened mediating session began to take shape. The Quakers, in their first meeting with all the parties, described conferences the Quakers had held in the past. In these conferences, Quakers only facilitated discussions; the outcome was up to the parties. As noted, the spokesperson for the Sri Lanka hardliners was receptive to the idea of such a session. The Tamil militants, while not committing themselves, did stress that, if such a session were to happen, it should be very private and definitely not in India.

Two options for a location were discussed. London was desirable because it would be easy to get Sri Lankans, including Tamils with Indian passports, into the city unnoticed. What is more, the Quakers had their own facilities there. The Quakers also had a mission house and facilities in Geneva, and, while it would be more difficult, participants could probably arrive unnoticed.

The possibility of a formal, Quaker-sponsored mediating session never got as far as determining representation, however. In mid 1985, before such a conference could be arranged, the government of India announced it was convening talks in Thimpuh, the capital of the tiny kingdom of Bhutan, with the Sri Lankan government and the militants. For Elder, who had worried about whether the Quakers could provide the necessary support for a conference (transportation, security, and so forth), the move by India was welcome.

"I was hugely relieved," he says, adding that it was "a bit alarming how much responsibility was going to be placed on a group of amateur Quakers to monitor and successfully carry off a meeting of the kind we had been discussing."

While he felt that the International Committee of the Red Cross or the United Nations was more adequately equipped to support such a meeting, what it came down to, Elder says, was a determination that "if we were the only group that was trusted, we would do it. But you always worried about possible betrayal . . . a trap. . . . [We just do not have] a lot of resources."

At the Thimpuh meeting, he notes, Tigers and two other groups had telecommunications to each group's headquarters. "This was much more sophisticated than anything we could have done," Elder said. "We asked the Indian government, the Sri Lanka government, and the militants if we should withdraw at this point; was it confusing to have another group, albeit very small and one not with a lot of resources, going between and trying to set something up? It was interesting that none of the groups wanted us to pull out." One of the hardliners explained this support for the Quaker effort by saying that although he was grateful that India was there offering its good services, one could not ignore the fact that India had vested geopolitical interests in the area.

While Elder was relieved, the Indian intervention elicited an adverse reaction among some Quakers. One said, "It seems to me Rajiv Gandhi has gotten our fox." Elder sees it differently. "At no point," he says, "should we Quakers feel that if this effort in Sri Lanka works out we are going to advertise, 'Ah, the Quakers did it again!' I think the minute that kind of self-aggrandizement gets into our activities, then the perception of all we Quakers are concerned about—bringing an end to the fighting and saving as many lives as we can—becomes distorted."

Once again, Elder reveals that Quaker intervention is the antithesis of a high-profile mediation effort where the advancement of national interests is paramount.

· · · · · · ·

The India-sponsored talks led to an agreement in mid 1987 between the Indian and Sri Lankan governments. The possibility of greater political autonomy for Tamil areas in the north was granted, in return for which the militants surrendered weapons to Indian troops. The Tigers initially objected, but later they acquiesced and moved out of Madras. Indian forces numbering twenty thousand were at first greeted in Sri Lanka as liberators. But after surrendering some weapons, the Tigers reversed themselves and launched attacks against both Sinhalese civilians and Indian soldiers. Rajiv Gandhi responded by ordering that the militants be disarmed and increasing Indian troop strength in Sri Lanka to fifty thousand. A year and a half later, Indian troops remained in Sri Lanka, unable to suppress the Tigers. Some of the other militant groups sided with the Indian army. One militant group aligned with the Tigers. An extreme Sinhala nationalist group, the JVP, reemerged at this time in southern Sri Lanka, conducting bombings and assassinations against Sinhalese moderates and anyone espousing a conciliatory approach. The JVP has been accused of several hundred assassinations of Sinhalese political candidates and party workers.

Elder and other Quakers continued to travel to Sri Lanka, but with most Tamil militants in hiding in the jungles and death squads at work throughout the island, message carrying was greatly restricted.

· · · · · · · ·

The conflict in Sri Lanka is almost entirely indigenous. Except for the intervention by India, foreign governments have stayed out. Why, then, would a few individuals from Europe and North America belonging to a tiny, obscure Protestant religion be acceptable as intermediaries? Part of the answer lies in the beginning—that is, how and under what conditions the intermediaries first involved themselves. Other reasons for Quaker acceptance include the nature and history of Quaker reconciliation work and the manner in which they establish and maintain their particular brand of neutrality. Elder explains these in the context of his message carrying in the Sri Lanka civil war.

In the initial meeting with each party, the Quakers would first describe their faith (especially the Quaker commitment to nonviolence) and give brief personal histories. Then, unlike in the India-Pakistan conflict where they started as fact finders, Quakers became involved in Sri Lanka with an offer to carry messages. As Elder expresses it, "We had a much clearer vision. We were going in saying, 'This is something we have acquired some experience in. We found in similar situations that people often want to talk directly—with leaders, with the opposition—and cannot.'"

Finally, Elder and his colleague stipulated two conditions all parties would have to meet for the Quakers to perform such a message-carrying function:

One, at no point would the disputing parties make any public statements about using Quakers as intermediaries, our explanation being that if we were identified in any way, the press would be on us. We would become part of the active dialogue of the struggle and conflict. To be effective, we have to be unseen, or at least in a position where we don't have to tell the press we can't tell them anything. We can't become a part of the politically active situation.

Two, if the time should come when either side felt we were not useful, that side should tell us, and we would stop carrying messages. So at no point are we going to feel we are coercing one side or the other. At several points during the last several years, we have asked each side, Do you think we are doing anything useful? So far [through 1988], all sides have asked us to continue.

These conditions were agreed to and adhered to by all parties. This fact has special significance. Referring to the "bombshell" revelation by the spokesperson for the hardliners about his willingness to talk with the militants, Elder says, "The fact the militants have never chosen to state publicly that they have this information from him I think is revealing. . . . It says that they have accepted us and that they know our position would probably be terminated. They would have violated their agreement that they would not say anything about the Quaker activity publicly."

Given these conditions for entering the conflict as intermediaries, why were the Quakers especially well suited? What advantages did they have that others apparently did not?

I am always astounded at how responsive people are to outsiders coming in. There is no Quaker history in Sri

Lanka. We don't have 150 years experience. . . . But among the elite of Sri Lanka, many were trained in England. Many had come across Friends House in London, or Friends lodgings, or they knew of William Penn House. In the Buddhist-Quaker and Hindu-Quaker overlap, there seems to be an awareness that Quakers are sort of like Hindus and a lot of Buddhists, and have a commitment to pacifism. At least the teachings are there ... and used as justification by different branches for being radical pacifists. And there are so few radical pacifists in the world; when you run into another, you sort of sense that you are like us.

To me, it is almost a miracle that the Quaker name conveys so much. To walk into the most security-conscious ministry in Colombo on the basis of the fact that you have a calling card that says Quaker, or walk in and talk to Prime Minister Indira Gandhi, is a kind of magic that is hard to reproduce. I assume that there would be other groups that could do it: Mennonites, the Pope, archbishops. According to Elder:

People we meet seem to have a sense that here is a person, even though they don't know that person individually, who comes from a tradition of integrity, credibility, sincerity, even if, in that instance, that person may be acting naively. You don't have to worry about that person's crafty deception. So that seems to be the starting point which we Quakers happen to have historically. That perception has to be maintained continually. One could lose credibility rather quickly at any point by what one says, being seen someplace, or saying something wrong in the newspapers.

I'm constantly struck by how very busy people will

stop whatever they are doing in order to talk with us. I keep thinking we really have no legitimacy. We have no power. We could easily be dismissed as do-gooders who should be back home minding our own business. The fact that we are taken as seriously as we appear to be taken is a never-ending miracle which I have only been able to explain in the context of our being able to provide a service which apparently is often not available through any other channel. So to this extent we have the power of the powerless of doing something which they can't do and they have no vehicle for doing. From their perspective, there may be some usefulness in using us, and there doesn't appear to be a lot of risk involved, or not enough risk to worry about.

After a certain point, we become credible as human beings, even if we weren't Quakers or pacifists. The fact that we do go back and forth and appear to report accurately and, I guess, thoughtfully, seems to build our credibility.

Even if the Quakers are well suited as intermediaries in this kind of conflict, each party still must see some advantage in accepting them. The reasons could be several, according to Elder:

I am aware of the fact that each party must feel they can use us for their own purposes. . . . [The spokesperson for the hardliners] is using us for a variety of things—for example, another source of information which he doesn't necessarily accept as true. We have contacts that his men don't have. In our meetings, there is always a brief period where he is interrogating us, I guess—what we are seeing, what the mood seems to be, and so on. We are able to be in places he can't.

The smaller Tamil parties probably felt that dealing with us would enhance their political status. To the extent they did feel this, it seemed a little unrealistic and also unfair. We really don't make that much difference: the fact that we talk with you and to the other Tamil groups doesn't fundamentally alter your relationship. It was certainly clear that they appreciated being talked to, especially after the Tamil Tigers took the political stance that they were the sole representatives of the militants.

I think there is even some of the old, unreal image of the importance of the West. It is the worst and best of the colonial legacy. People we have talked to may have felt: we Asians are being heard by important people from Britain and America. If we Quakers were Ghanaians or Indonesians, I don't think we would be accepted the same way, since people feel we come from the rich, powerful nations. It's an irrelevant consideration, in some sense, but I think it may enter into why we are being listened to.

It is one thing to claim a meaningful Quaker faith and a history of conciliation work; it is another matter to demonstrate neutrality in the daily acts of message carrying. In addition to imposing the two conditions of entry, Elder explains how Quakers regularly struggle to maintain—and limit—their mediating role:

In Sri Lanka, we define ourselves as message carrying. Sometimes they will ask for our opinion. We back off and say, "You who are involved will have to be the ones to work out the settlement, the range of possibilities. It really is not our position to make suggestions, but we are willing to carry all the messages back and forth."

Another thing is appearing to have no personal vested interest in how this thing comes out. Here again, I think having a pacifist tradition gives one a kind of neutral credibility. It is almost like the Swiss, where they have nothing to gain personally, but they have a kind of professional commitment to do this thing and do it right. You assume there is compassion and so on. I think if the people we talked to had the feeling that we were getting some kind of glory out of it, our role would be different.

As message carriers, Elder and the other Quakers agree that to set deadlines "would change the nature of our work. There is a separation between just carrying messages and working out a formula. We see ourselves as vehicles of communication. Deadlines would give the impression that we have something to gain. We would not want to say, 'You have got to get that mechanism set up by the first of the year, because we're walking out if you don't, and then you will have a real problem on your hands with no one to carry your messages.' A deadline would seem to say we have our agenda. But we don't have an agenda."

For Elder, the sporadic visits present a mixed blessing. "Each trip," he says, "is a different situation. Every time I go over to Sri Lanka I am out of touch; I miss so much during the months I am away from Sri Lanka. This is a weakness of the way we work. Once out there, I try to get up to speed by reading whatever I can and asking lots of questions. But the gaps between our visits leave me open to saying something really stupid. On the other hand, not being plugged in lends plausibility to the kind of amateurishness which is part of our strength."

. . . .

Neutral mediators are a strange breed of actor in international affairs. Most international actors—nation-states, international organizations, or transnational actors such as multinational corporations—have military-strategic interests or economic interests or organizational missions that put them in conflict with each other. In their dealings, they must be constantly vigilant to protect their interests and, at the same time, advance them when possible. States, in particular, act first to promote their own self-interests, and they do so strategically. Everything they say and do has strategic content. Whether the mechanism is force, coercive diplomacy, or negotiation, the consequences of what one does is due, in part, to what the other does. Concomitantly, each must act to anticipate and change the other's choices. Most important, this strategic imperative is known to all. It does not have to be spelled out or demonstrated. Strategic behavior is a fact of international life.

A fact, that is, for *most* actors—all those who have significant strategic or economic interests. The few who do not, the neutrals—neutral states, international organizations, and mediators of various sorts—shoulder quite a different burden. They must demonstrate convincingly that they are neutral. They must credibly commit to a position by which, in a dispute, they will not coerce the parties or favor one side. This is not easy in international relations. There is no overarching authority to guarantee such a position.

In short, neutrals, unlike other actors in international relations, must convince others that they are not like most other actors. They must do this visibly and credibly. Often, they must do it day to day, repeatedly and continually, for if they do not, their fragile reputation as a neutral can easily crumble. Much of what neutral mediators do, therefore, can be understood as attempts to demonstrate their neutrality.

This, then, is the framework I use to elaborate Elder's explanation of the role and function of a Quaker intervention. Neutral mediators must find ways to demonstrate convincingly that they are not acting like most international actors. But an additional mediating dilemma arises peculiar to individuals and many religious groups and small organizations. These actors must convince disputing parties they are credible, reliable, trustworthy, serious, knowledgeable, skilled, and so forth—in short, qualified. This task, too, is not easy. How do you convince another you are both a rare breed yet worldly, amateur yet experienced, knowledgeable yet behind on the news, committed yet willing to walk away? As Elder well knows, on the international scene there are plenty of do-gooders doing no good. The Quakers, especially where they are not well known (which is most everywhere), contend with this dilemma constantly.

The Quakers attempt to resolve these contradictory demands by the role they assume and the actions they take. Part of it is by design, part by chance. But the net result is that, under the right set of conditions, they provide disputing parties a valuable service.

Four features of Elder's brand of mediation highlight the strengths of the role and the difficulties of performing it: the Quakers' two conditions for operating, the aversion to deadlines, the irregular scheduling of trips to Sri Lanka, and the openness among parties.

When the Quakers require the parties to respect the anonymity of the intervention and give each party a veto over its continuation, the Quakers are doing more than avoiding the spotlight. The two conditions send several signals that reinforce the Quakers' neutrality and their qualifications as mediators. First, by giving each party a veto over the continuation of the message carrying and by restricting any publicity whatsoever, the Quakers are effectively saying, "This is *your* dispute, not ours. We have no interests in your disputed issues beyond seeing violence stopped and peace achieved. Moreover, the communication and reconciliation process we bring is *yours*; you have complete control over this process in the sense that you can single-handedly cancel it at any time by either exposing the operation or quietly asking us to leave. In addition, if you were to ask us to leave, you need not jeopardize any progress made. No one can accuse you of blocking a peace process because no one knows it is going on. You have perfect deniability."

In short, these two conditions—in combination with the historic, religious, and personal factors Elder discusses—make a message-carrying effort a very low-risk enterprise for disputants. When reputations and lives are at stake, getting hostile parties to communicate in some way other than with bullets and press releases is no small achievement.

A second signal these two conditions send is, "We Quakers are powerless. By giving you veto power—indeed, insisting that you have it—we demonstrate that we have no overriding interests in the conflict. In fact, in principle, we Quakers could become a key ingredient in a resolution process or a move toward negotiations or any other piece of an overall settlement process, and you could use us right up to the final step and then drop us. You would get the glory of being a peacemaker and nobody would be the wiser. There is no public record to show otherwise. And, once again, we have demonstrated that we have no overriding interest, not even to claim credit for a settlement, and thus have no incentive to expose your claim as a peacemaker." It is probably fair to say that most mediators in most contexts are used in exactly this way; their very expendability makes them unsung heroes.

With these two conditions, the Quakers bind themselves to a very limited role. They cannot demand benefits for themselves or push a particular solution. At the same time, they can resist efforts by either side to use them in ways inconsistent with

Quaker values and objectives—namely, employing nonviolent means and achieving a state of peace. As a result, a third signal is this: "Whether or not you share these values and objectives [and Elder's experience is that the parties do claim to share them and do believe they are operating in accord with them], we have to live by them. This puts a constraint on you, at least with respect to the message carrying; the alternative is to call it off."

This self-binding nature of the two conditions, then, is the essence of the "power of the powerless" Elder mentions. A Quaker mediator is powerless to impose terms of agreement. Unlike powerful mediators, "powerless" mediators cannot change the disputants' cost-benefit calculation through threats of pain or promises of aid. But they can change the nature of the disputants' interaction. They can set the standards for the intervention process—the message carrying, in this case—and thus influence the interactions between parties.

In difficult disputes, this standard-setting effect can be significant. It can establish different norms of interaction: the parties can refrain from accusing the other of malevolent intent because they need not fear looking weak; they can reveal their inner fears and suspicions with low risk; they can play with alternative approaches to a solution, again, at low risk. It can provide an outlet for conciliatory and nonbelligerent gestures. This is a form of influence that powerful mediators mostly do not have. They are playing the game of power politics, whether they like it or not. Everything they say and do is strategically tinged. And everything the parties say and do carries enormous risks. Not so with the "powerless" Quakers. They cannot impose a solution, but they can guarantee a low-risk means of communication and impose certain standards of interaction.

From this assessment of Quaker mediation, it follows that so-called message carrying is not merely transmitting words from one side to the other. Quakers are not human telephones. They do set conditions. They do constrain disputants' behavior. They do have influence, influence based not on great resources but on the very absence of such resources. In addition, that influence is targeted not at party payoffs but at party interaction. To the extent that ongoing party interaction sets up dynamics that perpetuate and escalate the conflict; a Quaker intervention, therefore, can serve to counteract those dynamics and contribute to an overall resolution process.

Regarding the second feature of his mediation style, aversion to deadlines, Joe Elder says that setting deadlines would suggest to the parties that the Quakers have an agenda. It would indicate that the Quakers have taken upon themselves to ascertain what is good for the parties. Moreover, a deadline would direct the target of the intervention away from the process—that is, the communication between parties and the nature of their interaction—toward specific proposals, positions, and the justifications of those positions. By eschewing deadlines, the Quakers are effectively saying, "We are here for the duration; whether or not you settle or make progress on the issues, we are here merely to help with the process (at this point, carrying messages); we will only carry substantive proposals, not make them." Again, they constrain the disputants' choices in that message carrying must be conducted on the Quakers' terms, not the parties'.

Sporadic visits are the third distinction of Elder's approach. The Quakers' low-budget, small-scale operation makes irregular scheduling of visits necessary. As Elder notes, this is a problem in the Quaker manner of mediating. At the same time, however, this mode of operation signals to the parties that, indeed, the Quakers are not professionals. It says, in effect, that the Quakers are not in this for their own benefit (other than to improve the chances of world peace), that they are not building a reputation on the backs of others' conflict.

Elder believes sporadic scheduling puts him in a position where he is not up-to-date on recent events and where he can easily say something naive or "stupid." Being in such a position may reinforce the image of being nonprofessional, maybe unqualified. On the other hand, it does convey the impression that the Quakers are not so involved in this dispute that they know every detail and have an answer for everything. In fact, a position of naiveté helps draw the distinction between being purveyors of a process—at this point, the message carrying—and being proponents of a solution. If the mediators had a solution in mind, or even a set of preliminary proposals, they would have to diligently keep abreast of developments and adjust their proposals as things changed, which would conform to traditional diplomatic practice. But if they are naive on details (*current* details; ignorance of the dispute's history would be insulting to the parties), they effectively say that it is the *process* and the intended changes in perceptions and attitudes that their actions address, not the details of proposals and solutions.

Elder's self-effacing description of Quaker mediation is consistent with the practice itself. When he proposes message carrying to powerful leaders who are caught in a horrible conflict, he would be foolish to offer anything more. Left at that, such an intervention amounts to little more than a story of small people in big places, of dabbling in others' affairs to enact one's religious beliefs. As a scholar of international relations, I have a realist side that suspects this is the proper interpretation; it is, after all, just "epiphenomenal." Traditional diplomats would certainly agree. On the other hand, the idealist or, maybe better, the transnationalist in me suggests that, on balance, the real peacemaking does not necessarily take place under the spotlight. Rather, it is carried out in many places and in many ways by quiet peacemakers like Joe Elder.

For me, resolution between these competing interpretations remains elusive. Just as the self-aggrandizing accounts of traditional diplomats skew our understanding of peacemaking toward power plays, the self-effacing accounts of Quaker mediators skew our understanding away from subtle effects. What is clear, however, is that people like Joe Elder get little glory. They do endure considerable hardship, even personal risk. To interview such a person is not merely to collect facts. It is to explore together an obscure form of global citizenship. It has been for me both an intellectual struggle and a moving experience.

Thomas Princen

Notes

1.   All direct quotes are from a series of interviews conducted with Joseph Elder at his home and in subsequent telephone conversations between mid 1988 and early 1989. A day-long interview with his principal co-mediator, who will remain anonymous for the reasons cited earlier, augmented the details and interpretation given here.

2.   One group, also with a religious association, composed of Sri Lankans, planned a series of meetings with the militants in Madras and, by announcing the trip in advance, attracted some press attention. When the group arrived in Madras for the meetings, none of the militants showed up. The government of Sri Lanka was not willing to ask for assistance from the International Committee of the Red Cross (ICRC), since to do so would have implied that the Tamil problem was an international, not a domestic, problem.

CONCLUSION

. . . .

The Realities of Making Talk Work

Our research team's study of twelve unusually thoughtful and influential mediators took place at a pivotal point in the development of the field of mediation. As the 1990s began, mediation programs were proliferating, and the number of aspiring mediators was growing exponentially. Increasing funding from foundations and other sources supported a wide variety of research projects, many of which sought to help those in the field define what makes for good practice. The twelve mediators we profiled were struggling with similar issues. We seem to have caught these mediators at a time in their professional lives when they were trying to articulate for themselves and justify for others what their work was about.

What we see in these profiles is a snapshot of a field caught in a mythology about mediation that is frequently at odds with the reality of the work. The mediators appear to be trying to clarify for themselves how to accommodate the mythology to the practical constraints and challenges posed by the kinds of disputes in which they become engaged.

Myths of mediation are not located in any single work, but we can reconstruct the major contours from the professional literature, especially works devoted to the training of novices. The mythic world of mediation is one in which one practitioner of the art is pretty much like another in regard to motives and orientation to the role. In the mythic world, mediators are impartial neutrals who have no authority and no wish to impose their views on the disputing parties. Also, the process is entirely voluntary and noncoercive (see Fuller, 1971; Goldberg, Green, and Sander, 1987; Moore, 1986). Additionally, the role of mediator is demanding, but ultimately uplifting and invigorating to all who can meet its stringent ethical, moral, and psychological requirements.

We are not the first to observe that the mythic world is not supported in practice. Scientific inquirers have persistently raised doubts about claims of mediators' "neutrality," noncoerciveness, and presumed unity of purpose and motive (Kolb, 1983; Silbey and Merry, 1986; Cobb and Rifkin, 1991). But these reports have been, by and large, about anonymous volunteers or employees of bureaucratic institutions, whose practices tend to be routine and structured. The departures from the myth that are documented in this volume occur at the very highest level of professional activity and commitment. This suggests that the divergence between the myths of mediation and the practice cannot be attributed to deficiencies of individual practitioners; rather, it has deeper roots in the structure of the field and the unique, and perhaps contradictory, demands of the work itself.

There are five major ways in which the terrain of professional life as depicted in the profiles departs significantly from the myths of mediation. First, mediators are not a homogeneous group. There are three distinctive and contrasting professional niches in which our profiles fit: the field builders, the "pros," and the outsiders. Each niche represents somewhat different motives for doing mediation, exposes its members to somewhat different stresses, and contributes differently to the field.

Second, settlement is not the primary means by which mediators judge whether their contribution has been a success.

Practitioners have different visions about the ultimate purpose and goals of mediation. In our sample, the mediators espouse two such visions: the transformative vision and the pragmatic problem-solving vision. Both visions seem to expose their adherents to disappointments and frustrations, albeit of very different kinds.

Third, when it comes to the actual practice of mediation, we also find contrasting perspectives in how mediators frame and organize the work. We call these perspectives the settlement frame and the communication frame. Each frame emphasizes different strategies and tactics, and pictures the mediator operating at contrasting levels of activity and power. These frames are useful to mediators, giving order and direction in a complex role, but they also impose blinders that can lead to unwitting mediator manipulation and coercion.

Fourth, in part because of the severity of the conflict in which they are engaged, but also because mediation is a business for most of those we studied, mediators are inclined to make extensive use of pressure tactics and arm twisting. Such tactics are often harnessed to achieve mediators' needs to "sell" themselves and demonstrate their prowess. Since the use of pressure tactics violates norms of mediator "neutrality," the masking of mediator pressure becomes a tactical issue of some importance.

Finally, the job of mediator is inordinately stressful. Some of the mechanisms by which mediators cope with this stress add an ironic element of additional tension to their practice.

We conclude by considering why myths about mediation practice are so persistent in the face of the kind of accounts we have assembled in this volume. We suggest that these myths have become more of a liability than an asset and that a new perspective is needed, one that recognizes the increased professionalization and practical realities of the work.

Their Place in the Field:
The Builders, the Pros, and the Outsiders

In the myth of mediation, there is one generic mediator, albeit one with many different personalities and styles. Our profiles suggest that the community of mediators is actually a diverse one, where practice intersects work lives in at least three distinctive ways: those who are public spokespersons and builders of the field, those who practice mediation full time, and those who mediate outside the profession. Not only are their motives different, but each group experiences different stresses and strains in the work.

The builders of the field are as well known for their public advocacy of mediation as for their practice. These mediators, who are on record in print and in front of national audiences, are, like others of their colleagues, the voices for the field, its purposes, and justification. People like Albie Davis, Eric Green, Larry Susskind, and sometimes Patrick Phear publicly articulate the ways in which mediation is a credible and legitimate alternative to other means available for resolving conflict. They make a case for mediation's efficiency and cost savings, community empowerment, transformation of personal relationships, and professional problem solving. Their public claims and visibility justify the work of others, and they contribute significantly to the expansion of the field.

They are also very busy. As mediation's public advocates, they bear a considerable part of the burden for "selling" mediation to potential users who may be skeptical, perhaps even hostile. People come to them for advice about entering the field and sometimes directly for jobs. Also, their performances before different audiences often inspire new recruits to enter the field. These demands have implications for their practice of mediation. Given their multiple activities (including public advocacy and speaking to national and international audiences), the time actually available for doing mediation is frequently limited. One sees in the profiles of Lawrence Susskind and Eric Green, for example, more demands for their services than they have time to contribute. These time pressures are inevitably felt in those cases they do mediate. Sometimes their busy schedules define the actual time available in a case, such that the parties have to accommodate their needs to those of the busy practitioners.

The field builders see themselves as public spokespersons for mediation. As such, they may unwittingly contribute to some of the myths as they make public claims for the uplifting quality of the work and the ease with which settlement and even more fundamental change can be achieved. While they are among the most articulate among the sample, one wonders whether their role as spokespersons and their track records as mediators may handicap them when it comes to seeing some of the difficulties that may be inherent in the role. Their very success, in both conducting their practice and representing it to a wider audience, pushes them to portray the work with an enthusiasm that other mediators may not be able to match.

Others profiled in this book speak from a different place. These are the full-time professionals, who make a living at mediation in either private practice or the public sector. Though they do on occasion speak and write about the profession, their concerns primarily cover a gamut of issues relative to their full-time work. Mediators like Howard Bellman, Bill Hobgood, and Patrick Phear are in private practice, and they worry about getting clients and about their niche in the market. Fran Butler and Patrick Davis work in large public bureaucracies. They seek to differentiate the humane and often caring treatment that clients get in their practice from what is likely to happen to them in the hands of impersonal, and often arbitrary, others.

The full-time professionals face considerable challenges to their credibility and legitimacy. They have to "sell" themselves at the same time as they are marketing their services. In contrast to the field builders, who are selling both the process and a vision, the professionals who are in private practice need to cultivate referral sources and convince specific disputants to use their services. Since they are in competition with others—Hobgood calls it the "peace and conflict marketplace"—they need to differentiate themselves from others. In the Hobgood, Phear, and Bellman profiles, for example, each subject takes pot shots at their competition. These are important matters when one's livelihood depends on a steady stream of clients.

Those who work in institutional contexts (such as Fran Butler and Patrick Davis) have the opposite problem: they have more cases than they can handle. Their concerns have more to do with stature and credibility. They have few mediation colleagues and no well-defined career path they can pursue. They all have moments when they wonder whether anybody in their organizations cares about their work.

Every mediator faces challenge in actually doing the work. Bringing recalcitrant parties to settlement is difficult, and there is considerable debate about how to do it. However, because the full-time professionals spend so much time mediating, they feel most acutely the impact of uncertain success and the lack of consensus in the field about innumerable strategic and tactical issues. It is they who are most apt to be affected negatively by the inadequacies of the mediation myths.

The field builders and full-time professionals are an important resource for those who mediate but do not consider themselves professional mediators. For these people, other professional and occupational cultures such as legal and bureaucratic decision making, as well as more traditional models of international diplomacy, compete with mediation in some of the new arenas where it is being tried. In the face of these competing claims for how to resolve disputes, the fact that mediation emerges as a profession with a recognizable set of techniques and practices associated with it lends credibility to people like Juju Atkinson and Linda Colburn, who are outside the immediate profession but choose to mediate. Intervenors like Jimmy Carter and Joseph Elder, who believe that mediation can serve important political agendas such as world peace and social harmony, infuse the profession with a higher purpose that serves the interests of all practitioners.

At the same time, these outsiders face their own challenges, some of which have implications for the field. Most of the outsiders bring their own agendas to their mediations. These agendas may be quite different from those of the parties. Jimmy Carter, for example, is clearly interested in developing institutions and mechanisms and a role for himself in inter- and intranational disputes. Linda Colburn's aim is to change the way homeless and poor people fight with each other. These are ambitious goals that cannot always be realized. Consequently, the outsiders are often disappointed in their performance. Some of them also combine their agendas with considerable clout and authority over the disputants. This combination has the potential for producing heavy-handed outcomes or ones that might be hard to describe as the result of a collaborative endeavor. A more modest agenda, like that of Joseph Elder, may buffer the mediator from disappointment, but it may also make for an intervention that may be inconsequential or whose effects are difficult to discern.

Outsiders are likely to have an uncertain impact on the field. Given the stature and visibility of some of these people, when they fail it can reflect negatively on the entire mediation enterprise. When they succeed, as with Carter's effort at Camp David, the field may be energized with a sense of purpose and vision. However, the outsiders' status may make it difficult to connect their experience to that of other practitioners and to the collective state of knowledge about competent practice.

The Ends Toward Which Mediators Work: Transformative and Pragmatic Visions

The myth of mediation holds that it is a process whose end is agreement. Specifically, the argument goes that mediation results in better agreements because the mediator can be more responsive to needs of the parties. But the mediators seemed much more interested in talking to us about larger issues than just settlement. They spoke to us a great deal about purpose, what they were trying to accomplish in the immediate situation and, often, in a larger context. Two broad visions emerge that form a rough divide among the practitioners.

A significant group, particularly those we have labeled the builders and outsiders, define their work in transformative terms (see Harrington and Merry, 1988). Joseph Elder, Jimmy Carter, Larry Susskind, Albie Davis, and Linda Colburn talk about their practice as part of a broader agenda to make significant changes at the institutional and/or individual level. Mediation is seen as a means to empower community members, further the goal of citizen participation, and set standards for responding to the current world challenge of ethnic, tribal, and cultural disputes. Such wide-ranging agendas give to mediation an almost messianic mission that is so attractive to many would-be practitioners and inspirational to potential disputants.

We note, however, that in most of the stories told in the profiles, the outcomes of mediation fall far short of these transformative aims. For example, Albie Davis admits that her goals of neighborhood change are hard to detect in the written agreement in which one person agrees to paint a door and the other to supply his phone number. There is also evidence that some who espouse the transformative vision find that, on occasion, even the more limited goal of settlement is elusive. Consider the odds against which Linda Colburn works. She talks about modeling conflict resolution skills through her interventions so that people can make use of the skills in their emotionally charged and often violent lives. But how can this goal be met when the parties have a deeply entrenched history of violence and when she lacks such basic resources as police intervention and support from social agencies?

Other practitioners espouse a change agenda as well, but theirs is couched in more local, pragmatic, and constrained terms. Bill Hobgood, Eric Green, Patrick Phear, Juju Atkinson, Fran Butler, Patrick Davis, and Howard Bellman are pragmatic problem solvers. The pragmatic vision is the one articulated most frequently by the full-time professional mediators, although some others subscribe to it as well. These practitioners mediate within existing institutional constraints and seek to make the systems in which they are involved work better. What it means to work better is a judgment that reflects the broader agendas the mediators pursue.

Efficiency is an important by-product of the mediation process, according to most of the pragmatists. From the perspective of practitioners like Eric Green and Bill Hobgood, pursuing business disputes and grievances to court or arbitration is wasteful of time and money. Thus, they make the case to the parties that mediation makes good business sense. But even the efficiency argument is usually couched in more ambitious terms—mediation can solve problems better than other choices available.

These mediators work in the context of ongoing relationships between formerly married couples, employers and employees, companies and suppliers, and community and governmental groups, among others. The relationships are marked by conflict and the potential for future disputes. Mediation has the potential to rescue these parties from the morass in which they find themselves by offering ways to deal with particular problems, at least temporarily. So, with the help of Patrick Phear and Fran Butler, divorced parents can deal with some of the mundane issues of child rearing that keep coming up. Bill Hobgood and Juju

Atkinson can suggest ways for parties to work out specific details of a problem. Patrick Davis can temporarily ease a little pain for parents of children with disabilities.

However, there are limitations in the pragmatic vision as well. Mediation is but a moment in these troubled relationships. Patrick Phear summarizes it well when he predicts that a divorced couple will be either back in court or with him in six to nine months. Mediation solutions are often ephemeral, and a specific problem solved will always reveal many others that can arise. Agreements fall apart in Howard Bellman's world; in Bill Hobgood's, grievance mediation is dropped from the next labor contract; in Patrick Davis's, parents return to the school committee the following year. Contradiction is embedded in these stories of pragmatic problem solvers. On the one hand, they believe that they do help make the institutions in which they work function more efficiently, professionally, responsively, and humanely. At the same time, there is more than a discouraging word about the difference they actually make.

In short, in pursuit of either a transformative or pragmatic vision, the goals may be unrealistic. Given the limitations of time and resources, the possibilities for making major changes in people's lives seem remote at best. Even the pragmatic agendas are rarely fully realized. While these broad visions bring inspiration and meaning to an emerging field, they may seem eerily irrelevant to the actual problems and dilemmas of daily work.

Deciding What to Do: Settlement and Communication Frames

The mediators justified their work to us with reference to broad transformative or pragmatic visions. At work on a particular dispute, however, their concerns are more immediate. What will they do? In the mythology of mediation, the days when it was an "art" with no science of practice are a thing of the past. Guidebooks for how to do it proliferate, and training programs specify the steps and stages. But both the "art" and the "science" metaphors are misleading. We prefer the metaphor of "framing," because it seems to capture both the structured patterns implied in the science metaphor and the ad hoc quality alluded to in the art metaphor.

Frames are the interpretive schemes that mediators use to make sense of and organize their activities while at work on a dispute (Schön, 1983). What a mediator does in a case is a blend of intentional and explicit technique, the tacit and taken-for-granted ways each has developed of dealing with the typical cases in the practice, and more general beliefs about the causes of conflict and the possibilities for its resolution. We see frames as a way to capture some of the implicit but nonetheless powerful orientations mediators have toward their role. This focus on frames derives from our observations that mediators are rarely passive actors in the process. Rather, they actively orchestrate the ways the dispute will be handled and let the parties know in no uncertain terms what is expected of them. Frames give focus to the myriad of choices mediators make while at work in a dispute, and suggest as well what comes to be seen as problematic and difficult (Scheff, 1984; Sheppard, Blumenfeld-Jones, and Roth, 1989). Our observation suggests two primary frames: settlement and communication.

Before we elaborate the specifics of settlement and communication frames, it is important first to clarify the way in which we are using the types. At some level all those we studied organize their work to achieve both better communication and settlement. What we suggest here is that there is a tendency for practitioners to define their roles and structure their activities according to whether it is settlement they seek or a change in the ways parties communicate with each other. Further, we do not want to suggest that these different frames are universally associated with particular structures and formats of mediation, but rather that a mediator's frame will be more likely to lead to certain kinds of activities than others and that what comes to be seen as a challenge or problem will likely differ as well. If mediators frame the process as one leading to settlement, then uncovering the elements of a possible deal, and moving the parties to accept that deal or some variant of it, occupies a lot of mediator attention. If enhanced communication is the frame, then more mediator effort goes toward keeping the parties in mediation so that they can better understand their conflict. Frames translate into specific actions within a dispute, but not in any preset formulaic fashion, since choices will always reflect on-the-spot decision making. But these too will be influenced by a frame.

Settlement

At some level, all mediators look for an agreement among the parties as an aim toward which they work. But for Juju Atkinson, Fran Butler, Jimmy Carter, Linda Colburn, Eric Green, Bill Hobgood, and Larry Susskind, getting agreements that work is the overriding goal that drives their activities and the primary basis that they use to judge themselves. Specifically, what it takes to get these settlements will differ somewhat depending on which of these mediators one consults. Butler's approach is highly structured and organized around a sequential discussion in which issues are introduced and explored, a proposal made and then worked through, and the process concluded with a discussion to reiterate the agreements reached. Hobgood's "conditioning" approach is similar—an ongoing, repetitive process in which he reiterates a series of arguments and tries to raise doubts about success in arbitration in order to gradually change the parties' beliefs.

One of the interesting features in working with these settlement-oriented mediators is that our conversations often centered around what it would take to get agreements. They frequently predicted what kind of settlement would result and discussed these predictions with us. They were not always correct, but this kind of thinking seemed to preoccupy them. Further, each of these mediators has a rather elaborate repertoire and detailed structures for discussing how to get the parties to make concessions so that agreement is more likely.

Settlement-oriented mediators want to find a substantive outcome that will result in a "deal." The substantive possibilities may be couched in broad, general terms, such as Susskind's preference for efficient and durable outcomes that maximize joint gain. Or they may be more focused, such as Hobgood's decision that Rosie's conflict should be used to change the safety program in the mine. They may be even more specific in scope, as when Linda Colburn wanted the parties to stipulate that neither would use physical violence against the other for at least twenty-four hours. Whatever the specific outcome they seek, these substantive matters seem to organize the practice of settlement-oriented mediators.

The structure of the mediation follows a particular iterative sequence for those who orient their work around the possibility of a specific outcome. First, the mediator interrogates the parties for some period of time until he or she develops a sense of how to deal with the issues presented or solve the particular problem. Susskind calls this sense a "concept," Butler describes it as the "contours" of a settlement, and Hobgood calls it a "fix" on the case. These ideas may be the mediator's own, but generally they take off on something said or suggested by one of the parties. Many of the most experienced among the group identify these concepts very early in the dispute.

Although ideas are often revised (and refined) as discussions unfold, the concepts seem to become the basis on which the mediators engage in rather directed conversations with the parties. In subtle, and often not so subtle ways, the mediator tries out the ideas on the parties and they react. In so doing, both go through a series of reiterations and modifications that are organized around the central idea. In this process, the initial concept may be modified (recall that Hobgood had to abandon his efforts to get the mine to drop the warning from Rosie's record), and a new one become the basis for persuasion.

As the mediators readily acknowledge, they are often ahead of the parties on these issues. They know what should happen, but the challenge is to make it occur. Thus, discussions often bog down as the parties get stuck and repeat their claims or are not yet ready to move to any new way of seeing their issues along the lines of the mediator's conception. Butler's persistent efforts to focus the parties on her proposal regarding visitation are offset by the parents' desire to discuss new emotional issues and grievances.

From a settlement perspective, many different kinds of situations present challenges to the mediator. Labeled as problems, these become the basis for the application of specific techniques. If you are interested in settlement, then the reluctance of the parties to move away from cherished positions may be read as a problem. It is not surprising, then, that specific techniques are used to address this kind of recalcitrance. Two seem especially worthy of consideration.

The art of questioning is highly refined in the practice of many of the mediators. Although occasionally questions are used to elicit information, part of the art here is in their use to promote the achievement of a specific end. Questions become suggestions in the guise of a query. According to Fran Butler, questions are useful because they are less likely than outright suggestions to cause resistance from the parties. Bill Hobgood uses pointed questions in a similar way. Larry Susskind sums it up well when he says that "questioning is a way to teach without lecturing."

When the parties balk at changing their explicit positions, the mediators try to create situations of choice in which settlement in mediation is preferable to other possibilities. Hobgood, for example, gives the parties informal readings on how he thinks they would fare if their case were to be heard by an arbitrator. Green uses a technique called "litigation decision analysis" to help the parties gauge how they might fare in front of the judge. Butler reminds the parties about their negative experiences in court, which were their original motivation in coming to mediation.

Carter reminds Begin and Sadat about the risks they will run in their relationships with the United States and the consequences for their personal relationships with him. Susskind keeps comparing the emerging ideas with the parties' BATNAs (Best Alternatives to a Negotiated Agreement). Colburn paints the alternative boldly: if the parties do not participate in her conversation, they could be out on the street. Mobilizing the consequences of not continuing in mediation becomes a powerful incentive for the parties to change their positions.

Those mediators who frame the primary task as one of settlement tend to be directive in their style. They orient their activities toward concrete problem solving and frequently make suggestions on matters of substance. Most are comfortable with the notion that they are expert in the particular substantive domain in which the dispute occurs, and they use this expertise as the touchstone of their efforts at persuasion and influence. These settlement-oriented mediators are quite willing to acknowledge that they make judgments about what is a good and bad agreement and try to influence the parties in the direction of good. Theirs is an activist view of the mediation role, and they are eager to campaign to persuade or motivate the parties to concur. They thrust themselves forcefully into the conflict and are strongly inclined to believe that without their substantive and procedural know-how, the parties would flounder and settlement would be elusive.

Enhanced Communication

The other mediators in our sample frame the task quite differently. They view mediation as a process to enhance communication. Their aim is to have the parties come away from mediation with a different, better understanding of the problem, if not with a definite settlement.

Joseph Elder, who describes himself as a "message carrier," probably best exemplifies this stance. In the kinds of disputes in which he and the Quakers become involved, the possibilities for agreement are slim and likely to take years to resolve, if they ever are. He sees himself in a limited role, a facilitator of dialogue and a "vehicle of communication." For Howard Bellman, mediation provides the forum for the negotiators to do their work, and it is his responsibility to activate them. Similarly, Patrick Phear describes what he does as "facilitated negotiation." While he is concerned that his clients achieve success in their work with him, "success" may or may not be an actual settlement. In introducing mediation to one of his clients, he said, "Here we try to find ways you both can understand your problems and try to help you figure out for yourselves what you want to do about them. Whether you end up agreeing or not, you should end up with a clear sense of what you have in common and what you disagree about." Phear sees this stance as protection for both him and the couples with whom he works.

If enhanced communication is the way the mediation task is framed, then what is labeled a problem or roadblock will reflect this agenda. First, mediators are concerned when the parties do not communicate in ways that further the task of better understanding and cooperation. While this is true for many of those we profile, it is a particular concern for the mediators whose very agenda it is to facilitate better communication. Albie Davis and Patrick Phear talk about the problems of people who do not listen to each other and whose response is to repeat the past. Howard Bellman and Joseph Elder believe that only if the involved parties live up to their responsibilities will any progress be made.

Because their emphasis is on communication, these mediators help us see some of the ways that mediators seek to influence the ways the parties converse with each other (Cobb and Rifkin, 1991). There is an effort to impel the parties to communicate about the future and not the past. As Patrick Phear tells his clients, "Let me tell you that mediation is really hopeless at deciding past rights and past wrongs. . . . I do believe it is excellent at looking forward to designing things." There is also the creative and energetic "summarizing" of the parties' positions. Albie Davis notes that when she summarizes the stories the parties tell her, it helps her conceptualize the problem and construct a *new* story that incorporates the others, a route to possible agreement. Similarly, Phear takes what the parties tell him and reframes it in ways that emphasize areas of agreement, not disagreement. Joseph Elder and Howard Bellman manage the conversation in less direct ways, by charging the parties on their own to make proposals or "work out language" that will meet some of the concerns of others involved.

A second problem that this group of mediators highlights for us is the challenge to keep the parties at the table and in mediation. As Phear describes it, he wants his clients to commit to a process that he controls. "I'm the orchestra leader. . . . If they want to play in this orchestra, they're going to have to play when I point at them." Both Elder and Bellman want the parties to stay in the dialogue as long as possible and talk in a productive way as these mediators define it. Patrick Davis tries to keep the discussion focused on the program for the sake of the children.

Keeping the parties engaged and increasing their investment in the negotiation process is important because it is by staying in the dialogue that possible new ideas and areas of compromise might be discovered. The way Howard Bellman rises to this challenge is instructive: "You have nothing to lose by coming into the process," he argues to the group he has convened. When the process threatens to break down, he calls attention to the investment of time and effort as the very reason to remain in the deliberations. Similarly, Joseph Elder strives to keep the dialogue open because it is a way to model norms of interaction in a context where agreements are incredibly difficult to achieve.

Challenges to the mediator's management of the conversation happen all the time. Some mediators use the private caucus to regain control of the situation. The mediator will single out one party or another and talk to him or her about how to participate in the conversation. It is in these settings, for example, that Albie Davis will try to change the way somebody is framing an argument. Bellman caucuses with the parties when he thinks they are not participating in good faith. Of course, some mediations are conducted almost entirely using a caucus structure, a situation that contributes considerably to the mediator's ability to manage the communication process.

Just because mediators in this subgroup talk more about the communicative process than about settlement does not mean that they are passive, inactive, or unconcerned with the substantive issues that are in dispute. Quite the contrary. In their focus on the ways the parties talk to each other, these mediators influence how issues are framed, the ways problems are understood, and the flow of information between and among the disputants. Indeed, influence over the conversations in mediation constitutes one of the primary ways that mediators can foster agreements even when they claim it is not a major aim they pursue.

Not surprisingly, the mediators who frame their task as one of enhancing communication between the parties take a less directive stance than the settlement-oriented mediators. More inclined to see themselves as behind-the-scenes catalysts or orchestrators of the parties' own coping and problem-solving skills, they recognize some of the limitations of the role. As Bellman notes, his contributions are inversely related to the technical quality of the issues and expertise of the parties. These mediators also seem to be particularly sensitive to the dangers of violating disputants' autonomy by using pressure tactics or by the intrusion of the mediator's personal standards or opinions. Mediator "power" is viewed with distrust and some wariness. These mediators emphasize, instead, the virtues of "less is more," as Elder puts it. By keeping a low profile and getting the parties to do the lion's share of the work, a mediator avoids the risk of becoming another party with an agenda to pursue. This stance, as articulated by some of these mediators, is one that fosters in the parties a more immediate sense of ownership and a better foundation for dealing with each other in the future.

There is no question that the settlement and communication frames are useful to mediators. The profiles suggest some of the ways in which these frames help give order and direction in situations that might otherwise overwhelm and frustrate practitioners. Frames are also an inevitable outgrowth of practice. The more mediators practice, the more likely they are to develop accustomed ways of dealing with recurring situations. The notion that mediators check their experience, with its biases and preconceptions, at the door is one of mediation's myths, not part of its reality.

On the other hand, framing is clearly not benign. Each frame carries with it its own limitations. The settlement-oriented mediators must struggle with the fact that the parties may not be ready to participate under the terms the mediator envisions. As Carter learned in the Ethiopian-Sudanese conflict, in these circumstances, mediation can be a front for the parties to pursue other agendas.

A second limitation of the settlement frame can occur when mediators pursue their agendas over those of the parties. The mediator gets a "fix" or a "concept" of the settlement and is reluctant to let it go. What starts out as an iterative sequence of ideas, questions, and revisions gets foreclosed as the mediator fails to attend or respond soon enough to the parties' concerns. Rather than back off and try a new tack, the mediator may get locked in, and the process moves toward an impasse.

The profiles are replete with examples of how a mediator's allegiance to a particular agenda can interfere with the parties' own problem solving, and expand or narrow the scope of what are deemed legitimate topics of conversation. In one of Hobgood's cases, for example, his efforts to have the parties expand their purview to consider solving a basic problem rather than a particular grievance not only was rejected by the parties but seemed to inhibit their efforts to deal with the actual grievance on the table. Finally, the settlement frame is rarely even-handed. Not everybody's ideas are attended to equally. Certain people—for example, parties the mediator works with frequently, or expects to work with in the future—find that the mediator responds to their interests more directly. Thus, the one-time plaintiff or grievant may feel in danger of having his or her agenda subordinated.

There are also limitations to the communication frame. Given the problems that bring parties to mediation, parties may expect more help on the substantive issues than they appear to get. Phear and Elder are challenged, for example, to do more. There is also a danger that the mediator, out of a conviction that the parties need to "communicate" without hindrance, will fail to protect a party during the process. Bellman, for example, was surprised when he was challenged by a member of the environmental coalition for his failure to deal with some sexist remarks that had been made. Communication-oriented mediators, when they tutor parties in how to speak to one another, are as selective and as subject to their own prejudices and biases as are their more settlement-oriented colleagues. For instance, the definitions of "appropriate" kinds of talk can limit participation and move the discussion in particular directions as surely as an iterative sequence that puts out substantive ideas. Placing blame on discussions of "right" and "wrong," while denounced by mediators like Patrick Phear and Albie Davis, ignores the distinct possibility that somebody's behavior *is* wrong and needs to be considered during mediation.

Frames are a feature of all the practices we studied. However, given their positions in the field, we noticed certain differences in the degree to which mediators dominate process and influence outcomes. Because of their experiences and extensive caseloads, professionals are most likely to display a consistency of approach and impose their frames, whether settlement or communications, across a range of cases. Outsiders and field builders are more likely to choose cases that they feel fit the frames they use. In sum, despite rhetoric to the contrary, many of those we profile go to great lengths to assure that their frames will dominate the process and influence the outcomes. This inclination derives significant impetus from a desire to be judged successful, to be seen as having made a difference. The source of these desires is, in turn, rooted in the "business" side of mediation practice.

The "Business" Side of Mediation and the Question of Mediator Power

Most of the mediators bow in the direction of the voluntariness of the mediation process and the need to respect the parties' autonomy. This is part of the myth of mediation. Yet nearly every profile illustrates the working mediator attempting to shape the process and substance using some very strenuous and powerful tactics. While the use of such tactics may contradict the pacific, laid-back mythology of the impartial mediator, the mobilization of some kind of mediator "muscle" would seem essential in many of the protracted, embittered conflicts described in this book. Further, in the interests of pursuing broader objectives or more pragmatic professional aims, most of these mediators feel impelled to drive the process in some very forceful ways.

The impetus to use pressure tactics comes not only from the process of mediation, however. For most of those we profile, and most intensively for the professionals, mediation is also a "business." Some earn their livelihood (or a significant portion of it) from their mediation practices in either the private or the public sector. Getting business through clients and referrals and accounting for one's contribution to organizations and individuals are thus among their concerns. Others desire to build institutions for handling conflict (Carter in the international sphere, Green and Hobgood in the business sector, and Albie Davis in the community area). To ensure a steady and reliable referral base, there is an implied demand to please important players, such as lawyers and judges in the cases of Phear and Green, and, for Hobgood, company and union "pros." Other mediators have a stake in building their reputations and visibility in the field. Here one would include Susskind, Bellman, Phear, and Green, among others. In an evocative phrase, Hobgood acknowledges some of the competition that exists in the field when he talks about a "peace and negotiation marketplace."

That these professional agendas exist is not surprising. Many of those we set out to study are leaders in the field and were attractive to us precisely because they are in this position. However, we need to consider some of the ways that these professional interests may insinuate themselves into the workings of the mediation process. And it is here that our attention is directed to the use of pressure and other forms of control to convince the parties to make agreements that will reflect positively on the mediators. We do not claim that these professional interests override others, but rather that they are among the factors that influence the mediators and their practice.

In the pursuit of settlement and the imperatives of their particular frames, the mediators describe a range of persuasive efforts. These tactics run the gamut from mild comment to blunt confrontations. Inducements are probably the most benign. Hobgood, for example, imagines aloud how great it will be for management to adopt the safety program that he has conceived as a central part of the settlement package. Carter intimates to the Ethiopian and Sudanese bargaining teams that if they work cooperatively, he will be motivated to use his contacts in the Bush administration to provide material assistance to each side. Strictly speaking, such verbal "carrots" are far from the conventional notion of pressure tactics, but they are also ways of reminding the disputants that the mediators are the ones with power and authority at their disposal.

At other times, these reminders are more explicit. Thus, at Camp David, Carter reminded Begin and Sadat of the unhappy consequences of no agreement. These consequences were made more pointed by Carter's telling Begin and Sadat in no uncertain terms how disastrous it would be for him personally if no accord was reached. In more immediate circumstances, Colburn was not shy about telling a violence-prone couple that unless they agreed to go for counseling, she would use her authority as manager of the housing complex to have them evicted. Green was not bashful about reminding the parties of his close ties to the referring magistrate, using that link to imply that the judge would probably view the defendant morally at fault if the case went to trial. He took his own moral stand when he bluntly asked the plaintiff, "How greedy can you get?"

When direct power and authority were less readily at hand, some mediators were adept at mobilizing their own expertise as a functional substitute. Butler and Hobgood could invoke their knowledge of the legal or arbitration system to make salient the uncertain, capricious, or unattractive result of an imposed agreement. For those whose approach is less directive, pressure for concession making is often mobilized by seeking some kind of moral high ground. Elder reviews with the parties their long, dismal past and the consequences in human life of continuing their conflict. Bellman reminds participants of their responsibility for pulling their weight in the process.

Mediator pressure is also applied in the way that parties are socialized, when they are reminded about the appropriate way to "behave" in mediation. The parties are to refrain from talking about past grievances and stay focused on the future; to put aside "emotions"; to think of the other side's needs as well as their own; to refrain from violence and provocative language; and to reciprocate offers with compromise. These exhortations often come at moments of high tension, with the clear implication that failure to comply is to be in some way at fault.

Pressure is also orchestrated by mediator decisions about format. Thus, Carter insisted that the parties in the Ethiopian-Sudanese conflict make a public announcement that they were embarking on mediation, as a way to force both sides to put forth their most attractive proposals and as a demonstration of their "good faith." Green's decision to invite a senior law partner to the negotiation was partly intended to bring pressure on the resistant junior partner, who had been the primary negotiator up to that point. Bellman, otherwise among the most nondirective of those we profiled, used a caucus to urge one of the parties to "get tough" with the others. Similarly, Albie Davis, Phear, and Susskind, among others, use the caucus to press parties to change their stance. Susskind talks about this influence when he describes how he tries to change their attitude by such appeals as

"If I were you, here's what I would do." Several feel that keeping parties at the bargaining table is a useful way of exerting pressure toward agreement. As Green remarks, the parties' desire to go home may be "the fuel for final settlement."

There is more than a little evidence here of the dual presence of what Bellman calls the "iron fist and the velvet glove" and the delicate balance of the two. One gets a sense from these profiles that masking mediator pressure in that velvet glove is a tactical issue of some importance. Sometimes this takes the form of sheer denial—the "I know it may appear that I am breaking your arm, but actually I am not" disclaimer. Such behavior tends to occur when the mediator is engaged in a strong press for a particular substantive line. At other times, one observes the iron fist cloaked in the guise of questions. Rather than suggest or recommend a particular course, the mediators press for substantive points by asking what Susskind calls the "tough" questions. In other situations, mediators exploit choice by claiming parties can leave at any time, but then making it quite difficult to do so. These efforts to keep the knuckles of the iron fist from showing through the velvet glove seem to signal some of the tension that exists in the mediation role between the mandate to be noncoercive and respectful of the parties' autonomy and the pragmatic requirement to get something accomplished.

This masking of pressure tactics has implications for the profession. On the one hand, we have a myth that says mediation is noncoercive. The reality of the conflicts in which they are engaged and the demands of their professional careers means that the impetus to use pressure and coercion is probably inevitable. Frequently, mediators resolve this tension through a kind of denial about what they do. The denial stands in the way of learning and keeps the field from better understanding the uses and limits of pressure.

The Stresses of Mediation

People are attracted to the practice of mediation. Many of the field builders, for example, find themselves inundated with prospective practitioners. Albie Davis has even developed a handbook that she can distribute to the many people who contact her about the field. Part of this attraction has to do with some persistent myths about mediation: that it is a "helping" profession in which mediators can make a difference in people's lives; that the work is inspiring and uplifting; that, like those with a religious vocation, aspiring mediators believe they are all but "called" to mediation.

Those we profile are not as sanguine. Most allude to the stresses involved in practicing mediation. At times these expressions are direct. Phear talks of mediation as "a lonely and difficult life." At the height of his success at Camp David, Carter confided in his diary, "I resolve to do everything possible to get out of the negotiating business." Colburn no longer mediates. Hobgood, Phear, Butler, and Albie Davis have expanded their practices to include other dimensions of intervention and social change and do not mediate on a full-time basis any more. True to his diary confession and after his chastening experience with the Ethiopian-Sudanese dispute, Carter has been less publicly visible as a mediator. Of those in full-time practice at the beginning of our study, only Patrick Davis remained by the end.

A good deal of mediator burnout appears to derive from the parties, whose emotional pain, limited motivation for resolving their difficulties, combativeness, and general resistance often conspire to frustrate and demoralize even the most tenacious and resourceful mediator. Colburn and Elder have been exposed to situations in which they could be literally killed by disputants who, in Colburn's understatement, "excessively validate anger." Carter and others have tried to mediate in situations in which the parties seem more interested in gaining a public forum for their grievances against each other than in working to resolve the conflict.

The work can be lonely and emotionally draining. Phear, Susskind, Butler, and Davis all refer to the emotional wear and tear of trying to help people whose anger or emotional wounds are raw and almost overpowering, but with whom the mediators must hold themselves in check or disguise their own painful or angry reactions. Susskind talks of the necessity of "soaking up anger without ever hitting back." Patrick Davis speaks of the emotional pain he feels under circumstances where he wants to help but can do so only to a limited degree. Colburn has had to listen to accusations that she is racist.

Shortages of time and money, as well as the narrow way that mediation has been traditionally defined, often add to the stress that many mediators experience. Colburn is forced into one-shot, "on-the-spot mediation," because she has no place to refer a suicidal person, no counseling center prepared to teach her disputants the rudiments of "anger management," and a police department unwilling to back her with reliable violence control. Atkinson, Albie Davis, Patrick Davis, Butler, and Hobgood operate in settings that are constrained by time and often resources. Hobgood has the additional frustration of being confined by a grievance process that limits how far he can go in addressing some of the serious problems that erode relationships between labor and management. There are economic costs as well. Hobgood, Susskind, and Green are paid lower fees for mediation than they can command from training and other forms of intervention.

There is also a tension that is endemic to the structure of negotiation itself: when multiple negotiators are working on each side, it is never completely clear who actually wields authority on a bargaining team. Much mediator time and energy is spent trying to make these evaluations, so that unanticipated resistance does not torpedo a possible settlement. The negotiating process also has its own inexorable pace. Susskind talks about his desire for things to go on "fast forward," even while logic tells him that the parties need to discover things for themselves. Phear, Butler, Hobgood, and Green also give voice to the frustrations engendered by the ever-present need to be patient, slow down, and recycle the same issues many times over. Carter and his team drafted no less than twenty-three versions of a proposed agreement during the Camp David talks. When the principal negotiators detest each other, as turned out to be the case with Begin and Sadat, there may be a need for endless caucuses in which much of the burden for representing each side's views to the other falls on the mediator's shoulders. Dealing with angry couples and hostile attorneys can also take its emotional toll.

Mediators must also cope with stresses engendered by ambivalent social attitudes toward mediation and peacemaking. Despite its highly touted virtues, mediation has not been a popular choice among disputants, be they divorcing parents or warring nation-states. Absent a determined push from judges or others with institutional clout, few combatants present themselves at the mediator's doorstep. Instead, mediators as noted must search for business—impressing possible referral sources, "outselling" rival practitioners, cajoling, pressuring, and "educating" ambivalent negotiators, debating with themselves and their key advisers (if advisers there be) whether the mess is even worth trying to mediate. Sometimes the contortions reach antic proportions, as with Colburn's capturing the attention of two violent, half-crazed disputants by posing as a pizza delivery person. Even when you think you have succeeded, the parties tell you differently. So Hobgood spends several years giving his best, only to have grievance mediation written out of the next contract.

The effort takes its toll. We see the signs in the occasional acerbic asides about other mediators' skills or concepts and the cynicism about the parties' resistance. They are observed in the ever-present calls for institutionalizing mediation as a way,

Susskind says, to curtail ambulance chasing and solve the "entry problem." And, of course, we notice the signs in the decision to search for other lines of work or shift the focus of practice.

Mediators must also deal with the fact that theirs is an emerging discipline in which there is little consensus on major aspects of practice. Susskind makes the point most clearly, perhaps, when he ticks off the major issues on which there is sharp debate: what is the best way to gain entry into a dispute? How "active" should a mediator be? How knowledgeable about the substantive issues in dispute? How accountable for the outcome?

This is also a field in which no consensus has been reached about what a mediator should be trained to know and do or, indeed, whether any training beyond some kind of generic education in negotiations and mediation is necessary. At times in the profiles, it is difficult not to wonder whether, on occasion, mediators may be in over their heads or struggling unduly because they lack knowledge about interpersonal dynamics or techniques of skillful interviewing or whatever else is involved in the process of change. Certainly, it is hard to resist the notion that they must sometimes ask themselves these questions and be pained at the response.

Finally, stress comes from the inherent contradictions and ambiguities of the mediation role. Mediators often experience tensions between giving the parties autonomy and their own obligation to control the process, and between the promise to address difficult problems and the often constricted settlement that results.

These tensions are managed in a variety of ways. We noted earlier the tendency of some mediators to deny that any contradiction exists. Others develop cynical or alienated feelings about themselves and their practice. Colburn, for example, found that her ideal of modeling peacemaking did not prevent her from behaving in contradictory ways when the situation warranted. But in so doing, she reports a painful degree of self-alienation that ultimately led her to leave her job. Still others resolve these tensions by taking a more pragmatic stance—what they do is simply better than the other choices available. This may be a realistic response, but less inspiring than many of their original motives for entering the field.

Allegiance to a particular frame of practice is another way that mediators manage the stresses of the role. As we have suggested, frames help give order, purpose, and direction to what might otherwise be an overwhelming sense of confusion. However, there is an ironic twist: frames create headaches of their own. Settlement frames require enormous expenditures of energy and time. As Susskind describes it, it means getting unrepresented parties to the table, providing them with negotiating skills, actively shaping the agenda by adding issues parties had not previously considered, and then pushing them hard. These efforts can leave the mediators open to attack for pushing their own ends, a lesson Carter learned from the Ethiopian and Sudanese negotiators. A communication frame presents its own problems. Sometimes the approach is so laid-back and quiet that parties have difficulty figuring out whether the mediator has contributed anything. Bellman, for example, has been accused of doing nothing, a rather painful thought given his own sense of practice.

Beyond Myth

That mediators have agendas not given them by the parties, that they are frequently heavy-handed, and that the work is often discouraging is not original news. What is noteworthy, we think, is that we find the disparity between the work as practiced and the mythic characterization of mediation occurring at the very highest levels of practice.

Why have these myths been so persistent? Part of the answer

must surely lie with the nature of the enterprise itself. Compared with other forms of intervention and social change, mediation is noteworthy for its almost complete absence of theory about social conflict and intervention. Nothing akin to the situation prevails in psychotherapy or organizational intervention, in which powerful and influential models—such as psychoanalytic, behavioral, and systems theories, among others—actively compete and provide at least a viable intellectual and emotional scaffolding for the otherwise beleaguered intervenor. Mythic views thrive in such a vacuum.

There is also the diversity of backgrounds and professional disciplines of those who contribute significantly to mediation and the wider field of dispute resolution. The cacophony of voices and perspectives has been tonic in some regards, but in others it makes forging agreement on the basic phenomena and ways of practice difficult. In the absence of better-grounded alternatives, or at least those with convincing appeal to such a diverse audience, the mythic image persists. Indeed, this image may be helpful in conditions of such diversity, providing a kind of lowest common denominator that is reasonable sounding and true to certain aspects of the work.

The diverse arenas of conflict in which mediators function—literally everything from fights about the kitchen sink to nuclear armageddon—stretch the limits of understanding and agreement beyond what is reasonable. Yet the fledgling field is understandably reluctant to compartmentalize and diminish itself by drawing premature boundaries between areas of conflict that look as if they might be related and, if they were, would increase the profession's scope and influence.

Some of the more pragmatic concerns of the professional practitioners—such as the struggle for clients and efforts to develop a reputation—are also highlighted in the profiles. So we witness competition among practitioners who seek to differentiate themselves from others, as well as institution building that might routinize and even outdemand. These efforts frequently translate into conflicts over the actual practice of mediation, leading to assertions that one approach is superior to another. All this occurs against the background of a myth about mediation that seems impossible to realize.

The mythic world of mediation contrasts sharply with what we learned from the practice of the mediators we profiled. Of course, these practitioners are not blind adherents to the myth. In reflecting on their practice, they make more than occasional acknowledgment that mythic virtues such as "neutrality" and mediator self-effacement are not among their highest concerns, nor are they naive about the hard realities that the mythic view tends to ignore.

What is interesting, however, is that the mediators we pro-filed rarely cite their departures from mythic behavior as cause for calling into question the mythic values themselves. They contin-ue to accept the myths, as least as formal virtues. Such, perhaps, is the inevitable posture of a field's founders and proselytizers. The mythic "frame" has as much value for establishing a new field as for mediating a particular dispute. It gives direction and inspiration amidst uncertainty, isolation, and complexity. There are liabilities as well. In the press to professionalize the work, these myths become the bases for selection and training of new mediators and so are perpetuated in the ongoing practice (Silbey, 1993). Without examining the myths, the risks of demoralized practitioners, oversold or misleading claims, and a general intel-lectual and professional stagnation are likely.

But what is to replace the mythic frame, now that the tasks of founding and converting have been accomplished? We suggest that the time is ripe for a shift to a new frame that accepts the practical realities of mediation and that recognizes and is straightforward about the dilemmas and inner contradictions of the work. Such a frame, which we label a "practice" frame, translates into an open and unapologetic acceptance of what we have observed in the work of these mediators, who

- inevitably bring their own agendas to any conflict in which they become involved;
- use pressure and other "robust" tactics prominently in their work;
- are often businesspeople whose motives and interests are not automatically congruent with those whom they assist.

For all these reasons, a practice stance also acknowledges that mediation has promised what it cannot always deliver. The process is unlikely to be totally voluntary, the parties' autonomy cannot be fully guaranteed, and settlements are as likely to bear the imprint of the mediator as that of the disputants. These are the practical realities of mediation as practiced today.

It has become commonplace in the field to criticize mediation for its faults along these lines. Indeed, the field has become increasingly polarized as critics and advocates endlessly debate the merits and faults, the promises and disappointments of mediation. We think that our observations about the dilemmas of practice can be accepted by proponents as well as critics. These admissions are but a point of departure. They can become the facts for an agenda whose aim is to explore and improve practice. Rather than bemoan or deny mediator biases, pressure, and self-interest, we need to find better ways to study and learn from these characteristics. Are some mediator visions or frames more useful and practical than others? A practice frame that forthrightly acknowledges its assumptions can foster the development of alternative models that are based on different assumptions. Some are beginning to surface. Sara Cobb (1993) articulates a new concept of neutrality that does not depend on the stance of the mediator, but on how conversations take place. Robert Baruch Bush and Joseph Folger (in press) promote a vision of mediation that has relationships and learning, not problem solving, as its goal. These kinds of shifts in theoretical concern and inquiry promise to move us away from the kinds of endless debates that mark the field and that have become increasingly irrelevant to the concerns of practicing mediators and those who see promise but admit failures as well.

Our call for a shift away from the myths of mediation to an open acknowledgment of the problems of practice in no way obscures or diminishes the very high regard in which we hold those we have profiled. They are the true pioneers in a terrain that is arduous and still poorly mapped. That we understand this terrain so much better now than we did a mere five years ago is a tribute to them and others like them. Our scrutiny of their work rests on the simple belief that the underlying spirit behind the mediation myths is more likely to be realized by casting the myths aside and finding more practical ways of making talk work.

Deborah M. Kolb and Kenneth Kressel

References

Bush, R. B., and Folger, J. (in press). *Mediation at the crossroads*. San Francisco: Jossey-Bass.

Cobb, S. (1993). Empowerment and mediation: A narrative perspective. *Negotiation Journal, 9*, 245–259.

Cobb, S., and Rifkin, J. (1991). Neutrality as a discursive practice: The construction and transformation of narrative in community mediation. In S. Silbey and A. Sarat (Eds.), *Law, politics and society* (Vol. 11). Greenwich, CT: JAI Press.

Fuller, L. (1971). Mediation: Its forms and functions. *Southern California Law Review, 44*, 305.

Goldberg, S., Green, E., and Sander, F. (1985). *Dispute resolution*. Boston: Little, Brown.

Harrington, C., and Merry, S. (1988). Ideological production: The making of community mediation. *Law and Society Review, 22*, 709–737.

Kolb, D. (1983). *The mediators*. Cambridge, MA: MIT Press.

Moore, C. (1986). *The mediation process: Practical strategies for resolving conflict.* San Francisco: Jossey-Bass.

Scheff, T. (1984). *On being mentally ill* (2nd ed.). Chicago: Aldine Press.

Schön, D. A. (1983). *The reflective practitioner.* New York: Basic Books.

Sheppard, B., Blumenfeld-Jones, K., and Roth, J. (1989). Informal third-partyship: A program of research on everyday conflict intervention. In K. Kressel and D. Pruitt (Eds.), *Mediation of social conflict.* San Francisco: Jossey-Bass.

Silbey, S. (1993). Mediation mythology. *Negotiation Journal, 9.*

Silbey, S., and Merry, S. (1986). Mediator settlement strategies. *Law and Policy, 8, 7.*

INDEX

• •